Literacy Development in the Storytelling Classroom

LITERACY DEVELOPMENT IN THE STORYTELLING CLASSROOM

Sherry Norfolk, Jane Stenson, and Diane Williams, Editors

LIBRARIES UNLIMITED

An Imprint of ABC-CLIO, LLC

A B C 🟫 C L I O

Santa Barbara, California • Denver, Colorado • Oxford, England

Library of Congress Cataloging-in-Publication Data

Literacy development in the storytelling classroom /
  Edited by Sherry Norfolk, Jane Stenson, and Diane Williams.
    p. cm.
  Includes bibliographical references and index.
  ISBN 978-1-59158-694-4 (hard copy : alk. paper)
1. Storytelling. 2. Language arts (Elementary)
3. Language arts (Middle school) I. Norfolk, Sherry, 1952– II.
Stenson, Jane, 1941– III. Williams, Diane, 1953– IV. Title.
  LB1042.N57 2009
    372.67′7—dc22   2009011550

British Library Cataloguing in Publication Data is available.

Library of Congress Catalog Card Number: 2009011550
ISBN 978-1-59158-694-4

First published in 2009

Libraries Unlimited, 88 Post Road West, Westport, CT 06881
A Member of the Greenwood Publishing Group, Inc.
http://www.lu.com

Printed in the United States of America

The paper used in this book complies with the
Permanent Paper Standard issued by the National
Information Standards Organization (Z39.48–1984).

10 9 8 7 6 5 4 3 2 1

Standards for the English Language Arts by the International Reading Association and the
National Council of Teachers of English, copyright 1996 by the International Reading
Association and the National Council of Teachers of English. Reprinted with permission.

DEDICATIONS

To Bobby, for his unwavering patience, support, shoulder rubs, and inspiration; and to every child whose eyes light up at the words, "Once Upon a Time ...."—SN

To my future ...
to Geoff, Geord, Ramsey,
Kate, and Zach
may you write your own stories
and
to the faculty and families of
The Baker Demonstration School;
may we continue to inspire the world
through our storytelling.—JS

To Ray and Gaie—When hands reach out in love, hearts are touched with joy.—DW

CONTENTS

Contents

Contents

FOREWORD

The genius scientist, Albert Einstein, was famous for his theory of relativity. But he had another theory that fewer people knew about. A reporter who wanted to know what parents and teachers should do to create great scientists asked Einstein what he thought. Einstein replied, "Tell the children stories. Read to them." It startled the young reporter, who asked the genius, "Yes, but then what else would you do?" Einstein's answer rings true today. "Share more stories with the children," he said. "Give the children more stories." *Literacy Development in the Storytelling Classroom* supports Einstein's assumption.

It has taken time for storytelling to be accepted as a credible discipline within the academic world. But now that it has, a plethora of books have been published to meet the new demands for information. But this collection stands out because the essays reflect the quality and high interest in storytelling as a teaching tool and have been written by some of the finest teacher-storytellers in the country. Each essay has been carefully selected by the editors to show practical uses of the oral tradition in the classroom and how through stories both teachers and students can increase their knowledge, expand their skills, and become more literate.

Long ago, hunters sat around fires and told stories about their adventures, while young listeners gathered important survival information and used that knowledge to make wise decisions and solve problems when they ventured into the dark forest as hunters. Children don't sit around fires any longer, but stories still help twenty-first-century kids survive in a contemporary forest of ever-changing and often-conflicting ideas.

I can read, write, speak, and listen with clarity and understanding. These skills, combined with my innate ability and interest, have prepared me to choose wisely and act responsibly as an adult. I owe a debt of gratitude to my teachers, but my family deserves full credit for establishing a solid foundation upon which my formal education was developed. And they did it long before "parents as first teachers" was ever conceived.

The first step toward literacy began in infancy, when as a child I was a listener. Research shows that children who are read to and talked to as babies acquire language faster and learn to express themselves easier. It was true for me at least. So I can say with sureness, storytelling provided an excellent pathway to a lifelong appreciation for words and the ideas they convey.

As far back as I can remember, my family gathered on the front porch and shared stories to teach, entertain, and encourage my brother, sister, and me. It was through their homespun storytelling that my love of the spoken word originated, family history and values were passed on, and my self-confidence was strengthened. The porch storytelling stage was that special place where my input was expected and respected within the circle of adults. My siblings and I thought we were just as brave and clever as the characters—who outsmarted foxes and captured the wind in our grandfather's tales. It is on those early memories that two of my early picture books are based: *Flossie and the Fox* and *Ma Dear's Aprons*.

I always enjoyed the times when we kids were invited to tell stories. I had no idea that I was acquiring skills that I would use throughout my life. By creating my own stories I was learning how to develop an idea with sequence and logic and tie it together with a beginning, a middle, and an end. By conceptualizing, sorting, organizing, and finally telling the story, I was later able to transfer those skills to my writing. As the author of more than one hundred books, I still begin the writing process by telling my stories—fiction, nonfiction, and concept books, too.

I am reminded by griot Onawumi Jean Moss, who is a "Keeper of the Word," that it is important to introduce youth to the traditions of our ancestors through personal experiences. Since every culture has stories that reflect their people's beliefs, customs, and history, there is a need for a variety of story motifs, especially in a multicultural environment. Whether building a storyboard, doing a compare-and-contrast exercise, or exploring various language patterns, storytelling offers a positive alternative to what's often missing in the classroom textbook.

It took a while for me to find my voice as a writer. Before I was published, I was an English teacher who stubbornly held on to rigid rules regarding grammar and usage. I thought standard English was the ONLY language pattern that students needed to be exposed to in the classroom. I was wrong.

Storytelling helped me realize that words are tools. There are no right or wrong words, just different ways of expressing an idea, describing a character, staging the action, etc. Sometimes I might create the setting with a single phrase: "It was just before dark." Then again, "It was jes' 'fore dark," might express it better. To help my students manage language, rather than the other way around, I began teaching them the skill of code switching: changing your language pattern to fit the social environment.

One special memory is of my grandmother telling horrific ghost stories. They were deliciously frightening, but I always begged for more. Being a good listener led me to become an avid reader and a budding writer. Without even realizing it, I had learned the five elements of story structure—character, dialogue, setting, action, and idea. In the author's note to the *Dark Thirty: Southern Tales of the Supernatural*, I recognized the tremendous gift my grandmother had given me through her artful storytelling.

One test of literacy should be measured by the extent to which a person can use his/her imagination. While working on my master's degree at Webster University in St. Louis, I had the opportunity to take a class in "Storytelling and Puppetry" from the award-winning storyteller Lynn Rubright.

Lynn was the first person I knew to model the use of storytelling in the classroom. After her class, I was convinced that her techniques could help my students break down their fear often associated with verbal communication. I gave them exercises that freed them up enough *to visualize*—to see with the mind, to *anticipate*—to believe without evidence and *verify*—to prove it. These skills are the basis for all scientific studies. Yet my students learned it from storytelling.

This book is full of ideas and teaching strategies that will excite teachers and encourage students throughout the school year. I know you will enjoy using it and watching the convincing results. I also know, firsthand, the positive influence storytelling will have in the lifetime of a person. I owe a debt of gratitude to my beloved family who helped shape my career as a teacher, a writer, and a storyteller—and of course, the little girl in my heart who still loves to hear a good yarn on the front porch.

—Patricia C. McKissack
St. Louis, Missouri

Patricia C. McKissack has written more than 100 books about the African American experience. They have won countless awards and received much critical acclaim, all the while bringing enjoyment and information to young readers. Before becoming a full-time writer, Patricia worked as a teacher and then as an editor of children's books. "My career as a teacher helped me recognize what books were needed and what children enjoyed reading; my career as an editor taught me how to develop an idea. After teaching for nine years and editing for six, I felt I was ready to launch my writing career." McKissack and her husband, Fredrick McKissack, have written several award-winning titles: a 2003 Coretta Scott King Honor Book, Days of Jubilee, *and* Black Hands, White Sails. *The research for* Christmas in the Big

House, Christmas in the Quarters *took the McKissacks on a writer's treasure hunt through the states of Virginia, West Virginia, and Tennessee. Pat has written several novels on her own, including her Newbery Honor title,* Dark Thirty: Southern Tales of the Supernatural *and* Porch Lies: Tales of Slicksters, Tricksters, and other Wily Characters, *a collection of stories that are very popular among storytellers. McKissack is a storyteller who enjoys a good porch lie. Fred and Pat McKissack live in Chesterfield, Missouri, a suburb of St. Louis. When they aren't traveling for research, they travel for fun. Web site:* http://www2.scholastic.com/browse/contributor.jsp?id = 3372.

ACKNOWLEDGMENTS

Our Heartfelt Gratitude Goes to ...

... our spectacular, dedicated, thoroughly professional contributors, without whom this book could not have happened. Each of you has willingly shared your unique perspective and creativity with us, and we are deeply indebted to you! This has been an incredible journey with teachers who took the time to write about what they do and tellers who wrote about classroom collaborations with teachers. These shared experiences spark and enrich curriculum learning and inspire thinking that ignites literacy learning. The generosity of our collaborators and their willingness to share their hearts and souls will have long-lasting effects on students for generations to come.

... Jamie Koss, Anne Patrick, and Juli Ross for technical help and help and help!

... Judy Sima, who once again volunteered for the thankless task of preparing the bibliography—we most sincerely thank you!

... Limeul Eubanks for drawing Diane's story; and Fellowship Bible Church, especially Brenda and Earvin, for understanding this wonderfully crazy life Diane lives as a storyteller and writer; and also to the Mississippi Arts Commission for knowing how important this work is.

... our marvelous editor, Sharon Coatney, who always responded instantly and knowledgeably to our frantic questions and concerns.

Acknowledgments

... Diane and Sherry also wish to acknowledge Jane, whose cry, "I've been thinking ... " is always met by our groans ("Oh, noooooo!"), but is always the precursor of a great idea.

... Sherry and Jane wish to acknowledge Diane, who has been heard to say, "My nerves are shot!" but continues to provide support, encouragement, laughter, and good work—no matter what!

... Jane and Diane wish to acknowledge Sherry, who handles our conference calls while driving in the dark and rain through unknown territory. Together, we have charted a new path and blazed a trail for teachers, tellers, and students!

... and we are grateful to all of the children who have inspired us, challenged us, and shown us time and time again that story is truly the most powerful teaching tool we can bring to the classroom.

INTRODUCTION

Sherry Norfolk, Jane Stenson, and Diane Williams

It has been two years since our last book, *The Storytelling Classroom: Applications Across the Curriculum*. Again, we have the collaborative effort of teachers and storytellers to show the many ways storytelling can inform and teach and express.

We'd like you to think about the gifts of the oral tradition—what it brings and offers to children and teachers and tellers—how we become whole and articulate and expressive as we listen to and tell stories. Simultaneously, we'd like you to think about the gifts of the literary tradition—the worlds that open to literate children and teachers and tellers, or how we become whole and articulate and expressive as we participate in literary communities. This collection is about how both traditions can intermingle and create worlds of possibility for children in school. And, how one does not preclude the other; each requires the other in order to be successful. The oral tradition and the literary tradition belong in schools as complements, as parts of the whole . . . to the benefit of children.

This book is about LITERACY! So, we begin with a discussion of literacy. We've selected six components of literacy and chosen articles that have inspirational and practical lessons to demonstrate possible interactions between tellers and teachers and between and among literacy components. We're excited to present as well as extend ideas about speaking and listening, reading and writing to include more current endeavors of visual literacy and information literacy as part of this collection.

Introduction

Speaking and Listening: The oral tradition is based on fundamental literacy priorities, that is, speaking and listening come first, develop concurrently, and need encouragement throughout school years and beyond. Oralcy should not stop being taught or experienced when the child jumps into print modality (kindergarten and first grade), or when the child shifts into content learning (fourth and fifth grade). The very young child learns language in a dyad because someone interacts and speaks and listens. How pleasurable is it to babble to and with an infant! First I coo and giggle, and then the baby coos and babbles and giggles. As the toddler begins speaking, adults compensate for the full production of sentences because the toddler's physical efforts "tells" the adult what he or she really wants. Layering language on top of a sensory experience and physical activity should be present as the child grows and knowledge expands. Note in chapter 3 an article titled "If You Can Read, You Can Cook" by Nancy Perla that applies the layering of language onto the physical activity of French tart making. Note in chapter 5 the lead article by Greg Weiss, "Use Your Words: Reimagining Literacy" that insists education remember its roots in speaking and listening. Or take a look at "Creative Book Making: Stories of the Seasons" by Sue Gundlach and Lea Basile Lazarus in chapter 5 where middle school students reexperience the sensory roots of language.

Reading and Writing: Well, here we are. You might think these two are the whole of literacy instruction in the schools—certainly, they are the easiest to measure and test. Certain tales such as "The Turnip" or "The Little Red Hen" or "Goldilocks and the Three Bears" appear early in a young child's experience. They are repetitive and the vocabulary is accessible. After they are known, they can be "read" by looking at the pictures in the book. Using wordless picture books helps a child form a story (narrative structure). In the kindergarten chapter, check out Andy Offutt Irwin's "(I Got those) Low-Down, Dirty, Emergent-Reader Blues," in which he teaches word families through music and whack. Reluctant readers are encouraged to "Read, Spell, and Tell" by Lynn Rubright in the same chapter. Articles in each chapter speak to the immigrant or bilingual experience, such as Carrie Sue Ayvar and Cathy Crowley in chapter 2, Antonio Sacre and Sadarri Saskill in chapter 3, and Luiz Da Silva and Sadarri Saskill in chapter 4.

Visual Literacy: When we read, one of the pleasures of the activity is the pictures that form in our minds about the characters and the setting. When tellers tell, the story comes from pictures in their minds; often they aren't thinking about particular words, they're speaking off of the images that roll along inside their minds. Hmm. This is important! There must be ways to encourage such pictures so that our reading and telling can develop. Three of our contributors have stellar articles for any age (their use is not limited to the chapter's age group). Cathy Ward in chapter 2 offers a way to encourage looking at and articulating the story found in works of art. In chapter 4, Janice Del Negro looks at the images in picture books to help children understand the story found in those images; in the same chapter, Mike Gnutek shares an inspired and inspiring integrated art, music, and storytelling lesson and how it develops higher-order thinking.

Information Literacy: What is information literacy? The American Library Association in the beginning of a definition says that information literacy is "having the ability or set of abilities to recognize when information is needed and have the ability to locate, evaluate, and use effectively the needed information." Because of the amount and variety of ways information is available, this is a critical skill. Schoolchildren, teenagers, adults, storytellers, and teachers all need the ability to recognize when information is needed, and they must be able to evaluate the information and use it appropriately. Many of the articles in this book adhere to information literacy standards, but most directly and notably in chapter 4 is "Hidden Memory: A Family History Project" by storyteller Anne Shimojima. What started with the purchase of a new computer expanded into a family photo album and a performance story about her family's immigration, time in the camps, and life in America!

In chapters 3, 4, and 6, we feature six contributions (three pairings) because their interaction shows how the teller informs the teacher and how the teacher becomes increasingly effective with story as the guide … and how children benefit. In chapter 3, Mary Gay Ducey, who never writes down her stories, tells "Canada Geese." You can hear her quiet, calm, encompassing voice through the words she put down on paper. You can hear how much she admires the grandmother and the granddaughter. Her counterpoint is Nancy Perla, a long-standing, wonderful teacher who cooks with children. What you discover is how much Nancy loved and learned from her grandmother and how her art is cooking. The article and the story mesh for your enjoyment.

The second pairing is storyteller Beth Horner, who never writes down her stories either, singing and telling an environmental story (it's about do-do-do-do-do-do-do or sewage), "The Pipeline Blues," which she performed for fifth graders and their teachers. The teachers Jackie Downey and Juli Ross crafted activities and assessments on persuasive writing that produced some terrific work by students. In these three examples rests the heart of this book about literacy. Children benefit when knowledge and art, technique and expression, and many ways of understanding are embraced in schools. The teller has a piece of that understanding and so do teachers. Collaboration among and between teachers and tellers, as well as increased attempts to understand each other, benefits children.

Chapter 5's feature is the collaborative act or art of two teachers who honor the children they instruct. Sue Gundlach and Lea Basile

Lazarus are artists in their own right who share their knowledge and love of their artistic processes with students as they teach.

In a broader context, we began this Introduction speaking about the gifts of the literary tradition and the oral tradition. We offer this collection to you, our readers, as a living gift—not stagnant, not that it has the answers, but as an attempt to encourage and develop integrated curricula, to remember that all language has a sensory base and that it is learned in human relationships, and that an investment in the arts is an investment in our creativity and cultural heritage, in our diversity, in our communities, and in our humanity.

"I am the Dancing Man, and I have a gift for you!"
—Ruth Bornstein, *The Dancing Man* (Clarion, 1978)

CHAPTER ONE

Foundations and Inspiration

CLASSROOM CROSSINGS: SERIOUS AND SWEET
Tim Tingle

In 2007, I was hired to conduct one-hour writing seminars for under-achieving students at a Texas high school to prepare them for the state standardized writing exam, a test focused on the personal-experience narrative. I soon noted that most of my underachieving students were African American and that they had been placed together in classrooms according to their race, with a sprinkling of Mexican Americans as well. Teachers heading up these in-school segregated groupings viewed their role as disciplinary rather than instructive.

As I entered the first classroom, I was met with students eager to display their disinterest. The first hour proceeded as the students hoped. Nothing happened. The usual story starters were met with derisive, though subdued, laughter.

By the second hour, I had realized the racial nature of the groupings, and I knew from being raised less than one hundred miles away that every student before me shared one common social experience. They had, every one of them, been the object of racism.

I told them so. "I want you to use that common experience, painful though it may be, and let's tell the story. Remember, you are not talking about an incident you've read about or seen in the movies, but something that actually happened to you."

I divided the students into pairs. At first, no one talked. I said to them: "You can't tell me you don't know what I am talking about. Now is the time, your partner has a story, too. Let's do it!"

Silence. Then a young girl said, "You really want me to tell about what happened to my sister and me at the mall last summer?"

"Yes, I do," I replied. "I want all of you to start talking, one partner at a time. This is not about getting angry or getting even, this is about us trying to understand why people do what they do. But first, the stories."

"You have ten minutes, five apiece, so keep it short. And keep the language school-appropriate."

A floodgate was released. Before the hour was over, I wished I could somehow unplug everything in my life and spend the next four months with these twenty students. I knew we could produce an unforgettable and very publishable collection of short stories, and I longed to help them do it.

But life moves on. I will share one story from the class. Following a highly energized half-hour, I chose several of the students to tell before the entire class. Time drew to a close and a young man said, "Enrique, you haven't told your story." Everyone turned to the only Mexican American in the class; all the other students were black.

"Come on, Enrique."

"Yeah, man, you tell your story."

Enrique was a man of my heart. "I love basketball," he said. "I go every Saturday to play at the courts in the 'hood, you know. Nobody plays on my side of town. One afternoon, some guys came over from the college and made us leave the courts. Hey, let's go to my neighborhood, I told everybody. The court's empty."

"So we did. As soon as my friends saw me playing basketball with guys from the 'hood, they started calling me N-lover, and darkie ... all sorts of names. Now I don't have any friends in my own neighborhood, just a few."

Nobody said a word. The largest student I would see all day broke the silence. "You got friends here, man. We with you."

At least ten students rose from their chairs and circled him, slapping him, high-fiving him. "Man, we had no idea," seemed to sum it up best.

Hoke. (That's Choctaw for OK). I am not suffering under the delusion that skies parted and angels descended because of the happenings that day. I have no way of verifying any changes, whether in test scores or attitudes.

But I did my best to bottle the miracle—and learn and teach from it.

Some relevant background material: in the summer and early fall of 2006, I was traveling and speaking on a book tour that took me to 120 communities, mostly small towns. Hurricane Katrina struck cities (mostly) along the Gulf Coast and I, along with thousands of fleeing refugees, struggled to find a place to spend the night, every night, for I was on the move.

During this life-changing trek, I was reminded almost daily that we as a people have yet to overcome so many of our attitudes regarding race and cultural differences. I watched as slurs and insults were heaped upon those who had lost everything. I saw tensions rise as vacationers now shared hotel lobbies and breakfast bars with "those people," as one matronly woman said, pointing at a family huddled together at a La Quinta Inn near the Oklahoma City airport. I was shaken and began to write with a renewed sense of purpose.

Midway through the tour, my first children's book, Crossing Bok Chitto, *arrived in bookstores. The following suggested classroom activities begin with a reading of the book.*

For elementary students, I approach each class with two primary goals: improved writing skills through an increased awareness of the narrative structure, and new insights into attitudes regarding ethnic and cultural differences.

I use *Crossing Bok Chitto* as the text, and it serves as more of a jumping-off point than a final narrative. I usually tell a brief version of the story with a follow-up classroom discussion. For those unfamiliar with the story, here is a summary:

(Summary of) *Crossing Bok Chitto*

In the early 1800s, a young Choctaw girl, Martha Tom, crosses the river Bok Chitto in search of blackberries. She loses her way and stumbles upon a forbidden slave church. Encouraged by his father, a young boy named Moses leads her home, and when they reach the river, Martha Tom shows him the secret crossing path, made of stones and lying unseen just beneath the water.

Moses witnesses a Choctaw wedding and a friendship is born. Every Sunday, Martha Tom joins Moses' family at the church service. When Moses' mother is sold, he convinces his father the family can escape by the stone path.

With their home surrounded, the family leaves "through the front door" and become invisible to the slave owners. Moses dashes to Martha Tom's house and alerts the Choctaws that his family is crossing over. Martha Tom's mother gathers the Choctaw women, who appear as angels in the night fog. The pursuers, with dogs and guns, lay down their weapons as Martha Tom leads Moses' family across the water, singing in Choctaw a verse she has learned at the Sunday services, "*We are bound for the promised land.*"

Resources

• Tingle, Tim. *Crossing Bok Chitto: A Choctaw Tale of Friendship and Freedom.* El Paso, TX: Cinco Puntos Press, 2006.

• Teachers Guide, Cinco Puntos Web site: http://www.cincopuntos.com/pdf/crossing_bok_chitto_guide.pdf.

Assessments

At the story's conclusion, I pose some of the following questions:

- Why did Martha Tom cross the river and how?
- Why did her mother need blackberries?
- Who were the African American churchgoers hiding from? Why?
- Did the story *Crossing Bok Chitto* take place before or after the American Civil War? How do you know?
- Why did the men pursuing the slaves put down their weapons and allow them to escape?
- In today's world, does a real Indian: Drive a car? Go to college? Shop at the mall? Play computer games? Ride a horse?

For students capable of higher-level thinking, I chose from among the following:

- In light of the scene depicting invisibility in *Crossing Bok Chitto*, discuss suspension of disbelief.
- Give examples from other books and films that require suspension of disbelief.
- Two types of invisibility exist in the book. One is depicted when Moses and Martha Tom walk, hand-in-hand and unseen, by the plantation house, in full view of the white family. The other is when the escaping family becomes invisible to their pursuers. What is ethnic invisibility?
- Were the men chasing the slave family free?

These questions, and the following, always elicit the most thoughtful responses: what is the real miracle of *Crossing Bok Chitto*?

These questions, and many others, are available on the Cinco Puntos Web site, http://www.cincopuntos.com/pdf/crossing_bok_chitto_guide.pdf.

To encourage students to make that all-important connection between their personal lives and the message of the story, I offer the following writing opportunity:

Using an everyday situation from school, sports, or home, write a fictional scene describing one person reaching out to help someone of another race.

For the Choctaw Labor Day Gathering of 2006, I was asked to perform *Crossing Bok Chitto*, previous to Chief Pyle's state of the union address in Mississippi. During his speech, Chief Pyle announced the donation of close to a million dollars of relief to Katrina refugees, and the opening of Choctaw facilities to provide housing.

We can become a nation of givers, people of compassion; lessons from our stories make these changes possible.

STORYTELLING IN THE 'HOOD
Susan Danoff

Long ago when the world was new, Raven was visiting the world he had helped to create. He entered a village and saw fear on the faces of the villagers. He was puzzled by this emotion he had never seen before, and the villagers told him, "Raven, fear is something you have never known. At the same time that you planted good in the world, evil was also placed here. You just saw the face of Axsuq, the evil one. He demanded our berries and we gave them to him. We do not know how to fight evil. And his mother is even more powerful than he. We fear them, Raven. We fear them. We do whatever they want to avoid their wrath."

Raven felt great anger toward Axsuq and told the villagers, "I will go, and I will destroy Axsuq."

Raven tracked Axsuq and because of Raven's great prowess with bow and arrow, he killed the great hunter Axsuq, but then he had to face an even greater evil: Axsuq's mother. When she looked at him, she laughed and said, "Raven, you cannot fight evil in your Raven's mask and cloak of immortality. I challenge you to fight me without them. Fight me as a man, Raven."

In his pride, Raven removed his mask and cloak of immortality. He beheld the terrifying evil in Axsuq's mother as she transformed into a giant writhing snake. Without his cloak of immortality, Raven felt fear for the very first time, but grabbing his spear he also felt courage for the first time. In a battle for his life, the life of a mortal man, he defeated Axsuq's mother.

Afterward, the villagers shouted their praises, but Raven told them: "I must go away from the world now. I have learned something I did not know before. You no longer need me. I never understood fear before because I did not know death. Now I know the fear that creates courage. You have the courage it takes to live in this world. You no longer need me."

After that, Raven left this world.

(My abridged version is based on the story in *Raven the Trickster: Legends of the North American Indians* by Gail Robinson, Atheneum, 1982.)

The day I told this Raven story, I was weaving the theme of identity through my work with three groups of middle school students at Martin Luther King Middle School in Trenton, New Jersey. I wanted my students to think about the masks we wear and the assumptions we make when we look at others. What do our masks hide and what do they reveal about us? What power do they hold over us?

To complement the story, I also shared "We Wear the Mask," a poem by the African American writer Paul Laurence Dunbar (1872–1906):

> We wear the mask that grins and lies,
> It hides our cheeks and shades our eyes,—
> This debt we pay to human guile;
> With torn and bleeding hearts we smile,
> And mouth with myriad subtleties.
>
> Why should the world be over-wise,
> In counting all our tears and sighs?
> Nay, let them only see us, while
> We wear the mask.
>
> We smile, but, O great Christ, our cries
> To Thee from tortured souls arise.
> We sing, but oh the clay is vile
> Beneath our feet, and long the mile;
> But let the world dream otherwise,
> We wear the mask!

The students were initially puzzled by the poem when I asked why its narrators wished to "wear the mask." We talked about the period when Dunbar had written the poem, and finally one of the students realized that the speakers of the poem, survivors of slavery, did not want to reveal the truth of their pain and suffering to those who would not understand or sympathize with them. Once the students understood this and discussed how they too sometimes chose to hide their emotions, they recited the poem together with great feeling.

I was the only Caucasian person in classes of mostly African American and a handful of Latino students, and the Raven story helped us to think about how we appear in the world and the assumptions others make about us as well as the conclusions we jump to before we get to know other people. I asked the students what they knew about me just by looking at me, and they told me that I was white (correct). But one asked me, "What kind of white are you?" meaning where was I from originally. The students proceeded to name every European country they could think of, but they didn't hit the right one (Russia). They told me they knew I was married because I wore a wedding ring (correct), but when they tried to tell me my age they guessed everything from thirty-two to fifty. By the time we finished talking about what they thought they knew about my "mask and cloak," we realized that they had guessed incorrectly on just about everything that they thought had been obvious from my appearance.

Yet they were even more astonished when I asked them what they knew about Mr. Perry, an apprentice storyteller who had visited their class several times. They said that Mr. Perry was African American, married (he too had a ring), and between thirty-two and forty years old. They were astonished to discover he was Latino and a native Spanish speaker.

Talking about big themes like identity with teenagers, it is more powerful to come in the back door with metaphor. But I wanted to do more than that. Using the story and poem as fodder for the imagination, I wanted the students to explore their own sense of identity metaphorically. In metaphor, we see ourselves as if in a mirror, but that mirror does not threaten us. It just helps us to see more clearly.

To do this, I brought in a bunch of art supplies—markers, crayons, glitter glue, glue, small pieces of colored collage paper, yarn, sequins, and white construction paper with a mask form traced onto each one. I had made a few simple models of my own to show the students how the empty facial form could easily become a face by drawing features or pasting on some of the ornamental odds and ends. They couldn't wait to claim the materials and many took great care with their masks, creating astonishingly beautiful faces in our seventy-five minute class period. The cool eighth-grade boys could not get enough of the glitter glue.

We left the masks to dry until the next time I visited, and then I passed them out again. "We're going to write poems," I told the students, "as if our masks are speaking to us. What would your mask say if you gave it a voice?" I had written poems from the points of view of the two masks I had made, and I shared these with the students to provide a model of what I was asking them to do. Then we talked about verbs—brainstorming every verb we could think of—and I put these up on the board. This would help our characters "act" in the world using their five senses, because we might consider what they tasted or consumed, how they moved, the textures of their environment, the sounds, the colors, and the smells. By the time we finished brainstorming, the students couldn't wait to write.

If I had asked the students to write about their own sense of identity, they would have been stuck. The question is too big and too daunting. Even as an experienced writer, I wouldn't know how to begin. But I wasn't asking them to write about themselves here, and the masks had so much personality, so much power, and so much emotional content, that the task was easy.

The super-cool eighth-grade boy who wrote this poem had not even picked up his pencil the first few times I visited:

> I wear my mask of power
> When I stretch to Mars
> It feels like the galaxy is in my hand
> When I whistle
> It sounds like the wind that blows
> Not evil
> Stay calm
> I won't hurt a soul.
> —J.M.

The sixth-grade girl who wrote the following poem missed class the day we made the masks, so she drew hers in pencil, a simple round face with large eyes, wrinkle lines of worry on the forehead, a big frowning mouth, and large teardrops. She was able to take powerful ownership of some of the verbs we brainstormed, and her last line blew me away:

> I wear my mask of sadness
> I paint dark blue sky
> I breathe cold air
> I stare wisely
> I scream slowly "GO AWAY"
> I kick the rock open
> —K.J.

One of the strongest writers I worked with was a sixth-grade girl who never smiled. Her mask had mouth and eyes slanted down in sorrow. This is what her mask said:

> In my mask of sadness
> I would cry out blue gems
> I would talk softly
> I would walk slowly
> I would sing out all my sad feelings
> I would let go the useless things in my heart
> I would fill my soul full of darkness
> I don't want to tell people how I feel.
> —H.D.

Most of the poems expressed sad or angry masks, but this sixth grader wrote one of the only funny poems of the day. His wild mask had small eyes and nose, feathers sticking up from the top of his head, a mouth opened wide with teeth showing, and a large black mustache and beard.

> In my goofy mask
> I sing "hoola hoola hoola"
> I dance in a triangle shape like I'm on Mars
> I burp loud as a hippo fart
> I eat bananas and cow manure
> I run till my feet sprout flowers
> I'm the goofy mask
> Watch out
> —M.S.

The eighth-grade girl who wrote the following poem was often absent from school, but when she managed to show up, her oversized attitude frequently caused her to get thrown out of class or suspended for the day. I saw her expression relax for the first time when she saw the art materials. She took a bunch of pink paper and glue and made an intricate collage out of pink, working hard and creating a piece of art unlike any of the other students. When I praised her creation, she said that she wanted to be a fashion designer. After that, she engaged in a positive manner in the class:

> Pretty 'n Pink
> It's me
> It's me
> Who else could it be
> looking this good
> in pink?
> Not you
> Not you
> And not you
> No one is like me
> No one can be me
> Because I was created
> to blow people away
> I was created to
> take your breath away
> I was created
> I was created
> I was created
> for my specialty
> I was created from
> the heart
> That's why
> No one else
> could ever be me.
> —A.J.

This is just a small sampling of the sixty poems written from the mask-making activity. I wish I had space to include all of them because each was powerful and personal, direct and vivid.

Writing unmasks and reveals our identity, but for many students, especially teenagers, writing can be a self-conscious process that closes rather than opens their writers' voices. Exercises such as this one, where students take on the voices of others, paradoxically free their own writers' voices.

I visited Martin Luther King Middle School fifty times over a two-year period between December 2004 and June 2006. The first day I visited, I asked the school secretary if I could park on the street, and she looked at me sort of funny and said, "I wouldn't." A friend who occasionally visited as a guest artist pointed out the drug dealing that was going on across the street from the school. One morning when I arrived, I asked about the numerous police cars outside. "A gang incident," someone told me, almost dismissively. Another morning, the students were chattering excitedly about an incident the night before when three drive-by shootings claimed a few lives. When I was signing in one day in the school office, I saw a boy being taken out in handcuffs. The metal detector was used only occasionally, though it was situated by the main entrance. One morning my class was interrupted so that the on-site police could frisk all of my students for cell phones, and another day all the girls were removed from class to have their lockers searched for a pair of shoes that had disappeared during gym class. I frequently saw skirmishes in the halls, and the first year I was there, the hallways were so noisy all through the day that I could barely hear and be heard in the classrooms. Whenever possible, we held class in the school library, which was insulated from the noise. The situation changed the second year, especially on the infamous day called "hall sweep" when students were sent home if they were caught in the halls skipping class. The noise was certainly reduced that day; almost no one was in school.

When it came to the mandatory standardized tests, between 2002 and 2006 only about 20 percent of the students tested proficient in language arts and less than 10 percent tested proficient in math. I carried pencils, notebooks, and folders for the students since they rarely brought their own to class.

During my residences the students wrote many pieces, and I published their best work in two anthologies. These children were easily the best writers I had ever worked with even though the test scores told a different story. They had seen and experienced a lot, their voices were honest and open, and yet they had come to my class with absolutely no idea that they had something special to offer that would be valued by others.

Although I have layered storytelling, poetry, modeling, and writing activities in the lesson I have just described, I want to focus on the power of story as the opening activity. The presence of the story within the lesson cannot be underestimated. I discovered at Martin Luther King Middle School, as I have for more than twenty-five years at many other schools, that stories have the capacity to transform the inner-city classroom. Students who enter the room with little sense of engagement become intense listeners. Once opened to the experience of story, their own thoughts and stories emerge like pinpoints of light in the darkness. Storytelling is education that passes through the heart before it reaches the mind, a path that our ancient traditions understood so very long ago. We engage, we remember, and we create meaning for ourselves when our emotions play an equal role to our intellect. And in environments where emotions are raw and it is difficult to make order from chaos, stories provide a safe place to experience and understand emotion.

Often I would feel that the children entered the classroom with anger and resentment. Once they began to listen to a story, they were able to leave behind the baggage that had come into the classroom with them and enter the peace of the story. A Trenton fifth grader described the experience of listening to a story this way: "What I felt was I can live in this world without being scared. I see a lot of colors. I love the way the environment was so nice. No trash on the ground. I didn't see nobody throw stuff out the car. It was beautiful."

Story language is vastly different from instructional language. It's more personal and carries no judgment. The storyteller, just by virtue of sharing a story, is sending the message: "I am telling you something real and important about me." The story does not have to be about me, but the emotional investment I have made in telling it shows that the story is a gift from me. I have taken a risk and have modeled how to take a risk.

Teaching and learning are inextricably connected. If I don't model what I am looking for—both in spirit and in practice—how can I expect the students to be able to do it?

Storytelling belongs in every classroom, but it is absolutely essential in the classrooms of our so-called failing schools. The schools may be failing, but these students have the capacity, as all children do, of being the outstanding thinkers and writers that I saw emerge at Martin Luther King Middle School in Trenton. Our children are starving for an education that speaks to them; let us nourish them with story.

LEAVING OUR CHILDREN BEHIND: LITERACY AND NATIONAL STANDARDS
Judith Black

The U.S. government suffers from the same malaise as most of us. If our nation's children are not reading, it is someone's fault, but not theirs. The Bush administration's Elementary and Secondary Education Act (2001), known as No Child Left Behind (NCLB), claims innocence for our constantly declining educational system. This legislation, like much that came before it, and much that will follow, is the Bush administration's magic-bullet answer to falling achievement in our public schools. The administration's plan: ratchet up testing, primarily of literacy and numeracy skills, and penalize schools that do not show adequate annual achievement. The irony of this and all punitively based educational legislation is that the very schools that exhibit lower scores are not infused with extra funds and resources to support higher achievement. They are penalized. The result is that schools are now hyper-focusing on bolstering students' tests scores, for a "national standard" (in hopes, that after the "test" dust settles, some authentic education might take place). Most educators secretly hope that once the "test" dust settles they might move on to some authentic education. Let us examine the obvious fallacy operating here and look to the storytelling classroom—an educational model that actually works for teaching literacy.

Ron Paul, a Republican candidate for the 2008 presidential race, has noted: "A better title for this bill is 'No Bureaucrat Left Behind.' National testing will inevitably lead to a national curriculum as teachers will teach what their students need to know in order to pass the mandated assessment ... There are continuing disputes about teaching all subjects, as well as discussions on

how to measure mastery of a subject matter." Here is a Republican who understands that these standardized, primarily multiple-choice tests are basically irrelevant. They measure the skills at a time in the child's development that will be
understood and utilized only by a small segment of the population.

What we have learned, as educators, from Jean Piaget and Eric Erikson is that cognition and emotional well-being are deeply intertwined and are
a growth industry. Larry Kohlberg taught us that moral reasoning and its
increasing sophistication emerges from the cognitive and emotional levels of
development that we have reached. Every stage of development and learning
is based on the foundation that precedes it. The knowledge of facts, those
things needed to pass compulsory state and national tests, are much like the
bricks in the Tower of Babel, the tower that goes straight up, with no supporting structure, and is easily toppled. A fundamental education that gives students the ability to think and reason and act emerges from a much broader
base of accumulated skills and experiences.

Educators understand that in order to create a strong foundation, they
must teach from the current knowledge base of the individual child. Forced to
fulfill a national standard that dictates that every child, by the age of eight, must
read at a standardized third-grade level (according to President Bush's NCLB
introductory speech) is absurd. It is only at this age that many learning disabilities begin to surface, that teachers are coming to grips with the best way to
teach students whose learning skills do not respond to traditional classroom
approaches, and that children coming from other languages and cultures are beginning to find a foothold into this system. Punitive national standards simply
don't work. They disempower teachers who know that in order to educate a
child, you must start where they are, cognitively, curricularly, and culturally,
and create pathways into this mainstream of learning. Compulsory standardized
testing will not improve education. Empowered, well-funded, and locally based
schools will. This is where the storytelling classroom can serve as a brilliantly
adaptive tool to meet the needs of students and the objectives of teachers.

In the teaching of literacy, possibly more than almost any other subject, true learning emerges from speech, and speech emerges from the immediate world the child inhabits. Thus, each student's road to literacy will begin in
their home and community. From urban New York City, to an Iowa cornfield,
to a Texas border town, a child's experience of their world is a unique starting
point for literacy acquisition.

One of the elementary schools that I have worked with in California
draws a large percentage of its population from Spanish-speaking homes. I was
hired as a storyteller-in-residence, sharing stories in public elementary and middle schools. It became clear, after finishing my first session to a polite but blank-
faced auditorium of students, that the material I used so successfully in my
native New England had no resonance for these students. That night, I reshaped
the program, pulling up stories from my repertoire such as "La Cama Grande"
("The Big Bed"). This tale is about el nino piqueno (a little boy) who was
allowed to leave the bed he shared at home with his tres hermanos (three

brothers) and go spend the night with su abuela, his grandmother. Thrilled, he arrived at her casa (home) and would be allowed to sleep in la cama grande, solomente (in the big bed by himself), which turned out to not be the heart's desire he had anticipated. As his grandmother kissed him good night and shut the squeaky puerto (door), he found himself distressed by images of ghosts, monsters, and bad guys. This story was a huge hit with the students. Not only did the story come from their culture, but there was enough Spanish language to create a bridge of understanding into the English language and the theme spoke to their developmental level. The group participation (which was orchestrated to sound like a creaking door, a howling ghost, a monster's yell, a bad guy's shout, and a little boy's frightened scream) allowed them to be active participants in an English-language experience. Once this tale was complete, they were engaged in the process of active listening. The students were now ready travelers, willing to reach for the unknown because they felt safely grounded in the known.

This is why there can be no one national standard. The learning must come out of the children's experiences. Storytelling has the flexibility to reflect almost any population's social and cultural experiences of language (both oral and written) and can be built into their literacy program.

The Storytelling Classroom

Oral language precedes reading and written language. For a learner of literacy, this means that exposure to literate, poetic, clear, and expressive spoken word, shared in a nonthreatening and emotionally engaging manner (that is, storytelling), becomes part of students' fundamental language use. Jane was a kindergarten teacher in Brookline, Massachusetts. Every day she told her young charges a story. Jane had been telling the story of Snow White to her students, who had asked to hear it multiple times. The school principal, trying to reinforce the school's distinguished academic reputation, came to talk to her during recess and questioned her use of time for this activity. She led him to the window where they could hear the children at play.

"Look out," said one girl. "You're gonna fall and get a black and blue shiner, as dark as ebony." The principal was floored that a five-year-old was using a word far more sophisticated than the average kindergartener's vocabulary, and never again questioned the time required for storytelling.

In a classroom, there is almost no time for children to verbalize a narrative to the attuned and receptive hearing of their peers and teacher. There is one instructor, twenty to thirty students, and forty-three minutes to cover a topic. You can do the math. Yet, we have learned that literacy rests not merely on hearing, but in the children's ability to create verbal pictures of their world. Using storytelling not only as an instructional tool, but in peer coaching sessions, enables children to express their images and stories as well as having their stories heard. In a study by the Massachusetts Institute of Technology, virtual peers as partners in storytelling and literacy, the power of story modeling, and listening were explored. A computerized storytelling buddy, Sam, was devised. Sam looked much like the preschoolers he was interacting with, telling stories collaboratively with them. Accessing the child's use of language, he "told" stories in a developmentally advanced way (for the individual child), modeling narrative skills important for literacy. "Results demonstrated that children who played with the virtual peer told stories that more closely resembled the virtual peer's linguistically advanced stories: using quoted speech and temporal and spatial expressions. In addition, children listened to Sam's stories carefully, assisting him and suggesting improvements" (*Journal of Computer Assisted Learning,* 2003). What this study does not look at is the subtle nurturing effects of being listened to. Now we venture into a world that no national standard wants to even address, that human growth and development (literacy, in this instance) is not only about the cognition. As Piaget, Erikson, Kohlberg have all shown us, human beings do not develop fully in single categories such as cognition or moral thinking when the emotional and social aspects of their lives are voided or abused. We are whole beings, and storytelling addresses that wholeness, inspiring literacy through all avenues of human development. This gift of the storytelling classroom is unquantifiable, but essential to nurturing humanity. It is the element that those of us who "grow" children cannot, and never want to, ignore.

A few years ago, I helped develop a grant proposal for work at a school in Lawrence, Massachusetts. Following are some of the beautifully flowered prose I assembled for that application:

Whereas:

- A majority of the student population (80 percent) represent learners whose primary/home language is not English.
- The teacher population is not familiar with the culture of origins of most of the student population.
- This particular student population reads English significantly below standard levels.
- This particular student population has been slow to acquire social and communication skills necessary for school success.

We propose a storytelling residency that will focus on language acquisition and communication via tales from the indigenous cultures of the student population ... blah, blah, blah, blah, blah.

Completed by the principal and myself, this was all well-intentioned and accurate. Then I arrived. The old brick schoolhouse resembled the home of the Little Old Woman Who Lived in the Shoe, as children seemed to be oozing out of and pouring into every nook and cranny of the ancient structure. The office was a tiny room jammed with the secretary and principal's desks and three children at various levels of distress. "Oh sure, we're expecting you honey," called the secretary. "Just hang your coat on the rack next to the desk and I'll try and find Sherry (the principal)." There were, in these moments before the day officially began, what felt like a hurricane of children running, screaming, packing the hallways, dashing up stairs, in a building with no gym, cafeteria, or auditorium.

I saw the principal at the other end of the hall with a child under her arm. Now, mind you, her arm was not around his shoulder. She literally had him under her arm, as if she was carrying a rug. The boy, seven or eight years old, was screaming, spitting, and pinching at her. She, meanwhile, continued down the hall waving enthusiastically at me and greeting every child in both English and Spanish as she passed them.

"This is my buddy Diego. He's having a bad morning." She put her hand gently on his head and lowered him to a standing position, his arms and legs still beating at anything nearby. She talked to him soothingly in Spanish, but he was not to be dissuaded. I stuck my tongue out at him and began making weird faces and strange sounds. He jumped track to hone in. We started playing a finger game. "Thanks," Sherry said without him hearing. "Part of it is neurological and he needs to have complete dissonance in order to change response. The other part is that he's just plain angry." It turned out that his father had just finished a jail sentence in the Massachusetts prison system, but would not be returning or even visiting home because he owed some time to the New Hampshire prisons. This seven-year-old, with wizened, hardened features, was thought to be angry about not being able to see his father between the two sentences, and it was difficult to consult with his mother, a junkie whose communication skills were not optimal. During this explanation a few other students passed. Not one of them got by without Sherry riffling their hair or touching a shoulder gently and offering an introduction. "This is Maria. She is a very good reader." "This is Pablo. Wait till you see him running on the playground. He has feet like wings." "Jose, come meet the storyteller. Jose is a math genius." No sooner did she complete her explanation of Diego's issues than the sound of flying furniture was heard from a nearby first-grade classroom. "Un momento," she said and was off to douse another fire. What made me think that our little plan, which outlined exactly what would be accomplished in each classroom session and how, might require some flexibility?

It turned out that I would be working intensely with Diego's second-grade class. The principal told me that he spent a lot of his classroom time sleeping, something he did infrequently at night. When he wasn't sleeping, he was often causing havoc. Any little thing could take him from an average day to a day headed down death gulch. A look from another kid, a perceived slight, or even hunger, and he could go from a pleasant, engaged kid to a violent one, throwing chairs at windows and knocking over desks. Since there was no counselor's office, Diego spent a lot of time at a desk alone in the downstairs hallway.

I preach the perks of storytelling so often that I forget it's real. One day on my way to lunch, I saw Diego at a little desk in the hallway pretending to read a book about Michael Jordan. His face was locked like a prison door. I looked at the book.

"Hey man, what ya reading?"

He was barely audible and didn't look up.

"Michael Jordan."

"Hey, he's the man isn't he? Find out anything interesting? Hey, what's that?"

There was a sketchbook on the table.

"May I take a look?" Diego nodded. "Woo. These are great drawings. You do them?' Another nod.

"Cool! What's happening here?" And he started to tell me about a kid climbing up a building to escape and how the guards were trying to shoot him, and that's what the zigzag lines were. But there's a really bad man in there and the kid has got to get away.

"Hey, want to hear a story about a really bad man?"

You bet he did, and without knowing exactly why, I launched into Bluebeard. Sitting in the basement hall with kids, adults, and lunch aides traipsing back and forth, his attention was riveted in that little sphere of energy that the story created between us. I had barely finished when the principal (by all reckoning, a woman soon to be sainted) appeared with Diego's mother. I wanted to tell her what an important part he had in the classroom story we were acting out (he was in "The Chili Plant" class), but my Spanish was much too halting and she was feeling diffident because he had disrupted his classroom ... again. He was taken away. The next day, while once again sitting in the hall, Diego called me over.

"Hey, storyteller lady."

"Hello, my man. What's up?"

"I want to tell you a story."

I pulled up a chair and hunkered into the intimacy of our circle. He took out his sketchbook, opened it to the same picture we were looking at the previous day, and began.

"This here is a castle and a really bad man lives in there. He has a black beard, so I call him Blackbeard. See this kid climbing the wall? He is super kid and he is climbing in to save a girl from Blackbeard ..."

Diego feared his father, but through the story he'd heard, he recreated his life and was the hero saving his mother.

He went on until school life forced us to break the circle. The circumstances of Diego's life will be deeply affected only by a new trend in social, political, and economic justice. I'm not holding my breath. His ability to see himself as a hero rather than a victim in his world can be affected by storytelling. I pray that this slight switch in vantage points will give him strength in his world.

Storytelling is not a panacea, but as a tool that can be personalized for any given population, it offers a wonderful model of language usage, encourages that usage, and addresses the whole life of a child. It is a tool that every classroom reaching toward literacy might well choose to employ.

Resources

- NCLB Background: passed in 2001, uses standardized testing to measure results. http://www.ed.gov/nclb/landing.jhtml.
- Perrault, Charles. *Bluebeard, Les Contes de ma Mere l'Oye*, 1697.
- Ryokai, K., C. Vaucelle, and J. Cassell. *Journal of Computer Assisted Learning*, vol. 19, issue 2. Oxford, England: Blackwell Publishing Ltd, 2003, 195–208.

ASSESSMENT OF STORYTELLING
Ann Bates, EdD

Teachers in storytelling classrooms provide rich testimonials about its impact on children's learning. Whether students are listening to stories being told or learning to tell stories themselves, they are engaged in language arts in an elemental yet joyful manner. The listening and speaking that storytelling elicits invites response and participation. Both the listener and the speaker are immersed in the story, its narrative form comfortably familiar and its details distinctive and mesmerizing. To tell a story effectively before an audience, one must interpret it and convey this to the audience, an act that requires a deep understanding of the narrative and the deft use of language. Furthermore, it is possible, through story selection, to expand the students' knowledge of and appreciation for the stories and oral traditions of different cultures and eras.

Teachers who use storytelling in the classroom are confident about the benefits that these experiences hold for children; it almost seems unnecessary that storytelling be justified or somehow proven to be a worthwhile activity for pupils. But the need for accountability in all learning experiences we provide for children today is a reality. Stakeholders, including parents, administrators, community members, and, most importantly, students themselves, must be informed about the learning that occurs when storytelling is part of the curriculum. This learning needs to be documented and further linked to learning standards. Indeed, we can see this as an opportunity to grow, rather than limit, the use of storytelling in the classroom.

Assessment data has the potential to provide us with the tools we need to educate our school communities about the benefits of storytelling. But the aesthetic and experiential nature of storytelling makes it an uneasy fit for the assessment measures favored and sometimes even required today: tests of isolated reading skills, timed measures that focus on the speed of print processing, or paper-and-pencils standardized tests. Further, the research on storytelling itself is scant, providing us with little direction when it comes to assessment. This chapter will attempt to weave the assessment of storytelling into an instructional plan that is linked to learning standards. The goal is to document student progress in the learning associated with this time-honored and powerful language and literacy activity in order to both strengthen our teaching of storytelling and inform others of its benefits for children of all ages.

Using Informal Assessment

Storytelling lends itself to *informal* assessment practices, in which observations, anecdotal records, and artifacts of student work are used to document and evaluate progress. The term "informal" can be somewhat misleading when used to characterize this type of assessment, for it connotes a somewhat unplanned and spontaneous approach to evaluation, especially in contrast to formal assessment, which includes measures such as standardized, statistically normed tests. Perhaps "authentic" is a more descriptive term for what occurs. In authentic, informal assessment, the student is evaluated while actually engaging in the task being assessed, rather than while doing a representative act, as is the case with most formal assessment measures. Thus, the data collected through informal assessment can be considered the most accurate and valid possible, since we are seeing the real application of learning. This makes it especially useful for evaluating and planning instruction, as well as for assessing student learning.

In the classrooms of effective teachers, authentic, informal assessment is woven so naturally into instruction that its planning and design processes are often obscured. Storytelling seems to be especially prone to this. It has an overt, visible quality to it; the students' learning is easy to see, hear, and respond to. While it may seem unnecessary to assess or document it in any systematic way, opportunities to do so must be captured, documented, and celebrated. This will help secure a role for storytelling in the development of language-rich, literate classrooms.

Beginning with Instruction

Sound assessment practices always start with instructional planning. Simply put, we must assess what we teach. This begins with the identification of those features of storytelling that we want students to learn and demonstrate. Given the nature of storytelling and its various components and facets, it is important to limit this list to those specific elements that we plan to teach and expect students to demonstrate based on their ages and their experiences with storytelling. Table 1.1 is such a sample list: it itemizes the features of storytelling that a teacher might identify as important for her students to learn as they prepare and perform their stories.

Beginning with instructional elements allows the teacher to feel ownership of the assessment process, to see it as a tool for his or her own use. This makes the next step, connecting the instructional elements to learning standards, easier and more palatable. Table 1.2 links the storytelling elements from Table 1.1 to the National Standards for the English Language Arts, provided by the National Council of Teachers of English (NCTE). It is here that ideas for possible data sources begin to emerge, for implicit in the standards are

Table 1.1 Sample List of Instructional Elements for Storytelling and Story Listening

Storytelling Elements	Story Listening Elements
Story selection	Attentive listening
Sequencing of story events	Appropriate participation
Oral expression	
Clear, audible language	
Interpretation of story characters	
Use of unique vocabulary	

Table 1.2 Linking Storytelling Elements to Learning Standards

National Learning Standards, English Language Arts	Storytelling or Story Listening Element	Data Collection
NL−ENG.K−12.1 Students read a wide range of print and nonprint texts to build an understanding of texts ... Among these texts are fiction and nonfiction, classic and contemporary works.	Selection of an appropriate story	Reading record
NL−ENG.K−12.3 Students apply a wide range of strategies to comprehend, interpret, evaluate, and appreciate text.	Sequencing of story events; interpretation of characters	Storyboards, observation checklist
NL−ENG.K−12.4 Students adjust their use of spoken, written, and visual language (e.g., conventions, style, vocabulary) to communicate effectively with a variety of audiences and for different purposes.	Clear language; oral expression; use of unique vocabulary	Observation checklist
NL−ENG.K−12.9 Students develop an understanding of and respect for diversity in language use, patterns, and dialects across cultures, ethnic groups, geographic regions, and social roles.	Selection of an appropriate story; attentive listening; participation	Reading record, observation checklist

broad and useful guidelines for gathering data. Organizing for data collection must be done at this point in the process so that opportunities to observe and document student learning are captured in a variety of ways.

Collecting and Analyzing Data

Connecting the storytelling elements to learning standards does not ensure that students have made progress toward meeting them; it merely

Table 1.3 Sample Reading Record

Title	Fiction/ nonfiction	Classic/ contemporary	Origin, source	Print/ nonprint
The Lion and the Mouse	Fiction	Classic	Aesop's Fables	Print
Bear Attack!	Nonfiction	Contemporary	*Time for Kids* magazine	Print
Grandpa's Ghost	Uncertain	Contemporary	Family lore	Nonprint
The Master Swordsman	Fiction	Classic	Folktale of Ancient China	Print

articulates the potential or possibility for that to occur. The next step involves collecting, analyzing, and interpreting data that document student performance in each area, allowing the teacher to show the student's or the group's progress toward meeting the standard. The data collection step calls upon the classroom teacher's observational and record-keeping expertise and the ability to find data sources in perhaps unexpected places.

While storytelling lends itself to anecdotal data, it is important to build in opportunities to quantify the data for analysis and interpretation. The following sections outline some possible data sources that can likely be found in storytelling classrooms and used in the service of assessment. A close reading of the learning standards provides guidance in choosing or even designing data sources.

Reading Records or Logs. Standard 12.1 calls for "wide reading" in a variety of materials. A reading record or log, in which the student records titles read for general reading or while selecting a story to tell, becomes a useful artifact. It can be analyzed according to several variables, one of which could be the amount of reading done by the student; another might be the variety of genres and cultures the child explored during the selection process, which addresses aspects of diversity as described in Standard 12.9. A checklist can be added to the reading record to document the variety and diversity of the materials read and considered during the selection process. Table 1.3 is an example of a student's reading record; these data can be used to demonstrate quantity of reading as well as diversity and variety in genre, story origins, and forms.

Storyboards and Story Maps. Standard K–12.3 calls for the student to be able to use strategies to comprehend. Sequencing story events, retelling, and summarizing are some indicators of comprehension that can be practiced and demonstrated through storytelling. Knowledge of story grammars and the ability to sequence the events of a story can be aided by the use of storyboards or story maps produced by students and used as they learn and prepare their stories for telling. Storyboards (Refer to the article on storyboarding and the computer in chapter 3.), which should not be viewed or evaluated as art projects, provide rich artifacts for assessing students' abilities to synthesize and sequence key story elements, an important aspect of comprehension.

Observational Checklists. The observational checklist, completed while observing students as they tell and listen to stories, is frequently used in

Table 1.4 Sample Observation Checklist

Student_____

Storytelling/Story Listening Element	✓	Comments
Oral Language		
Audible, clear		
Expressive		
Eye contact		
Body position and gestures		
Unique vocabulary		
Language that facilitates visualization		
Comprehension		
Interprets characters		
Summarizes		
Sequences		
Listening		
Listens attentively		
Responds/participates appropriately		

Table 1.5 Sample of a Completed Rubric for a Class

Data source	3 Points (Exceeds)	2 Points (Meets)	1 Point (Does Not Meet)
Reading Record:			
	IIIII	IIIII IIIII III	III
Wide reading	5–6 stories considered for selection.	3–4 stories considered for selection.	1–2 stories considered for selection.
Variety	Student read material from all 4 genre categories. IIIII IIII	Student read material in 2–3 genre categories. IIIII II	Student read material in 1 genre category. IIIII
Storyboard	Complete story grammar represented in 6 frames; uses as retelling aid to learn story. IIIII IIII	6 frames used to represent story. IIIII IIII	Fewer than 6 storyboard frames. III
Observation Checklist	5–6 ✓ in Oral Language IIIII II	3–4 ✓ in Oral Language IIIII IIIII I	1–2 ✓ in Oral Language III
	3 ✓ in comprehension IIIII IIIII	2 ✓ in comprehension IIIII II	0–1 ✓Comprehension IIII
	3 ✓ in Listening IIIII IIIII	2 ✓ in Listening IIIII I	0–1 ✓Listening IIIII

storytelling classrooms: it is often the primary assessment tool. The checklist categories below are taken from the list of storytelling features identified earlier and linked to the national learning standards (Tables 1.4 and 1.5). Observational checklists that will be shared with students or used by them should be written using age-appropriate, child-friendly language. Developing the checklist with student input demystifies the evaluation process for students and allows them to see the connection between assessment and learning.

The checklist data, collected as the students tell and listen to stories, is analyzed later using a teacher-designed rubric. This last step, described in the next section, ensures that the checklist data is measured against the school's or classroom teacher's curricular goals and expectations.

Using Rubrics to Analyze and Interpret Assessment Data

What constitutes wide reading for a fifth grader? How many events can we expect a third grader to include in a story? What should a first grader be able to produce in a storyboard? How a teacher establishes expectations, or benchmarks, for storytelling achievement and progress should be based on the age and experience of the students, the resources available, and the curricular goals established. Rubrics allow us to make judgments about data collected using descriptors in a gradient of increasing quality and capability. A well-constructed rubric clearly sets forth the criteria for evaluation, providing some means for quantifying the data where appropriate. The sample rubric in Table 1.6 uses the data-collection methods described earlier to evaluate an individual student's progress.

Below, the same rubric is used to evaluate data for a sample class. Tally marks represent the number of students who performed in each category. This class rubric is particularly useful for instructional planning; it provides

Table 1.6   Sample Uncompleted Rubric for an Individual Student

Data source	3 Points (Exceeds)	2 Points (Meets)	1 Point (Does Not Meet)
Reading Recording:			
Wide reading	5–6 stories considered for selection.	3–4 stories considered for selection.	1–2 stories considered for selection.
Variety	Student read material from all 4 genre categories.	Student read in 2–3 genre categories.	Student read in 1 genre category.
Storyboard: *Comprehension*	Complete story grammar represented in 6 frames; uses as retelling aid to learn story.	6 frames used to represent story.	Fewer than 6 storyboard frames.
Observation Checklist	5–6 ✓ in Oral Language	3–4 ✓ in Oral Language	1–2 ✓ in Oral Language
	3 ✓ in Comprehension	2 ✓ in Comprehension	0–1 ✓ in Comprehension
	3 ✓ in Listening	2 ✓ in Listening	0–1 ✓ in Listening

clear indicators of which storytelling and story listening elements should be emphasized in the next unit of instruction.

Conclusion

Informal assessment of storytelling, particularly using observational checklists and rubrics, is not new; indeed, this is likely the method favored by teachers in storytelling classrooms. The framework presented here connects selected storytelling elements to national learning standards early in the planning process, uses observation checklists and authentic artifacts as data, and then analyzes and interprets the data through the use of a teacher-designed rubric. It is in this step that we document individual or group achievement and progress and show that learning standards and curricular goals have been addressed through storytelling.

Assessment of student learning in storytelling must not impede or limit our teaching of the aesthetic principles associated with this art form. Rather, well-designed assessments capture, affirm, and celebrate the efforts of teachers and the progress of students and point us in the next direction for guiding classroom storytellers in exploring their craft.

LEAPING THE BIGGEST HURDLE: HELPING SHY ADULTS OVERCOME THE FEAR OF PUBLIC SPEAKING
Delanna Reed
Speaking, Listening, and Visual Literacy

At the end of the first day of class one fall semester, a young woman in her early thirties waited to talk to me. She introduced herself as Debbie and told me that all of her life she had been too frightened to finish a public presentation of any kind. She would get nauseated, her mind would go blank, and she would have to sit down to avoid fainting. We discussed how natural her fear was, and I gave her several tips to begin using to work on overcoming her fear of public speaking. A couple of weeks later, when we finished a personal story assignment in small groups and I invited the students to tell their story to the whole class, Debbie was the first one to get up and tell hers.

I teach storytelling and literacy to K-6 education majors at East Tennessee State University with two primary outcomes in mind: to enable pre-service teachers to tell a story competently and to make storytelling a viable teaching tool in the classroom. Two of the strongest challenges in this bifurcated goal are the reluctance of the majority of education majors to speak in front of their peers and their lack of belief in their own creativity. These two core issues often make them resistant to the use of storytelling in their future classrooms. I would like to first address their fear of public speaking.

Like the children discussed in Sue Black and Beverly Frett's article in this book, many of my students have strong speaker apprehension in regard to speaking before their peers. Among this reluctant majority, I occasionally encounter a college student like Debbie who has never been able to stand in front of an audience of peers without being totally overcome by anxiety. Students who enjoy public performance bring a zest to the storytelling experience that enthuses everyone in the class. However, the true rewards come when the reluctant student overcomes her fears and excels in storytelling by the end of the semester.

Addressing Anxiety

How do we overcome those fears and learn to face an audience with ease? I use a combination of approaches.

- Create an empathetic audience, in this case a group of students who will all take their turn at standing in front of the group to tell a story.
- Encourage students to practice the story sufficiently and in advance of the date they are to tell. By doing their utmost to internalize the story, they are much less likely to forget it.
- Encourage students to learn stories from the oral tradition—they don't have to be memorized word-for-word.
- Teach the use of visualization to envision telling a story to a rapt audience instead of imagining failure.
- Begin to immediately use positive self-talk to change the way students think about their ability to speak before an audience. Telling yourself statements such as "I am a wonderful storyteller" and "People hang on my every word" does much to change the way you look at yourself and your abilities.

Another way I ease my students into public speaking is to begin with short storytelling assignments that take place in small groups. When telling stories in small groups, students don't yet face the pressure of being evaluated by the instructor. In this way, they have the opportunity to develop skills before telling in front of the entire class. These assignments include telling a short personal story and telling a brief story such as a fable with a flannel board and puppets. The final group assignment involves scripting and staging a story and presenting it as a group to the rest of the class. At this point, students are standing in front of the class but they are not alone. This prepares them for the final storytelling assignments told in front of the class and evaluated by the professor.

In addition to gradually preparing students to speak in front of others, peers are encouraged to give only positive feedback in the small groups. Before the final performances, I give the students guidelines for doing evaluations. Fellow students are expected to participate in the feedback sessions, following my example of identifying positive performance choices before giving suggestions for improvement. The guidelines I give on conducting evaluations are based on our oral interpretation textbook, but over the years, I have also adopted approaches practiced by skilled coaches like Doug Lipman, Jon

Spelman, and Connie Regan-Blake. The important point to keep in mind when giving feedback is to honor the storyteller's style and performance choices as valid even if they are different from your own.

Even though students come to the point that they must tell their story in front of us all and receive my evaluation, some opt to tell their stories with a partner. I introduce them to tandem storytelling early in the semester. Although they must find the time to script and rehearse the story together, some students find that the advantage of having a partner when in front of the audience is worth the extra work. The first advanced storytelling assignment is to tell an oral traditional story. Because stories from the oral tradition can be put into your own words, the stress of memorization is relieved. Some students can't let go of memorization as a way of learning the story and, unfortunately, they are usually the ones who suffer memory loss in front of the audience.

Convincing pre-service teachers that telling stories in the classroom is worth the anxiety, time, and effort involved is also a key to success. That work begins with the syllabus, which identifies Tennessee State reading standards, Tennessee State technology standards, and six Interstate New Teacher Assessment and Support Consortium (INTASC) principles that are met by the course. Since East Tennessee State University (ETSU) interdisciplinary K-6 students are required to take this course, they need to know up front what they are gaining by doing so. I also have found that they need to read the research and anecdotal evidence of those who have used storytelling to teach children. *Children Tell Stories: A Teaching Guide* by Martha Hamilton and Mitch Weiss is most helpful for accomplishing this goal. Not only does the book establish the benefits of storytelling as an instructional tool, it offers methods to teach children how to tell a story that instructs the adult who reads them.

In addition, one of the major assignments in the course involves selecting a story for a target age group and creating learning activities to go with it. As Susan Trostle Brand and Jeanne M. Donato point out, "... story reading is most beneficial when it is accompanied with extension strategies" (Delmar, 2001, p. 9). Along with their activities, students must list the Tennessee State standards being met. By doing so, they can see for themselves that storytelling teaches curriculum. Students are encouraged to study lesson plans and activities designed for stories and books found online and in various texts. One recommended text is *The Storytelling Classroom: Applications Across the Curriculum* (Libraries Unlimited, 2006) by Sherry Norfolk, Jane Stenson, and Diane Williams. While Web sites and textbooks offer many excellent and creative teaching ideas, students are required to think of their own activities. They can borrow ideas from other sources, but they need to adapt and change them to fit the story they are telling. It is important in designing these activities that they spring directly from the story that inspired them. In other words, if the activity can be done without hearing the story, then it is not designed correctly. This assignment for pre-service teachers was developed by Dr. Flora Joy, professor emeritus and founder of the ETSU master's degree in storytelling. When I began teaching with her in 1999, I inherited this well-designed activity. Although I have made adaptations over time, it still retains key features that make it unique.

The assignment requires that students begin with the story selection, not the lesson. Only after they have selected a story that they really like and have chosen their target age group are they to begin creating lessons to go with the story. A central feature of this assignment is to be as creative and imaginative as possible in designing the activities to go with the story. These need to be fun and original while remaining directly connected to the story itself. For example, if the activity focuses on language arts, it uses the vocabulary found in the story. If science or social studies are involved, the subject of the activity (animals, the environment, other cultures) must relate back directly to the story. There are excellent teaching tools already in place such as doing a storyboard, a comparison with a Venn diagram, and word puzzles. However, if they are used, the student is expected to use them in such a way that they will work only with that particular story.

Fostering Creativity

The biggest challenge to overcome with pre-service teachers is their perception that they are not creative, so in addition to giving them example story lessons to study, I also lead them through a brainstorming activity. We start with a well-known folktale such as "Little Red Riding Hood" or "Jack and the Beanstalk." While writing everything on the board, I ask them to name the subjects they will be teaching. We list everything from language arts, math, and social studies, to various arts, good character traits, and psychomotor skills. Once our list is on the board for all to see, we recall together the basic story line of the example folktale. Next, I ask them to look at what happens in the story and suggest ways they can link that to a subject. I offer some suggestions to get started, but by the end of the session they have generated a number of excellent ideas that are fun and educational. I use Susan Trostle Brand and Jeanne M. Donato's *Storytelling in Emergent Literacy: Fostering Multiple Intelligences* (Delmar, 2001) to introduce students to the many ways that storytelling connects with multiple intelligences. This helps students expand their activities to include learning modes that go beyond the verbal linguistic.

Here's an example lesson from one of my students. She chose Dr. Suess' *Horton Hatches the Egg* (Random House, 1968) and designed activities targeted for second and third grade. One lesson she designed was a creative way to develop critical thinking, listening, and writing skills by writing a news report based upon the facts in the story. An art project of decorating an egg promoted life skills, writing skills, and creative skills. Still another was a mock trial scenario in which the students debated who would make the better parent. Each of her activities was integral to the story. The activity that most impressed me was a math activity that incorporated the concepts of probability, percents and ratios, counting, time, measuring, and an optional activity involving estimation.

Lesson: "I said what I meant, an elephant is faithful 100 percent."

Objective: Students will develop an understanding of percents and ratios in everyday life and develop higher thinking.

Materials: Sandwiches, colored water and containers, apples, and a dollar bill with four quarters.

Project: The teacher will ask the students to explain how much 100 percent is and give examples of how Horton illustrated 100 percent in the story. Then students can form groups, and the teacher will pass out different materials to each group. After each group has had time to examine their materials and develop a plan, they are to demonstrate 25 percent, 50 percent, 75 percent, and 100 percent, as well as the ratios 1/4, 1/2, 3/4, and 1 to the class with their items. Each group will be demonstrating a different item (sandwiches, apples, colored water). Afterward, the students will be asked how they can apply this to other items and activities (pizza, cooking, sharing, homework, shampoo bottle, how they spend their time, and so on).

These are just a few of the numerous activities created for this assignment. Various creative writing assignments, nature walks, dramatic skits, and writing lyrics based on the story have all been incorporated into story lessons. Those students who have the opportunity to test their story and activity in a classroom are impressed at how engaged the children are.

By the end of the semester, Debbie, the woman frozen by stage fright, was the best storyteller in the class. For her final story, she brought the whole class to tears with a first-person telling of her mother's struggle to bring up four children after their father died from being exposed to Agent Orange in Vietnam. I'll never forget the joy and pride I felt in her growth into an accomplished, confident storyteller. Although this class came late in her educational career, it opened the door to a wondrous world of learning never before imagined.

References

- Brand, Susan Trostle, and Jeanne M. Donato. *Storytelling in Emergent Literacy: Fostering Multiple Intelligences.* Albany, NY: Delmar, 2001.

- Hamilton, Martha, and Mitch Weiss. *Children Tell Stories: Teaching and Using Storytelling in the Classroom,* 2nd ed. Katonah, NY: Richard C. Owen Publishers, Inc., 2005.

- Norfolk, Sherry, Jane Stenson, and Diane Williams. *The Storytelling Classroom: Applications Across the Curriculum.* Westport, CT: Libraries Unlimited, 2006.

- Seuss, Dr. *Horton Hatches the Egg.* New York: Random House Children's Books, 1966.

STORYTELLING IN SCHOOLS: QUANTITATIVE STUDIES AND INNOVATIVE PROJECTS
Kate Dudding and Jackie Baldwin

We believe that storytelling belongs in every school around the world, and we want to encourage and support that goal. Here's how we went about it with our project, Storytelling in Schools.

As pressures build in schools for national testing, reporting, and accountability, many feel storytelling can be eliminated in schools. However, we knew that there were many quantitative studies documenting the methods and effectiveness of using stories and storytelling techniques in traditional classrooms to help teach the standard curriculum. But these studies were not easily accessible nor were they widely publicized. We wanted to make this information readily available to anyone interested in storytelling in schools so they could examine, learn from, and emulate these studies.

We defined four elements to our project:

1. A free downloadable booklet for school and arts administrators containing brief descriptions of classroom projects, broken down into quantitative studies and innovative projects, with follow-up links to the Web site: http://www.storytellinginschools.org/booklet.pdf.
2. A free downloadable brochure to be handed out at appropriate venues containing information about this project, backed up by position statements from national agencies on the value of storytelling in classrooms: http://www.storytellinginschools.org/brochure.pdf.
3. An online searchable Web site for school and arts administrators, which describes each classroom project in detail with contact information for the program director: http://www.storytellinginschools.org.
4. An online searchable how-to Web site specifically for storytellers, including detailed information about varied topics such as state standards, marketing and fee structures: http://www.storytellinginschools.org/how-to.

For our first edition, we found twenty-five quantitative studies and books and sixty-five innovative projects covering art, music, drama, history, language arts, mathematics, physics and science, oral interpretation and presentation, cultural awareness and understanding, classroom behavior, behavioral problems, student/teacher relationships, teacher training, libraries, and museums.

To give you a flavor of the material covered by our project, below are descriptions of six of the twenty-five quantitative studies and books.

"Storytelling and Story Reading: A Comparison of Effects on Children's Memory and Story Comprehension," a thesis presented to the faculty of the department of Curriculum and Instruction, East Tennessee State University by Matthew P. Gallets, May 2005. Keywords: Storytelling, reading, comprehension.

Abstract: For years, storytellers have been going to schools to share stories with children. However, to date only limited research has been done on the effects of storytelling on children's learning. This project was part of an ongoing study involving several researchers. In this portion of the project, the effects of storytelling and story reading were compared. The population studied consisted of kindergarten, first-, and second-grade students. Half the students were read stories aloud and the other half were told the same stories by a storyteller. Data were collected regarding the students' ability to recall facts they had heard, as well as their skill in using formal story elements. The students' interpretations of story meaning were also examined. Students in both the reading and storytelling groups improved on most measures. However, on some measures, notably regarding recall ability, students in the storytelling group improved more than students in the reading group. (The thesis is available at http://www.storynet-advocacy.org/edu/research/gallets-abstract.shtml.)

Stagebridge's 2004–2005 Storybridge Program by M. Parks and D. S. Rose, 2005. Keywords: elementary education, language arts, listening, teacher education.

Abstract: Stagebridge's 2004–2005 Storybridge Program, part of the U.S. Department of Education's Arts in Education Model Development and Dissemination Program, provided direct instruction and teacher training to eight fourth- and fifth-grade classes in three schools in the Oakland, California, Unified School District.

Senior storytellers modeled storytelling for students and teachers in these classrooms once a week for six weeks. Next, professional storytellers worked with the students and teachers biweekly for eight weeks to help them gain an understanding of storytelling principles and skills. At the end of the program, students were given the opportunity to tell a story on stage in front of their peers. Additionally, three teacher workshops were held to further develop the teachers' knowledge and skills in storytelling and its use as a classroom tool. Students showed improvement in language arts and listening comprehension skills as a result of the program. Participating teachers gained a deeper awareness and understanding of storytelling as an art form and its impact on the core subject matter curriculum. (A report is available at http://www.storynet-advocacy.org/edu/research/parks%202005.shtml.)

Storytelling for Middle Grades Students, Fastback 482 by John W. Myers and Robert D. Hilliard, Phi Delta Kappa Educational Foundation, 2001. Keywords: middle school.

Abstract: Preparing and telling a story in the classroom is fun for both teacher and student, and stories have great value as motivational tools to enhance instruction. Students who have difficulty recalling facts from the textbook easily remember the concepts that are contained within a story. Stories seem to provide frameworks that aid understanding and retention.

This Fastback offers tips for using storytelling in middle-grade classrooms, noting that having students tell the stories may have greater motivational benefit than having the teacher tell the stories to the students. The Fastback states that storytelling by students helps to develop higher-level thinking skills, such as analysis and synthesis, as well as skills in oral composition. (This source lists sixty-seven books and two periodicals as resources.)

"The Effects of Storytelling versus Story Reading on Comprehension and Vocabulary Knowledge of British Primary School Children," *Reading Improvement*, vol. 35, no. 3 (Fall 1998): 127–36, by Susan Trostle and Sandy Jean Hicks. Keywords: elementary school, language arts.

Abstract: This article compares effects of storytelling versus story reading on comprehension and vocabulary development of thirty-two British primary children. The article states that one group listened to stories in storytelling style; the other group listened to stories read by a student teacher. Findings show that children who witnessed storytelling scored higher on comprehension vocabulary measures than the children who listened to story reading.

"Thinking and Doing Literature: An Eight-Year Study," by Judith A. Langer in *English Journal*, vol. 87, no. 2 (February 1998): 16–23. Keywords: elementary school, middle school, high school.

Abstract: A series of studies conducted over an eight-year period by the National Research Center on Literature Teaching and Learning examined the ways people think when they read literature and the ways in which instruction could support that kind of thinking. The research studies were based on both a constructivist and social/communicative tradition. Some ten field researchers collaborated with about fifty teachers and their students. The participating classes included pre-kindergartners through adults, with a major emphasis on the middle and high school grades.

The studies demonstrated the ways in which the open-ended exploratory nature of considering possibilities from a variety of stances helps enrich and complicate meaning. It was also learned that supporting students' development of literary understanding is often difficult for teachers to sustain for lack of instructional models.

Findings led to the development of an alternative pedagogy and procedures for ongoing assessments of students' progress. Interactions with students convinced the researchers that literature and storytelling can play an important role in enriching students' understanding across subject areas, and the process of exploring horizons of possibilities can be helpful in content classes even when literature is not read and point of reference learning is the goal. (A report is available at http://www.storynet-advocacy.org/edu/quantitative-studies. shtml. This article contains sixteen references.)

"The Effects of Storytelling Experiences on Vocabulary Skills of Second Grade Students," by Gail Froyen, a research paper presented to the faculty of the Library Science Department, University of Northern Iowa, in partial fulfillment of the requirements for the degree of master of arts, 1987. Keywords: elementary education, language arts.

Abstract: Success on academic achievement tests has been largely based on the student's facility for using language. Thus, the acquisition and use of words has enhanced and become a predictor of one's aptitude for future learning.

Second-grade students at Lowell School in Waterloo, Iowa, were taught storytelling techniques and given opportunities to practice these techniques for thirty-five to forty minutes per week for six months. This activity, held during lunch, was self-selected and conducted in small groups of eight to nine students in each group, with forty-three students in total.

Each session started with memory game activities, which helped develop both good listening skills and the ability to concentrate. A common goal, with everyone helping one another and the accomplishments of each storyteller celebrated by all, was an undoubtedly powerful inducement to learning. The group feeling was cooperative rather than competitive. Behavior boundaries and expectations were set high; they were clearly expressed and consistently enforced. The fun and success aspect of telling and listening to stories was enhanced because of each student's responsibility for his/her behavior. After six months, these students significantly increased their performance on vocabulary and reading comprehension tests beyond what was expected for that six-month period, as measured by pre- and post-Iowa Tests of Basic Skills. (A report is available at http://www.storynet-advocacy.org/edu/quantitative-studies.shtml.)

CHAPTER TWO

Preschool and Kindergarten

THE INEXTRICABLE LINK BETWEEN LANGUAGE AND LITERACY
Donna Washington

In the 1960s, Betty Hart and Todd Risley were studying language development in preschool children. Their research led them to a startling discovery. They found out that a child's exposure to language at a very early age had a profound affect on whether or not they became lifelong learners. Children who came from homes where the parents did not use complex language and expected simple answers to their questions heard, on average, 30 million fewer uses of language than their peers by the age of three. They called this discrepancy the 30 million word gap. By the time these children entered kindergarten, their deficit was even more extreme. The gap profoundly affected their abilities in every subject in school.

If you cannot understand the text, then history, algebra, geography, and science books are of no use to you. Novels are boring or bewildering. Reading for fun is not pleasurable in the slightest. Without a good grounding in language, education is impossible.

Andrew Biemiller has worked with language and literacy for many years and notes that our schools are not set up to help children who come to kindergarten with the word gap. We should be working hard to improve their understanding of complex language and literature. Instead, we do the opposite. We spend the first years of elementary school trying to teach children how to read and write, and we do not expose them to language more complex than their abilities. They are learning how to spell cow, they are reading a book about a cow, and they are drawing cows. Ideally, at the end of the lesson you can spell the word cow, you can say the word cow, and you can identify a cow. How does this further your language development if you already knew the word cow going into the lesson?

The only way the word gap can be addressed is if our schools begin instituting language programs that focus on all facets of literacy, not just phonics and sight words. For Biemiller, literacy is not about being able to say or recognize words printed on a page, but is about being able to process a string of words and get meaning out of them. In order to do that at advanced levels, students must spend their early educational years soaking in language that expands their understanding of how words can be used. They must learn how literature is put together and how to approach various forms of fiction and nonfiction in order to figure out how to understand it. We must expose students to language beyond their abilities to read.

For a number of years, I worked as an artist-in-residence at an alternative middle school in Raleigh, North Carolina. The students who attend this school have either been expelled from traditional schools or transferred over because they are not succeeding. My task was to come into the eighth-grade classes and help the students write plays set in medieval Europe. I used a combination of discussion, writing, oral editing, recording, and improvisation over the course of the week, and by Friday they had managed to get the first drafts written. My favorite part was coming back at the end of the year. The students finished making drafts with their teacher, rehearsed, and then acted out the plays. They videotaped all of them and every class got a chance to watch them while we had a "feast." These students, some of whom were reading and writing at a second- or third-grade level, were able to accomplish this task because it was introduced using the four facets of a literate person: listening, speaking, reading, and writing.

Biemiller points out that there are many consequences to not giving students enough training in how to approach literature and understand complex language. One such consequence is called the fourth-grade slump. This occurs when you have a child who has successfully sounded out words since kindergarten and can read simple text after third grade. Literature changes pretty drastically from third to fourth grade.

Educationally, we go from learning to read to using reading to learn. There isn't any transitional step. The idea is that if you can sound out words then you can read. This is not true. Many children arrive in the fourth grade and their teachers discover that though the child can sound out every single letter and say each word in sequence, they have no idea what they are saying. The student cannot grasp the concept the words represent. This is the biggest curse of the 30 million word gap. It prevents students from using reading to learn other subjects. It also makes them hate reading at an early age and shun books. Unfortunately, fourth grade is only the beginning. Middle school and high school teachers assume students are grounded in how to approach text and they don't offer any instruction in that process at all. This system of education is a recipe for disaster for many children.

E. D. Hirsh Jr. is an educator who agrees wholeheartedly with the need for students to have a solid grounding in language in order to succeed. In fact, he offers his own language-based theory about what is needed to become a life-long learner. Hirsh identifies three different elements of language and what role they play in literacy.

Aural language is all of the language you have ever heard. The more often you hear the word, the more it is reinforced. You may never use the word in conversation, but you have been exposed to it. Any word that is not in your aural language storage does not exist as far as you are concerned.

Oral language is the language you use in everyday conversation. You might know the word "octogenarian," but you might not use it. If the language concept is not in your aural language, it cannot be in your oral language.

Experiential language occurs when you encounter concepts outside of your normal understanding and adapt the meaning contextually. For instance, if you read the sentence, "The old man was bitter," it is safe to say that nobody walked up to the old man, licked him, and found he had a terrible taste. Bitter must mean something other than flavor. However, if you have never heard the word "bitter" and you have never seen anyone use it, then you might be under the impression that this old fellow sinks his teeth into people when he gets upset.

Comprehension stops cold when you cannot decode language. If a word is not in your aural or oral language, it cannot be used in your experiential language decoding. Having a vast store of aural language is a key to being successful in education, but, as Drs. Betty Hart and Todd R. Risley discovered, many children come to school with a very thin arsenal of language in their aural storage. This is definitely a problem, but it is only a part of it. Biemiller points out that without comprehension, none of your language stores matter.

Dr. Gerald Duffy has written a great deal on the subject of comprehension. He explains that in order to comprehend what we are reading, our brain must be able to go through quite a few processes at the same time. You must:

• Understand what you are reading.

• Remember what you just read.

• Predict the next event. Absorb the next event.

• Check your prediction.

• Alter your prediction if it was wrong.

• Update your expectation.

• Make long-term predictions.

When you can do all of that at once, you become a master at comprehension. Not surprisingly, there are a lot of people in the world who don't pick this skill up naturally. It must be taught. If the person does not have a good foundation in language, then mastering comprehension will be very difficult. Currently, most schools do not teach the comprehension process. They assume that if you learn how to say the words, you will understand them.

Drs. Hart, Risley, Biemiller, Hirsh, and Duffy are all looking at different sides of the same puzzle. How do you synthesize all of this knowledge into a tool that will help children become better learners? How can you address the language gap, improve comprehension, help the brain stay flexible enough to adapt to different forms of literature, encourage reading in the upper grades, and impart the basic skills needed to be successful in every other subject in school? Fortunately for us, such a tool exists.

Storytelling provides many of the skills that are necessary to overcome language deficits. The brain is like any muscle: its parts must be used or they do not function. Hart and Risley noted that when they implemented games that used words in an imaginative story line, children in the gap were able to remember the words and incorporate them. Biemiller says that the mechanism for learning language is the same for people from the time they are newborns right up until puberty. We learn by watching people's faces, eyes, and expressions and listening to the tones of their voice. Storytelling enhances learning because the information is presented in a visual episodic form that emphasizes the use of voice, face, and gesture. Because of this, it is possible to use complex language and interesting words with very young children. This teaches the brain that context is important for understanding language. There are no prefabricated pictures or images for the listener to draw upon; they must create everything themselves. It forces the brain to convert language into images. Words mean nothing if they are not converted into ideas.

Stories for very young children tend to be repetitive. They are encouraged to participate and repeat the same phrase or hand gesture over and over. This teaches the brain about sequences and the importance of remembering what you have just heard. Usually there is some kind of change, very slight, that happens in each episode. Children learn they have to listen carefully and anticipate that there is going to be a change. They usually become quiet and focus more intently in order not to miss it. As they get older, they begin to try to predict what the change is going to be and anticipate it. Sometimes they are right and sometimes they are wrong. It is not unusual for a child to tell you what they thought was going to happen in your story. It is also not unusual for someone to blurt out, "I knew it!"

Storytelling also increases a child's aural language. There has always been discussion about whether early childhood intervention works. Often, it seems that the advances children make in those early years are washed out by the time the child gets into first or second grade. Recent studies tell us that this is not so. The information doesn't disappear. What we have discovered about Head Start and other programs is that if you get the information into the child, it will be stored for future use. Biemiller points out that it is not until puberty that a person's ability to read, write, and speak integrate well together. Prior to puberty, a person's brain is trying to learn the skills that will help them compete in life. Once puberty happens, the brain turns everything else off and starts focusing on sex.

The number of children who don't know basic folktales and fairytales is often very discouraging. Sometimes children only hear these stories in preschool. They need to be grounded in basic oral literature in order to build more complex literature on top of it. We should be spending more time telling stories to children in first, second, third, fourth, and fifth grade. There is a need for this type of foundation. You may personally never have the opportunity to see your work with a child blossom, but if you get the information into the child before puberty, it will show up somewhere else in his or her life.

Storytelling also enhances writing. Children who have been exposed to storytelling know full well that every tale has a beginning, a middle, and an end. They know what happens in each movement of that story and they understand descriptive language. Character development, epic movements, imaginative story lines, and interesting plot twists are second nature to these children. Writing is a very difficult thing to teach to someone who does not understand narrative structure.

Children who have been exposed to stories have encountered an abundance of language and understand that complex words break down into smaller words. These children are much more likely to play word games and explore interesting literature. They are much less likely to be stumped and completely stop just because they don't understand one word. They learn to continue and focus on the shape of the material as they decode the language.

Storytelling is not the curative for all that ails us in the educational system. We have a long way to go to achieve the level playing field that we long to create, but storytelling is a tool that can flatten out some of the larger mountains that we have to climb. There can be no doubt about the inextricable link between language and literacy. Storytelling is one of the best bridges between the two.

Resources

- Biemiller, Andrew, PhD. *Reading Research to Practice: A Series for Teachers.* Cambridge, MA: Brookline Books, 1999.

- Duffy, Gerald G., PhD. *Explaining Reading: A Resource for Teaching Concepts, Skills, and Strategies.* New York: The Guilford Press, 2003.

- Hart, Betty, PhD, and Todd R. Risley, PhD. *Meaningful Differences in the Everyday Experiences of Young Children.* Baltimore, MD: Paul H. Brookes Publishing Co. Inc., latest reprint 2000.

- Harvey, Stephanie, and Anne Goudvis. *Strategies That Work: Teaching Comprehension to Enhance Understanding.* Portland, ME: Stenhouse Publishers, 2000.
- Hirsch, E. D. Jr., PhD. *The Schools We Need: Why We Don't Have Them.* Garden City, NY: Doubleday, 1996.
- Zimmerman, Susan, and Ellin Oliver Keene. *Mosaic of Thought: Teaching Comprehension in a Reader's Workshop.* Portsmouth, NH: Heinemann, 1997.

WHAT DO YOU SEE? VISUAL LITERACY AND STORY STRUCTURE

Cathy Ward

Speaking, Listening, Writing, and Visual Literacy

National Standards

> NCTE: 1, 3, 4, 6, 9, 11; CNAEA—Visual Arts 1: Understanding and applying media, techniques, and processes; CNAEA—Visual Arts 3: Choosing and evaluating a range of subject matter, symbols, and ideas.

Objectives

Students will practice visual literacy skills by observing, reflecting, and discussing a work of art. Students will understand basic story structure and elements of a story. Students will work together to write a story based on discussion and observation of a work of art and using knowledge of story elements and story structure.

Materials

- Artwork
- Construction paper
- Colored pencils

Instructional Plan

This lesson has two parts. Try Part One with your students to practice talking about art before combining Parts One and Two with a new artwork.

Part One

I selected an artwork with which my students were not familiar and that told a story, meaning that the characters and setting were evident and *something was happening.* The artwork was perfect for kindergarteners who were learning about basic story structure. A poster reproduction of *Dance Before the Hunt* by Lee N. Smith hung in the room a few weeks prior to this lesson. The artwork was in the room as a piece in the environment. Students gazed at the artwork at various times during the day, thinking about the scene that lay before them. At the very least, the artwork should live in the environment—at the students' eye level—for a few days prior to discussion.

I began this lesson immediately after our morning rug meeting by calling their attention to the poster reproduction of *Dance Before the Hunt.* We quietly reflected on the artwork for about fifteen seconds, allowing our eyes and minds to focus. Wanting the students to create their own observations and conclusions, I did not tell them the title or artist of the piece. I did not tell them about my initial impressions or what art critics said. I asked one simple, powerful question, "What do you see?" Hands shot up, eager to share what they saw!

"I see boys. I see a forest."

Students first stated what they noticed in the artwork. The following questions move students beyond their initial impression to delve deeper: "What do you think they are doing? Why do you think that? Tell me more about that." With encouragement and a bit of prodding, observations became more substantive.

"They are playing a game." "The boy in front isn't happy, I think he is sad." "I think it is at the end of the day, the sun might set soon."

In discussing artwork, students form the discussion based on their thoughts and observations. Students require "think" time between questions, and I repeat their responses for validation and allow "wait" time for responses to sink in.

We move from simple observations, noting the characters, what they are doing, and defining the setting, to *inferring* why the characters are behaving so and what might happen next. Reading between the lines is a skill that is developed and can begin before one learns how to read words. Visual literacy—the ability to *read images*—is an integral piece of literacy.

Part Two

Now, what can you do with this conversation? Extending Part One of this lesson is to invite your class to collaboratively write a story based on your chosen artwork. Students are divided into three groups where they would collaboratively write a part of a story: beginning, middle, and end. White poster board is placed on both sides of the artwork to delineate physical space for the "beginning" and "ending" of the story. The artwork serves as a base for the "middle" of the story, while the white poster board represents the beginning and ending that is yet to be written.

The first small group collaborated on the beginning of the story. Their story led to the middle part, which was the artwork that we just discussed as a group. In this case, their story must end with the boys in the forest. The first student begins, and the next adds a line (or lines) to the story, and so forth. Each student writes and illustrates their sentence and I keep the story in order, in order to type the dictated line. This process repeats with the "middle" and "ending" groups.

After all groups have written and illustrated their story, we have a class reading. Each student reads and displays their page to the class. I place each student's page in clear protective sheets in a binder with separation pages labeled "beginning," "middle," and "ending." As children picked up our story binder, the labeled sections strengthened the concept of basic story structure.

For the remainder of our school year, students picked up our "Dance Before the Hunt" story and read with each other. Students smiled as they read and enjoyed their peers' work. Not only did students learn about basic story structure in this lesson, but they did so in a meaningful and connective experience. They also learned how to critically look at and think about an image.

Adaptations

Though this lesson is built upon a steady framework, the details are organic and it is meant to be adapted to your students' needs and interests. Experiment, have fun, and listen to your students' ideas and suggestions; broaden your approach as you become comfortable with the activity.

Here are a few suggestions to get you started:

- Rather than a poster of an artwork, try to bring in sculpture, an interesting painting from a tag sale, quilts, family photographs, etc.

- The next time you take your class to an art museum, rather than having mediocre and shallow experiences with many artworks, try an adaptation of this lesson with one or two artworks for a meaningful visit!

Assessment

In kindergarten, the key to assessment is participation. Raising your hand and saying something about the picture is very important. And it's vital that the contribution be accepted positively. Because this activity happens five more times during the school year, the kindergarten student will have opportunities to watch and listen to peers who contribute in meaningful ways to the classroom discourse. Over time, the child understands he/she must participate and say something important about the artwork.

Bibliography

- Barrett, Terry. *Interpreting Art: Reflecting, Wondering, and Responding*. New York: McGraw-Hill, 2002.
- Burnham, Rita, and Elliot Kai-Kee. "The Art of Teaching in the Museum," *The Journal of Aesthetic Education*, vol. 39, no. 1 (Spring 2005): 65–76.

THE ROOT CHILDREN: FICTION OR NONFICTION?
Jane Stenson
Listening and Writing

National Standards

NCTE: 3, 4, 5, 11, 12; NAS 1: Science as Inquiry; NAS 7: History of Nature and Science.

Objectives

Children will tell a story by acting it out together from a narrator's direction; they will animate or dance the cycle of the seasons; they will express actions suitable to the words used by the narrator; they will write books based on their observation of a plant's cycle; they will understand the plant cycle and the seasonal cycle.

Materials

For the Dance

- One scarf for each child, some opaque and some translucent.
- A small, hand-held musical instrument such as a glockenspiel.
- Narrator will need to know the story well enough to ad-lib or respond to children dancing with scarves!
- You may find Sibylle von Olfers' book *The Story of the Root-Children* helpful in elaborating the telling.

For the Children's Book

- Narcissus bulb or a lima bean (substitutions are fine) for each child and planting material.
- White construction paper approximately four by six inches for each observation/ drawing.

Instructional Plan

The Story

The Story of the Root-Children
Sibylle von Oflers
Etwas von den Wurzelkindendem (1906)

It was winter and the root-children were sleeping deep in the earth. Mother Earth knew that soon she would wake the children. When the snows began to melt and the first warm breezes were felt, she decided that the time had come. Spring would soon greet the earth. Awakening each root-child, she told them it was time to make their beautiful clothes in preparation for their spring journey to the surface of the earth. The root-children worked very hard. Some even helped the insects polish their wings and get the sleep from their eyes.

When the rivers were flowing again and the first birds appeared, Mother Earth told the root-children and the insects that it was time to go. In a stately procession they went adorned with their newly made colorful clothes to the surface of the earth. Some went to live and grow by the river-banks, while some went to the meadows or forests. Wherever they went, they took root and grew to become honeysuckles, poppies, primroses, and sunflowers. They loved the warm breezes, the gentle winds, and the cheery sun. The root-children blossomed and lived happily throughout the spring and summer. Too soon the air became colder and the winds fiercer. Their beautiful clothes became faded and tattered or fell to the earth. Autumn had arrived. The root-children knew it was time to go back to Mother Earth.

When they saw Mother Earth again, she helped them prepare for the winter, saying, "Now it is time to sleep, for winter will bring a blanket of ice and snow. When spring comes again, you will be refreshed, ready to make your beautiful clothes again, ready to make your journey to the riverbanks, meadows, and forests of the earth."

The Dance

The narrator distributes scarves, one to each child, and asks the children to pretend they are asleep "under, way under the ground." The narrator uses a glissando—a sweep striker from low to high across the glockenspiel—to signal the beginning of the story, saying, "I am going to tell you a story that you can act out as we go along."

As the story proceeds, the music (free-form as it is) should suit the words, for example, the gentle, gliding sound of "they sat in a cozy circle to sew their beautiful clothes" versus the marching beat of "they formed a stately procession." The scarves are meant to encourage movement and adornment as a pillow/blanket or a cape/headpiece/tunic. Some children may need encouragement to respond creatively to the music and the scarves!

It's lovely to stretch the story during the summer section with perhaps a hopping dance, or a windy and warm day, or fuzzy bees and flitting butterflies. Then contrast those movements with the fierce winds of autumn and the cold air that causes shivers. And the narrator should be certain to really welcome the children (hug?) back into the ground for sleeping as the earth is covered with a blanket of snow and ice. Yes, by all means, leave them sleeping!

Writing and Illustrating a Book

Discuss later with the children what they liked about the activity and what pictures they had in their minds during the story. Be sure to use the words "cycle" and "seasons" and have the children articulate their meanings.

Prepare a planting activity of a lima bean or narcissus, one bean or bulb for each child. Start the growth cycle and have each student draw "what you see." Have them draw what they see (over time—perhaps one drawing each week) and keep all the drawings until the root-shoot-bud-flower-seed-dying cycle is complete. Teachers scribe the children's thoughts about their plants and what is happening to them and how it differs from the previous drawing. Then put the drawings together in a book, a science or nonfiction book.

Articulate "fiction" and "nonfiction," saying that both are stories about the same topic: nature. One is the cycle of the seasons and one is the plant cycle. Ask, "How are they alike?"

Keeping knowledge whole and meaningful is important for young children, who have many ways (languages) to understand the world. Some children will excel at the dance while others will excel in the creation of their nonfiction narrative. Either way, the content is learned, the interdisciplinary skill is experienced, and literacy is served.

Assessment

In kindergarten, everyone has something to say *and* everyone has the opportunity to dance! How a child participates can be recorded anecdotally. The student is also expected to accomplish a book about the plant cycle. If the book was written and the dance was danced, how wonderful this is!

BRINGING THE STORY TO LIFE WITH PUPPETS
Marilyn Price
Speaking, Listening, and Visual Literacy

National Standards

NCTE: 1, 4, 9, 11, 12.

Literacy Development in the Storytelling Classroom

Objectives

Stretch the imagination through multiple examples. Increase the life of the story outside of the classroom with recognizable visual reminders. Add humor and wit to an existing tale. Increase the possibility of interaction with different skill sets such as recognizable voice and noises that will be available to all. Make the visual a partner of the oral and double its learning power.

Introducing the Craft of Puppetry

Puppets as a teaching tool have existed for about 3,000 years in an unending variety of uses. Traditionally used as religious implements, their use has been broadened into the storytelling venue in most cultures while holding onto their initial purpose. Their ability to add color to a story and add multiple characters with one director makes for classroom magic, and the size of the characters helps the audience (classroom) to focus visually while listening, thereby doubling the impact.

Puppets can be given roles in the classroom with opportunities for drama and discipline. The options of having simple hand puppets available for:

- Storytelling introduction
- Actors and actresses in the drama
- Birthday announcements
- Foreign-language skills (the puppet only responds in the language being taught)
- Clean-up chairperson
- AND endless other opportunities in literacy

There are many easily available puppets to purchase for the classroom, but this puppeteer/storyteller recommends the creation of the characters by the class for particularly outstanding results. The story suggested (and there are many more listed) is the classic "Little Red Hen," which adds not only the option of interspersing new characters who live in the house, besides the traditional ones, with the hen, but this magnificent tale has a wonderful message and infinite opportunities for wit and wisdom. It is also extremely easy to tell with many opportunities for the class to add their voices and animal sounds.

The Characters

- The hen
- A dog
- A cat
- A cow

All of the above characters can be made out of everyday objects: the hen from an envelope and a red sock, the dog from paper plates, the cat from a cat food box, and the cow from a milk carton with a picture of a cow's head attached to it.

I recommend that everyone in the class make at least one of the characters that live in the house with the hen and that the teacher makes the hen or uses one already made. Besides the ideas given here, there are many options, including photos of the students' pets mounted on sticks and made part of the telling or puppets that could easily live in the house with the hen, such as a mouse, frog, or any fantasy character in the puppet box. The story won't be affected by a change in characters as long as the drama remains.

Now that the cast has been created (or purchased), it is time to set up the room and the scene.

The setting in which your students best listen to stories is how you should incorporate the use of puppets. I do not recommend circle time as it is difficult for some children to see what is immediately next to them. I do recommend a comfortable distance of approximately three feet away so little necks do not have to bend to see the action.... Depending on your volunteers, they can join you and the narrator, in front, or they can even be disbursed around the classroom setting.

In the case of the "Little Red Hen," I like to teach the sounds first. When I point to the cow, we say, "moo," and you know the rest! I recommend other props for all good cooking stories; bring in bowls to make the bread, spoons to stir the dough, etc. If the classroom has a play oven, make sure it's handy. And if it's near snack time, bring in a loaf of fresh bread. The hen will share it when the lesson is learned. The little red hen gets all the good lines and you get to help her say them. She greets her friends in the morning (as a warm up) with "good morning, cow" and the cow says, "moo." You then interpret the cow's language by saying "good morning" said the cow and the scene gets set up in that way. However, you tell the story in all its repetitive wonder.

Assessments

The "Little Red Hen" is a powerful story told without props or puppets, but the impact of telling it with both is magic. The everyday object characters serve as constant reminders of the value of helping and working together cooperatively. The use of puppets will help to focus students' attention and serve as reminders (especially the everyday variety of puppets) as they go through everyday tasks of drinking their milk and feeding the cat and mailing the mail, even setting the table, etc.

Stories and puppets impact the lives of students—wherever the stories take them.

Resources

- Andersen, Hans Christian. *The Ugly Duckling*. New Fairy Tales, First Book, First Collection, 1844.

- Heiner, Heidi Anne. *The Gingerbread Man.* St. Nicholas Magazine, 1875.

- Nettleton, F. T. "Old MacDonald Had a Farm." Traditional ballad. *Tommy Tunes* (collection), 1917.

- Williams, Sue, and Julie Vivas. *I Went Walking.* Pine Plains, NY: Voyager Books, 1992.

- Zemach, Margot. *It Could Always Be Worse: A Yiddish Folktale.* New York: Farrar, Straus and Giroux, 1992.

(I GOT THOSE) LOW-DOWN, DIRTY, EMERGENT-READER BLUES
Andy Offutt Irwin
Listening, Reading, and Writing

National Standards

NCTE: 4, 5, 12; CNAEA—Music 4: composing and arranging music within specified guidelines.

Objectives

Students will compose short narratives using the twelve-bar blues pattern.

For four years I was involved in a program in Atlanta through Young Audiences, Woodruff Arts Center called smART stART. (Cute, huh?) SmART stART is a ten-week reading enrichment program for kindergarteners in Title I schools. After three years of serving in this program on two different campuses, the czarina of Young Audiences Special Programs, Susan Williams, assigned me to Garden Hills School. My job as a musician/storyteller was to help improve the reading skills of the school's kindergarten children, 90 percent of whom were Hispanic ESL (English as a Second Language) students. Most of these children spoke no English at the beginning of their kindergarten school year.

Bear in mind, I am not a Spanish speaker. Indeed, I am the living punch line to that old joke: someone who speaks three languages is trilingual, someone who speaks two languages is bilingual, but someone who speaks one language is American.

I am much too lazy to do actual research, but I am conceited enough, and I have been around long enough, to take great stock in my own anecdotal evidence. I can play a little guitar, and I have found in my travels that children respond to music and will even make up their own songs if given the proper mix of freedom and instruction. One of the easiest cultural-crossing musical forms is the twelve-bar blues.

Aha, you say. *This is a book about storytelling and you, Andy, are talking about music!* Fair enough. But storytelling and music are not mutually exclusive. The storytelling part is forthcoming, so stick with me.

Indeed, twelve-bar *is* music, and music does something special: it is used for emotion-based cognitive development. In other words, music adds the extra fun element that opens up another section of the brain. If you're like me (and I'm sure you're relieved you're not), you simply can't recite the alphabet without putting a pause after G and after P. That's because you most likely learned your ABCs to the tune of the old French song, *"Ah! vous dirai-je, Maman."* (Later, the English poem "Twinkle, Twinkle Little Star" was plugged into this same melody.) (Tangent: no, Mozart did not write it; he merely composed variations based upon it. Your Trivial Pursuit game is wrong. Sorry.) We all know lots of other musical-learning examples, and as with a great many of us in arts education, I stand on the shoulders of the creators of *Sesame Street* and *Grammar Rock.* I bow to them (carefully, or I may fall).

Without getting into a whole lot of music theory, twelve-bar blues is what happens when you play very simple rock 'n' roll. (Tangent: isn't it cool that it's spelled rock 'n' roll? . . . Not rock and roll, or even rock & roll?) In its most basic form, the lyric line will read as such:

This is a song about writing the blues
This is a song about writing the blues
Follow this little pattern and you can't lose.

Note that the repeated first line rhymes with the third line. I enjoy offering this conundrum of arithmetic: "When you write the first line, you are two-thirds finished."

Badda-bing!

Now, gentle reader, I'm going to ask you to change your thinking a bit. For our purposes, don't think of twelve-bar as only a *musical* form, but think of it as a poetic form as well, the way you might think of haiku, say, or the less noble, but fun as-all-get-out, limerick. A song, by its very definition, requires words. In the classroom, we ask the children to give us a short narrative in the twelve-bar pattern. I always put the above example on the dry-erase/chalkboard. I tell them to write three lines, repeating the first and rhyming the third. For example, ask the children to write (make up) a twelve-bar song about the first thing they do when they get home from school. A child in Atlanta wrote this:

I pet my cat, it makes her purr
I pet my cat, it makes her purr
My cat has very soft fur

This is a simple example, but it was a great start. Asking the children to make the rhyme forces them to use a little more vocabulary. I asked her to create a second verse. She wrote:

I feed my cat from a can
I feed my cat from a can
I take care of her the best I can

Well sure, technically, this verse didn't actually rhyme, but an opportunity arose allowing us to point out the homonym "can" and its different meanings. I'm a big believer in these serendipitous teaching opportunities—I not only *believe* in them, I've seen them take place!—and these opportunities come up constantly when the students are making up their own stories. Each story becomes an individual thing. At this point, the teacher may move the writing along by asking the student questions such as, "What is your cat's name?" "Why did you name her that?" "What's the funniest thing she ever did?" The answer to each question will be a start for a new verse of the song.

Once the songs are created, the teacher puts them on a newsprint pad where all the students can see them. Using colored markers, the teacher and the students go through the lyrics as the teacher underlines the rhyming words and circles the sight words. Later, different colored markers can be used to make squares around long vowel sounds and short vowel sounds. For example: blue squares around long vowels, red squares around short vowels.

There are all kinds of subjects one can give the students to get their juices flowing: seasons and weather, games and toys, etc. At one school, each of the five kindergarten classrooms wrote a song about different community helpers, such as mail carriers, teachers, police officers, firefighters, garbage collectors, doctors, actors, and the like. The art teacher was involved, working with the children on costumes and set design. We had an evening performance; pictures were taken, videos were made, snacks were eaten, and lives were changed.

For Older Students

I have used the twelve-bar exercise as a catalyst for story creation, again giving the students subjects from which to draw ideas. For older students, this form can open up opportunities for word play and introduce the idea that wit is a spontaneous and intellectual practice (but I don't tell them that at the outset). Students who would never know how to begin a story might find making up a silly song an easier task. And with older students, "making up" is the term I often use. It is my hope that they still know how (or at least have a memory of how) to play, and for many students—let's face it—writing is homework drudgery. But makin' up stuff, in the vernacular of the South, and probably other regions as well, the word "story" is another term for a lie, especially a longer made-up narrative. As it is with a lot of people in my business, when I was a child, in order to make the lunchroom half-hour a bit richer, I embellished those anecdotes of my daily life that I told to my peers. Socially speaking, when I was found out, this practice was not seen as simply playing, and often as I told these false accounts, that goody-goody kid quickly drew in a noisy breath, covered her/his mouth with one hand while raising the other, gave that shocked look, and shouted in fake sotto voce, "You're telling a STO-ry!"

But the twelve-bar form can not only fertilize the creative germ, it can also serve as yet another tool used in giving license to the creation of fiction (or the creation of *anything*). Twelve-bar, or any kind of songwriting, can bestow onto students a means to lose themselves, bringing out what may have been secret thoughts and observations and helping them to know that their ideas are valid. And this may be its most important use. When a child reaches a certain age, publicly displayed flights of fancy can be frowned upon. Indeed, somewhere around the time when recess and play become physical education and exercise, there is the danger that a creative spirit can be forever snuffed out. Twelve-bar, in its inherent goofiness, allows those flights to take wing. In some classroom environments, a spirit of friendly competition may emerge between the students as they try to out-create one another.

But, Andy, um . . . I can't play an instrument.

Pish-posh. Just run down the hall and fetch your music teacher. It can be fun to involve folks in your music department in working out a team-taught class and even creating a culminating event (show). But, for the sake of argument, let's say you don't have a music department or a music teacher. Well, I'd bet that somebody you know plays a guitar or keyboard or harmonica. This might be a good time to involve a community member, or a parent, or someone in your Parent-Teacher Association (PTA) or Parent-Teacher-Student Organization (PTSO).

Okay . . . so that's not working. How about going to the pawnshop and buying an Autoharp? (Tangent: Autoharp is in a league with Frisbee, Kleenex, and, for your great-grandma, Frigidaire; it is a brand name. The generic term is "chorded zither." Now, say THAT three times without laughing. No really, it's easy!) Check it out:

There are only three chords used in the twelve-bar form. Theoretically speaking, in a given key, the chords used are the tonic (I), subdominant (IV), and dominant (V). Bladd- bladda. In GIT-guitar talk, in the key of G, the chords would be: G, C, D7. In the key of E: E, F, B7. In the key of C: C, F, G7. Those three keys can get you through nicely. If you're playing an Autoharp, simply press down the chord buttons and strum across the strings. (Tangent: Remember that musician you asked to come and help you in the classroom who said he was too busy? Give him a call and guilt him into tuning your new/used Autoharp. It's the least he can do.)

In the key of G, the chords would land as in Figure 2.1.

But wait! Who says you need an instrument anyway? Try doing this *a cappella* by having a couple of students sing the accompaniment. (No more than a couple; too many cooks spoil the broth.) Or use some of those rhythm instruments that are in the closet in the back of the auditorium. (Tangent:

$$
\begin{array}{lll}
G & C & G
\end{array}
$$
My Cap'n Crunch is soggy, the milk's been on it way too long

$$
\begin{array}{ll}
C & G
\end{array}
$$
My Cap'n Crunch is soggy, the milk's been on it way too long

$$
\begin{array}{lll}
D7 & C & G
\end{array}
$$
And now it's Cap'n Mushy, to eat it now would just be wrong

You'll find them in the old box next to that older box of mid-twentieth century microphones buried in a tangle of cords.) The same warning: Let there be peace on earth and let it begin with you not giving too many kids rhythm instruments.

And now it is I giving *you* license to be creative. Everything I know about education I learned on the streets. The one thing I do know is this: the more I plan, the more room I have to diverge from the plan when things change. When kids are making up their own stuff, things do change. Above all: don't be afraid to be amazing. Who knows, you just might put on a show and save the town.

Assessment

Student poems will follow the twelve-bar blues format, with rhyming words in the first and third lines.

STORY-SONGS, STEPPING-STONES TO LITERACY
Pam Lindsey
Speaking and Listening

National Standards

NCTE: 4, 12; CNAEA—Music 1: students sing expressively, with appropriate dynamics, phrasing, and interpretation; CNAEA—Music 3: students improvise "answers" in the same style to given rhythmic and melodic phrases; students improvise short songs and instrumental pieces using a variety of sound sources, including traditional sounds (for example, voices, instruments), nontraditional sounds available in the classroom (for example, paper tearing, pencil tapping), and body sounds (for example, hands clapping, fingers snapping); NAS 4: students should develop an understanding of properties of earth materials and objects in the sky.

Objectives

To encourage enthusiastic participation in a variety of musical activities in order to: encourage singing expressively; apply and improve communication and language/literacy skills by singing alone and with others; interpret and improvise sounds, rhythms, and lyrics through dramatic play using a variety of vocal, sound, and visual resources.

Bye oh baby bunting
Daddy's gone a' hunting
To get a little rabbit skin
To wrap up Baby Sheila in.

It's been said that lullabies are the first stories children hear. This lullaby is one of the first stories I remember hearing as a child when my mother rocked my baby sister. Songs are stories put to music. They are the means that our ancestors have used for generations to share events about their lives, whether love, war, tragedy, celebrations, or silliness and fun.

Even now, I can remember at the age of five visualizing my Dad hunting for the rabbit skin. I also remember the emotions the song brought forth of how much my Dad must love us to go hunting for the skin to keep us warm (imagery). It didn't matter that we were never really wrapped in rabbit skin; the emotions the song evoked were real then and still are when I hear the song. It made me connect with my father's love for his children.

Hearing, listening, and visualizing are pre-literacy skills learned without knowing we are learning and are vital to emergent literacy in years to come. Likewise, these skills are cultivated by exposing young children to music.

I have taught music enrichment classes to toddlers through pre-K students for almost twenty years and have seen firsthand the value of introducing and exposing children to music at a young age. The toddlers who joined me in a circle during music time enjoyed bouncing to the rhythm of the song "Matilda the Gorilla" by Mary Rice Hopkins. They couldn't talk or sing yet, but they enjoyed singing the chorus "Ooh, ooh, ooh, ooh, aah, aah, aah," and listened intently to the story in the song while I used a gorilla puppet as a visual aid. For months whenever I entered the room, the toddlers would begin singing "ooh, ooh, aah, aah," and bouncing to the rhythm of the words. These children were learning pre-literacy skills through the rhythm and chorus of the song.

Rhythm is an important part of music, just as it is in reading. Good readers need good rhythm. Through the rhythm of music and motion we can help children develop this rhythm so they can become rhythmic readers. In music, we work with expressive terms, lyrics, and poetry. We use introductions, themes, phrases, development, and rhythmic structure, all of which parallel language arts expectations. If we as teachers can recognize and use these and other similarities between musical and literacy skills, we can strengthen both.

I prefer to concentrate on American children's folk songs in the music curriculum I use. Let's use the song "The Cat Came Back" to demonstrate how music can be a launching pad for literacy.

Instructional Plan

"The Cat Came Back" (A Traditional Children's Folk Song)

I begin by telling the children that we are going to sing a song about a man named Mr. Johnson who doesn't like cats. I explain that we don't really know why he doesn't like cats and I ask the children to give me reasons that they think he may not like cats. I then discuss real and make-believe things that Mr. Johnson might do in the song to get rid of the cat and ask them which things could really happen and which things could not really happen. Next, I teach them the chorus of the song because this is the part they can sing easily. It is simple and very repetitive. "The cat came back the very next day. The cat came back, we thought he was a goner. The cat came back, he just wouldn't stay away ay, ay, ay." To the question, "Ms. Pam, what's a goner?," I explain that it means the cat is "gone forever."

The children snap or clap on the first part of the chorus until they sing the words "away, ay, ay, ay," at which time they sway their arms from side to side (crossing the midline) in time with this part of the song.

The verses of the song encourage the use of a variety of teaching methods, that is, visual, auditory, or tactile. Using a multifaceted music presentation helps the children remember the song and lyrics. In addition, this approach increases their ability to imagine and visualize pictures—both essential for reading comprehension.

> **First verse:** "Old Mr. Johnson had troubles of his own. He had a little cat who wouldn't leave his home. He tried and he tried to give the cat away. He gave it to a man going far away." (For "a man going far away," pretend to be holding a steering wheel and blowing the car horn.)
>
> **Chorus**
>
> **Second verse:** "He gave it to a man with a great big box. He covered it in chains with a thousand locks. With the cat inside he threw it into the sea, then rushed back home and swallowed the key."
>
> *Movement: While singing the lyrics "great big box," draw a big box with your hand in the air and wave your arms around it as if putting the chains around the box. Then pretend to turn the key in the locks, pick up the box, and throw it into the sea. Move your arms quickly on "rushed back home." Use pretend actions on "swallowed the key" (of course, tell them you'd never want to do that and they shouldn't, either!).* Emphasize rhyming words: box, locks, sea, key.

Chorus

Third verse: (Science vocabulary: Mars, stars, asteroid, space, trace, rocket-ship, days, nights, gravity—"pieces floated everywhere") "He put him in a rocket ship bound for Mars. For seven days and nights it zoomed through the stars. It crashed with an asteroid in the middle of space. Pieces floated everywhere but there was no trace."

Movement: At "rocket ship," lift your arms above your head, putting your hands together in a point for the rocket ship. Hold up seven fingers for the days and nights and then zoom your hands through the air. At "crashed with an asteroid," clap loudly and then wiggle your fingers gently down to the floor as if pieces are floating downward. Rhyming words: Mars, stars, space, trace.

Chorus

Fourth verse: "Once a crazy scientist took that little cat." *Movement: use the pointer finger of each hand to circle around each side of your head to demonstrate crazy.* "He put him in a time machine with one small rat. He zoomed him back ten million years to the dinosaurs and apes. The cat took one look around and said, 'There's no possible escape!' " Rhyming words: cat, rat.

Chorus

Story songs encourage children to listen and hear in new ways. Children not only listen to the music of the song, but they hear the story as well. This attentive listening allows them to visualize the action in the story and use their imaginations to hear many other types of sounds. They use their imaginations to "hear" the *clanking* of the chains around the box, the *rattling* of the keys to lock the chain, the *honking* of the car horn as the man drives far away, the *soaring* of the rocket ship, the crashing of the asteroid, and the *zooming* of the time machine. Interpreting the song in dramatic play encourages voice development of a wide range of pitches and volumes as well as creative expression. Adding sound effects by using instruments improves aural discrimination.

With the addition of props, instruments, and movement, we address sequential learning. By using gross and fine motor skills in the movements, we develop midline crossing skills. This development can easily transfer to fluid eye movement for reading. Improvisation and creativity are encouraged as the children become more familiar with the song and desire to develop the characters to a greater degree. Often children have asked for more than one Mr. Johnson and more than one cat. This is easily accommodated with additional props and creative imagination. I let the children decide how these additional characters—such as Mr. Johnson's brother, wife, or sister—came into the story.

As the children become more familiar with the song, I add a visual poster for each of the four verses, with lyrics below the artwork. Each child holds one of the four posters representing his or her verse. The class helps them decide the order in which to stand by recalling the sequence and details of the story. The lyrics are on each poster and we point to them from left to right while the children sing the song. At the end of the month, each child is given a page of the artwork from which they may cut the verses apart to make a songbook or just take home to share with their parents.

One day a teacher thanked me for demonstrating how to use music to teach across the curriculum. She and her students had integrated the song into other areas of their learning experiences. They made a song-and-picture book from the artwork to share with their parents and siblings and to encourage family literacy. They created an art project by making their own "Cat That Kept Coming Back." Finally, they used the song to inspire a science lesson in which the children, like the crazy scientist, built their own spaceship.

Assessment

The enthusiastic participation of the students' dramatic musical presentations allows assessment of how well children comprehend the story and understand its sequence. Allow the children to "tell" the story of the song, rather than sing it, to demonstrate their ability to use oral language to retell the story; have them identify rhyming words in the song and discuss what parts of it could be true and what could not be true to help them distinguish fact from fiction. Videotape the children at the introduction of the song and again after all learning has been completed as an effective tool for assessing which children choose to participate and enjoy participating in an increasing variety of experiences. Assessing all of these areas determines how well the children have improved their communication skills and how well they can apply these language skills for their own purposes.

ADVENTURE TO THE UNNAMED PLANET
Randy Taylor
Speaking, Writing, and Visual Literacy

National Standards

NCTE: 4, 6, 7, 11, 12; CNAEA—Drama 2: Acting by assuming roles; CNAEA—Drama 3: Designing by visualizing and arranging environments for classroom dramatizations; CNAEA—Drama 5: Researching by finding information to support classroom dramatizations.

Objectives

Students will use appropriate language to comprehend, evaluate, interpret, and communicate their understanding of project content.

Shhhh! The members of the Space Exploration Enterprise (SEE) team are reporting on their encounters with the inhabitants of the Unnamed Planet. The kindergarten explorers are presenting their reports while images of the creatures are projected onto the "communication bubble." Each member of the team is listening closely to what each explorer is reporting—these reports mean much to the mission of the SEE. Listen ... (and note: the spellings and grammar are all theirs!)

"He lives in a tent and he eats everything."

"The one I spoke to eats trees."

"It eats worms and will give us food and drink and lives at worm's house. They taste like chocolate."

"This is a him. He told me the food is free. They have long purple noodles. His name is Joshua. You might want to laugh at him. The drinks come from wind cups. This guy wants to help us find food. He is a copper kind and gets mad real easy. If you ignore him he will get mad."

"He eats trees—dinks sap."

"It was standing on water that was like a pink slide."

"It eats spiders. They dinks juice and live in a bubble."

The reports go from the SEE explorers who are captive on the Unnamed Planet hoping to find food and water—and eventually, the ability to return to Earth. Each kindergarten explorer has journeyed to a different part of the planet to explore the terrain and the possible inhabitants (the planet was divided into a grid, each with its own code using words and numbers, such as A3 or B4). The explorers were able to talk to the inhabitants through a special "decoder" (it was explained to the children that the engineers developed these decoders; each explorer then modified it to his/her own needs).

This team is part of a kindergarten class at Winnona Park Elementary School in Decatur, Georgia, that uses expeditionary learning. This is a unique program that emphasizes hands-on, project-based group learning, where much of the academic work is done in "learning expeditions"—long-term investigations of important questions and subjects that include individual and group projects and performances and presentations of student work. I met with the four teachers to decide what the focus of our residency would encompass. They wanted to explore community, mapping, the four elements, and imagination, while keeping in mind that they were going to see the wildly creative *Seussical the Musical* at the Alliance Theatre.

My chore as a Wolf Trap Early Learning teaching artist with the Alliance Theatre was to construct and implement a program that would engage the students and weave a story inside which they could manipulate and become co-creators while staying true to the wonders and curiosities of the students. The residency, which would encompass ten sessions, needed to meet the teachers' educational objectives as well as the Alliance's overarching theme of story with specific drama objectives dictated by the Arts Curriculum in Education grant from the Georgia Council for the Arts, which funded the program. Out of these parameters, SEE was developed.

The first meeting with the students was to ensure their buy-in for the project—so I told them the story that would be the foundation of the project and which we would explore and expand together. I came in wearing a cap with a SEE logo and addressed the class as a fellow scientist. I introduced the information about a new planet that had just been identified beyond Pluto. (I was quickly informed that Pluto was no longer a planet.) I told them that this new Unnamed Planet seemed to be emitting a kind of communication which we could not decipher, and we were curious about how to find out about this. There was an immediate suggestion to go to the planet.

I told them that SEE has the capabilities to make just such a venture, and wondered if they might want to join SEE in this enterprise. They agreed, with a wealth of questions. I told them they would have to have a security badge before they could work for SEE. They totally agreed on the need for such security.

After taking an oath to be loyal to SEE, they were each given a badge with the SEE logo. They filled in their pictures and their names and proudly placed their badges on their chests. So began the exploration of the Unnamed Planet.

Over the next five weeks, the story unfolded. I met with each of the four kindergarten classes twice a week. While focusing on mapping and language skills, students in their role as employees of SEE mapped out the solar system and arranged the parts of the special spaceship that was designed by SEE's engineers (the students).

The solar system was created by using a long rope with various large glass beads placed on it. Each student held a different bead as the rope was unrolled to reveal the expanse of the solar system. Individual specialists reported what they knew about each planet. The final planet was the Unnamed Planet, where we were to venture. A modern tape dispenser symbolized our spaceship, which was to go from Earth to the Unnamed Planet, emphasizing the great distance we would have to travel. Each group reported on the difficulties they predicted with such a long journey.

A plan for the spaceship was presented to each group. It was a drawing of a hollow shell with an outline, a few windows, and some floors. The SEE explorers had to decide how to fill the empty spaceship: what would be needed for such a long journey? They drew images of items to fill the ship, and these pictures were placed on the ship in strategic locations. We ended up with gardens, sleeping areas, control panels, exercise rooms, communication devices, oxygen storage tanks, medical labs, electrical wiring, and of course, toilets—both boys' and girls'.

To actually go on the spaceship, a large inflatable black bubble was unrolled in the classroom. The bubble was constructed out of plastic drop cloths and held together with duct tape. A window fan provided the air needed to inflate the bubble. Each SEE explorer removed his or her shoes, entered the spaceship, and entered a new world. A recording of a spaceship blasting off provided the auditory clues to the event.

Once in space, the explorers encountered problems, which we addressed: there was oxygen escaping from the ship; the garden wasn't producing enough food for us to eat; the controls for the engine weren't working right. Thanks to the expertise of the crew, most of the problems were solved so that we could arrive at the Unnamed Planet.

We also took time to remember our families whom we had left behind on Earth. We weren't sure exactly how long this adventure might take—some said a year, some said maybe a lifetime. Each explorer dictated a message they would like to send their family: "I will miss you." "I will be older the next time you see me." "I'm not sure I really want to go on this trip." "I hope we well meet some aliens." "Don't worry about me, I am brave."

Throughout our expedition, the children talked and talked and talked about their experiences. Their spoken language reflected acquisition of new vocabulary on a daily basis; their observations reflected comprehension and evaluation of our strategies and mission; and their enthusiasm reflected a total engagement in learning. Mission accomplished!

Assessment

Students' print and non-print texts provide examples of their ability to use language to describe, report, comprehend, and evaluate their surroundings. Special note should be taken of appropriate use of new vocabulary words in these contexts.

THE TURNIP: THE GREAT, BIG, ENORMOUS POWER OF STORY
Sherry Norfolk
Speaking and Listening

National Standards

NCTE: 4, 6, 12.

Objectives

To recognize the beginning, middle, and end of a story; to understand and be able to identify story elements such as characters, settings, problems, and solutions; and to be able to identify and use story sequencing.

During the planning meeting for a ten-session kindergarten residency, the teachers explained that one of the classes would include a group of five children with special needs.

"Don't worry about them—they probably won't get much out of it, but maybe they'll enjoy the stories," their teacher told me. Well, wave a red flag in front of me—I love a challenge!

The teachers determined that the main objectives of the residency would be for children to recognize the beginning, middle, and end of stories; to understand and be able to identify story elements such as characters, settings, problems, and solutions; and to be able to identify the sequence of the story. My personal (but unspoken) objective was that the kids in the special needs group would get more out of our sessions than just enjoyment.

One of those children was Jeremy, a child with fetal alcohol syndrome. Among the many common symptoms of this brain disorder are a short attention span and difficulty organizing and retaining information. Yet from the very beginning, Jeremy paid attention. He made constant, unvarying eye contact, and his expression reflected an understanding of the story. When we retold stories through large- and small-group creative drama, he always demonstrated comprehension by doing what he was supposed to do when he was supposed to do it. He didn't have a large vocabulary, but he used the few words he had appropriately. And during our reflection sessions, he was able to answer questions about the characters and sequence correctly.

Each day, the students heard and learned to retell a complete story, and each day, the number of participants in each group was reduced: the first day, the whole class retold the story together through creative drama; the second day, groups of six children worked together to tell a story; the next day, groups of four children performed, etc. Eventually, the day arrived when students would retell a story on their own, demonstrating their ability to use their math/logical intelligence by correctly sequencing and their linguistic intelligence by using complete sentences and story structure.

The Lesson

Our story was a very simple version of "The Turnip," a cumulative Eastern-European folktale found in many picture books (see below). For teaching purposes, I tell it with repetitive, rhythmical phrases, distinctive character voices, and stylized body language to help visual, auditory, and kinesthetic learners succeed. Each character is represented by a specific gesture: the Old Man grabs his suspenders, the Old Woman holds her apron, the Little Boy has a baseball bat, the Little Girl cradles her doll, the Dog begs, the Cat licks her paw, and the Mouse flexes her paws. (Yes, these are stereotypes, but that's why they work!)

As I told the story, the repetition and patterning allowed the children to begin to tell along with me, repeating the phrases and mimicking the actions. After the first telling, we identified the characters and listed them on the board (unsurprisingly, the children produced them in perfect sequence). We talked about what was happening at the beginning of the story (the Old

Man wanted a turnip, so he planted a seed); what happened in the middle (the turnip wouldn't come up when pulled, so the Old Man got help from all of the other characters), and what happened at the end (the Mouse pulled it up, the Old Woman cooked it, and they all ate it because they all helped). We identified the problem and the solution. They didn't miss a beat.

Having reviewed the story logically/sequentially and linguistically, we reviewed it for the visual and kinesthetic kids, retelling the story using only actions. This allowed the linguistic learners to retell it in their minds; the kinesthetic learners to review the sequence through their body language; and the visual kids to watch the action.

Next we did round-robin telling: we got in a circle and I started the story, then clapped and stopped, turning to the child beside me to continue. She told until I clapped again, and so on. We went around the circle a few times. If a child had trouble remembering what came next, I provided the visual cues to help her remember. When it was clear that everyone had a good grasp of the story, they paired up to practice telling it to a partner.

At this point, I noticed that no one paired up with Jeremy, so I asked him if he would like to tell me the story. He was sitting directly at his teacher's feet, and she shook her head, rolling her eyes. Let me say here that she is a very good, caring teacher. She wasn't being cruel—Jeremy had been diagnosed as unable to learn and she simply did not believe that he could do this. I figured whether or not he could do it on his own, he could at least do the actions with me or listen to me tell it again. I sat down.

"So, Jeremy, what happened?" I asked him.

"There was Ol' Man," he began. "He wanted Turnip. He planted sheed. It grew. It grew. He shaid time to pull. He pull, he pull, it wouldn't come up. He got Ol' Woman. She pull, she pull, it wouldn't come up . . ."

He told the whole story in perfect sequence.

The teacher was agog and I was thrilled, but Jeremy was unmoved. He had always known that he could do it.

When the practice session was complete, I gathered all of the children and asked who would like to tell the story to the whole group. Hands went up, and a little girl got up and told a very elegant version of "The Turnip." We all clapped (because we had learned our audience manners). But before the applause ended, and even before I asked for another volunteer, Jeremy stood up and walked to the front of the group.

"Onsh there was Ol' Man. He wanted Turnip. He planted sheed. And the sun came down and the rain came down. It grew, it grew, it grew . . ."

He told the whole story in perfect sequence, adding details. Everyone cheered. Jeremy grinned from ear to ear—he liked applause, and he rarely got to hear it directed at him. All four teachers were in tears.

The next day, the teachers and I met to discuss plans for our grand finale, which was scheduled to take place in four days, complete with video cameras, special guests from Young Audience-Woodruff Arts Center, and the principal. I asked the teachers to decide which of the several stories that the

Figure 2.1. Practicing for Performance

children had learned would be featured in the performance. Nobody mentioned Jeremy and his story.

"I'd really like for Jeremy to tell his story," I said hopefully.

"Oh, no, let's not put that kind of pressure on him," his teacher replied quickly. "It will have been five days by then—he won't remember it."

So we agreed to let the whole special needs class act out the story with me serving as narrator, thus removing any pressure while allowing all of the students a chance to participate. We practiced it that way the day before the finale.

Grand finale day arrived, along with all of the promised suits and equipment. The children performed with lots of giggles and impressive stage presence. Then it was time for "The Turnip." I gathered my troupe and quickly reviewed our roles: "Who is the Old Woman? Who is the Little Boy?" When I reached Jeremy, he said matter-of-factly, "I de Ol' Man."

Well, the Old Man is the narrator, and that was supposed to be my role. So what? I moved Jeremy to the front of the line and stepped offstage. I could narrate from there if necessary, but . . . maybe it wouldn't be necessary.

"So Jeremy, what happened?" I asked.

"Onsh there was Ol' Man. He wanted Turnip. He got sheed. He dug, he dug, he planted. And the sun came down and the rain came down. It grew, it grew, it grew. He shaid time to pull. He pull, he pull, it wouldn't come up. He got Ol' Woman—" at this point he turned, grabbed the child playing the Old Woman, pulled her into position, and continued, "she pull, she pull . . . "

He not only told the whole story, in perfect sequence, with some new language—he *directed* it!

When the story was finished and the children had taken their bows, the teacher came over to me.

"Jeremy's life has changed as of today. He was tested and diagnosed as unable to learn, but he obviously *can* learn and remember what he's learned. I'm going to have him retested. His IEP [individualized educational plan] will change and his whole educational future will be different." She was delighted by the discovery—and frustrated with a system that had wasted nearly a year of Jeremy's educational life.

Providing multiple points of entry into learning (visual, aural, and kinesthetic), and engaging all ways of knowing through linguistic, logical, kinesthetic, rhythmical, spatial, interpersonal, and intrapersonal methods may have been the key to unlock Jeremy's ability to learn. Or maybe it was just the great, big, enormous power of story.

I've used this lesson plan with kindergartners all over the country, and even in Hong Kong. It always works, and has repeatedly yielded small miracles such as Jeremy's. Try it—and watch your own small miracles occur!

Resources

- De la Mare, Walter. *The Turnip*. Boston, MA: D. R. Godine, 1992.
- De Spain, Pleasant. "The Turnip" in *Twenty-Two Splendid Tales to Tell from Around the World*. Little Rock, AR: August House, 1994.
- Hester, Denia. *Grandma Lena's Big Ol' Turnip*. Morton Grove, IL: Albert Whitman & Co., 2005.
- Morgan, Pierr. *The Turnip: An Old Russian Folktale*. New York: Philomel, 1990.
- Oxenbury, Helen, and Aleksei Tolstoy. *The Great Big Enormous Turnip*. Pan Macmillan, 1972.
- Parkinson, Kathy. *The Enormous Turnip*. Niles, IL: A. Whitman, 1986.
- Peck, Jan. *The Giant Carrot*. New York: Dial Books for Young Readers, 1996.
- Tolstoy, Aleksei. *The Great Big Enormous Turnip*. New York: Scholastic, 1969.
- Tolstoy, Aleksei, and Niamh Sharkey. *The Gigantic Turnip*. Brooklyn, NY: Barefoot Books, 1998.
- Ziefert, Harriet. *The Turnip*. New York: Viking, 1996.
- Zunshine, Tatiana. *A Little Story About a Big Turnip*. Columbus, OH: Pumpkin House, 2003.

Assessment

Use an observational checklist to determine the teller's understanding of story elements and proper sequencing of story events.

MOVE IT!
Sarah Howard
Speaking and Listening

National Standards

NCTE: 11, 12; HCOF Language Development: Demonstrates increasing ability to attend to and understand stories; understands and uses an increasingly complex and varied vocabulary; HCOF Literacy: shows increasing ability to discriminate and identify sounds in spoken language; shows growing awareness of beginning and ending sounds in words; progresses in matching sounds and rhymes in familiar words, songs, and poems; HCOF Book Knowledge and Appreciation: shows growing interest in reading-related activities; and demonstrates progress in abilities to retell and act out stories and predict what will happen next.

Objectives

Children will listen longer, understand more, increase phonemic awareness, increase vocabulary, and increase ability to retell and act out stories and predict what will happen next.

In my work for a public library, I like to find material that can be modified for use with different ages by tweaking the way the stories and songs are presented. The Move It! theme has been used successfully with children ages two and on up to early elementary.

Hattie and the Fox by Mem Fox, illustrated by Patricia Mullens (Bradbury Press, 1987), is a story that's easy to tell and easy for kids to retell. I have found it fun to use a fox puppet to tell this story. For younger audiences, I hold the puppet in my lap with most of him hidden; as the story cumulates, the children help with the naming of body parts ("Goodness gracious me! I can see a nose in the bushes!" "Goodness gracious me! I can see a nose, and two eyes, in the bushes!" "Goodness gracious me! I can see a nose, two eyes, and two ears ... in the bushes!") as they appear. You can encourage the kids to find their own nose, eyes, legs, etc. Even in programs for infants, this title works as a tactile story as parents hold their babies and repeat the names of the body parts.

For older audiences, I make a simple box or panel with fake paper grass, put the fox puppet behind, and reveal the body parts more sneakily as audience members try to figure out what animal is causing all the trouble.

If you are not a puppet person, this story tells well with different inflections and body postures for each animal. In fact, in a second-grade classroom I assigned each child an animal. I gave them their phrase and they each developed their own voice for the animal. The fact that all the animals are at first unfazed by the problem lets the students portray different emotions. The lackadaisical response of Hattie's animal friends at the beginning and their frightened response at the end lead to talking about opposites, assumptions, discoveries, changes of mind, and other developmental aspects. Taking this idea a step further, older kids can act out the story for younger kids with minimal props. You can also use the format of telling in which you prompt the lines to the children as you tell. In my mind, this works only with stories such as this one, which have short phrases that keep the story rolling. Nothing is more annoying for an audience than having to wait too long for things to happen and the story flow breaking up.

Each child can have a puppet and recite the repeated lines of their animal. Depending on their age, they may need help with this. Younger kids will participate by holding up their puppets when their characters speak. It is wonderful to see the amount of pride on the children's faces when participating in this simple way. Keep in mind that you can make stick puppets for the animals. You can also tell the story using whatever puppets you happen to have. You can even have more than one of each animal, and the kids can participate from the audience (five pigs, five horses, or whatever you have).

We have a puppet stage in the library's public area for kids to put on their own shows. Years ago, I was entertained by watching a child putting his own nose, eyes, and ears, through the curtain as his parent played the part of the cow.

Since the hero of this story is a hen, it pairs easily with *Big Fat Hen* by Keith Baker (Harcourt Brace & Company, 1994). This is a version of the traditional rhyme "One, Two, Buckle My Shoe." With the young crowd, we simply pat our legs while parents hold up fingers representing the numbers. For older kids, we hold up fingers and act out parts of the story. Repetition is very important, so we often present this rhyme again at the end of a program, asking parents to get out their car keys and use them as rhythm instruments as we chant.

Silly Sally by Audrey Wood (Harcourt Brace & Company, 1992) is great fun. As you share the story, older kids are able to join in on the rhymes. It is possible to add on to the story; for example: "On the way she met a loon, a silly loon, they sang a tune." You can stop the story at this point and sing a little song. I suggest one verse of "If You're Happy and You Know It." Other opportunities such as jumping for leapfrog, snoring, and dancing exist. If parents are involved in your program, they are able to participate one-on-one with their child—this has even been successful with the infant program, as parents lift their babies in the air for leapfrog and tickle and sing with their children. A simple extension activity is to create a small stick puppet of a "Silly Sally" for kids to hold, turn upside down and move forward and backward as the story progresses.

If you do not have the time to make stick puppets in advance, just grab some stickers. Give each child a sticker (something large and round works well), and after the story, do this little rhyme or make up a simple tune:

Put a sticker on your nose and cock-a-doodle-doo (three times)
Cock-a-doodle, all day long.

Sing many different verses, replacing "nose" with other body parts. Don't forget to use this as an opportunity to build vocabulary and expand to knuckle, ankle, and shin, as well as the more popular chin, knee, and foot. And yes, "bottom" is an all-time favorite. There is also much wing movement and head bobbing and pecking as they act like hens during the cock-a-doodle-doo portion.

Another perpetually winning song is "Head and Shoulders, Knees and Toes." Present this the traditional way and then with a twist—sing the list backward to go along with the silliness in "Silly Sally." Beware, as it takes some thought—and many mistakes and giggles will take place!

Toes, knees, shoulders, head
Shoulders head (two times)
Nose and mouth and ears and eyes
Toes, knees, shoulders, head
Shoulders, head

One strategy with the theme-based program is to end on something opposite from the way you started. We started with stories with characters moving in different ways, so we end the program with a bedtime story. Over the years I have learned how important it is to balance my program with quiet stories and songs as well as the raucous; thoughtful stories and songs as well as the silly; and sad stories and songs as well as the happy.

Goodnight Moon by Margaret Wise Brown, illustrated by Clement Hurd (Harper & Row, 1947), is a classic that lends itself to many fun extension activities in the program or at home. I like to start off by reading it with the lights turned down or even with a large flashlight on the page. The rhyming in this story lends itself to some vocal participation from the kids, and it is great to hear them trying hard to say "Hush!" quietly. I also tend to draw out the "shhh" part longer then usual. After reading the story (in big-book format), it is possible to have the children look up close at the pictures, allowing for some open-ended questions and letting them point out different objects in the book. Finding the mouse on the page is a favorite activity. It is also fun to give each child a chance to take the flashlight and point it at an object in the room and say goodnight to it. This allows them to name objects and practice that important skill of taking turns. (Be prepared to have a hard time ending this activity.) Also, since the three bears and the cow jumping over the moon are mentioned in the story, children enjoy talking about those rhymes and stories.

It is logical to end with singing "Twinkle, Twinkle Little Star" or perhaps the rhyme "Tick Tock Clock":

Tick tock, tick tock,
I'm a little cuckoo clock.
Tick tock, tick tock.
Now I'm striking one o'clock.
Cuckoo!!

With this rhyme, you can strike the clock up to 3 or 5 o'clock. You also control the amount of movement depending on your audience and their needs. The kids (or the parents behind the kids) can shift their weight from side to side. Participants can be sitting down (with the child on the parent's lap if very young) or standing. On the "Cuckoo" part, the child can jump, or the parent or adult can lift the child into the air—or the child or the parent can lift the child's arms in the air. As the clock strikes higher numbers you can also make the swaying and lifting into the air go faster to simulate winding the clock tighter.

Assessment

There are many statistical ways in which we measure success in our programs. Sometimes, we are not aware of the day-to-day influence we have since we see the kids for only a short amount of time at the public library. Last month, a mother grabbed me at a community event and asked me for my e-mail address. She sent me a video clip of her two-year-old sitting in a chair with her stuffed toy kitty on the floor in front of her with the book facing out, right side up, turning pages from front to back, "reading" to the kitty. When her mom asked her what she was doing, she answered, "I have a book and I'm being the story lady."

THE ESL STORYTELLING CLASS
Catherine Crowley
Speaking and Listening

National Standards

NCTE: 11, 12.

Objectives

Increase English-language acquisition skills of speaking and listening, and familiarize students with the experience of public speaking. Students will be able to choose a familiar story from a list of stories on the whiteboard; they will be able to perform the story in front of the class and include all five elements of performance: 1) give an introduction for themselves and the story; 2) use appropriate volume to tell the story; 3) tell the story completely, with a beginning, a middle, and an end; 4) include movement and gesture where it advances the story; and 5) conclude the performance of the story with thanks and a bow. In addition, students will be able to listen to the story performances of other students with a critical ear and determine if the others have included all five parts of the performance requirements.

One day, after telling a good tiger story to an audience of Chinese-speaking ESL students at a private school in Chai Yi, Taiwan, my school director, Julie Wu, informed me that she would like me to start telling stories every day in addition to my other teaching duties. I broke the bad news to her that I was receiving only the pay of a poor English teacher, and "good storytellers get paid a small fortune for their valuable performances." But I told her that I would be happy to teach the students themselves how to tell stories. I told her I believed storytelling offers many ways for an English-language student to improve speaking and listening skills.

Wu was delighted with the idea and immediately put a proposal to the school's board of directors. They approved and the classes were offered for enrollment. I assumed the classes would be for the same older students that I taught every day, who already spoke quite a bit of English. To my dismay, the class in storytelling was offered to the preschool and kindergarten groups.

When I tried to object and back out of the plan, I was informed that the students' parents actually fought for places in the class, and that two classes had to be offered. Not only were these classes for very young learners, but the class sizes had grown from the seven students per class I had recommended, to fifteen students per class. The two storytelling classes were to start immediately and be offered every Wednesday afternoon over a ten-week period.

It was too late to back out. So with the brainstorming help of other storytellers, especially my mentor, Elizabeth Ellis, Web sites like Heather Forest's Story Arts (http://www.storyarts.org), and the book *Children Tell Stories: Teaching and Using Storytelling in the Classroom* by Martha Hamilton and Mitch Weiss, I was able to cobble together a program that actually proved more successful than my wildest expectations. Oh, the power of story!

These classes began in March. The students had already been in full-time English preschool and kindergarten since September. They had been exposed to English songs and stories for at least six months if they were of preschool age and for more than one year if they were kindergarteners. They knew the ABCs and had beginner's English.

The classes were to be fifty minutes long. I was worried about their attention spans. So I divided the class time into several activities to keep them focused. The first part of the class would be a very short story told by me, the second part would be story performance by them, and the last part would be doing an art project that complemented the day's story.

The first thing I decided to do was to alter the mood of the class-room. I turned off the fluorescent lights and put on low lights. I put classical music on at a soft volume before the students arrived. I took all the small chairs away from the long tables and arranged them in a small audience fashion before the whiteboard. When the students were all seated, the music would be turned off to signal the beginning. I wanted them to feel that this was an environment where something special could happen, maybe even something magical!

I put up big color photos of children telling stories to large audiences that were taken by Paul Porter at the Tejas Storytelling Festival. I put up photos of all the Asian tellers I knew as well. I took Linda Fang's beautiful photo from her Web site and put it up next to pictures of Robert Kikuchi-Yngojo and Nancy Wang of the storytelling duo Eth-Noh-Tec. Then I put up large color copies of children's art from *Children Tell Stories*. The pictures the children had drawn showed different aspects of using good storytelling techniques: a boy bowing, a girl looking in a mirror and practicing her story, and a boy using gestures. All of this was done to create an environment in which the children could visualize themselves as storytellers.

When the children arrived in the class, they were with a Chinese-speaking teacher who was there to help them and to interpret when necessary. The children oohed and aahed at the theatrical effects of lighting and music, but the Chinese teacher quickly turned on the lights. Chinese parents are always worried that their children will develop bad eyes from working in poor light, she explained. I turned the fluorescents off again and assured the Chinese teacher that this class was for their other senses, especially their hearing.

After they were all seated in the little chairs, I told them "The Story in Five Words" that Elizabeth Ellis had taught me. I demonstrated the basic storytelling technique that I wanted them to master as I told the story. I stood before the seated group, took a bow, and said, "Good Afternoon. My name is Ms. Cathy. My story is 'The Story in Five Words.' "

Then I told/showed them the story. I held my hand out flat about three feet above the floor and said, "Boy." Then I used my hands to make a bird flying and said, "Bird." Then I made a fist and said, "Rock." Then I gestured a throwing motion with a fist and said "Threw." And lastly I made my hands look like bird wings flying and said, "Flew."

Next I had the whole group repeat the actions and the words. We reviewed counting the words to five. As I performed each action, they called out, "One, Two . . . ."

They demonstrated varying degrees of ability and attention, but they seemed to like it. I then asked for volunteers to perform the story in front of the group.

After recruiting the first volunteer, I wrote his name on the white-board. As he performed each part of the story, I drew a large red star next to his name. I coached him to take a bow, say his name, speak so we could hear him, say the story name, tell the story with gestures, and then take a bow and say thank you at the end. I showed the students that this boy got a star for each thing he did, up to five stars.

First star, if you introduced yourself and gave the name of the story.
Second star, if we could hear you.
Third star, if you used good gestures.
Fourth star, if you told the complete story.
Fifth star, if you thanked the audience and took a bow.

I pointed to the pictures on the wall of the boy bowing and using gestures. We repeated the process with several students, each time demonstrating that the stars were given only if the desired action was performed. For example, as soon as the student said his or her name and bowed, I drew a star next to his or her name on the whiteboard.

I would ask the group, cupping my ear and pointing to it, "Can you hear her?" If they said, "Nooooo!" then I would erase the star I had started to draw and look very sad. Then we all would gesture and demonstrate speaking louder. As soon as the volume of the speaker's voice rose, the star was immediately drawn next to her name, and we would all cheer. Then the storyteller was encouraged to continue the story.

Everyone who wanted to try telling the story was given a chance to do so. But many were shy and stayed in their seats. At this point, the lights came back on and the children brought their chairs to the tables. There were crayons and a paper with a picture and word illustration of "The Story in Five Words" that I had created from graphics I found on the Internet. As they colored, I stood at the end of the long tables and told several stories I thought they might know. They knew "The Itsy Bitsy Spider," "Five Little Monkeys Jumping on the Bed," "Baby Bumblebee" and several other nursery rhymes and poems. This became the list of performance choices that I put on the board for the following week. As they finished coloring their pictures, each child was shown the notebook where their illustrated stories would be kept. These art pieces would later serve as prompts for them to show their parents the stories they knew.

When the children arrived the following week, the room setup was the same. They immediately went to their seats. But this time on the whiteboard was listed every child's name. And there was a list of names of stories they could choose to tell. I would call out each child's name and bring them to the front of the group. I would ask them which story they would like to tell and read off the choices. When the child told their story all of the students would hold up one finger for each star as it was earned.

"Good introduction! One star!"

"Can you hear him? Two stars!"

And as they finished up the story, wild applause and cheering ensued with the students chanting, "Five stars!"

Often the group would join in the recitation with the storyteller, but I would gently encourage them just to listen until it was their turn. As each week passed, we had less and less time to do the art project at the last part of the class because once all fifteen students in each class had overcome their shyness enough to tell a story, they could not get enough of doing just that. Small groups formed to tell stories in tandem and in ensemble style, especially stories like "Five Little Monkeys Jumping on the Bed." They loved playing the part of the doctor and using a deep voice to say, "No more monkeys jumping on the bed."

Even extremely shy students overcame their reluctance to stand in front of the group, for example, the very shy twin sisters. One was taller and more developed physically than the other. The littler one clung to her. The day we began to use the story, "In a Cabin in the Woods" the twins reacted. They loved the part of "come little rabbit, come with me, happy we will be." They loved the gesture of petting the rescued rabbit. They stood before us and we watched as their mouths moved, but no sound came out. The rest of the class watched fascinated and breathed out the words softly to the twins.

They did not get five stars for several weeks, and then one day, we got volume and their classmates cheered. To my amazement, one day soon after that, the twins told (separately) two different stories. Their preschool daytime teacher told me later that when the twins had first come to school, they had cried all day, everyday, until they were picked up by their parents. Their teacher stood at the back of our story class slack-jawed in wonder to see them perform their stories with volume and gestures.

The list of stories in the students' repertoire grew each week and began to include stories that were more complex and not based on nursery rhymes or songs. For example, they reveled in telling the story using a tissue as a prop for "The Poor Girl Who Could Not Pay the Rent," a melodrama.

Some stories came from short, one-minute versions of stories that I had prepared for easy memorization, like "Talkative Turtle," a Cherokee story, and "Ant and the Dove," an Aesop's fable (both found on Heather Forest's Web site). Students with stronger English skills took home the printed stories which their parents helped them memorize.

By the end of the term, every student in the class had mastered several stories and could tell them in front of a group. Each student understood volume, gestures, and expressions of body and voice. Each achieved a significant measure of self-confidence and comfort expressing him- or herself in English. And each had experienced a little of the magic of telling a story.

Assessment

The "five star" strategies above provide the framework for assessment.

Resources

- Forest, Heather. *Story Arts.* http://www.storyarts.org.
- Hamilton, Martha, and Mitch Weiss. *Children Tell Stories: Teaching and Using Storytelling in the Classroom.* Katonah, NY: Richard C. Owens, 2005.

- "The Poor Girl Who Could Not Pay the Rent," in LaRue, Thurston, *The Complete Book of Campfire Programs.* New York: Association Press, 1965. Full text of the story can be found at http://www.archive.org/stream/completebookofpr006444mbp/completebookofpr006444mbp_djvu.txt.

YOUNG CHILDREN CAN INSTINCTIVELY NAVIGATE THE STORYTELLING LANDSCAPE

Diane Williams

Reading and Visual Literacy

National Standards

NCTE: 3, 4, 6.

Objectives

Students will have an opportunity to participate in a reenactment of a story. Repetition will ignite the child's ability to retell the story, and students will learn story sequence by performing the story as a group, then retelling it as individual storytellers. Students will explore vocabulary words; explore the story characters' (animals) habitats, foods, and social lives; discover the emotional intelligences of the characters (happy, sad, greedy, uncertain, unsure, trickster, etc.); explore narrative setting/landscape (presentation setting); and explore and discuss geographic settings.

The Lost Boys of Sudan were displaced by war and the tragedy of losing their parents and adult family members at a young age. In our minds, it is unimaginable that these children, so young, could learn to navigate the landscape and find their way to an uncharted land of hope. But children are endowed with the ability to imagine and believe—that is, until they are taught differently. It is when the idea of obstacles is placed before them that they become focused on what could be considered the drudgery of learning. When classroom learning is presented in a matter-of-fact way, when it is presented in a text-only format, when it is taught with the only outcome being to test on prescribed knowledge, then we are not respecting the child's creative and inquisitive nature to navigate the landscape.

I would be the first to admit that the displaced children of Sudan had to learn to utilize a technique we call "learning the hard way." I don't know many adults that could have persevered through what the survivors of Sudan's unrest survived. Children learn; they have a resilience that kicks in when they look around and contemplate the landscape. Our society has tried to mimic that landscape with laudable TV programs such as *Mr. Rogers' Neighborhood, Captain Kangaroo, Sesame Street*, and *Barney & Friends*. These were all good models that served children a menu of imaginative and creative sparks. What was lacking was the interactive thrust that came from the child's own spirit. The spirit was now in the "boob tube," and the child sat patiently waiting to see what it was going to do next, rather than learning and even taking the initiative to explore the landscape by leading the exploration.

The Centre for Applied Research in Education at the University of East Anglia, United Kingdom, conducted a study of stories written and told to children. In the article there is a discussion about the meaning of "imaginative response," suggesting several senses in which imagination may be engaged by a stimulus. Based on illustrations from the data of the study, it goes on to examine previous relevant media research and ways in which television and videos may be considered either to stimulate or stifle the imagination processes and products of story making.

Turn off the television for a moment and let's examine another possibility. From the time children learn to talk, their imaginations start to explore. Imaginary play pals are a very important tenet to early childhood development. Imaginary play pals teach children language skills that parents spend hours, days, weeks, and months trying to impart. Young learners, one-and-a-half to five years old, spend a lot of time listening to the voices inside their own heads. They are very attentive to this mode of language development. The language structure of the imaginary play pal is very eloquent. It teaches the child using the natural and social environment. The imaginary play pal, or IPP, takes a child (or group of children) by the hand and guides him on a journey of exploration in the home, along the playground, in the car, in the community, and beyond. The child fearlessly follows. I don't think there is a study that shows the exact moment when the child begins to take the lead, but he does—and when this happens, you can be certain that it will not be much longer before the child realizes that there is no further need for the IPP.

A study on childhood IPPs was done by Marjorie Taylor, head of psychology at the University of Oregon and a leading researcher on children's pretend play, and University of Washington researcher Stephanie Carlson. They explored the hidden world of imaginary companions. (An article referencing this subject can be found at http://seattlepi.nwsource.com/lifestyle/202632_imaginary07.html. In the article, it is said that nearly two-thirds of children have had an IPP and that the IPP is a catalyst for youthful creativity.

Some children transfer the responsibility of the IPP to a doll, toy soldier, toy car, etc. The reason children put down their dolls, soldiers, and cars when they get closer to puberty is because they learn that they are fully capable of taking on the responsibility of their language skills at this point. They take ownership over navigating their environments. Sometimes there is a pull and tug with parents, and sometimes the child will seek independence (I'm referring to language literacy and children expressing themselves).

In John Dewey's pedagogical creed concerning education, first published in *The School Journal*, vol. LIV, no. 3 (January 16, 1897): 77–80, he states:

"I believe that the image is the great instrument of instruction. What a child gets out of any subject presented to him is simply the images that he himself forms with regard to it.

"I believe that if nine-tenths of the energy at present directed towards making the child learn things, were spent in seeing to it that the child was forming proper images, the work of instruction would be indefinitely facilitated.

"I believe that much of the time and attention now given to the preparation and presentation of lessons might be more wisely and profitably expended in training the child's power of imagery and in seeing to it that he is continually forming definite, vivid, and growing images of the various subjects with which he comes in contact in his experience."

Lord of the Flies by William Golding (Riverhead Books, 1954) is a good story to compare and contrast for adults to find more information about the child's instinctive nature of survival using the landscape. Let's look at the book *Anansi and the Moss-Covered Rock* to understand how one can create a social and environmental landscape for children to explore and learn the oral tradition.

You have probably heard the saying, "I'm in my element now!" Creating the right atmosphere for storytelling with children who are embarking on a journey with language learning is key to helping them take ownership of the story. It provides early childhood learners with the prescriptive methodology and format needed to ease them into their "element."

Anansi and the Moss-Covered Rock: Providing a Socially and Environmentally Safe Place for Young Language Learners

Let's take a look at the folktale *Anansi and the Moss-Covered Rock* by Eric A. Kimmel. Years ago, Eric graciously gave me permission to retell this story. His book has been a classic in libraries and schools for years. It is beautifully illustrated by Janet Stevens to pique the interest of young learners. Eric's approval letter to me had a caricature of himself drawn in red on yellow paper. I knew that this man had children's best interest at heart because his letterhead was humorous in a youthful, artistic way.

Invited to a preschool to provide a session for two- to four-year-olds, I knew that I had to carefully craft a plan so that this varied age group would feel welcome in the story environment. I started out by telling the story and followed up with a discussion on the book and the illustrations. We talked about the animal habitats: where the animals lived, what kinds of food they ate, and how they interacted with one another. The discussion ended with a lesson in emotional intelligence and character education. Talking with these young language learners about how the animals felt was easy because the students were used to making decisions about sharing and not sharing, and this story was certainly one about greed.

Is Anansi a nice creature? Is he a trickster? Did he treat his fellow animals fairly? Was he greedy or just hungry? What about the other animals? One by one they all went "on a walk in the cool of the forest with Anansi," when Anansi suddenly played a terrible trick on them. It all happened so suddenly—"kapow!"

It should be noted here that this lesson can take place in a day or over a period of time, with the storyteller talking about the environmental landscape one day and animals and their habits and reading the story the next day. A discussion of the book can happen on still another day, but the place where the story really sinks down deep—where students will learn to make meaning for themselves—is when you put *them* in the story.

Activity

Let's take a look at how that happens systematically and review how this methodology can lead to freeing the child to go from being a picture book learner to a text learner to an audio/visual learner, and then finally—helping her to learn the value of using her language and taking ownership of learning new words—to retelling stories.

Whenever I plan story time with young language learners, I start by explaining words, characters, and places (geography and landscape) with which children may not be familiar. Then I tell the story. Now the fun is about to begin. At this juncture, I frame the story by asking the students what happens first, next, etc.

By the time I get to the point where the students can get inside the story, they are ready to become actors playing their parts. I've done this exercise with other stories such as the "The Three Billy Goats Gruff" and "The Boy Who Cried Wolf" for students who are a bit older than preschoolers. There are never more than three stage locations, or settings, in the room. More than three changes the dynamic of the story. Students anxiously raise their hands because they remember the story and want to get involved. Next I assign roles: Who will play Anansi? Who will play Bush Deer? Who will play the other animal characters? Anansi lives in one location on the far end of the setting, Bush Deer lives in the tree, and all the other animals live on the other end of the setting. The moss-covered rock is key to this story and it resides somewhere in the middle.

I do not get into a discussion about Anansi because these young learners have enough to do as it relates to the logistics of the story. But for older children, you will want to explain to them that Anansi is a spider and that his stories have been told for generations by the Ashanti people of Africa. It is also interesting to note that Anansi is half-man and half-spider depending on his character at the time. The spider is a trickster character.

Because of the repetitive nature of the story, children quickly learn what to say and do.

Anansi And The Moss-Covered Rock
(Story Synopsis)

Anansi goes for a walk in the cool of the forest and stumbles upon a rock covered with moss and says, "What a strange-looking moss-covered rock." Kapow! He falls down in a dead faint (Note: I explain to the children what it means to faint.). *Anansi lies on the ground for what seems like an hour and then wakes up. He repeats his actions not knowing what was really going on, but he figures it out after fainting a second time. There is something about repeating the phrase "Isn't this a strange moss-covered rock" that makes the characters faint. Anansi is a quick thinker and he decides to go on an adventure by tricking all the animals in the forest. One by one, he visits them and asks, "Isn't it a beautiful day? Wouldn't you like to go for a walk in the cool of the forest?" and the animal goes walking with Anansi.*

(Note: Young language learners enjoy making sounds to describe action. Each time the animals go walking, you can incorporate a sound strategy; for example, the sound of the walking, "ah boom, ah boom, ah boom-boom-boom." [Repeat.])

When they arrive at the rock, Anansi states, "What is that?" and the animal responds, "Isn't this a strange moss-covered rock?" Kapow! The animal falls down in a dead faint and Anansi quickly goes to its house and steals all of its food. (Note: This is a good opportunity to talk about animal habitats and the foods they eat.) *When the animal wakes up, it doesn't realize what has happened and goes home to find out that its food is gone.*

Each time the trick is played, the Bush Deer watches from its hiding place nearby.

At the end of the story, Anansi tries to play the trick on Bush Deer, but Bush Deer has seen this before. He tricks Anansi into saying, "Isn't this a strange moss-covered rock?" and Kapow! Anansi faints. Bush Deer quickly runs to the homes of all the other animals and they all go to Anansi's house to get their food.

Anansi learned a lesson. It doesn't pay to play tricks on anyone, but for some reason, he is still playing tricks on animals and people to this day.

Activity Continued

You'll have to repeat this interaction over and over with students. As they become familiar with the story, everyone will want to have a chance to play the part of one of the characters. You can be creative with the number of students that get to participate; therefore, the story would be repeated four to six times with a class of thirty students. Just be sure to pick an Anansi and a Bush Deer that you know will not be shy—someone who doesn't mind being the star of the show.

The first and possibly second time that the story is performed, the entire class can say the repetitive phrases in unison, but by the third time the story is performed, individuals should be able to recite their parts; if not, then ask the class to assist the student.

Assessment

After everyone has had a chance to act out their part, it will be easy to assess the learning by asking one student to come up and retell the beginning of the story. Another student can tell the next segment of the story, and so forth until the end of the story is retold. It's easy for them to retell the story now because they are telling you what they have just seen.

The students' recollection of animal habitats and the foods they eat is another way to assess learning.

Young language learners can be engaged in a discussion of the emotional intelligences of the animals. They are all happy to go walking with Anansi, confused when they awaken from a dead faint, and sad when they find that their food has disappeared. Anansi is greedy and a thief who has done something he shouldn't have. Bush Deer's character takes a bit more explaining and conversation, as he is an observer throughout the story, but dares to be tricked in the end. Bush Deer turns the tables on Anansi and tricks him.

Telling this story and allowing students to use hand puppets is a wonderful, fun way to get them to take ownership as presenters of this story. They will want to tell it over and over again.

Conclusion

Value students' language. They do not have to recite the phrases word-for-word as memorization. As long as they are relating an accurate description of the action in the story, that's fine.

One of the ways I encourage students to learn the repetitive phrases is to get them to practice chanting the phrases at the beginning when I'm telling the story.

Stories such as Keith Faulkner's *The Wide-Mouthed Frog* and Janet Stevens's *The Three Billy Goats Gruff* are great for young language learners to learn to retell. In each of these stories, children navigate the landscape and discover story settings. By visually acting out the action in the story, they learn to transfer the images into words. From the text and pictures in a storybook to acting out and repeating actions and phrases, children learn to transfer this knowledge to retelling.

After telling stories at a library in my town of Madison, Mississippi, one of the children from the local day care center said, "I have a story to tell!" I gave her permission to stand in front of the group, and this wonderful three-year-old retold the story of "The Three Little Pigs." I was fascinated! The day care provider told me, "Our children retell stories every day before nap time in their own words."

Your students will, too, if you allow them to navigate the landscape.

Resources

- Faulkner, Keith. *The Wide-Mouthed Frog.* New York: Dial, 1996.
- Kimmel, Eric A. *Anansi and the Moss-Covered Rock.* New York: Holiday House, 1990.
- Stevens, Janet. *The Three Billy Goats Gruff.* San Diego: Harcourt, Brace, Jovanovich, 1987.

CHAPTER THREE

Primary Grades

STORIES MAKE A DIFFERENCE
Jane Stenson

Nothing in all my years of classroom teaching has been so exciting or empowering as telling a story with children gathered 'round. When I arrived at the Baker Demonstration School in 1986, a kindergarten teacher, Betty Weeks, was one of the sublime teachers down the hall. She told "The Gunniwolf," "Sody Sallyraytus," "The Smell of Eels," and 100 other stories. She told right before she dismissed the children for the day so that the story would be carried from the school, through the carpool line, and into the child's home. It was glorious. Betty has died, but that tradition lives in our school; all children from the toddlers through eighth graders hear and tell stories, the world's stories and personal stories.

One of the gifts Betty Weeks gave me was her version of the Grimm's tale "The Queen Bee," which I tell near the beginning of the school year. In it, the third son is maligned by his older brothers because he won't scruff up the ants or kill the ducks or smoke out the bees because, "They have done us no harm and we shouldn't harm them." The brothers enter an enchanted kingdom where everything has been turned to stone, "There is nothing that was not stone." Three tasks are performed, and it is the youngest son who completes the tasks and returns the kingdom to its natural form, because of his compassion and intelligence; he is a good person. This story tells the children everything I expect of them—they must be their best selves. They must be friendly and generous and they must try hard and must not harm any living thing.

One year in the spring, my students and I went on a field trip and saw an old, gray, crusty, huge (as in three feet across) snapping turtle, safely removed from visitors in his tank. Every twenty minutes or so the turtle rose to the surface, snagged a breath, and floated back to the bottom of the tank. What a life! A boy stood next to me and tugged on my sleeve, "Look, look at that," he said. "There is nothing that is not stone." How had he remembered? And we looked openly and happily at each other, strengthened across the years between us, by our understanding and shared language.

A wonderful teller from Michigan, La'Ron Williams, visited our school and shared stories from his tradition. The drum was beating, he was singing, we all were singing, and the characters in his stories were their very best selves. At the conclusion of the tellings, a boy in the front row of the auditorium raised his hand to ask a question: "Will you be my friend?" The child understood the messages transmitted through music and words and smiles and the choice of characters.

Stories make a difference in our understanding. It is the teller's job to bring the story to a transformed place where each of us can be a head taller than before, where each of us can be our best selves, if just for a moment. Stories give us a path through the forest we call the world.

"But, but ... ," this is the primary chapter. Students need to read. They need to write and you've given us anecdotes about children and stories. Yes, that's right. The child who hears stories *craves* the story found in a book and can critique it, "Oh, that's a good one! *Let's read it again.* Where does it say wolves? Show me." The child who hears stories knows how the story is supposed to go and has a million pictures in her head, so she can *write* in a clear and meaningful way, with a strong structure, about important subjects. The child who hears stories is likely to become a strong *teller* of tales.

And, above all, the child who hears stories is probably going to be a great *listener*, because that's how the tales are accessed.

As tellers, I encourage you to try some of the following activities when you're in a classroom. As teachers, I encourage you to tell stories with your children; you will have fewer management issues and you and your students will be smiling more. Try some of the activities found in this chapter to make a difference in the lives of your students and in your own life.

Memory begets story, story begets learning, and learning begets memory, which in turn begets story: the never-ending circle. In the following two articles, which are featured together, this circle is demonstrated in the seamless synthesis of a teller whose work informs and inspires a teacher and her students.

CANADA GEESE
Mary Gay Ducey

On a brisk March day some years ago, I told stories of women's lives at the Women's Center on the campus of UC Berkeley. The hall was packed and women lined the walls at this unusual offering, for it was the first time stories marked the Center's celebration of International Women's Day.

I told stories for a while and then suggested that women come up and tell their own. Several generations of women were in attendance, some of them in family groups numbering grandmothers, mothers, daughters, and granddaughters. So began an exhilarating hour of spontaneous tales, filled with adventure, pathos, surprises, and howls of laughter. When the stories ended, women drifted toward the exit, still telling, still remembering.

One woman was left and she said: "I am not much of a storyteller, but I do have a story that needs telling. If I tell you, maybe you will use it."

"Very likely," I said. "Let's hear it."

She began.

"When I was a little girl, I spent time with my grandmother, my mother's mother. She was a quiet woman, and always busy; but good, good company. I was in her kitchen one day, watching her make an apple pie. She had always cut a design of Canada geese into the top crust. Really! Not just slits, but cutouts of geese flying across that pie. So I said: 'Grandmother, why do you do that? Why do you cut those geese?' 'Ah,' she said, 'I have been waiting for fifty years for someone to ask me that question.'

"Your grandfather and I grew up neighbors. His family's farm was the only one we could see from ours, and our land met theirs. Each night we could look out and see their farm light no matter what the weather and we knew that we could always get there if something went wrong. It's good to know that neighbors are there.

"He was a good man, your grandfather. We were the same age and we played together all the time. I was the youngest and he was too and no one was left but us. Our folks were glad we had each other. When it came time for us to go to country school, my father plowed a furrow to the road so we could walk there together. He was a patient man, your grandfather, and a good thing, because I was often late. Our desks were right next to each other in school. He was good at arithmetic and reading. I was good at geography and drawing. I always liked to draw, even little pictures in the frost on the windows.

"When we went into town to the big school, we stood on our road for the bus. Both of us had tin pails for our lunches. I remember the first day we were there. He was a kind man, your grandfather, but not much for words. We sat in the back of the bus tight against each other, a bit scared. I took an art class at the big school. I never knew there were classes where you could draw, and my teacher, she was an artist. An artist. I wondered, could I be one?

"I don't recall your grandfather ever asking me to keep company. Not really. Our families went to the same church and sometimes we would go to choir practice together, or on a sleigh ride. No one talked of our marrying. No. But everyone knew that if we did, our farms would be joined someday. That would be a big farm then. I knew that and he did, too. He was a hard-working man, your grandfather.

"We were in high school soon, the first ones in our families to go there. I took art classes, but only after I had taken the practical classes. I couldn't tell you how fast the time passed in the art class. Like lightning. Your grandfather took agriculture courses and such. Sure he did; he was going to farm. Everyone knew that. What would I do? I had a good number of thoughts, but well, times were so hard and there was no money.

"By that time we had taken to going to town, sometimes by ourselves. I suppose you could say we were courting then. We never talked about it, but I guess you could say that is what we were doing. I don't think your grandfather ever asked me to marry him. No, I don't. It was just expected; everyone just thought we would. I guess I thought so, too, though he never asked.

"That is how I found myself, one fall day, in the back parlor with a wedding dress on. My mother had made it from her own. She was finishing the veil as it sat on my head, her mouth a line of pins. Then I heard the sound of a flock of Canada geese flying south. You never forget that cry. I looked out the window and saw them climbing, climbing, and just for a moment, I wished I was among them. Flying, flying.

"Then I pulled the veil down and I married your grandfather. He was a good man, yes he was. It wasn't long before I made him an apple pie. Now I admit it; I am pie-proud. But pride goeth before a fall, and when I tried to fit the top crust, darned if it wasn't short. I knew better than to stretch it too far. Marriage is like that I have found; you need to stretch some. I looked at the crust and then my hand had the knife and before I knew it I had cut out little Canada geese, just flying across that pie. I served a piece to your grandfather ... a big piece. He looked down at the geese and he said nothing. He was a quiet man, your grandfather.

"That was such a long time ago now. Years and years. The world has changed so much since then, hasn't it? It's hard to believe how much it has changed.

"I am glad. For you, granddaughter, you ... can fly."

IF YOU CAN READ, YOU CAN COOK
Nancy Perla
Speaking, Listening, Reading, and Writing

National Standards

NCTE: 3, 4, 6, 12; NCTM—Measurement 1: understands such attributes as length, area, weight, volume, and size of angle and select the appropriate type of unit for measuring each attribute; understand the need for measuring with standard units and become familiar with standard units in the customary and metric systems; understand that measurements are approximations and how differences in units affect precision; NCTM—Measurement 2: apply appropriate techniques, tools, and formulas to determine measurements: develop strategies for estimating the perimeters, areas, and volumes of irregular shapes; select and apply appropriate standard units and tools to measure length, area, volume, weight, time, temperature, and the size of angles.

Objectives

Using a hands-on approach, students become familiar with cooking terminology, measurement, and baking techniques as they create a hand-made, free-form fruit tart. Students rewrite the recipe in their own words to describe cooking procedures, techniques used, and connections made during the process. Using their own written recipes, students work together on their own to create a second tart.

Introduction

I have such tender memories of visits to my grandmother's home when I was young. I loved our walks to and from the library, carrying armfuls of books. I remember how she also checked out several movie star magazines that sensationalized the glamour queens of the day—Grace Kelly, Elizabeth

Taylor, and Natalie Wood, and their handsome leading men—Cary Grant, Eddie Fisher, and Robert Wagner. Armed with my cache of books and balancing a bowl of fresh, sweet cherries, I disappeared into the cozy daybed on the screened porch. It looked out onto my grandfather's impeccably maintained vegetable garden, flowerbeds, and neatly pruned plum tree. Resting against propped up pillows, I monitored the swift comings and goings of the homing pigeons my grandfather banded, raised, and trained. I imagined their travels to and from exotic, far away places that I only read about. Listening to the peaceful cooing of those pigeons, I was content.

It seemed my grandmother was always in her kitchen, and it was from her that I discovered my passion for cooking and baking. She made everything from scratch! And, she taught me how to cook many ethnic foods from our Slovenian heritage. We carefully rolled handmade "struklji," or strudel dough, across a large, flour-dusted tablecloth placed atop her kitchen table . . . and gently and tenderly stretched and coaxed the stubborn dough across the entirety, using our floured fingertips to extend it so thinly that, if we tried, we could read a book right through the dough! Finally, we spread finely sliced apples, sour cherries, or ground walnuts and honey all over the rolled-out dough, dotted it liberally with butter, carefully rolled it up into a jelly roll, and baked it. The result was always sweet and flakey . . . perfection.

The best was, of course, plum dumplings that used the purple fruit from my grandfather's tree. Each plum was encased in a soft pillow of dough (flour, potato, and butter), and the dumplings were boiled until they billowed to the top of the pot. Served warm with a generous drizzle of buttery breadcrumbs, my fork caused steam and aroma, translucent red juices, and memory to spill across the plate.

To Begin the Baking Activity

I donate this activity to the school's annual fund-raising event. It's a serious baking project for two students at a time, and we use a respectable recipe that is broken into steps easy for young children to follow. It has tremendous taste appeal that is fantastically delicious and unforgettable. This is a four-hour event!

Materials:
For the dough - 1.5 cups (7.5 ounces) flour

1/2 tsp salt

10 T cold, unsalted butter cut in half-inch cubes

3–6 T ice water

For the fruit filling - one pound of ripe peaches, nectarines, apricots, OR plums

One cup berries (about half of a dry pint)

3–5 T granulated sugar

Figure 3.1. "Glad" to be at the Farmers' Market!

- The activity should take place on a summer Saturday morning and be located in proximity to a farmers' market. I bring all of the ingredients and cooking equipment.

- We work together to make the dough for the first tart, during which the children learn a French pastry technique called *fraisage*, or "smearing the dough with the heel of your hand, thereby spreading the small pea-sized butter pieces into long, thin streaks between skeletal layers of flour and water" (*Cook's Illustrated* Magazine). Next, the dough is gently gathered into a four-inch disc (nicknamed the hockey puck by students Riley and Libby) and, using the outside edge of the hand, a crosshatch is impressed in the dough. This gives the rolling pin something to grab onto when the disc is eventually rolled out.

- The dough is chilled for at least one hour.

- We visit the local farmers' market to purchase the best fruits and berries we can find (fresh peaches, apricots, pears, raspberries, blueberries . . . whatever looks good).

- Preheat the oven to 400 degrees and wash and prepare the fruit. Berries need to be completely drained, peaches sliced into half-inch slices, etc.

- The dough is rolled into a twelve-inch circle on floured parchment paper. I give each student a twelve-inch aluminum pizza pan and show them how to trace a twelve-inch circle onto their parchment paper to use as a guide for rolling the dough. After it's rolled, it's chilled for fifteen minutes.

- The prepared fruit is then sprinkled with a little sugar and placed in the center of the chilled circle of dough. The edges of the dough are folded up around the fruit and it's baked until it's brown and bubbly, for about fifty to fifty-five minutes.

- With the first tart in the oven, the students rewrite the recipe in their own words using a blank greeting card (I have brought a selection for their choosing). This reinforces the process of making the tart as well as offering an opportunity to clarify parts of the process. Students always invent words to remind themselves (visually) of detailed steps, such as the "hockey puck." I suggest they slip these cards into a

Figure 3.2. Almost in the oven.

family cookbook, and I mention that I frequently bump into recipes in my cookbooks and they always bring back fond memories.

- After the recipes are written, students use them to make a second tart by themselves. (It's the zone of proximal development applied to tart making!) It is wonderful to see how quickly they become expert French bakers and how they use the language they have coined for themselves, especially "Now, it's time for the first tart to come out of the oven . . ."

Assessment

"The proof is in the pudding . . . or in this case . . . the tart." Although this is a casual summertime activity, as a teacher, I am naturally curious to see how children follow verbal directions, learn from visual demonstrations, how students work together as they prepare the second tart, the neatness and proficiency of their handwriting and spelling, and their fluency as they read the recipes they have written. Most of all, I am in awe of the exquisite finished product and the look of pride in the children's eyes as they show their tarts to their parents. Finally, it's the end of a lovely day, and I think how thankful I am to my grandmother for sharing her passion for reading and baking so lovingly with me.

Mrs. Perla's Rustic Fruit Tart

Dough: 1.5 cups (7.5 ounces) flour, 1/2 teaspoon salt, 10 tablespoons cold, unsalted butter, 3–6 tablespoons ice water

Fruit Filling: 1 pound peaches, nectarines, apricots, or plums; 1 cup berries, 3–5 tablespoons sugar

Making the Dough

1. Put flour and salt in processor . . . 3 pulses
2. Add butter . . . 12 pulses until coarse . . . pea size
3. Add ice water 1 tablespoon and 1 pulse at a time until it holds together when pinched
4. Empty dough on work surface
5. Gather dough into 4″ × 12″ mound
6. Fraisage or smear with heel of hand, starting at top sixth and working down
7. Remound dough with scraper and fraisage one more time
8. Form into a 4″ disk, wrap in plastic, put in fridge for about an hour

Preparing the Filling

1. During last 30 minutes, cut fruit into 1/2″ slices
2. Rinse and dry berries (drain very well)
3. Set oven rack in low mid-position and preheat oven to 400 degrees

Assemble and Bake

1. If dough is in refrigerator longer than an hour, let stand at room temperature for 15 minutes
2. Roll dough out on floured parchment into a 12″ circle, dusting with flour as needed
3. Slide parchment onto baking sheet and put in refrigerator 15 minutes
4. Sprinkle fruit with sugar and toss
5. Mound in the center of the dough leaving a 2 1/2″ border
6. Fold dough up around fruit, gently pinching pleats
7. Lightly brush dough with water and sprinkle with one tablespoon of sugar
8. Bake 50–55 minutes
9. Cool on rack. Yum.

GRANDMA—MY FIRST TEACHER: LESSONS LEARNED OUTSIDE OF SCHOOL

Dovie Thomason

Speaking and Listening

National Standards

NCTE: 1, 3, 4, 6, 7, 9, 11; NCTE—Foreign Language 2: Students demonstrate an understanding of the relationship between the practices and perspectives of the culture studied.

Objectives

Students gain appreciation for oral history; exposure to another culture's attitudes/uses of storytelling; understanding of the role of listening in learning; understanding listening and speaking as essential to literacy; self-control.

My grandmother, Dovie, was Kiowa Apache (Plains Apache-Texas) and was the first of our family to learn to speak or read or write in English. Her schooling was from missionaries and lasted only a few years; by today's standard, she would scarcely be considered literate. As both her granddaughter and namesake, much was expected of me: achieving fluency in English, becoming the first high school graduate in our family, imagining the remote possibility of attending college, and working as an "educated professional" person. I achieved these goals and, most importantly, I achieved them thanks to the early and lifelong influence of my grandma and her stories.

"My Grandma Dovie told me the old stories, not only to teach me our Indian culture and history, but because I needed them." These words are the dedication to one of my recordings of the old traditional stories and remain the inspiration for a lifetime of work with the stories of the First Nations of North America—our Indian peoples.

When I was a child, she would sit me beside her as she gently and humorously shared the antics of the Animal People in stories older than time itself. Those animals were often unruly and misbehaving, making bad choices without any thought of their inevitable consequences. Their squeaking and snarling and growling voices are still in my mind half a century later, and they delight the new generations as they delighted me when I was young.

I was small, and occasionally unruly, with a tendency toward bad choices. It was Grandma who was charged with straightening my crooked ways so I would be in harmony with what was held to be of value in my family and the larger Native American community. The stories were (and are) the traditional way to guide the young (and not-so-young) without punishment or embarrassing confrontation. Through the mistakes of the story characters, we are shown human weaknesses and gently, with humor and respect, are reminded to look at our own mistakes and correct them ourselves, rather than needing to be controlled by being admonished by others.

I remember when I was in second grade when I was visited by my grandma and learned the first story that I was ever able to retell. She beckoned me to sit beside her as she began to tell the story of a turtle who wanted to learn to fly. That turtle would talk and talk, trying to get the birds to take him with them on their long, annual journey to warmer climates. The birds assured him they could never teach him to fly unless he could close his mouth around a stick and keep it closed, holding on tightly, while they carried him on their flight. Was that turtle able to control himself and his need to talk nonstop long enough to get south with the birds? Of course not! And he fell to the earth, cracking his shell and carrying the scars on the shells of all turtles even to this time. And did he learn his lesson? Well, he never tried to fly again and he's been pretty silent ever since the day he tried to be someone he wasn't!

That story made an impression on me, as it has on thousands of young listeners through the years. And in my sharing of the story, it remains fresh and current for me; I've learned that it has many "lessons" within it. Of course there's the obvious lesson about needing to learn to keep your mouth closed sometimes. But that lesson wasn't apparent to me the first time I heard the story. It was my grandma's patient repetition *sixteen* times during that long-ago visit that finally taught me the important lesson about being quiet so that I could listen and learn. I guess I had fidgeted and fussed during the fifteen attempts to teach me the lesson about self-control. She never scolded me or told me to be quiet and pay attention; she just told the story again and again without ever losing her sense of humor or patience.

Hearing the story again and again as a child (and telling it, as both a parent and visiting storyteller) has shown me how much can be contained within a "small" traditional tale. There are levels of meaning and lessons contained therein that are revealed only through multiple tellings and many different listeners. Turtle's story also teaches about respecting your own talents/ gifts and the diverse talents of others, taking responsibility for what happens as a result of your behavior/choices, thinking things through before jumping to action, having empathy for the needs and feelings of others, and so many more valuable lessons. For the young listener, there can be no "wrong" answer in their interpretations of the stories, as they will refine what they've learned with each repetition. Soon, just mentioning the word "turtle" was all Grandma had to do to cause me to immediately look closely at my behavior at that moment to determine why she'd mentioned turtle.

Beyond the specific lessons of a particular story, Grandma was teaching me how to listen. And, through listening, I was "learning how to learn." I was anticipating the next part of the story, whether new or familiar. I was predicting the outcome based on other stories she'd told me. I was visualizing the characters and the settings held within the stories. I was acquiring vocabulary and fluency as she described and elaborated her stories with words far beyond my reading or writing levels. I was comprehending mood and tone, imperative or interrogatory, before I'd ever heard of punctuation. I was imagining alternative endings and stories of my own as I effortlessly absorbed the form and shape and structure of stories. She was readying me for reading and writing long before I was exposed to the printed word by creating a world of words that opened an internal space that would later be filled with books, books, BOOKS!

Before my eyes scanned a printed page, decoding and memorizing the letters that I would need to enter its pages, I learned to listen and enjoy the playful and instructive nature of the spoken word. So, many years later, as a former writer and teacher and now as a storyteller, I can see how those earliest lessons about oral language became the foundation for the definition of true literacy that guides my work: speaking, listening, reading, and writing all combine for true "literacy"; but the grandmother of them all is SPEAKING . . . .

Resources

- Thomason, Dovie. *The Animals' Wishes.* Barrington, IL: Rigby Reed, 2000.
- Thomason, Dovie. *Fireside Tales.* Audio. Somerville, MA: Yellow Moon Press, 2001.
- Thomason, Dovie. *Lessons from the Animal People.* Audio. Somerville, MA: Yellow Moon Press, 1997. (These resources are available from http://www.doviethomason. com.)

MY GRANDMOTHER'S BOUQUET OF FRIENDS
Limeul Eubanks
Speaking, Listening, Writing, Visual Literacy, and Information Literacy

National Standards

NCTE: 4, 7, 9; NAS 1: All students should develop abilities necessary to do scientific inquiry and an understanding about scientific inquiry; CNAEA—Visual Arts 1: Understanding and applying media, techniques, and processes; CNAEA—Visual Arts 2: Using knowledge of structures and functions; CNAEA—Visual Arts 3: Choosing and evaluating a range of subject matter, symbols, and ideas; CNAEA—Visual Arts 4: Making connections between visual arts and other disciplines; AASL 1: Learners use skills, resources, and tools to inquire, think critically, and gain knowledge.

Objectives

Students will identify the unique quality of their family's history by interviewing a family member about a belonging, keepsake, or treasure; students will focus on evoking visual imagery using the mind's eye; students will gather stories and look for things that remind them of a person or experience. The images will help them retell the stories and create an artistic representation of the story.

Introduction

Have you ever wondered why a thought or memory from the past pops into your mind? What about tasting something and remembering your parents making your favorite meal? Or does the smell of cotton candy remind you of the fair?

A personal experience of an event can be triggered by our five senses: smell, taste, touch, hearing, and sight. These senses can prompt one to recall an experience as it relates to a memory.

A vivid memory I have is of my grandmother's garden. It was full of aromas and bright and colorful flowering plants of all shapes and sizes. Each one had its own story of how it made its way into her garden. Even today, I can close my eyes after seeing a flower and I am quickly transported back to my grandmother's garden, where I see her cutting flowers to be placed in an array of vases that accented every room of the house year-round.

My grandmother told me once not to thank anyone for a plant or it will not live. Instead, she would say, "I will think of you every time it blooms." She would often refer to the plants by the name of the person who gave her the plant cutting. The references always made me smile.

Another fond memory of my grandmother is of her cutting flowers from the garden for a friend that was ill. We would place the flowers in a jar that we had decoupaged on the outside with cutouts of flowers and birds from an old garden magazine. Decoupage is the art of decorating surfaces by applying cutouts (as of paper) and then coating the surface with several layers of finish (such as lacquer or varnish). When the bouquet of flowers entered the colorless hospital, the room was transformed. I would listen carefully as my grandmother would tell stories and I remember thinking it amazing that a vase of flowers could guide an hour of tales.

Memories are important because experiences shape our lives. By sharing life stories, we are able to form a mental image that helps recall experiences. An account of a personal experience or an event can remind us of someone close. For example, a quilt is much more than fabric patterns cut into geometric shapes. Quilts were often pieced together using fabric from old garments previously worn by family members. Stories were told about each piece of fabric and the family member that it belonged to. We are immersed in a variety of personal stories in everyday life.

Essential Questions

1. Why are personal stories important to everyday life?
2. How can listening to stories told by others improve our lives?
3. How can my story make a difference in the lives of others?

4. What kinds of plants are given as gifts, and when?
5. Why is it important to remember experiences from life?
6. What kinds of emotions do we experience when someone gives us an unexpected gift?

Activity/Session I: Collage

Have students select a flower and ask them to discuss their selection. You can use old magazines to find flowers or research them on the Internet and create a collage. Ask your students what they liked about it. Does the flower remind them of someone? The flower can become the symbol or metaphor of that person. This is a good opportunity to discuss symbols and metaphors.

Collage is the art of making pictures by sticking pieces of paper or other objects of different things onto a surface.

Procedure: Arrange the items into a design or picture. When satisfied with the arrangement, paste or glue the items onto your background. Tell the students to be careful with the amount of paste or glue that they use. Ask them if they would like to give their collage a title or write a statement. Display their artwork. Make sure that students have a clear understanding of each meaning before going on to the other exercises.

Activity/Session II: Writing

Often stories are passed down from one generation to another. Ask your students to interview a grandmother, aunt, neighbor, or someone else they feel comfortable talking to. Students should ask the person being interviewed to share a memory about their favorite flower and to explain why the flower leaves them with this impression. Sometimes these stories reflect on life-changing events or focus on something else that has happened in a person's life.

Students should write down or record the interview and then follow up with research to learn about different types of flowers and relate the information to the interviewee's favorite flower. The flower becomes the metaphor of that person's life. This same exercise can be done with a belonging, keepsake, or treasure. Written stories should be no longer than one page. Be sure that the metaphor serves as the theme for the memory and retelling/storytelling that will take place in Activity/Session III.

Activity/Session III: Storytelling

As part of a group activity, students can hold a flower and the teacher can walk around the room as if he/she is walking through a garden. As the teacher picks the flower from one of the students, they become the voice of the flower, sharing facts and other important information. Students can relate the flower to the person they interviewed and go on to tell their story. Students may even relate themselves to the flower. The recounting should be no longer than three to five minutes. These activities can take place over the course of the semester.

Additional Activities

- Make a memory book with drawings and writings of stories from interviews for family members.
- Place the collection of students' stories in a booklet and make copies for each student and place a copy in the school library.
- Create decoupage collages of flowers from magazine cutouts and place decoratively around a box. Finish with a coating of medium gloss.
- Have students bring seeds and plant a garden. Once the garden blooms, students can research and learn more about what has grown.

Assessments

Take the information from the flower/plant research and compare and contrast the findings with the characteristics they have collected. Invite students to tell why the story is important to them and how their lives were shaped by this experience.

Have students create a family tree with leaves. On the back of each leaf, they should write something about each family member that reminds them of a flower (based on previous class discussions). Encourage them to create illustrations of each other's stories to help them recall and become better listeners.

STORYBOARDING AND THE COMPUTER
Jane Stenson
Writing, Visual Literacy, and Information Literacy

National Standards

NCTE: 1, 2, 4, 5, 6, 8, 11, 12; AASL 1. Learners use skills, resources, and tools to inquire, think critically, and gain knowledge; AASL 2: Learners use skills, resources, and tools to draw conclusions, make informed decisions, apply knowledge to new situations, and create new knowledge; AASL 4: Learners use skills, resources, and tools to pursue personal and aesthetic growth; CNAEA—Visual Arts 1: Understanding and applying media techniques and processes; CNAEA—Visual Arts 2: Using knowledge of structures and functions; CNAEA—Visual Arts 6: Making connections between visual arts and other disciplines; ISTE 3: Students use technology tools to enhance learning, increase productivity, and promote creativity; students use productivity tools to collaborate in constructing technology-enhanced models, prepare publications, and produce other creative works.

Objectives

Children will practice story structure with graphic organization, keyboarding experience, and computer graphic program experiences.

Materials

- Computer
- Color printer
- Story

Instructional Plan

A classroom teacher's and technology teacher's culminating project for first graders led to increased use of the graphic storyboard in first, second, and third grades and ultimately helped the children tell and write their stories. The project also gave them increased familiarity with using the computer, which is an ability to be cultivated as they seek information.

Computer instruction begins in first grade in our school. Because of family computers, teachers find many children with high familiarity of computer gaming systems rather than with the actual computer. Facility with the mouse is a major emphasis in first grade, and using drawing tools such as Kid Pix or Windows Print grants the opportunity to use the mouse in a fun and exploratory way. The mouse is what ultimately gives the child access to the joys of the computer! First-grade technology experiences are about the exploration of the computer (the mouse, the space bar, directionality, etc.). The technology curriculum emphasizes learning to use the mouse to access interesting Web sites, exploring graphic programs, and, by the end of the year, producing a small (six frames) document of either a research report or a folktale storyboard.

As in the acquisition of writing skills, the child's ability to put words into print doesn't match his/her quick thinking, (im)patience, and phonetic ability! The Type to Learn Program begins in second grade, so the storyboard activity bridges the graphic/writing expression and knowledge of the young child.

The child's drawings, often used as a means of expression and as a way to show knowledge, are adapted to the graphic exploration on the computer program. Graphics are much more fun and forgiving than the tedious "hunt and peck" to find the correct letter to spell a word. Kid Pix has drawing and painting tools in abundance to provide an enormous variety of mouse experience that can be self-directed. From the storytelling point of view, graphics rather than words increase the "telling" aspect of the story; you can't memorize the words if you are using pictures.

The color printer is the key. Kids are completely excited to see their colorful, imaginative graphics in print!

Graphics are key. Children are quite proud to show their research and their stories to anyone who will look!

Storyboarding is used to help children get to the essence of their story for writing or telling. So, in the six-frame document:

- The first frame draws the main character and should show some reference to the setting;
- The second frame has a picture of the conflict or problem which drives the action;
- The third frame extends the problem, or "sure enough" everything gets worse;
- The fourth frame shows attempts to solve the problem;
- The fifth frame shows the solution;
- The sixth frame pictures the transformation that occurred or why the story is important.

In the first example, a first grader placed what she knew about the story neatly into the six frames. Note that she chose a story that easily fits into the six frames, that is, she understood the directions for the storyboard and chose appropriately.

The TROO!!!!! Story of Balto by Helen B., Age Seven

Figure 3.3. Balto is a dog who lives in nome alaska.

Figure 3.4. One day people got sick and they did'nt have the medison to cure them.

Figure 3.5. There was metison in another town but the trains wer blocked with snow and the planes wer stuck in the storm.

Figure 3.6. So they had a big meating and one man said ... we shuld have a dog slead relay and they had one were balto led the way!!! It was a long trip but ... THEY MADE IT!!!

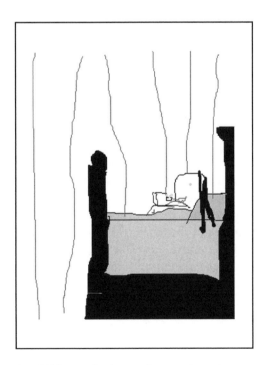

Figure 3.7. Soon the children tulk the medison and got better.

Figure 3.8. Balto is the kids favoret dog EVER!!!

In the second example, quite a conversation (with me) was had about why this second grader chose this particular story. He wanted "a story from Tibet and he knew China didn't like Tibet so he wanted to find out what a Tibetan story would be like. You know," he said, "if you know a person's story, then you know a lot about him." And that is enough sometimes for a child to hang on to a story and work with it, even though it doesn't quite fit the assignment. Next, as he worked (hard), he said he needed more frames because the story was complicated; I asked for six frames in order to get to the essence or bare bones of the story. He said there were three problems in the story and he needed more frames. I asked, "What problem is fundamental? What problem causes the other problems?" Here is Owen B.'s excellent storyboard of the Tibetan folktale "The Tower That Reached from Earth to Heaven."

The Tower That Reched from Earth to Hevan retoled by Owen B., Age Nine

<u>Part 1: The Pigs</u>

Figure 3.9. Farmer Wue is a man living in Tibet and loves his cute litle pigs.

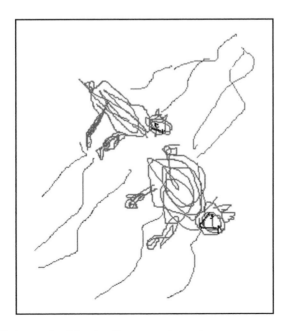

Figure 3.10. But one day his pigs flue away in a storm.

Figure 3.11. Farmer Wue loveing his pigs, went after them and than found himself in hevan and saw his pigs! But when Farmer Wue said he wanted to stay, the gods told him 'NOOOOO'.

Part 2: The Tower

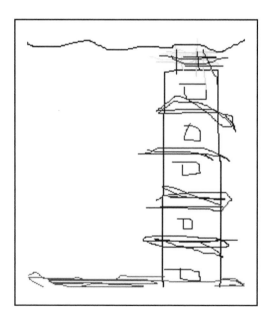

Figure 3.12. So Farmer Wue went back to his town and talked to the towns pepole about getting to hevan. So they finely disided to build a tower from earth to hevan.

Figure 3.13. So after the towns pepole disided to build a tower from earth to hevan, it went upfast and they only neded one more floor so, they disided to use rope and started to yell down...'SEND US ROPE!!!!!!!!!!!!'.

Figure 3.14. But it had been repeted and missheared so meny timse that when it reched the botome it was 'CUT US DOWN!!!!!!' and that's what they did.

The storyboard work that children use frames and reframes their stories whether for writing or telling. Pictures form in their imaginations and begin to move; why not use graphics to help the narrative structure process? Information literacy is all about understanding how to secure and evaluate information, a lot of it from the Internet. Storyboarding on the computer can be a beginning of the process of familiarity with the computer and of securing an understanding of narrative structure.

[Note: See Ann Bates's article "Assessment of Storytelling" in chapter 1 in which she has children creating storyboards as part of a storytelling unit assessment; see also Sue Black and Beverly Frett's article "Student Storytelling in the Classroom and Beyond" in chapter 4; see also Elizabeth Ellis's article in The Storytelling Classroom: Applications Across the Curriculum *(Libraries Unlimited, 2006.)]*

DRAWING STORIES
Diane Williams
Listening and Visual Literacy

National Standards

NCTE: 3, 4, 11; CNAEA 6: Making connections between visual arts and other disciplines.

Objectives

Students will listen to a story and follow instructions for drawing a coinciding picture; students will use simple lines and shapes to complete instructions for drawing a picture; students will participate in active listening.

This lesson plan uses a story that talks about one thing while drawing a picture about something different—and yet the two parallel as they draw on the same conclusion.

If you were to ask students to draw a picture of a school bus, a few would come up with a very nice drawing, while others would struggle with the overall concept. By telling a story that engages the listener, you can help students use lines and shapes to accomplish the goal of a well-designed picture.

The School Bus
By Diane Williams

Alice and Kevin did not like to get out of bed and go to school in the morning. Their mother always had to call them two or three times before they would wake up. They were dreamers with vivid imaginations.

Alice would often dream of being on an island that had coconut trees and where all the people would live happily.

Figure 3.15.   Draw four to six circles in a row to represent coconuts.

Kevin would dream of a parade of floating balloons.

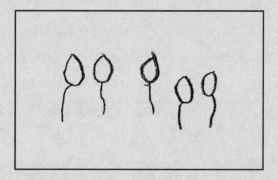

Figure 3.16.   Draw a line underneath each circle to represent a balloon and string.

They both knew that their mother's watchful eyes were not far away. They really didn't want to make her angry, but couldn't help it, especially when their dreams were always fun and took them on great adventures.

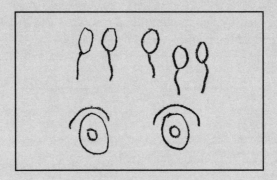

Figure 3.17. Draw two circles with inner circles spaced evenly underneath the balloons and place an eyebrow over each eye.

Kevin imagined meeting a great island chief who allowed him to rule over his land as kinsman and friend.

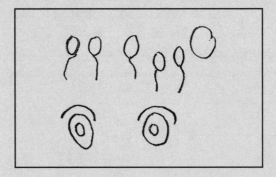

Figure 3.18. Draw a bigger balloon to the left of all the other balloons.

In Kevin's dream, people lived together in one community and the houses looked just alike. In fact, they lived in small houses, inside a big community house.

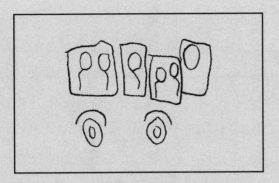

Figure 3.19. Draw squares around each balloon, including the big one.

Everyone inside followed the leader who was able to drive the people around, house and all.

Figure 3.20. Draw a big square around the entire group of pictures, but do not draw the line through the eyes that were previously made.

Figure 3.21. Draw a steering wheel in front of the big balloon.

Kevin's mind started to wander as he pondered houses on wheels. If I had a house on wheels, I could stay in bed and ride to school at the same time! I wouldn't have to get up until the last minute.

Figure 3.22. Write the words - S C H O O L B U S below the windows.

Just then, Kevin heard his sister Alice say, "Wake up! We've overslept. We're going to miss the school bus again!"

As much as Kevin didn't want to get up, he knew all along what he needed to be doing. His vivid, imaginative dream was telling him all along to get going because the school bus would be outside very soon.

This is a simple exercise to get students to draw a picture.

To create your own drawing stories, start with the end in mind. What sort of drawing exercise would you like to facilitate with your students? Look for pictures with simple lines and shapes, like houses, a room in a house, cars, outdoor scenes, etc. Then take time to envision how each line and shape can represent a segment of the story elements. The first time you create your own activity, you will want to try something that is easy to accomplish. The Internet is a great resource for finding "draw-and-tell" stories.

Resources

- Oldfield, Margaret. *Lots More Tell and Draw Stories.* Minneapolis, MN: Creative Storytime Press, 1973.
- Oldfield, Margaret. *More Tell and Draw Stories.* Minneapolis, MN: Creative Storytime Press, 1969.
- Oldfield, Margaret. *Tell and Draw Stories.* Minneapolis, MN: Creative Storytime Press, 1963.
- Pellowski, Anne. *The Story Vine: A Sourcebook of Unusual and Easy-to-Tell Stories from Around the World.* New York: Macmillan, 1984.

STORYTELLING WITH ORIGAMI/FOLD-AND-TELL STORIES
Kuniko Yamamoto
Speaking, Listening, and Visual Literacy

National Standards

NCTE: 3, 4, 6, 11.

Objectives

Students will learn about the Japanese paper folding tradition of origami; interpret relative positions and space between paper folding to complete origami models; recognize and create geometric shapes repeatedly by following folding instructions; connect the two disciplines of storytelling and origami; use simple shapes to communicate with audience; and older students will explore math problems learned by folding paper.

Materials

Use one square sheet of paper per student. Paper size should be 4″ square for small hands of second graders and 6″ square for third and fourth graders. Avoid construction paper; it is easy to rip and hard to crease when folding. Colorful square origami paper packages can be purchased at a local art supply store or from an online origami shop. Another option would be to cut regular twenty-pound letter-size paper into squares evenly measured on all sides.

Note: This activity is recommended for grades two, three, and four. Origami is appropriate for all grade levels. Grades five through eight participate enthusiastically. Kindergarteners and first graders will need extra help with folding each step. Origami models that are easy to fold can be found at http://www.kunikotheater.com/study.cfm.

Preparation

Teachers should be using a larger piece paper for instruction. Cut a letter-sized sheet (8 1/2″ by 11″) of office paper into an 8 1/2″ square and prefold so that it's easy to show step-by-step origami instruction. For a classroom or library setting, 8 1/2″ square will be big enough. If you are demonstrating this activity to more than thirty students, a larger sized sheet of paper is recommended. *Note:* The teacher should practice first before demonstrating to the class.

Procedure

Explain to the students that you are about to show them origami (pronounced or-ih-GAHM-mee). *Ori* means to fold, *gami* means paper; it is Japanese paper folding. While you are folding the paper, you will tell the story.

Story and Origami Instruction (*Note*: story is in the gray text boxes)

#1

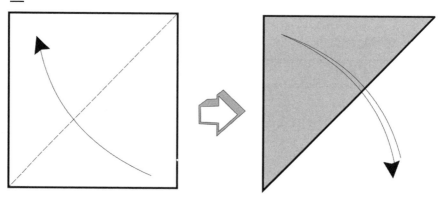

Figure 3.23. (#1) Fold and unfold.

STORY: Once upon a time, there was a kite maker who lived in a **square** village on the North Pole. His name was Kite. Every morning, he liked to walk over to the other side of the village. He would meet his friend Penguin and play for a while, then he would return to his backyard and make kites.

#2

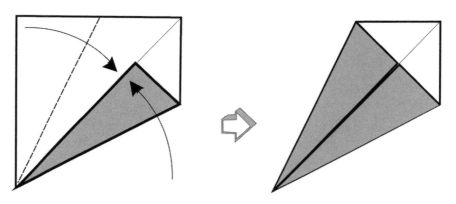

Figure 3.24. (#2) Fold each side diagonally to the center crease. *TIP: At the center, the two sides meet like a double door, not overlapping.*

STORY: Kite liked to fly his **kite** high in the sky.

#3

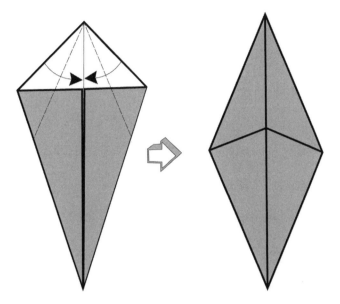

Figure 3.25. (#3) Fold the top edges diagonally to the center crease.

STORY: Kite saw a **diamond** in the sky. He wanted to touch the diamond in the sky. He made a big kite and flew up to the sky on his kite.

#4

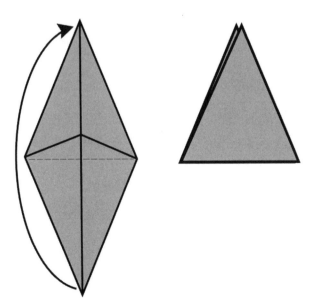

Figure 3.26. (#4) Fold the bottom point up to meet the top point and crease on the fold.

STORY: As he got closer to the diamond, he met a **bird**. (Use the origami model as a beak/mouth by holding it between thumb and the rest of the fingers.)

#5

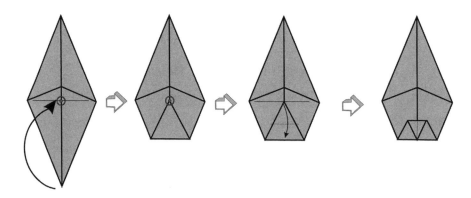

Figure 3.27. (#5) Follow the illustrations step by step. Fold the bottom point up to the center and crease on the fold. And fold the same point to meet the bottom edge. Press the creases hard so that they are all flat.

STORY: The bird said to Kite, "That diamond is mine, but I am willing to share it with you because this world is to be shared. Would you like a piece of the **triangle**? If it is too big, how about **half of the triangle**?" "Thank you very much, my friend," Kite smiled.

#6

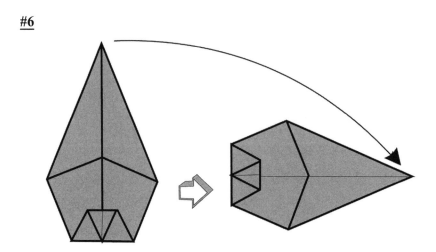

Figure 3.28. (#6) Rotate 90-degree angle.

STORY: Kite continued on his journey across the sky toward the **east**. (Use the origami model as an arrow pointing east.)

#7

Figure 3.29. (#7) *TIP: This part is the whale face. Keep this part on the left.* Fold in half horizontally by pushing the bottom half to the other side. As a result, on the left you will see the whale face.

#7a

Figure 3.30. (#7a) Pull down the small triangle flap. (Move this flap up and down like a jaw and make it look like it is talking.

STORY: When Kite looked down, he saw the Pacific Ocean and a whale. Kite swam with the whale all the way to Japan and learned to say things like, "**Kon-niche-wa**," which is how you say "hello" in Japanese.

#8

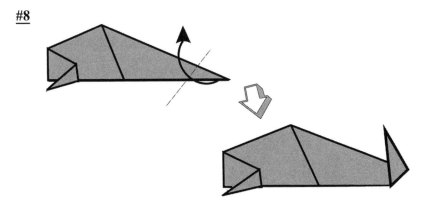

Figure 3.31. (#8) Fold the tail up. You have a completed whale!

STORY: But now Kite misses home, so it is time to say goodbye, "Say-o-na-ra …" The **whale** was kind enough to give Kite a ride to the South Pole.

#9

Figure 3.32. (#9) Just rotate the whale 90 degrees counterclockwise, as if the whale is doing a headstand. Then it looks like a penguin!

STORY: Kite could not wait to see his friend Penguin again so that he could tell him about all of the things he met that day: the big diamond, the friendly bird, the islands of Japan, and the whale. **Penguin** loved listening to Kite's story and asked Kite to tell him more.

Now Kite is your friend, too. When you experience your next origami adventure, tell him your story!

RAINSTICKS AND RHYTHMS: STORYTELLING WITH CRAFT, RHYTHM, AND MOVEMENT
Lynette (Lyn) Ford
Listening, Speaking, Writing, and Visual Literacy

National Standards

NCTE 1, 11; CNAEA—Drama/Theatre 2: Acting by assuming roles and interacting in improvisation; CNAEA—Visual Arts 6: Making connections between visual arts and other disciplines; literacy communities.

Objectives

Encourage linguistic, visual, rhythmic, and physical expression; nurture interpretive skills regarding the sounds and actions of a story shared in the oral tradition and reinforce their connections to descriptive words and phrases that might be used to share the same story in a literary format; provide narrative experiences that encourage pre-writing skills for all types of learners.

Resources and Materials Required

- Songs, poems, and/or stories about rain, rivers, water, etc. Some favorites: "Coyote's Rain Song," a Navajo tale in *Twenty Tellable Tales: Audience Participation Folktales for the Beginning Storyteller* (Margaret Read MacDonald, H. W. Wilson, 1986, 20–23), and, in a one-minute, thirty-second version, in *Three-Minute Tales: Stories From Around the World to Tell or Read When Time is Short* (Margaret Read MacDonald, August House, 2004, 34 and 35); "Stamping Land," in *Sing Through the Day: Eighty Songs for Children* (Marlys Swinger, Plough Publishing House, 1999, 49).
- One or two traditional rainsticks to use as examples during the introductory story; these may be found in local percussion or music stores, school supply catalogues such as Lakeshore Learning Materials (http://www.lakeshorelearning.com, or at Lark in the Morning (http://www.larkinthemorning.com.
- One paper towel tube per child.
- Two pieces of heavy-duty aluminum foil, 6″ wide by 11–11.8″ long, folded together then scrunched and bent into a slithering, snake-like shape.
- Two "daisies" per child—spoked circles cut from heavy construction paper or paper bags; the daisy center is the same size as the end of the paper towel tube; the petals should be at least three inches long.
- 1/3 cup (approximate) birdseed or small dried beans for each rainstick.
- Colorful masking tape.
- Markers or crayons.
- Yarn (optional).
- Bowls and measuring cups for birdseed or dried beans.
- Extra hands (volunteers—parents, classroom assistants, students from older grade levels, etc., particularly when working with students in grades two and three, or special-needs groups; students in grades four and five often "buddy up" in groups of three and help one another) to assist with rainstick construction.

Process for Sharing a Rain or Water Story, Verse, or Song, and Making Rainsticks

1. Set out all materials on tables of floor areas prior to the students' arrival.
2. Tell a story, read or recite a verse, or sing a song, using the traditional rainstick to reinforce the rhythm of the song or verse or to add to the sound effects of water or rain in the story.

3. Share background information about rainsticks: they were used by many cultures as musical instruments in ceremonies to bring rain; they are made in several different places where cacti grow, but mostly by people who live in northern Chile; in Chile and other desert areas, dry, dead cactus branches are gathered, and the cactus thorns are pushed or hammered into the inside of each branch; small gravel, lava pebbles, grains of sand, and seeds have been used to fill the cactus branch and run down the inside of the branch to make soothing rain sounds; nowadays, people still enjoy this rain-like sound. After sharing this information, explain that the group will make rainsticks, suggest and practice their sound effects, and use them to enhance a story, verse, or song.
4. Make rainsticks:
    a. Decorate the outside of the paper towel tube with markers or crayons.
    b. Using colorful masking tape, secure a daisy end-cap to one end of a paper towel tube, covering the daisy petals completely and taping at least one inch beyond the petal tips.
    c. Drop the aluminum-foil snake into the paper towel tube.
    d. Pour about 1/4 to 1/3 cup of dried beans or birdseed into the tube. Covering the open end with one hand, slowly tilt and move the tube, listening to the sound of the birdseed or dried beans; add more birdseed or beans if needed.
    e. Cover the other end of the paper towel tube with a daisy end-cap (see "b" above).
    f. If desired, wrap five or six lengths (about one inch) of colorful yarn around the tube as decoration, and carefully tie a secure (double or triple) knot.
5. Test the rainsticks (this is always a loud and exciting time!) by standing in small groups and gently tilting them, then rocking them back and forth, then holding them in a horizontal position and rhythmically shaking them to various beats: 4/4; 3/4, 6/8, etc.
6. Ask students for sound-effect suggestions: How could we hold and move the rainstick to make the sound of soft, gentle rain? The sound of ocean waves? The sound of rain tapping on a roof? The sound of someone walking on a gravel road? The sound of running feet?
7. Use students' ideas as the group shares first in a retelling of the introductory story, verse, or song, then in another presentation.

This is a popular activity with kinesthetic, tactile, visual, musical, and interpersonal learners, as well as students who have difficulty sitting through story presentations. Such students usually remember the stories more easily, and become excited by anticipating actions; their movements and participation help to reinforce the story's actions or the words of a verse or song.

To encourage positive use of the rainsticks, we create a word list of action verbs and descriptive words or phrases that will be enhanced with the rainstick sounds, and we agree on a cue signal for sound effects, if needed (watching the storytellers' movements is enough for some groups; knowing that the storyteller will point or nod at the audience may help others). We also use two simple rules:

Figure 3.33. Making a rainstick.

1. Rainsticks remain silently on our laps or on the floor unless they are being used to help create sounds in a story, verse, or song.
2. Rainsticks that can't follow the directions for movement in a story rest in a box on a table away from the group until the story, verse, or song is ended. These rainsticks always have another chance to participate.

Extensions

Geography and social studies: Locate South America's desert areas, particularly northern Chile, on a world map; research cacti and other desert plants.

Science: Discuss local materials that could be used as rainstick filler and various types of tubes that might be used to create rainsticks and how these items might be collected for recycling into instruments. Discuss recycling. Create other instruments from "garbage" (I like to explain this as "creating treasures from trash").

Music and art: Music teachers often use the rainsticks as percussive instruments and rhythmic accompaniment for songs in music class or as introductory topics or enrichment items for studies of multicultural music. Whenever possible, art teachers should be a part of this storytelling experience. I request their assistance, their input through accompanying arts activities, and the use of their space whenever this is a reasonable option.

Figure 3.34.   Dropping the aluminum foil snake into the tube.

English language arts: Students create original stories in which they can use the rainsticks to express action or essential descriptive sound effects. The stories are written, illustrated, shared in oral presentation, and discussed for content before the rainsticks are introduced into the telling. After editing, the stories are retold with rainstick sound effects.

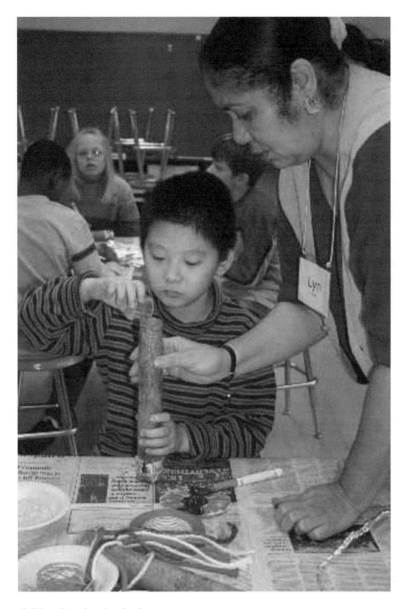

Figure 3.35. Pouring in the beans.

Assessment

Learning is demonstrated in the students' ability to follow directions in creating their rainsticks and in enhancing a narrative presentation, their reflections on sounds and ways to create them, their participation in characterizations and actions in the presentation, and their interpretation of sounds as descriptive words or actions.

Figure 3.36. Play!

LI'L WILLIE AND HIS DIDDLEY BOW: HOW ONE BOY'S IMAGINATION (AND PRACTICE) HELPED HIM TO LEARN TO PLAY AN INSTRUMENT

Charles "Wsir" Johnson

Listening, Speaking, and Writing

National Standards

NCTE: 1, 3, 4, 5, 6, 9, 11, 12.

Objectives

After hearing the story about Li'l Willie and the diddley bow, students will create a diddley bow and experience making musical sounds; students will write an original blues song using a 2-1 lyrical format: the lyrical form should include a pattern of rhythmic talk or narrative monotony line that is repeated once, followed by a single conclusive line.

Blues songs usually deal with the reality of living with troubles and perceived woes relating to love and injustice and the hope of returning to a normal frame of reference. Students can write about an experience they face each day, such as going to school, wanting a new pair of shoes or a bike, or doing homework. Example:

My homework is hard and my mind is about to stray.
I said, my homework is hard and my mind is about to stray,
But my mama said, "You'd better get it done today!"

Writing blues songs in this format is comparable to writing couplets. Assist students in understanding the formula for writing their lyrics:

• State the dilemma or situation.

• Add emphasis to the beginning of the next line ("I said") and repeat the first line.

• The third line should either be a conclusion, retribution, or alternative.

The diddley bow is a one-stringed instrument that is played like a slide guitar. It is usually handcrafted and generally consists of a wooden board slat and a single wire string stretched between two screws. It is played by plucking the string. The pitch is altered with a metal cylinder or small glass bottle that is used to slide over the strings using the other hand.

The diddley bow is significant to traditional blues music in the South. It has been said that the musical bow was introduced to America by African slaves. Today, it is primarily found in the Appalachian Mountains and remains a novelty in the Mississippi Delta.

Musicians who were poor usually made their diddley bows by simply nailing wire and a block of wood to a wall. Often, they didn't even have a block of wood.

Li'l Willie and His Diddley Bow

Story synopsis:

There once was a boy named Li'l Willie. He was born in a rural area of the Mississippi Delta. Li'l Willie's favorite thing to do was to make a bow and arrow and pretend that he was hunting wild game. Now, Li'l Willie would not hurt a fly on a summer's day, but he had an imagination for hunting in the great outdoors. Occasionally, he told his mother that he was going out in the woods to hunt for bears . . . sometimes, lions, big long boa constrictor snakes, and even alligators. When Li'l Willie didn't find the big game animals, he would pluck rhythms on his bow to help pass the time while he walked around looking for animals.

As Li'l Willie rounded the bend toward his house one afternoon, he saw his favorite uncle.

"Uncle Joe!" he yelled. Then he ran toward his uncle as if his pants were on fire.

Uncle Joe gave him a great big hug and threw Li'l Willie high in the air and when he caught him, he gave him another hug. That's what Uncle Joe always did and it always gave Li'l Willie's mother a scare. She was afraid that one day Uncle Joe was going to drop that boy!

Uncle Joe was a traveling musician who went to Chicago and made money playing his guitar in a band. Li'l Willie always wanted to hear the stories of Uncle Joe's travels. This time, Uncle Joe told him about a musical instrument he learned to play from an old gentleman he met a long time ago in a town called New Africa, just outside of Clarksdale in Mississippi. Uncle Joe said the instrument was originally called an African "slap bow." It was mostly played by children, but adults played it sometimes at gatherings.

Li'l Willie couldn't wait to hear each and every tale that Uncle Joe had crafted just for him. "Tell me! Tell me!" Li'l Willie said with excitement.

Uncle Joe said, "I'll do better," with excitement in his voice. "Let's make one!"

Uncle Joe got one of Li'l Willie's mother's old broomsticks and took the wire off. Then he nailed two nails on a board arms' length.

"Ooohhh, Mama's going to be mad if she catches you," Li'l Willie said. Uncle Joe took the wire and tied it to the nails. It was tight, like the string on Willie's bow. Uncle Joe plucked it with his finger and it made a twang sound, like a string on a guitar. Next, Uncle Joe took one of Li'l Willie's mother's old pill bottles and slid it up and down the wire while he plucked the string with his other hand.

Repeating his previous warning, Li'l Willie said, "Ooohhh, Mama's gonna get you ..."

Li'l Willie's eyes grew large as he listened to Uncle Joe play music with that old wire on a slat of wood and a pill bottle. Then Uncle Joe told Li'l Willie that it was his turn. Li'l Willie tried it. It was a little awkward at first, but Uncle Joe just said, "Keep on listening and take your time ..." All day long, Li'l Willie played that old-fashioned guitar.

Li'l Willie's mom had been sitting on the back porch of the house shelling pecan nuts to use in one of her delicious pies. She came around the side of the house to hear the commotion and saw Li'l Willie singing and doing some strange movements with his hand—on the wall of the house!

"Li'l Wil-lie!" his mother said excitedly. She was worried that her boy was having a heat stroke or had gone mad. "What are you doing? Where did you get that wire, and is that my old pill bottle?"

Uncle Joe couldn't help but laugh.

"Why are you laughing?" Li'l Willie's mom asked furiously.

Uncle Joe looked at Li'l Willie and said, "Ooohhh, you are in trou-ble ..."

Li'l Willie explained to his mother that he was playing a musical instrument. All she knew was that she heard a sound that mimicked a screaming cat, and Li'l Willie was using one of her pill bottles.

Uncle Joe realized that he needed to explain what kind of instrument it was that he gave to Li'l Willie. He then told her to have a seat, handed her a present from Chicago, and told her to relax and listen. Uncle Joe started playing and singing a song. Soon Li'l Willie's mom's feet started tapping to the rhythm of the beat that Uncle Joe was playing. She even joined in on the merriment by singing along with Uncle Joe.

Li'l Willie's mother told him that if he learned how to play the diddley bow like Uncle Joe, then he could keep the instrument. If not, it would have to go.

That night while gazing up at the stars, all Li'l Willie could think about was getting up and playing his diddley bow and hoping that one day he would become a famous guitar player. He was no longer using his imagination to hunt animals. Each time he played the diddley bow, he thought about the day that he could finally play like Uncle Joe and maybe even become a musician performing in Chicago.

The next day, Uncle Joe told Li'l Willie, "You don't always have to have everything to make music ... just use your imagination." Well, Li'l Willie practiced the diddley bow all summer long. The only time he stopped playing was when his mother was entertaining company.

Li'l Willie made his own old-fashioned guitar with an old piece of $2'' \times 4''$ wood, two nails, and wire. Now, he could carry his diddley bow and play anywhere.

They say there are still people all over the world playing the diddley bow.

How to Make a Diddley Bow

<u>Difficulty</u>: average
<u>Time required</u>: one hour
<u>*Note*</u>: This activity works well with smaller class sizes
<u>Materials</u>:

- A slat of wood twelve to twenty inches long
- Two nails
- Guitar string
- Small block of wood $1'' \times 1''$
- Metal cylinder or small glass bottle (approximate size equivalent to a medicine bottle)

Instructions: Place two nails (or screws or tacks) at both ends and pound them in halfway. String the wire tightly around each of the nails. Tighten the nail at one end of the slat of wood. Wedge the small block of wood under the string on the other. Push the wood close to the nail to increase the tension. Tighten the nail at this end of the slat of wood.

How to play the diddley bow: Use a metal cylinder or a small glass bottle to slide up and down the string with one hand. Use your other hand to pluck the string near the block of wood.

Tips: Piano wire works the best, or wire from an old mountain bike. But any wire will do as long as it is not too thin. Wire can be purchased from a musical supply store. You can mark the board and reference varying tones.

Option: Try to make a diddley bow using a wooden box to get a more resonant sound.

Assessment

Blues songs should follow the traditional 2-1 format, with rhythmical, rhyming lines that 1 and 2) state and repeat the dilemma or situation, and 3) conclude the piece. Successful blues songs can be presented in a blues concert!

CREATING AN AMAZING TEN-MINUTE GROUP STORY
Annette Harrison
Listening and Writing

National Standards

NCTE: 5, 6, 11, 12.

Objectives

Develop a group dynamic of cooperation, trust, and acceptance; demonstrate that an understanding of the components of a story setting, characters, and plot, combined with freed imagination, can easily create an amazing story.

For twenty-nine years, I have been telling stories in the classroom. I perform many programs for large audiences, but the intimacy and the connection I achieve with students can be done only in a classroom setting. My one-hour workshop, "From Student to Storyteller," includes the Amazing Ten-Minute Classroom Story. I call this process "story creating." Years ago, my friend and fellow storyteller Lynn Rubright taught "storyweaving," which is a lengthy, rich, multifaceted process of creating a group story or embellishing an already existing one. Through the years, I have modified and simplified this method into a ten-minute, high-energy, interactive language experience.

Once the students have taken ownership of their funny, adventurous, collaborative stories, there are numerous ways to extend the lesson. There is creative writing, mask making, playwriting, and dramatic play, to mention just a few. Teachers, librarians, parents, and storytellers can use story creating to teach, to develop class community, or just for fun!

The workshop is only an hour so I quickly create a safe place where the students can relax and express their ideas. I walk around the room smiling and making eye contact with each student and reading their name tags aloud (lots of laughter at my mispronunciations). I am letting them know they are all important and included. Next, I explain what to expect in this storytelling session. They become familiar with the three basic parts of a story (setting, characters, and plot), experience storytelling, and listen to the five simple rules. Then they are ready for story creating. The result is usually an interesting, funny story with a simple but compelling plot. Students are learning to create a story *and*—miracle of miracles—they are listening to each other!

Introduction

I put a word web on the board with the word "storytelling" in the middle and brainstorm with the students about words that pop into their heads, such as book, fairy tale, adventure, scary, funny, dramatic, etc. If they do not mention setting, characters, or plot, I try a different tactic. I ask them about the books they are reading. What keeps them interested? Here is an example of an exchange:

Me: How many of you are reading a good book? What do you like about it?
Student: I like the cat in my book.
Me: Why?
Student: Because he outsmarts the mouse. He's big and furry and funny.
Me: So the cat is the main *character* in the story. You like your book because of the *character*.

I add the word "characters" to the word web. I elicit "setting" with questions such as, "Who likes their book because of *where* it takes place?"

To add "plot" I may ask, "What happens in the story that makes it interesting?" In this way, the students learn the basic story components.

Tell a Story

To give the students a sense of story with its beginning, middle, and end, I tell a story with a simple plot and use gestures and voices to define the characters. After the telling, we go back to the word web to see if my story relates to the words on the board.

Example: Who was the main character? What was the setting? Was it funny or scary or dramatic? Explain.

Create a Ten-Minute Story

First go over the rules:

- Wait until you hear the words, "What happens next?" before you raise your hand with your ideas. The teacher will call on one person at a time.

- Listen carefully to what your classmates say so that you can add to it.
- The teacher will weave all reasonable responses into the ongoing story.
- If you have an idea you are excited about and the teacher does not call on you, write it down and make a new version of the story!
- We can have lots of fun with the story and even have scary parts, but NO VIOLENCE!

Here is the story-creating process:

I usually begin with the setting, so we all have a sense of where the story takes place. Since we have a limited amount of time, I give students a choice of three settings: their classroom, the gym, or outside on the playground. I will call on a child who is engaged but has not yet been called on to choose. I have never heard grumbling from the rest of the students; they remember the rules and go along with it. I also ask, "What season is it?" I choose one of the students to decide.

We know the setting and the season, now we need characters. I call on three students to give me a character that can be a person, animal, or creature. I often include students who appear to be outsiders, and they and their answers seem to be instantly accepted. Popular suggestions are an elephant, a cougar, a snake, a lion, a dinosaur, or a monster. We are creating our own characters and do not want any Disney or book characters in our original story. I begin the story:

Me:	It is fall and the children in Mrs. Rob's class are outside on the playground having a wonderful time. Can you hear the laughter? [The children laugh.] And suddenly ... WHAT HAPPENS NEXT?
Student:	It starts to rain!
Me:	Yes, and the winds are blowing and leaves are falling. Oh no! Look at that! WHAT HAPPENS NEXT?
Student:	Falling from the sky is a baby dinosaur!
Me:	I see it! A baby dinosaur falls out of the sky—and onto the playground.
Me:	[*I turn to the teacher*] Now we are going to have some dialogue where the characters speak to each other. A baby dinosaur has fallen out of the sky—what will you do?
Teacher:	[*Some teachers look stunned for a minute, but they all rally.*] I'll call the principal!
Me:	Good. Who would like to be the principal? [*I always pick the most unlikely child.*]
Pick up the phone. [*Both teacher and student are miming holding a phone to their ear.*]	
Teacher:	There's a dinosaur on the playground, he fell out of the sky, what should I do?
Student/Principal:	Run! [*A typical child's response.*]

Me: [*I need to remind the student that he is the principal, the adult person in charge.*] What would the principal say?

Student/Principal: Call the zoo!

The dialogue between the zookeeper and the teacher usually continues for a while, at least until a decision is made. The story continues with my guidance and many more times asking, "What happens next?" I like to include a television reporter on the scene to add more dialogue and give another student a chance to act out a part.

I keep my eye on the clock and when I think we need to find a conclusion, I ask, "The story is almost over. Who wants to tell us how it ends?" A student always comes up with a clever ending. I often add the following: "and the students in the class write up the story, take it home, read it to their parents, *and* no one believes them!"

The class is so happy and proud at the exciting story they created together that they often ask to do it again. I tell them what an amazing story they created. They can write up the story in their journals and illustrate it and they can tell it to their families.

Many teachers have told me that they now use story creating as part of their curriculum. And so can you!

Assessment

Observe students to assess their ability to follow directions; their grasp of story elements is demonstrated through their participation and ability to respond appropriately. The story created in the group process provides evidence of the class's grasp of the story creation process.

FINDING AND USING PATTERNS IN STORY
Sherry Norfolk
Listening, Speaking, Writing, and Information Literacy

National Standards

NCTE: 4, 5, 6, 11, 12; AASL 2: Learners use skills, resources, and tools to draw conclusions, make informal decisions, apply knowledge to new situations, and create new knowledge; AASL 4: Learners use skills, resources, and tools to pursue personal and aesthetic growth.

Objectives

Students will create, write, revise, publish, and orally present an original story based on the pattern of a folktale.

The brain thrives on making and detecting patterns. The more one reads about brain research, the more evident it becomes that the key to our intelligence is the recognition of patterns and relationships in all that we experience. Stories provide opportunities to identify and build on patterns of language, behavior, and action—and story patterns provide wonderful scaffolds for creating new stories that are fun for primary students to write.

I start this lesson by explaining that all over the world, people tell stories that pretend to explain how the sun got to be in the sky. In stories from Australia, Central America, Africa, Siberia, and North America, these stories follow a very similar pattern. Then I tell my *very* simplified version of the Cherokee story "Grandmother Spider Brings the Light," (found in *More Tellable Tales*), followed by *How Snowshoe Hare Rescued the Sun: A Tale from the Arctic.*

"Grandmother Spider Brings the Light"

Sherry Norfolk

In the beginning, there was darkness, darkness, darkness. The animals couldn't see where they were going, and they were always bumping into each other!

"Ouch! Stop that! Get off my tail!"

So they called a great council of all of the animals, and tried to decide what to do. "We need light!" said the Bear. "We can't see a thing in this darkness."

"That's right," the other animals said. "We need light. But where do we get it?"

"Well, when there is a thunderstorm, I sometimes see a crack in the sky, and light shines through. I figure if we send someone to the crack in the sky, he can bring back some light, and then we can see!" answered Bear.

"Great idea!" they all said. "Who will go? Who will go get light?"

"I'll go," said Buzzard. "I will go get light." Buzzard was big and tough, with long, strong wings, so the others agreed. Buzzard spread his long, strong wings and started off toward the crack in the sky. When he got there, he broke off some of the light.

"Hmmm. Now how am I going to carry this light back to the other animals?" thought Buzzard.

"Oh! I know! I have all of these thick, beautiful soft feathers on my head. I will make a nest of the feathers to carry back the light!" And he put the light on his head. Now Buzzard didn't know about light—he didn't know that it was made of fire. He didn't know that it would burn through the feathers on his head. So he started flying back, flapping his long, strong wings. Suddenly, the light began to burn through the feathers.

"OOOOUCH!" yelled Buzzard. He rubbed his head. The light had burned all of the feathers off of his head! He was bald!

And the light had burned out. There was darkness, darkness, darkness.

"Who will go? Who will go get light?"

"I will go," said Possum. "I will go get light." Possum started out, heading for the crack in the sky. She broke off a piece of the light.

"Now, what will I do with this light? I know! I'll be smarter than Buzzard. I won't put it on my head. I'll put it in my nice, bushy tail!" So Possum put the light in her tail, and she started back. Suddenly, the light burned through the hair on her tail.

"OOOOOOOWWW!" yelled Possum. She looked at her tail. The light had burned all of the hair clean off—her tail was naked!

And the light had burned out. There was darkness, darkness, darkness.

"Who will go? Who will go get light?"

"I will go," said a tiny voice.

"Who's that? It's too dark to see. Who's talking?"

"It's me, Grandmother Spider. I will go get light." "You're too small. And you're too old. You'll get lost and forget your way back. You can't go!"

"Well, I may be little and I may be old, but I think you oughta let me try."

"Let her try!" the animals said.

So Grandmother Spider started off toward the crack in the sky. She knew that she might forget her way back, so she spun a web all the way from where the animals were waiting, all the way across the sky to the light. When she got the light, she remembered what had happened to Possum and to Buzzard, so she scooped up some cool, wet mud and she placed the light into the mud so that she wouldn't burn herself.

Then, she started back, following the web back to where the animals waited. On the way, the light baked the mud until it was dry and hard. It was the first bowl in the world!

When Grandmother Spider got back to the animals, she flung the ball of light into the sky. Now, ever since that time, Buzzard has had a bald head. Possum has had a naked tail. Spider's web has been shaped like the rays of the sun.

And there has been LIGHT!

After hearing the two stories, the kids discuss the pattern: in each story, the sun is hidden somewhere, and only one animal knows where it is. What does that animal do? Well, s/he never goes to get it, that's for sure! But s/he does call the animals together, tell them where it is, and ask for volunteers. How many go? Three—but only one (the smallest) succeeds. That's the pattern in a nutshell—so now we can create a new story together!

To create a new story, we need to answer these questions:

1. Where is the light in the beginning of the story? (Explain that the answers can be creative—it can be in a dragon's belly, or in the bottom of the ocean, or inside a pyramid . . . the possibilities are endless.)
2. How did it get there? (For example, the dragon was hungry, so it swallowed it; the sun got tired of being in the sky so it let go and dropped into the water; a mummy wanted more light inside the pyramid, so he stole it.)
3. Who knows where it is? (I insist on animal characters for the rest of the story in order to avoid SpongeBob, Spider-Man, and the names of classmates.)
4. Who goes first to get the light? Why does this animal fail?
5. Who goes second? Why does this animal fail?
6. Who succeeds? How?

Once the questions are answered, I ask, "Do we have a story?" Their answer is almost always, "YES!" Nope, it's not a story—but it has most of the elements of story. It has a setting and characters, a problem, and a solution to the problem. But it's not a story. What's missing?

A title? We give it a title—still not a story. A beginning? Nope, we know the beginning—and the middle, and the end, but it's not a story. After some thought, someone will usually pipe up, "Details!"

Yep, we need details! Where do you get those? From your brain—from your imagination! And that's the most important part of a story! Whether you're reading a story, listening to it, or writing it, you have to *imagine* the way things look and the way they move and the way they sound. So I use *my* imagination to turn the outline we've created into a story, and tell it immediately, putting in as many details as I can think of, and adding voices, sound effects, and action to bring it to life.

After the modeling, it's the students' turn. I hand out blank forms printed with the story pattern and ask the kids to come up with all-new answers to the questions. As each child finishes, s/he stands, finds another standing child, and they pair up to tell their stories to each other. Many will be using character voices and sound effects and lots of body language—all of which will need to be translated into words on the page. This telling becomes the first draft of the story. When they are finished telling, they immediately begin to write their stories. I remind them that each of the animals needs to *talk* in the story so that we can hear their voices—important for when they begin to share the stories.

I have used this lesson plan with hundreds of second graders, and the stories are simply fantastic! This pattern makes it easy to write a story with a beginning, a middle, and an end. It requires the writer to think through and develop a logical, cause-and-effect sequence, and to practice their problem-solving skills in order to help the final character succeed. It encourages

Figure 3.37. Telling before writing—the kinesthetic approach.

Figure 3.38. The sun gets kicked into the sky!

Figure 3.39. Kindergartners dramatize: Bear called a meeting.

interesting dialogue and nearly always turns out funny—a real plus to second graders!

The story pattern can be successful from kindergarten through fifth grade. With kindergartners and first graders, I follow the same procedure up to the point when they begin developing individual outlines. Instead, I put them into groups of four or five, ask them to answer the questions together, and then dramatize the story together as a group. Someone needs to narrate the story (often the child who plays the One Who Knows).

Children take the parts of the other animals—shy children often take the part of the sun (no speaking required!). In third, fourth, and fifth grade, the same pattern can be used, emphasizing the how-and-why aspects of the Cherokee story.

Assessment

Published stories can be assessed for use of pattern, inclusion of descriptive verbs and adjectives, appropriate punctuation, spelling, capitalization, etc. Oral presentations should include facial, vocal, and kinesthetic expression—and enjoyment!

Resources

- Bernhard, Emery, and Durga Bernhard. *How Snowshoe Hare Rescued the Sun: A Tale from the Arctic*. New York: Holiday House, 1993.
- Holt, David, and Bill Mooney. *More Tellable Tales*. Little Rock, AR: August House, 2001.

GOLDILOCKS AND THE THREE BEARS, OR ...
Mary Kay Will
Listening, Speaking, and Writing

National Standards

NCTE: 1, 2, 3, 4, 5, 6, 7, 12; AASL 2: Learners use skills, resources, and tools to draw conclusions, make informal decisions, apply knowledge to new situations, and create new knowledge; AASL 4: Learners use skills, resources, and tools to pursue personal and aesthetic growth.

Objectives

Students will recognize characters, story settings, plot, and sequences of familiar folktales; compare and contrast traditional tales with modern-day versions; recognize that stories can change through different versions and retain common elements; write, rewrite, and perform their own versions of a folktale.

Resources

- Ernst, Lisa Campbell. *Goldilocks Returns*. New York: Simon & Schuster Books for Young Readers, 2000.
- Galdone, Paul. *The Three Bears*. New York: Clarion, 1972.
- Lester, Helen. *Tackylocks and the Three Bears*. New York: Houghton Mifflin Books for Children, 2002.
- Marshall, James. *Goldilocks and the Three Bears*. New York: Dial Books for Young Readers, 1988.
- Meyers, Cindy. *Rolling Along with Goldilocks and the Three Bears*. Bethesda, MD: Woodbine House, 1999.
- Rosales, Melodye. *Leola and the Honeybears: An African-American Retelling of Goldilocks and the Three Bears*. New York: Scholastic, 1999.
- Stevens, Janet. *Goldilocks and the Three Bears*. New York: Holiday, 1986.

There are other variants out there. A simple Internet search of "three bear variants" will pull up lots of ideas for other titles to use. Also to be found are recordings and films to further augment the selections.

As a teacher-librarian in a small elementary school, I always start my year out (after orientation) by sharing some traditional folktales such as the "Three Little Pigs," "Jack and the Beanstalk," and "Little Red Hen" in the earlier grades. It is still amazing to me how many children do not know these timeless stories. I share some simple versions of the tales, and we talk about stories, where they come from, and how they can change over time.

In one of the earliest versions of "Goldilocks and the Three Bears," Goldilocks was represented by an old woman. Throughout time, the character changed to a young girl, and eventually had "golden" hair. Information about the history of this story can be found at http://surlalunefairytales.com.

More versions continue to be created to this day. The purpose of this unit is to introduce folktale variants and for the children to be able to recognize the bare bones of a story.

The time line for this can be fairly loose. As the teacher-librarian in a school, I may see the students only once a week, so I introduce a new story each week. This unit also provides an excellent collaboration opportunity between the teacher-librarian and the classroom teacher, and can take place over two to three weeks.

The unit begins with a telling of "Goldilocks and the Three Bears, Ms. Will's style." I tell a jazzy, beefed-up version with changes in dialogue. It can be as creative as you want since it is really a bare-bones kind of story. Mine tends to change from year to year and what I can get away with depends on the students I have.

Usually when I am done, the students are asking to see the pictures— and of course, I tell them that the pictures are in their heads. This leads into a discussion of storytelling and where stories come from.

I ask them if they have heard the story of Goldilocks. A few will realize that it is the same story, just different. Others don't seem to understand that concept. This is where we get into how stories change over time and from different perspectives. I will then let them know that we are going to be studying "Goldilocks and the Three Bears" from different perspectives. The word "variant" is introduced.

The next step is to introduce them to the most basic original version of the story (Paul Galdone's version is a fine example). I tell the story using the book. This is a good time to do some comparing and contrasting of the version told the previous week; sequencing activities will also come into play.

Each week or lesson, you will introduce a new version of the story and do the same comparing, contrasting, and sequencing activities. The students will become very used to refrains and be able to join in. Four or five versions are all that will be needed—you don't want them to get burned out!

You can also create a group story. Ask the class to list the elements needed and write them on the board. Have them as a group create the outline or sequence of the story. Then take each element and ask for alternatives: that is, the bears can be lizards, the house a cave, the porridge could be Cheerios— anything goes. You can then tell the story using these elements or ask the students to write one of their own using them. In this way, you are showing how they are "changing" the story, or helping a story evolve into a new version.

Now comes homework! Give the students a copy of the elements that they produced. The assignment is for the students to come up with their own original version. They can retain the original elements or deviate from them. Several things can happen at this point, depending on the students: they might take a week to write their stories, allowing you to go over them individually and make suggestions or adjustments; they can pair up to share their stories with partners and exchange ideas and/or tips in the telling of the story; or they can rewrite and finalize their versions.

A storytelling festival is a must! This can be done in the classroom, for the parents, and for other classes. Perhaps you'll want to make smaller groups of tellers so that the class they are visiting will hear three or so versions instead of twenty. Have one of your tellers be prepared to introduce the activity. You can have them tell the original version or just ask the audience if they know the story of "The Three Bears" and that they are in for a surprise! Be sure that the student is supplied with the bare-bones version of the story to introduce the new series.

As a final product, you might want to create a classroom book complete with illustrations. You can purchase blank books for students to write in at http://www.teacherparadise.com; another source that actually binds books but is a bit more complicated is http://www.studenttreasures.com. These can be a bit pricey, so if you have access to a binding machine, that's the way to go.

Assessment

Students will participate in class discussions regarding story elements, characters, settings, plot, and sequence. From these discussions they will create their own story using the above information. These stories will follow the logical sequence and have a beginning, a middle, and an end.

GINGERBREAD FUN
Jeri Burns and Barry Marshall (The Storycrafters)
Listening, Speaking, Writing, and Information Literacy

National Standards

NCTE: 1, 3, 4, 5, 6, 9; NCSS—Geography 1: Students should understand how to use mental maps to organize information about people, places, and environments in a spatial context; NCSS—Geography 2: Students should understand the physical and human characteristics of places; AASL 2: Learners use skills, resources, and tools to draw conclusions, make informal decisions, apply knowledge to new situations, and create new knowledge; AASL 4: Learners use skills, resources, and tools to pursue personal and aesthetic growth.

Objectives

Students will compare different stories, discuss tale components with classmates, develop oral and written retellings of the story, and, with extension activities, will appreciate culture through variants of the tale. In addition, they will adapt the story to their own community.

Resources

- Baumgartner, Barbara. *The Gingerbread Man*. New York: DK Ink, 1998.
- Blair, Eric. *The Gingerbread Man*. Minneapolis: Picture Window Books, 2005.
- Kimmel, Eric A. *The Gingerbread Man*. New York: Holiday House, 1993.
- Mackinnon, Mairi. *The Gingerbread Man*. London: Usborne Pub., 2006.
- Rowe, John A. *The Gingerbread Man: An Old English Folktale*. New York: North-South Books, 1996.

"This was a great activity to get my students excited about the writing process."
—Deborah Osvald, second-grade teacher

One of our favorite stories to tell is "The Gingerbread Man." It is a classic tale about a runaway cookie chased by many characters before being devoured by a fox. Our version is told as if we baked the cookie and chased him around the neighborhood. Children love to hear the tale in this new light and delight in the juxtaposition of familiar images, unexpected characters, and plot twists.

This lesson helps your class create an original version of the tale. In addition to learning about setting, character, and plot, students learn about first- and third-person narrative styles. This unit can be accomplished in two to six days.

Step One

Select two versions of the story from the resource list. If none are available at your school, select others that begin with a farmyard setting and end with a fox devouring the cookie.

Read the first book. Then introduce the concept of setting (time and place of the story). Ask students to identify the setting of the story. Include the places where the cookie is baked and has its adventure. Write this information on one part of the board.

Introduce the concept of character (people and animals who take part in the story's action). Identify the characters in the tale. Include those who bake the cookie and those whom the cookie meets along the way. Write this information on another part of the board.

This process allows you to illustrate characters and setting in a story.

Step Two

Read the second version of the tale to your students. In our experience, students become highly engaged at this point. With every turn of the page, they wonder what will be the same as the first story and what will be different.

Ask students to identify setting and characters; note their answers on the board. Use a Venn diagram to compare and contrast the setting and characters of both tales. This process allows for an authentic assessment of the students' grasp of the text and their ability to compare one text to another.

Whenever we present story variants to students, we point out that although there are differences between tales, the plot remains the same in both versions. We explain plot as the events that happen in a story.

Ask your students to help you identify the plot elements that remain the same in both versions that you read. (Teacher's note: Someone bakes a cookie that runs away. It meets others that want to eat it, and eventually approaches a body of water. Since it cannot cross the water, the cookie gets help from a fox).

This process introduces the concept of plot and allows you to make an authentic assessment of student understanding of plot in a story.

Step Three

Now you are ready to begin the writing of your class version of the tale. We start by telling the students that authors often write about things that they know well. It helps them imagine their tales and gives them a chance to explore familiar things in new ways.

Because your students know the school setting and the characters that people it, they will write their tale as if it started in their classroom, with you and your students baking the adventuresome cookie.

Certain characters and places will remain as they are in most versions of the tale: a Gingerbread Man will run away; the Fox will be the evil culprit who eats him; the final obstacle will be a body of water; the cookie will recite, "Run, run as fast as you can, you can't catch me, I'm the Gingerbread Man."

After trying this lesson in her classroom, second-grade teacher Beth DePolo said that her students were more invested in writing this story than others because they knew the characters. Furthermore, all of her students were fully engaged by the storytelling and writing process, including those who typically don't pay attention in class.

With older students, we discussed the concept of point of view in stories. The stories that were read to the students demonstrate a third-person narrative style or point of view: the narrator describes the story as it happened to others. The class tale, told as if it happened to me or us, is in first-person narrative style. This relatively simple shift of perspective puts a new, interesting spin on an old, familiar tale.

Step Four—Brainstorming Session(s)

Students contribute ideas for a class story of "The Gingerbread Man." Allow all students to have a say. Accept all ideas, even if they are repetitive of others.

We have seen that the process of how hearing other ideas sparks the imaginations of students who might not have contributed otherwise. It also allows for the inclusion of students who act best with the modeling of their peers. Lastly, open acceptance of all ideas encourages student creativity and willingness to contribute. One teacher told us that she liked how the brainstorming process allowed all students to feel that their ideas were valued.

Brainstorming Task One

Tell the class the new story's setup: your teacher has brought a toaster oven into the classroom so the class can bake cookies for an event. One particularly large cookie runs away and becomes the Gingerbread Man. The task is to generate a list of possible reasons for the class to bake cookies; keep that list on the blackboard.

Brainstorming Task Two

Students generate a list of people and animals from the school and neighborhood that might follow the Gingerbread Man. Some ideas include the nurse, the cafeteria employees, a class rabbit, the principal, the bus driver, the storekeeper down the road, etc. This provides an authentic assessment of their grasp of character.

Brainstorming Task Three

Students make a list of places that the Gingerbread Man runs. Some ideas include the cafeteria, the gym, the playground, the buses, the road, the town, and a nearby ice cream stand. This enables an authentic assessment of the grasp of setting.

Brainstorming Task Four

Students brainstorm ideas for the obstacle that forces the Gingerbread Man to accept assistance from the Fox. Are there creeks or ponds in the vicinity of your school? If not, think of alternatives, such as a neighbor with a pool in the yard or a large rain puddle in a field. It is also possible to invent a body of water. As authors, take license to imagine a stream or a pond in some location along the cookie's journey.

Alternatively, substitute another traditional plot device. Sometimes it is not water that stops the Gingerbread Man, but the Fox himself. He feigns deafness, and asks the Gingerbread Man to come closer and closer. When the cookie is near enough . . . chomp!

Step Five—Making Choices

Select one reason for baking cookies in the classroom. Pick five or six characters, other than the Fox, whom the Gingerbread Man meets along the way. Unfortunately, we cannot recommend a surefire uniform selection procedure that works with every group. We vary our approach with each class and change our approach midstream if it seems warranted. Suggested procedures include voting on each character, one at a time; helping students recall the characters who earned the most enthusiasm from the class when first suggested, and select those; or guiding students to choose characters that would make the tale most interesting. Honor your instincts here!

The choice of characters will logically indicate where the Gingerbread Man runs. Go through the list of places to make sure you have chosen five or six as you did for the characters.

Lastly, select the body of water that stops the Gingerbread Man.

Step Six—Making More Choices

Decide who the Gingerbread Man meets first. This is mostly a logical exercise; a local storekeeper wouldn't be first to join the chase. Rather, it would be someone physically near your classroom. Encourage students to make logical, sequential choices. One teacher reported that her class was very excited at this point, watching the tale unfold.

Ask students to describe how the character appears in the location. We provide an example first, to model the process: the principal in the hallway with her briefcase; the old lady outside the store with a dog on a leash. Student creativity can be unleashed here; encourage students to invent unexpected images or pictures. For instance: the nurse with a stethoscope on the swings; the custodian dancing with his broom on the bus, etc.

Sometimes it is best to have teams describe a character. We further break down the steps in this case. Suppose one student suggests the custodian. Ask next for suggestions from the class about what the custodian was doing or what he held in his hand. This gives students practice and appreciation of descriptive language.

Step Seven—Putting It All Together

List, in order, all selected class-created sequences and character descriptions. Tell the tale to the students following the blackboard notes as if you are reading a book; in so doing, point to class-created sequences as you come to them.

Retell the tale again the next day. With a fresh look, the class may see editorial changes that would improve the story flow. This exposes students to the step of revision in the writing process.

Do a group retelling of the story, complete with everyone joining in on chants. This allows an authentic assessment of the students' ability to listen and use spoken language. It also puts their new take on an old oral story back into the oral tradition.

Have kindergartners illustrate the sequence of the new story. Older students can write it down in their own words.

One teacher wrote to tell us her plan to make a PowerPoint presentation of their tale, complete with photos of the new characters. Who knows what your class will be inspired to do!

Extension Activity

Read at least two of the stories listed below. Then use Venn diagrams to compare characters, settings, and plot elements. Identify similarities and differences and discuss what they might suggest about similarities and differences among cultures or regions represented.

Additional Resources

- Amoss, Berthe. *The Cajun Gingerbread Boy.* New Orleans: MTC Press, 1994.
- Browne, Marcia. *The Bun: A Tale from Russia.* New York: Harcourt Brace, 1972.
- Cauley, Lorinda Bryan. *The Pancake Boy: An Old Norwegian Folktale.* New York: G. P. Putnam's Sons, 1988.
- Compestine, Ying Chang. *The Runaway Rice Cake.* New York: Simon & Schuster Books for Young Readers, 2000.
- Egielski, Richard. *The Gingerbread Boy.* New York: HarperCollins, 2000.
- Ginsburg, Mirra. *Clay Boy.* New York: Greenwillow Books, 1997.
- Squires, Janet. *The Gingerbread Cowboy.* New York: HarperCollins, 2006.

DOGGONE GOOD STORIES OF AESOP
Darlene Neumann
Listening, Speaking, Reading, and Writing

National Standards

NCTE: 4, 6, 12.

Objectives

Students will listen to fables being read aloud, reread the fables, and create their own fable, telling it first and then writing it.

Second grade planned to perform the musical *Bebop with Aesop* with both English and dual language Spanish-English classes. I appreciate any efforts by classroom teachers to integrate dual language classes with our monolingual classes. As the media specialist, I taught half the students while the other half practiced.

Bebop with Aesop includes five fables: "Grasshopper and the Ant," "Milkmaid and her Pail," "Tortoise and the Hare," "Shepherd Boy and the Wolf," and "The Frogs and the Well." I would be introducing Aesop, teaching the parts of a fable, and discussing the moral. Teachers would introduce the five fables integrated into the musical. In the library, we would culminate by having students write their own fables. I chose dog, wolf, and sheep stories to share.

Week One

I told the story of Aesop, the slave who became a storyteller.

Students listened to Heather Forest's song of "The Dog and His Bone" from *The Animals Could Talk*. Heather's words, copied with her permission, were handed out so that the students could read in pairs. Next, students read the traditional translation from Aesop Online and compared the two versions of the tales.

Using creative drama, we played with the story. Kids chose partners. While one dog stood before the water, the partner dog became the reflection. Some children stood face to face, mirroring each other, while others had one partner sitting and the other lying down. Only one set of partners had the reflection actually lie down with her feet at the standing dog's feet. Interestingly enough, the students who reflected correctly were both students in special education. Most children said they'd never really looked at their reflection in still water. They had great fun growling and snapping at their reflections; their reflections happily growled back. Both partners were sad when the bone was gone, gone, gone. The session ended by singing "The Dog and His Bone."

Our second session involved another dog story, "The Wolf and the Dog." Children listened to Heather's version, reading the lyrical story together in pairs.

I asked who agreed with the dog's point of view, that it was perfectly fine to wear a collar in exchange for food and shelter. Who agreed with the wolf, that being free is better? We formed two lines, one that would rather live as dogs and one that would prefer to live as wolves. Wolves and dogs tried to change each other's minds.

One boy wolf said, "I love being a wolf. I eat whatever I want, whenever I want," to which a girl dog replied, "Well, how's that working for you? You're awfully skinny! Ready to change your mind and join me for hors d'oeuvres?"

Only one dog defected to the wolves' side, while all the wolves remained free. Sometimes two friends have to go different ways and believe different things.

We made Venn diagrams comparing the two dog-and-wolf stories. Children could choose to draw pictures or write words in Spanish or in English.

Our next task involved examining the structure of fables. What did these two dog fables have in common with other fables they had heard? We discovered that fables are short, teach a lesson, and have a moral. They usually have animals that act like people. Since second graders love big words, "personification" was introduced.

Week Two

For the second week, I chose three fables with wolves and sheep, rewriting the fables for storytelling and for reading by the children: "Shepherd Boy and the Wolf," "Wolf and the Lamb," and "Wolf in Sheep's Clothing." I chose to repeat "Shepherd Boy and the Wolf" to make second-language children feel more comfortable when presented with a packet of three fables.

Guided imagery helped the students understand a shepherd's life: lonely, with no CDs, cell phones, or refrigerators to keep water bottles cold—just sheep, sheep, sheep. In our noisy world, we can hardly imagine such silence.

Since their musical included "The Shepherd and the Wolf," I thought the children would enjoy another look at the fable through picture books. *The Boy Who Cried Wolf*, retold by B. G. Hennessy, brings to life what shepherds of old would do while watching sheep.

Today, we use literary allusions without even realizing we've done so. A commonly used phrase is "a wolf in sheep's clothing." To show students that society really does still recall Aesop's fables and morals, I told the story of "Wolf in Sheep's Clothing." After discussion, I read Helen Lester's book *Sheep in Wolf's Clothing*. We compared Lester's retelling with the traditional translation; children enjoyed Lester's humor. Coincidentally, Lester was scheduled for an author visit, which added another level of excitement to the reading.

Children read my retellings of wolf and sheep stories with partners or in small groups. Dramatic reading could be heard in each nook and cranny of the library. The favorite line seemed to be "Yum, Yum! Sheep!" Those reading in a group used "popcorn" reading: one child read aloud, pausing to say "popcorn" and a group member's name. That child then read. Students stay focused well in a group if they don't know exactly when their turn is coming.

Week Three

By this time, the children had heard and read many fables. Visiting a Web site to read fables written by third graders helped the second graders realize they too could write fables. We reviewed fable elements that they had previously discovered, and they were eager to begin writing. When Donald Davis visited our school, he told the students that a good story needs to involve people or animals acting like people, places, plot, and a problem. To create their fables, the children worked with a simple story web with five boxes, the additional one being for the moral. Writing a fable is easiest if a moral is chosen first, so the children selected from a list or made up their own moral. After finishing their webs, they told their stories to a partner and then to small groups.

In the next session, the students made a story map with pictures showing the beginning, the middle, and the end of their stories. After telling their stories with their maps, they wrote their stories. An extremely popular notebook of their original fables is in the library for everyone to read. Children brought fables alive with creative adaptations and up-to-date ideas.

Assessment

The students' written fables were expected to include the parts of a fable as discussed in class: people (or animals acting as people), place, problem, plot, and moral.

The students' participation was assessed through observation of contributions in creative drama. The media specialist listened to each child read for fluency and expression.

Adapting the Unit

This unit was used with second graders but can be easily adapted for younger or older students. Kindergartners may need help filling in their fable chart or writing their stories. Since students wouldn't necessarily be performing the *Bebop with Aesop* musical, those five well-known tales could be used with any age group. Parts of the musical could be done as readers' theater. Older students would write more complex fables with a more intricate story web, but they would still enjoy the creative drama.

And the moral of the unit is . . . Aesop's fables are still just as relevant today as they were hundreds of years ago.

Bibliography

- Brisas Elementary School. *Original Fables Inspired by Aesop*, http://www.kyrene.-k12.az.us/schools/brisas/sunda/fable/fable.htm#amy. 2007.
- Forest, Heather. *The Animals Could Talk*. Little Rock, AR: August House Audio, 1994.
- Gallina, Michael. *Bebop with Aesop*. Indianapolis: Shawnee Press, 2005.
- Hennessy, B. G. *The Boy Who Cried Wolf*. New York: Simon & Schuster, 2006.

- Lester, Helen. *A Sheep in Wolf's Clothing*. Boston: Houghton Mifflin, 2007.
- Long, John R. *Aesop's Fables Online*, http://www.aesopfables.com/.

DORA AND THE DIAMONDS
Flora Joy
Listening, Writing, and Visual Literacy

National Standards

NCTE: 4, 5.

Objectives

Students will explore oral, written, and psychomotor activities in response to a shared story. More specific objectives of this lesson are further explained in later sections labeled Skill Notes.

At a recent seminar about inspirational living, the speaker asked each of us to respond to his question, "Why were we put on this Earth?" Before a second had passed, he looked at me to give an answer aloud. I heard myself saying, "To help students connect storytelling with the academics." He was disappointed. He had wanted a much more "religious" answer. His subsequent questions to me were intended to lead me to an entirely different response, but I disappointed him again by saying, "That's my answer, and I'm sticking to it." Although my answer might strike you as being odd, it reflected at least *one* of my life's goals. "Dora and the Diamonds" has become one of my favorite stories to use with kids. They seem to love it, and they will do ALL of the activities without blinking. Then they beg for additional activities and for stories presented in the same manner. What more can we ask?

Practically all stories can be used to help boost a student's desire to develop and fine-tune academic skills. "Dora and the Diamonds" is just one example. This printed version was inspired by a tale I heard as a child, and my adaptation has gradually evolved after using it as a story lesson for several decades. You can find other versions (with a very different sequence of events leading to the climax), and all will work for story lessons. When I initially told the more standard folktale version, I realized that by 1) giving the old woman a name, and 2) having the rising action more closely resembling logical reasoning, the story discussions could cover more of the academic skills.

Story Mind-Set

Prior to telling the story, I informally ask listeners the following questions and either allow time for a few responses to each question or I ask the students to ponder their answers silently. (Note: Throughout this section, an approximation of the actual words I use are printed in italics. Feel free to use this same dialog or modify it for your own educational purposes.)

What is the most unusual birthday present anyone has ever given you?

Have you ever received a birthday present that you either couldn't use or didn't want? Maybe the giver just didn't know what kind of present someone your age might like. Sometimes an older person might select a gift for others without knowing their desires. After all, what if you were going to give a present to someone who was 100 years old? What gift might you select?

This story is about a present given to someone for her 100th birthday.

Notes for the Reader/Teller

Before telling this story to any group, I practice an "elderly" voice for Dora until it sounds both natural for me and respectful to older people. This was easy for me because of a close family member who lived to be 109 years old! Her voice was lovely, but it definitely had a "quiver" that was suggestive of one who had lived many years. I often notice that students choose to mimic this same voice during some of their post-story activities. You may use any character voices, gestures, or delivery styles that fit *you* as a reader/teller. These might change as you continue to use the story. For example, after about thirty tellings, I added a gentle "spit" on the ground (in Dora's character) to "finalize" the story at the end. That works for me. It may or may not suit the telling style of others.

Skill Notes

During the telling of this story, students may engage in the pleasure of listening to the story itself—thus developing skills in the affective dimension of learning. They will also be improving listening comprehension skills.

"Dora and the Diamonds"

© 2008 by Flora Joy

In the early days of long ago, a very old woman named Dora lived peacefully by herself in a tiny cottage. She was quite happy with her simple life, and she had no desire for material possessions. Dora arose each morning, puttered through her daily chores, and then reflected on the day's events for a few minutes each night in her rickety old rocker before she went to bed.

One night as Dora sat and rocked, she realized that on the following day she would be 100 years old! "Salivating salamanders!" she exclaimed aloud with a broad smile on her face. "I'll declare! I'll declare!"

So rare was it in those times for anyone to reach the age of 100 that the king decided to give Dora a very special gift. He filled a pouch with his brightest diamonds and set off to her house. He left early in the morning because at that time the night skies were completely starless, and nothing in nature brightened the roads for an evening journey. Every night was always pitch black.

Even though Dora neither needed nor wanted any diamonds, her kind and gracious spirit allowed her to accept the king's gift. When he left, Dora spread out the diamonds and stared at her new treasure. Oh, how they shone!

"Scampering scorpions!" Dora shouted. "I'll declare! I'll declare!"

She had no idea what to do with such a gift, and there was practically no place in her tiny house to store them. So she decided to stuff the diamonds into her mattress. But that night, just after she closed her eyes, an eerie glow crept from her mattress. So bright was the glow that she couldn't sleep. Nary a wink!

"Squirming skeletons," Dora muttered when she got up the next morning. "I'll declare! I'll declare!" The lack of sleep had taken its toll, and she knew that something else had to be done with those diamonds. So she decided to put them in an area where a bright light might be expected: *in the fireplace.* One by one she carefully tucked them into the ashes that still remained from earlier winter fires. Satisfied, she went about her chores, and before long she was asleep for the night. Shortly a bright flicker beamed from the fireplace and soon became a glow so brilliant that her entire house radiated. So strong it was that her distant neighbors awakened. Their curiosity caused them to rush to her cottage. They had no trouble finding her tiny dwelling on that dark night because the glow from the diamonds illuminated the entire path to her house. They were quite surprised to discover the source of the light, and all agreed that Dora couldn't leave the diamonds where they were. So they stayed and helped her remove them—one by one—from the ashes. That tedious task was completed by early morning, and Dora thanked her neighbors as they left. Then she sat down in her rocker to think.

"Shimmering shrubbery!" Dora muttered when she realized that her problem of storing the diamonds was certainly not to be an easy one. "I'll declare! I'll declare!" She sat down in her rocker. All day she rocked. And thought. And rocked. And thought.

By nightfall she had a plan. She took all the diamonds out into her backyard, and she brought along her slingshot. As soon as the sky was dark (as it always was in those days), she tucked a diamond into the leathery pouch of the slingshot, stre-e-e-e-e-tched back the rubbery band, aimed it high into the air, and then released that diamond!

She did the same with another diamond. Then another. And another. Each diamond soared high into the sky until it found a permanent resting place (one it liked far better than a mattress or a fireplace). As Dora shot one diamond after another, that dark sky began to lighten. And by the time she had shot her last diamond, the entire sky was twinkling with a new brightness that had never before been seen at night. Dora gazed into the heavens in amazement.

"Stammering starfish . . . *STARFISH! That's it! Stars! I'll call this new light stars!* And now *everybody* can enjoy my present from the king!" And not only that—now all of *you* know just exactly how the stars got into the sky!

Story Activities

Correlating Story Comprehension with Creative Dramatics

Practically all students enjoy role-playing after a story has been told. These activities shouldn't be forced or "required" even if your educational goal is to give young learners experiences in "public speaking." Instead, use activities that will beckon the shy ones to attempt oral language activities in front of their peers (always in an environment that will prevent embarrassment). You will know the "shyness levels" of your own students, and you will know when to gently encourage them to engage in less intimidating exercises. My actual words appear in italics. Modify them as you wish.

Today we might all envy a gift of diamonds. However, for 100-year-old Dora, this gift became a problem. Perhaps we can conclude that what can be extremely valuable to one could be quite a nuisance to others. (Skill notes: The above thought is one of the main ideas of this story, although it is deductively rather than inductively presented.) *For this activity, pretend you are Dora. Think about the way she might have felt about receiving such a gift and the predicament she was in regarding what to do with it. Picture in your mind how she looked, how she talked, and how she reacted at different times in the story. I am going to give some of you a chance to show how you think she appeared, sounded, or acted at various times. You may volunteer what Dora might have said, how she might have said it, or how she might have acted. Think about her possible posture and the sound of her voice. You do not have to remember her exact words (for in some cases, the words were not provided), but try to get close to what really happened as the story unfolded.*

Situation 1: The king has just given you the diamonds for your birthday. Show your response.

Situation 2: Pretend you have just lain down to sleep after stuffing the diamonds in your mattress. The glow mystifies you, and at first you aren't sure what it is. You begin to "talk to yourself." Let's hear your chatter.

Situation 3: Your neighbors have just come to your house after they saw the glow from your fireplace. They are telling you some things they thought the light might be. Describe their responses and give your reaction to some of them.

Situation 4: You will soon be attending a very important banquet at which you will be given an award for "inventing the stars." Deliver a possible "acceptance speech."

Skill Notes: As the students engage in the above activities, they are building the speaking skills of content (grammatical/dialect choices, word selection, sentence formation, etc.) and the speaking skills of delivery (vocal speed, vocal volume, enunciation, articulation, intonation, eye contact, gestures, posture, facial expressions, body positioning, spirit of delivery, etc.). They are also delving into their knowledge base to create language and new experiences for both fun and academic development.

Creative Writing Experiences

Below are some pretend situations relating to this story. I will describe a situation that might have happened, and you will write a response. (These activities may also be used as oral language experiences—or they may be dramatized rather than written, if desired.)

Skill Notes: In addition to skills described earlier, students are now engaging in the development of the comprehension skill of prediction/projection as they write or tell about or enact a possible "future" situation with Dora. They are also engaging in simulated experiences that they may face at future points in their lives and are preparing/practicing acceptable responses to such situations.

Writing Fun 1: Dora wants to write a thank-you note to the king for this present. Write a possible note that would be appropriate for her to send.

Writing Fun 2: A magazine reporter needs to write a short article explaining why Dora didn't just give the diamonds to all of the poor and needy people in her town instead of "throwing them away." Write a possible article.

Writing Fun 3: A year has passed. The king plans to give Dora a present for her 101st birthday. Write him a note of advice regarding what this gift should be.

Writing Fun 4: Examine the two-word expressions (such as "Salivating salamanders!") that Dora made during her times of bewilderment. All were alliterative interjections that were often unrelated to the context. If you were to compose some two- or three-word alliterative interjections for Dora, what would they be? Write five creative ones, following the pattern of 1) adjective-noun, 2) adjective-adjective-noun, or 3) a different pattern of your choice.

Writing Fun 5: Dora also uttered the expression, "I'll declare! I'll declare!" quite often. Many older folks acquire such expressions and say them often simply for emphasis. Make a list of some expressions you have heard from any of your older relatives or acquaintances. What expression do you think *you* might utter if you lived to be 100 years old?

Writing Fun 6: The name Dora in this story comes from a Greek word meaning "gift." Do you know what *your* first name means? Your last name? If not, investigate their origins.

Writing Fun 7: Dora chose to stuff the diamonds inside her mattress—a place where many "old-timers" used to hide their cash. Where would *you* hide some extra cash? Where would you hide a whole pouch of diamonds? Write a short description for either of these situations.

Recalling Literary Styles and Writing Poetry

1. *We have had an interesting time listening to, dramatizing, and writing about a story that is classified as a myth. A myth is a legendary narrative that explains a practice, a belief, or the origin of something. "Dora and the Diamonds" is a myth about how the stars got in the sky.*

   Skill Notes: Students are learning about literary characteristics by identifying this story as a myth and recalling other examples of this genre.

2. *We all have heard several poems about stars. Who can think of some?* (Let students relate those they know, such as "Twinkle, Twinkle, Little Star," etc.) *These poems, however, do not tell how the stars got into the sky. Write a very short poem explaining how the stars did get into the sky. You may use the reason provided in this myth, or you may make up a reason of your own.*

   Skill Notes: Students are building the language skills involved with poetry-writing tasks. They are also engaged in all creative writing skills while composing this poem.

Added Note: The poems created by the students in the above activity may be written on the folded star in the following activity.

Correlated Experiences with Star Folding

Paper-folding experiences are always a highlight in story follow-up. This story correlates nicely with a simple folded star. I begin by demonstrating how the star is folded, and then I give each student a sheet of paper (generally cut to size with step one already folded). Not all students achieve a "perfect fold" on the first try, but the goal is not perfection. If you have extra scrap paper, allow them to continue folding stars until they are proficient and comfortable. [See the reproducible sheet for student instructions in star folding. Feel free to photocopy the sheet for each student.] This is a great "take-home" experience for everyone, with the added bonus being that the youngsters can all go home with both a story to tell and a star to fold. That can be SUCCESS!

Another added bonus occurs when the students actually write their poems on their paper stars. These may be displayed in an area labeled "Star Search." Classmates may "search" for interesting or favorite poems.

Folding a Six-Pointed Star

(Student instructions to accompany the story *Dora and the Diamonds*, adapted by Flora Joy)

Step 1: Find a sheet of paper that can easily be folded. This can be copy paper, construction paper, or any type of art craft paper. The sheet will need to be a perfect square, so fold this sheet on a diagonal until two sides meet.

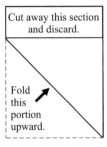

Cut away this section and discard.

Fold this portion upward.

Now cut away the TOP section that is NOT part of the newly formed square. You will be using only the square section of this paper.

Step 2: Fold this trimmed paper in half (forming two rectangles).

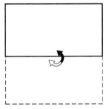

Step 3: The point at which these two folds cross indicates the center of the square. Noting this center, fold the paper in thirds by folding the right flap toward the left side of the paper.

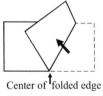

Center of folded edge

Step 4: Fold the left flap behind the center and right flap. These three sections should be practically even.

Step 5: Fold the entire design in half (from side to side).

Step 6: Draw a diagonal line as shown in the diagram. This line should START slightly below the halfway mark on the folded edge, and should extend upward to the TOP of that flap.

Step 7: CUT on this drawn line, discard the top portion, and unfold for a six-pointed star.

Figure 3.40.

146

For a more challenging experience (but one that greatly intrigues both the advanced learners and those who immensely enjoy paper folding), consult origami books for how to fold a three-dimensional star. One example appears in *Origami for Fun* by Toshie Takahama (Shufu No Tomo-Sha, 1980). If this story is presented during the winter holiday season, these stars may be used as decorations.

Correlations with Science

Activity 1: *In this story, Dora received some diamonds as a birthday present. When she tried to hide them, they not only glowed in the dark, but they shone far beyond her own cottage. Is it possible for ANY kind of diamond to shine in this fashion? Are there any elements that DO have these properties? If so, what are they? Explain how this happens.*

Skill Notes: Students are investigating scientific facts about specific elements and properties.

Personal Note: Before doing this activity, I tell the students the true story about the time I had to stay in a dormitory room on a college campus (during a summer storytelling conference) and was quite surprised after I turned out the lights to try to sleep. Suddenly there were TONS of lighted stars in the "sky"—the ceiling of my room. (Fortunately I'm a teetotaler, or I would have thought I was hallucinating!) This was my first experience with a prankster (a former room occupant) who had used a glow-in-the-dark "sky kit" that had left the room "lit" for all future residents. That experience caused me to dig into my Halloween paraphernalia and find items (like painted skeletons that actually do glow in the dark) to use with this story. Also, if I can find a room in the school that is completely dark, I use that room to show these items and to help create an interesting science discussion later. I also use my black light unit to demonstrate how black light bulbs can cause some neon colors to give an eerie glowing effect. Although the latter is a bit of a stretch, students thoroughly enjoy it.

Activity 2: *This story is a myth that explains how the stars got into the sky. Before, the night sky was supposedly black. Now that there are stars, can we still have any "black" nights? Do all "starry nights" provide adequate illumination for travel? Explain this.*

Skill Notes: Students are investigating scientific facts about nighttime illumination.

Psychomotor Experiences

Psychomotor Activity 1: *How difficult do you think it would be to remove diamonds from ashes? I have mixed together a quarter cup (or handful) of sugar and a quarter cup of rice.* (The amounts may vary.) *How long do you think it would take you to separate the rice from the sugar?* (Let some volunteers try to do this, if the learning environment allows it. If a competitive spirit exists, have two or more groups do this simultaneously. You may waste a little rice and sugar, but you'll have an interesting experiment and discussion.)

Author's Note for Activity 2: In today's society, "weapons in the school" is a tricky and touchy topic. (The logic is obvious.) This activity involves a slingshot—which is technically a legal "weapon." Some school systems do not allow the use of slingshots in their schools—for obvious reasons. Be sure to inquire about this in advance. If this activity would cause ANY concern or consternation with either students or parents, then don't use it. If you are able to explain it appropriately and cautiously beforehand, then it makes an excellent exercise for both psychomotor and physics skills.

Psychomotor Activity 2: *I wonder just how strong Dora had to be to get those diamonds into the sky. I wonder if any of us could shoot the diamonds that far. I have brought a slingshot to class today.* (Show the slingshot and demonstrate it.) *I have also brought some pom-poms (or cotton balls) that we will pretend are diamonds. We are going to draw a target on the chalkboard and "shoot" these pom-poms toward the target.* (At some point in this exercise, explain the dangers of using slingshots with items heavier than pom-poms.) As each student shoots the pom-pom toward the chalkboard, the one getting closest to the bull's-eye will be declared the winner. Students become quite intrigued with this activity and may want to continue it after class. Again, exercise caution with this.

The above are only a few examples of some activities that may be used with this story. Our goal as educators should always be to give students *positive* experiences with academics!

IMMIGRATION AND LITERACY IN AMERICA: SOMETIMES IT PAYS TO SPEAK ANOTHER LANGUAGE

Antonio Sacre

Speaking, Listening, Reading, and Writing

National Standards

NCTE: 1, 2, 3, 4, 5, 6, 7, 8, 9, 10, 11, 12; NCTE—Foreign Language 2: Students demonstrate an understanding of the relationship between the practices and perspectives of the culture studied. Students demonstrate an understanding of the relationship between the products and perspectives of the culture studied; NCTE—Foreign Language 3: Students reinforce and further their knowledge of other disciplines through the foreign language. Students acquire information and recognize the distinctive viewpoints that are only available through the foreign language and its culture; NCTE—Foreign Language 5: Students use the language both within and beyond the school setting. Students show evidence of becoming lifelong learners by using the language for personal enjoyment and enrichment; NCSS—Geography 1: Understand how to use maps and other geographic representations, tools, and technologies to acquire, process, and report information from a spatial perspective; NCSS—Geography 2: Understand the physical and human characteristics of places. Understand that people create regions to interpret the Earth's complexity. Understand how culture and experience influence people's perceptions of places and regions.

Objectives

Students will share their own stories (written and/or orally) of immigration and culture after listening to the teacher or storyteller's personal stories and folktales from their culture.

Materials

• A map of the world big enough for students to see.
• Sacre, Antonio. *The Barking Mouse.* Morton Grove, IL: Albert Whitman & Company, 2003.
• Collections of folktales from each child's heritage.

Chances are, if you live in the United States, you have someone in your background who was an immigrant. Even if you are American Indian, or have ancestors who were brought here against their will through slavery or other means, it is highly likely that someone along the way married someone who came from another country.

I often am asked to speak about immigration in schools, and I begin with the very personal story of the forces, choices, and decisions that set my ancestors in motion. I love to use a large map or globe to show students the places from which both sides of my family came. This was the case at the Baker Demonstration School on November 14, 2007, and is a model for what I have done countless times in schools and at festivals in the United States and Europe.

I start with my father's side of the family. His father, my grandfather, was born in Lebanon. He fled Lebanon during World War I and went to Cuba. I point out where we are on the map (on that day, near Chicago) and travel with my finger all the way across the oceans to the tiny country of Lebanon. Then I ask students if they can tell me where Cuba is on the map. When they do, I follow the route through the various oceans that my grandfather might have taken until I land in Havana, the capital of Cuba.

When my finger-as-imaginary-boat arrives, I tell some stories about my father. My father was born in Havana, Cuba, became a doctor, and came to the United States after Fidel Castro took power in the Cuban revolution—of 1958. With older students, I go more into the history and politics of this turbulent time. My father and his family didn't agree with the revolution, so they settled in Miami. This was a painful time for them. They had worked hard to buy a house in Havana and to establish a business, and when the budding

Communist government took it away, along with their freedom of speech and religion, they went to the United States with nothing more than the clothes on their bodies.

My mother's side of the family comes from another small island, Ireland. I ask the kids to help me find this on the map, and do the same finger-along-the-map journey until I end up in Boston. All the while, I tell stories about my mom's side of the family.

Her grandparents, my great-grandparents, left Ireland during the turbulent times surrounding the Irish Potato Famine and settled, like many other Irish people, in Boston, Massachusetts. My mother is a nurse and worked at a hospital in Boston.

My father did all the jobs that immigrants often have to do in the United States when they can't speak English. He was a busboy, a taxi driver, a dishwasher, and a factory worker. When he finally learned enough English to pass the medical boards and become a physician, he got hired as a doctor in Boston, where he met my mom.

I think of all of the big historical events that set my ancestors in motion: the Irish Potato Famine, World War I, the Cuban revolution—they made it possible for my mom and dad to meet.

At this point, I ask students to reflect on the events that set their ancestors in motion. If I were in the classroom, I might ask students who know where their families are from to come in front of the class and trace on the map the journey their ancestors made.

If the students don't know, it's a perfect homework assignment: where did their parents come from? Their grandparents? Can they go farther back?

The reasons why their families left are powerful. Equally compelling are the stories of how they arrived in the United States. I believe strongly that once we begin to learn some of these stories about each other, or discover these stories in our own backgrounds, that their power will help bring about some deeper understanding of each other that will lead to the beginnings of solutions to some of the problems we face.

After this brief discussion of immigration in my family, I tell stories about what it was like for me to be a child of immigrants in a small town in Delaware. While I spoke both Spanish and English fluently until I got to kindergarten, some kids at my school made fun of me for speaking Spanish and made fun of my dad's accent. I did what many other children of immigrants do: I decided to stop speaking Spanish and become as American as possible. Whenever my dad tried to talk to me in Spanish, I would answer him back in English, until little by little my first language slipped away. Luckily for me, my grandmother taught me Spanish again as a teenager, and the lessons I learned from her during those magical visits to her home in Little Havana became the strong foundation that helped me reconnect with half of my heritage while discovering a storytelling career.

I think teachers, if they are willing to share some of their stories of immigration in their family, may be surprised at how much in common they have with their students, and the students will be interested in the aspects of the story that are different.

Relearning Spanish and reconnecting with part of my heritage helped me immeasurably as I met people from around the world while I lived in Chicago and Los Angeles. Living in those places, I met many people from Mexico, and this led me to a desire to learn as much about Mexico as possible.

This prompted me to travel to Mexico many times over the past ten years, and this intimate knowledge of the country, the culture, the food, and the language has broadened my world outlook. I understand some of the forces that send Mexicans to the United States, and I know intimately what they are giving up in Mexico when they do so. Many of them do not make this journey lightly, and many have risked their very lives to come here.

When I tell a story that many Mexican children know, or remind them of something wonderful from their part of Mexico, a deep connection is made that is thrilling to see. This connection is deepened when I include the Spanish language in my stories. Often, I leave a phrase or word in Spanish. Then I will pause the story and ask if anyone can translate that word or phrase into English. Often, many hands will shoot up, and when they translate correctly, I have everyone clap for the translator, mentioning how useful and powerful that skill can be.

The pride that they feel and the excitement they show when they recognize one of their famous stories, often told in Spanish, makes them the star of the classroom or assembly. I encourage the other students to ask the kids from Mexico more questions about the stories I told, and get the real story from them.

By sharing some of these stories with the students, I hope to inspire them to do the same, starting in their home with their family. Then share with their classmates, and continue working outward as far as they have the desire and the time to do so, until they have many stories to share.

The fear of the unknown may be hardwired into our DNA. This may be what helped us as humans in our earliest stages of development to avoid dangerous passages through the jungle or plants that might have killed us if we ate them. However, it seems that we are also hardwired to be empathetic, and once we know someone's story, it becomes harder to hate them. If we can connect some of America's older stories of immigration (Irish, German, Jewish, Chinese, etc.) with some of the newer ones, this may be the beginnings of some cross-cultural understanding, where we continue to take the best the world has to give, reject some of the old ways that don't work, and move to a place where no child has to endure being made fun of for his or her own culture, but rather celebrates it.

SPICED-UP STORYTELLING:
ADDING A SECOND LANGUAGE
Carrie Sue Ayvar
Speaking and Listening

National Standards

> NCTE: 1, 3, 4, 6, 9, 10, 11; NCTE—Foreign Language 5: Students use the language both within and beyond the school setting. Students show evidence of becoming lifelong learners by using the language for personal enjoyment and enrichment.

Objectives

To understand and respect cultures and languages and people who are different from us; to encourage students to express themselves in more than one language, without fear or embarrassment.

I love to travel because I get to meet people and learn new things about different places, cultures, and customs. However, sometimes it is difficult to travel the globe and still make it back in time for supper. In a story, though, we can do just that. Stories are an integral part of all cultures. Our customs and traditions, our geography, even of the foods we eat are woven into our tales. Sharing stories can also help develop an awareness and appreciation of our own backgrounds, as well as those of others. This can be the foundation for better communications. It can help us understand others—those whose values, ways of life, religions, and languages are different from our own.

To begin, I explain to a classroom of students that storytelling is made up of three parts: the story, the teller, and the listener. They are all equally important, just like the three legs of a stool. If you want the stool to be straight, the legs must be even or it will become unbalanced. So I explain to students that their part is just as important as mine. I then ask them to "Open your ears. Open your minds. Fasten your seatbelts—you never know where we are going in a story, and we always wear our seatbelts!" Students usually join in physically miming the motions along with me.

Before you begin the story, invite the students to join you on an imaginary journey. First and second graders enjoy playing pretend and are happy to have an excuse to do it! This can give you an opportunity to tell a little bit about the country or place that you plan on "visiting."

There are several ways to incorporate a second language into a story. You can add a little *sabor*—flavor—to the tale by including individual words or phrases in the second language. For example: *Buenos Días* for Good Morning or *Señor Gato* for Mr. Cat. Make a little bit of language go a long way: "Once upon a time, there were three *björn*: Papa Björn, Mama Björn, and Baby Björn." (Björn is bear in Swedish.)

Illustrate portions by context. One character might say, "*Esta lloviendo fuerte.*" While another answers back, "What do you mean it's raining hard?" Or "*¿No te dije mil veces?*" "Yes, yes, you've told me a thousand times!"

You can tell the story completely in one language and then again in the other. If children are not bilingual, I personally usually do this only with short stories such as poems or nursery rhymes. Here is one from Mexico:

Sana, sana, colita de rana. Si no sanas hoy, sanas mańana.

Heal, heal, little tail of the frog. If you don't heal today, you'll heal tomorrow.

Another technique is to mix the languages, flowing back and forth between them, explaining or translating as you go along. For example: "*Había una vez,*" "Once upon a time," or " *¡Gato malo! ¿Cómo hiciste tal cosa?*" "Bad cat! How could you do such a thing?"

I encourage you to play with the story and the different techniques. Step out of your comfort zone and experiment to discover which style is right for you. If you are not sure of the correct pronunciation, ask someone who knows.

When I introduce the Latin American cumulative folktale, "Why Rooster Wakes the Sun," I ask if the children know what a rooster says. Invariably, most will say "Cocka-doodle-doo." "That's correct," I tell them, "If it's an English-speaking rooster. However, this story comes from Spanish-speaking countries like Cuba, Mexico, and Puerto Rico. This rooster or *gallo* in Spanish says *¡Quiquiriquí!* (KEE KEE REE KEE) Can you say that?— *¡Quiquiriquí! Muy bien* (very good)."

"Why Rooster Wakes the Sun"

There once was a rooster. He was a very good singer and was invited to sing at his *Tío Perico*/Uncle the Parrot's wedding. On his way, he saw corn sitting on a pile of trash by the side of the road. Gallo loved corn, ate it, and got his beak dirty. Embarrassed, he looked around for a solution. He saw a flower and told it to clean his beak. She answered, "No, no *quiero*. I don't want to." Rooster ordered (in turn) a sheep, a dog, a stick, fire, and water to help, but each answered, "No, no *quiero*. I don't want to." At last, he looked up and asked the sun, "*Por favor*, please dry up the water who won't put out the fire, who won't burn the stick, who won't hit the dog, who won't bite the sheep's tail, who won't nibble the flower, who won't clean my beak!" The sun agreed to do it, but only if rooster would sing to wake him up in the morning. Rooster agreed. Sun dried up the water, water started to put out the fire, fire burned the stick, stick hit the dog, dog bit the sheep, sheep nibbled the flower, and the flower cleaned the rooster's beak. Rooster went to the wedding, and ever since that day, rooster sings to wake the sun. *¡Quiquiriquí!*

Vocabulary: *gallo*/rooster, *flor*/flower, *borreguita*/sheep, *perro*/dog, *palo*/stick, *fuego*/fire, *agua*/water, *sol*/sun.

I have the children join in with the refrain "No, no *quiero*. I don't want to." I wiggle my finger as we say it, giving a visual cue. The children love participating, especially when given permission to "refuse" with attitude!

Assessment

Stories can help us see things from another point of view and encourage tolerance and better communication. Look for comparable tales from other cultures. Talk about the similarities and differences between these stories. Ask the students if they have ever thought about how animals speak differently. Ask them to think of other languages they have heard and to name the language and where it is spoken. Remind students that we already use words from other languages. (Examples from Mexico—canyon, lasso, piñata, and taco; from Australia—kangaroo and koala bear come from the Aborigines.) Ask students if they were familiar with the other language used in the lesson, or if they learned it during this activity. Discuss how it feels to speak in another language: was it comfortable? Familiar? Awkward? Define these words even if some of your students are familiar with the meanings. Was it fun? Easy? Hard? Do any of the students hear another language used at home? What languages do they hear at home?

Resources

- Ada, Alma Flor, *Medio Pollito/Half Chick*. New York: Dragonfly Books, 1997.
- Gonzalez, Lucia. *The Bossy Gallito/El Gallo De Bodas: A Traditional Cuban Folktale*. New York: Scholastic, 1994.
- MacDonald, Margaret Read. *El Conejito: A Folktale from Panama*. Little Rock, AR: August House, 2006.
- "No Way, José!/¡De Ninguna Manera, José!" in Hayes, Joe, *Tell Me a Cuento/ Cuentame un Story*. El Paso, TX: Cinco Puntos Press, 1988.

IDIOMATIC EXPRESSIONS, STORYTELLING, AND THE ENGLISH-LANGUAGE LEARNER
Sadarri Saskill
Speaking, Listening, Reading, and Information Literacy

National Standards

NCTE: 1, 6, 9, 10, 12; CNAEA—Dance 1: Students demonstrate kinesthetic awareness, concentration, and focus in performing movement skills; CNAEA—Visual Arts 1: Students use different media, techniques, and processes to communicate ideas, experiences, and stories; CNAEA—Visual Arts 3: Students select and use subject matter, symbols, and ideas to communicate meaning; ISTE 3: Students use technology tools to enhance learning, increase productivity, and promote creativity.

Objectives

This lesson plan was designed mainly for grades three to five. However, most activities can be adapted for a broader age range. Students will be able to differentiate between the literal meaning and the idiomatic meaning of various expressions; use idioms in everyday language situations; contribute to the ongoing development of context-based interpretation skills; and use storytelling as a literacy tool for understanding idiomatic expressions.

Lesson Background

Often, when presenting teacher in-services, I run into educators who just can't seem to wrap their heads around the idea that they, too, can be storytellers, as if this somehow mystical realm of the imagination has been delegated to a talented few who have been miraculously birthed through the womb of "the performing arts." I have to admit that, before my storytelling career, when I first started teaching years ago, I felt exactly the same way. However, that all changed one summer when I was co-supervisor of an exchange program between Strasbourg, France, and Evanston, Illinois. Motoring across the French countryside with a busload of overtired, understimulated, jet-lagged students soon led to a desperate cry to ease the exponentially mounting tension. ENTERTAINMENT! My French teacher counterpart looked at ME, pleading, "Do something! Anything! Can you sing? Dance? Tell a story?" Now, I may have been an exemplary teacher, but a storyteller? Yet desperate times call for desperate measures. I quickly synthesized the three portions of her request into one AHA! My response: "The Jazzy Three Bears." My musical version of the traditional tale was an instant success. The cogs on the gears of my teacher/storyteller wheels had, in one spontaneous moment, been set in perpetual motion as coexisting entities.

My host teacher couldn't wait for me to teach "The Jazzy Three Bears" to her elementary school students who were learning English. That was the first time I deliberately used storytelling-based lesson plans. Since then, I have used the same story-song as a springboard to activities encompassing a broad range of student ages, needs, and literacy objectives. I have found it particularly helpful when working with ELLs, English-language learners. The following English lyrics can be found on my CD, *Shake Your "TALE" Feathers* (also recorded in Spanish). There are many versions of this story-song floating around the world. The original is said to have come from Canada, created during the big-band era. Those who learn best through kinesthetic learning modalities enjoy the upbeat rhythm and actions. A description of the movements as I learned them is included below:

"The Jazzy Three Bears" © 1998

Adapted by Sadarri Saskill

[Students stand if possible. Hands form a tent peak above their heads.]

In a wee little cottage in the forest lived the three bears. [Show three fingers.]

(A CHACKA CHOO POW!) [Repeat two times—arms move twice to the left side, then twice right.]

One was the papa bear; one was the mama bear; one was a wee bear. [Show one finger each time.]

(A CHACKA CHOO POW!) [Repeat two times—arms move twice to the left side, then twice right.]

One day they were walkin', [Move both arms as if walking.]

Through the deep woods a talkin', [Move both hands as if they are talking to each other.]

When along, along, along, [Move hands out and away as if measuring something big—three times.]

Came a little girl, [One open hand shows her height.]

With golden hair [Pretend to twirl hair.] . . . and her name was Goldilocks,

And upon the door she knocked, [One hand makes a knocking motion.]

But no one was there. [Wag one finger as if to say "NO."]

No, no, no, no one was there. [Wag one finger as if to say "NO."]

[Take a few steps as if dribbling a basketball.] So she walked right in,

Had herself a ball! [Pretend to throw a ball into a hoop.]

No, she didn't care. No, she didn't care. [Shake one finger as if to say "NO" each time.]

And when she got tired, [Form hands into a pillow.] . . . she went upstairs,

Then home, home, home, [Whisper the word "home" two times, then yell it a third time.]

Came the three bears! [Show three fingers.]

(A CHACKA CHOO POW!) [Repeat two times—arms move twice to the left side, then twice right.]

"Someone's been eatin' my porridge," said the papa bear. "HMPH!" [Throw back shoulders.]

"Someone's been eatin' my porridge," said the mama bear. "WHOO!" [Throw both hands up.]

"Hey Baba Ree Bear," said the little wee bear, [Shake both index fingers around in the air.]
"Someone has broken my chair!" CRASH! [Clash both hands together like cymbals.]
Up woke Goldilocks, [Move arms as if stretching and yawning.]
Broke up the story, [Pretend to break a big stick.]
And beat it out of there! [Clap hands forward past each other in a single sliding motion.]
Yeah, she beat it out of there!

"Hey, bye-bye," "Bye," said the papa. [Wave good-bye.]
"Hey, bye-bye," "Bye," said the mama. [Wave good-bye.]
"Hey Baba Ree Bear," said the little wee bear. [Shake both index fingers around in the air.]
And that's the story of the three little bears. [Show three fingers.]

[Wave hands back and forth in sweeping motion, palms out, as if washing windows.]
Nah, nah, nah, nah, nah, nah, nah, nah, nah, nah, nah, nah, nah, nah, nah ... YEAH!
—Oh, a chacka chooka skiddly bopple skeedle doo POW!—

Figure 3.41. Mother/daughter storytellers (left to right) Sadarri, Misty, and Amber jazzing up "The Three Bears." Photo by Armando Salazar.

Idiomatic Expressions

One of the main lesson plans you can develop around this story variant involves idiomatic expressions. These can be especially challenging for ELLs. The Scholastic Dictionary of Idioms explains, "Idioms come from all different sources, from the Bible to horse racing, from ancient fables to modern slang ... Some idioms go back in time to the ancient Greeks and Romans, thousands of years ago. Others are more recent."

Taking such expressions literally can be quite confusing. The idiomatic meaning of the whole often has little or nothing to do with the meaning of the actual words as separate components. Begin by making sure that students understand that you will be taking them on an exploration of "hidden" meanings. For example, in "The Jazzy Three Bears," you can highlight any of the following idiomatic expressions: 1) "She had a ball"; 2) "She broke up the story"; 3) "She beat it out of there." First discuss what these expressions mean in the literal sense. Then explain their idiomatic connotation.

Next provide a list of idiomatic expressions. On one side of the paper, have students draw a literal interpretation of the word or phrase. On the other side or at the bottom of the page, students can write the real meaning. For an added challenge, they can also research and write down the origin of their selection. These student-generated visual learning tools can then be displayed on the walls or bulletin boards or organized in a book format. Some choices that my students have had fun with in the past include the following idioms: "I'm all ears"; "blow your top"; "butterflies in the stomach"; "cat got your tongue"; "chill out"; "cold feet"; "drive you up the wall"; "eat your words"; "eyes in the back of your head"; "green thumb"; "hot under the collar"; "keep something under your hat"; "like two peas in a pod"; "on pins and needles"; "pay through the nose"; "piece of cake"; "ring a bell"; "spill the beans"; "take the bull by the horns"; "two-faced"; and "with flying colors."

Finally, after students have shared their idiomatic expressions with each other, they can write or tell their own short story. Each story must include a specified number of idiomatic expressions used correctly in English.

Additional Mix-and-Match Lesson Plan Ideas and Activities

- Listen to various audio versions of "The Jazzy Three Bears." (See resources.)
- View this contributor's online version: http://www.prattlibrary.org/home/eStory. aspx.
- Making storyboards can be an excellent graphic organizer of images for sequencing. In addition, this technique helps teach and reinforce vocabulary. Knowing the vocabulary helps build a solid foundation for learning idioms.
- Compare idioms in the target language with idioms in the mother tongue. This validates student language, bolsters self-esteem, and creates a fascinating cross-cultural perspective.

- Investigate regional variations of English idioms between diverse geographic locations where English is spoken as the principle language.
- Put together individual dictionaries of idiomatic expressions or make flash cards.
- Play an idiom bingo game. Students fold a sheet of paper to form sixteen squares. From a predetermined list, students write in one idiom into each of the sixteen squares. The teacher calls out real-life situations, one at a time. Students mark on their idiom bingo sheet the expressions that best applies (there will be more than one correct answer at times). The first student with four correct situation/response matches in a row is the winner.
- Play the game Concentration using idioms. Using only one side, make one set of cards with idiomatic expressions. Make another set of cards with the English meanings. Mix together and place facedown in rows. Each round, students turn up two cards, trying to match the expression with its corresponding meaning. If it is not a match, those same cards get turned facedown. As play continues, students must remember where the matches are hidden.
- Using a digital camera, students can use programs like Apple's iPhoto to create books to illustrate and explain the accepted meaning of various idioms. Another option is to use a program like Nero's PhotoShow to create online slideshows to share similar work.
- Explore other stories that include idioms. One example that I used to teach idioms to my own children was the Amelia Bedelia series of books written by Peggy Parish. The author's quirky but humorous main character does not understand idioms and interprets them literally. She ends up doing exactly what the words in the idiom say to do. (See http://www.dallasartspartners.org for specific lesson plans and terms of use.)
- Emphasize vocabulary building by generating age-appropriate synonym lists from the story. (Examples from "The Jazzy Three Bears:" small, wee, tiny, minuscule . . . golden, blonde, flaxen, tow . . . tired, sleepy, weary, exhausted . . . story, tale, yarn, account.) This activity will particularly help ELLs when they write or tell their final story.
- Work in small groups to create an original fairy-tale rap, chant, or song that includes terminology learned from the lesson plans.
- Students can learn "The Jazzy Three Bears" and teach it to other classes. They can also highlight the idiomatic expressions from this story-song along with other pertinent information that they acquired throughout the lesson. They can also share the short stories and drawings that they created with other classrooms.
- Each week, have student(s) share a different idiomatic expression with its meaning and origin via the school's public-address system or newsletter. Thus, the opportunity for new learning can overflow from the one classroom to the entire school community.
- Teaching focus can center not only on general idioms, but it can be expanded to include proverbs and sayings; slang and expressions; phrasal verbs; and collocations of words that commonly occur together.

Assessment

There are a number of ways to assess student progress relative to the aforementioned standards and objectives. Some of these could include activities and/or quizzes involving sentence creation, matching, real-life situation/response (written, oral, or pictorial), fill-in-the-blank, or multiple-choice. Prior to story-writing activities, teachers can familiarize students with a teacher-made assessment rubric. From the outset, this can help to insure that students understand the expectations.

Resources

- Ifft, Mary Anne. "Vocabulary & Idioms." De Anza College, http://faculty.deanza.edu/ifftmaryanne/stories/storyReader$255, 2008.
- The Internet TESL Journal. "ESL: Idioms and Slang," http://iteslj.org/links/ESL/Idioms_and_Slang, 1995-2008.
- Pearson Education, Inc. "Paint by Idioms." FunBrain.com, http://www.funbrain.com/idioms, 2000-2008.
- Rosen, Gary. "The Three Bears," in *Animal Playground.* Audio recording compilation (CD). New York: Putumayo World Music, 2007.
- Saskill, Sadarri. "The Jazzy Three Bears (English and Spanish)" in *Shake Your "Tale" Feathers.* Audio recording compilation (CD). Kenosha, WI: Global Communication, 2001.
- Sperling, Dave. Dave's ESL Cafe: ESL Idiom Page by Dennis Oliver. http://eslcafe.com/idioms, 1995–2007.
- Terban, Marvin. *Scholastic Dictionary of Idioms.* New York: Scholastic, 1996.

POP, PLOP, AND TELL: HAVING FUN WITH VOCABULARY
Kim Cheves
Listening, Speaking, Reading, and Writing

National Standards

NCTE: 3, 4, 12.

Objectives

Increase phonemic awareness (initial and final consonants and vowels); reinforce comprehension and use of vocabulary words; practice oral language skills.

Materials Required

- Foam letters
- Vocabulary words
- Vocabulary pictures
- Emergent to early literacy level books

Once upon a time, there was a list of vocabulary words just waiting to enhance the stories children love. The words were overcome with joy when they were chosen for a sentence. They wanted to jump with pride when a child chose them for one of their own sentences. However, over time, the new words were forgotten. Sadness and emptiness filled the vocabulary list, which was once lively. What can be done to help children acquire and retain vocabulary? Is there a fun method that will make it stick?

While collaborating with kindergarten teachers at East Fannin (Georgia) Elementary School on ways to enhance vocabulary through oral language, we began to play with stories. Through kinesthetic techniques, we created a game out of the vocabulary words called Pop or Plop. We would read a story, retell it in our own words using the vocabulary words, and then the children would retell the stories in the same manner. This game can be incorporated into the story as the kids advance in the techniques.

In *Writing as a Second Language* (August House, 2000), Donald Davis says that "If language development is to be kept flowing, there must be opportunities after entry into school to try out language orally and kinesthetically. In fact, a good writing model will recognize talking as the basic creative language with which our children arrive at the door." In *Smart Moves: Why Learning is Not All in Your Head* (Great Ocean Publishers, 1995), Carla Hannaford tells us that "the most natural way, then, for children to learn when first in school at age five and six is through image, emotion, and spontaneous movement." We felt it was necessary to add movement into our plans.

Once a child enters kindergarten, literacy takes on a different focus, mainly toward reading and writing. It is amazing how well kindergarteners read these days; however, they need to be able to practice their oral skills as well. By offering movement games to link aural language to oral language, we can help bridge the literacy gap, thereby enhancing reading and writing skills. Pop or Plop can be adapted to lesson plans in any number of ways to accomplish a wide variety of objectives. Here's the basic version of how to play the game:

1. Choose the vocabulary words (that is, scraggly, romp, plump, witty).
2. Use foam letters or laminated die cuts. Pick the first letter of the vocabulary word. We'll start with just two words: S-scraggly, R-romp.
3. Hold one letter in your left hand (S). Ask, "What is this letter? Great! Now all the girls will be Ss for scraggly." Review the meaning of the word.
4. "Now let's practice. When I hold up the letter S, all the girls will pop up. When I lower the letter S, all the girls will plop down. S-up, S-down, S-down, S-up." Make up various patterns for the children to follow.
5. Now it's the boys' turn. Hold the letter R in your right hand. Ask, "What is this letter? Awesome! The boys will be Rs for romp." Review the meaning of the word.
6. "Now let's practice. When I hold up the letter R, all the boys will pop up. When I lower the letter R, all the boys will plop down. R-down, R-up, R-up, R-down." Use various patterns for the children to follow.

7. "Let's see how well we do together." As you raise a letter, say the letter and say up or down. Mix it up so some kids are up and some are down, that is, S-up, R-up, S-down, R-down, R-up, S-up, etc. As the kids catch on to the game, vary the speed and volume.

8. Encourage the children to use just their sense of sight. This time you will not tell them the letter or the direction. They will have to watch you and watch their letter to know whether they should be up or down. Make up patterns as in Step Seven without using words.

After starting the game with two words, you can increase the number of words to about five at the most. Select a couple of children to help hold each beginning letter. Allow each to make up the patterns for the letter he or she holds. Divide the class into groups of four to five kids to fit the number of letters used.

Vary the Pop or Plop game by using beginning sounds, ending sounds, or vowel sounds. For "scraggly," you could use "sc" or "ly" or "a." To reinforce the meaning of the vocabulary word, use the spelled-out word and the corresponding picture. When the teacher holds up the word "scraggly," the kids in the section holding the picture describing scraggly would pop or plop. Have fun adapting this game to fit the desired objectives.

Now it's story time. We chose emergent to early fluency level books, such as Denise Fleming's *Mama Cat Has Three Kittens* (Henry Holt, 1998), to help with reading readiness. These books do not have to mention the vocabulary words. After reading the story, retell it in your own words while embellishing it with the weekly vocabulary words. The challenge is to see if you can use all the vocabulary words while you tell the story! Filtering in finger-plays, music, or movement with the story helps the kinesthetic learners.

Once the children have heard the story through, it's time to play Pop or Plop. Each time they hear a vocabulary word, they get to pop up. When they hear another vocabulary word, they plop down. At first the storyteller will need to pace the story so that the kids will notice the vocabulary words, but the children catch on quickly and soon try to be the first to pop or plop.

The next time the story is told, tell the children that instead of playing Pop or Plop, they get to help *tell* the story. Tell the story again, but pause and let the kids choose the appropriate vocabulary word to help complete the sentence. The story takes on different meanings depending on how the vocabulary words are used. As long as a vocabulary word is used in the correct context, it's okay if it's not the exact word originally chosen.

Finally, the children get to retell the story in their own words. Ask if the child teller wants the "audience" to play Pop or Plop. This helps encourage the teller to use the vocabulary words often in their story. Below is an example of how we retold the story "Mama Cat Has Three Kittens":

What a fun way to review or introduce vocabulary words! When the children began to retell the story, they also wanted to pick new vocabulary words

Synopsis of *Mama's Window*

Mama Cat loves her three little kittens so much. Fluffy is the **witty** one. Skinny is really the **plump** one. And Boris, well, he's the **scraggly** one. One day Mama Cat decided it was time to teach her little kittens a few things. First, she washed her paws—slurp, slurp. Then Fluffy and Skinny washed their paws, too—slurp, slurp. But not Boris; that **scraggly** little kitten just napped. Purrrrrrrrr, purrrrrrr. Then Mama Cat saw a mouse run up a tall stone wall, so she chased it. Fluffy said, "Arrrr, that's my mouse, ye mates!" Skinny just rolled his eyes and said, "He thinks he's so **witty** when he's playing pirate kitty. Well, I'll show him, I'll get that mouse." It's a good thing the wall was **plump**, or Fluffy and Skinny would have had a hard time **romping** around on it. They are just little kittens. But Boris, that **scraggly** little kitten, just napped. Purrrr Purrrr. At the end of the wall was an enormous weeping willow tree. Mama Cat was so excited. She just couldn't wait to sharpen her claws on the rough bark—scratch, scratch. She'd be ready the next time she saw that **plump** mouse. Fluffy and Skinny wanted to be ready for the mouse, too, so they sharpened their claws as well—scratch, scratch. But Boris, that scraggly little kitten, just napped. Purrrr, purrrr. Just then, something started to fall from the trees. Leaves! Mama Cat **romped** in the leaves. But Fluffy said, "Arrrr, the sky is falling. I must go tell the king." Skinny just rolled his eyes again. "He must think he's a pirate-little, like Chicken Little. That silly little hairball!" Then Fluffy and Skinny **romped** in the leaves, too. But Boris, that **scraggly** little kitten, just napped. Purrrr, purrrr. Then Mama Cat started looking for that mouse again. She said, "Here mousey, mousey, mousey, I know you're here somewhere!" Then she smelled something. It had to be the mouse, so she began to dig in the sand. Fluffy said, "Arr, that's me treasure, stand back, ye mates!" Skinny wasn't about to stand back, and with his **plump rump** (boom), he simply bumped Fluffy out of the way. Soon both Fluffy and Skinny were digging for their treasure. But not Boris; that **scraggly** little kitten just napped. Purrrr, purrrr. After a long and adventurous day, Mama Cat finally curled up for a well-deserved nap. Fluffy even curled up, while saying, "Arr, this pirate's not tired yet (yawn)." Skinny was so tired he just rolled up next to Mama Cat and purred. But not Boris: that **scraggly** little kitten was wide awake! Just when all the others were fast asleep, Boris pounced on Mama Cat. "Arrrrrr!" said Mama Cat and then Boris, that **scraggly** little kitten curled up and napped.

to use. The child teller would pick two or three new words and determine the beginning, ending, or vowel sounds—whichever he or she chose. Then he or she would pick a few kids to help with Pop or Plop. The child teller then told his/her story using the new words chosen. We were excited to see the children's creativity expressed so well. We had not anticipated the children choosing more vocabulary words until further down the road; however, almost immediately the kids wanted to experiment with the vocabulary words they had already learned. The children added new characters, settings, events, mishaps, and endings based on the variety of words chosen. One child chose "slither," so he changed the mouse to a snake in his story. We even noticed that a little girl who usually didn't participate was eager to hold the letters and help with the game. Her fellow students were surprised and encouraged her. This was a huge step for her socially.

The children also suggested various movements for the Pop or Plop game. They came up with arm patterns, rhythm patterns, and foot stomps. We matched these patterns to the syllables of the vocabulary words. Allowing the kids to use movement helped the creative processes immensely. The teachers commented on how this process helped the students integrate the vocabulary words into their everyday sentences. It was almost a game to see how many new words the children can use each day. The teachers also mentioned that several children are teaching their parents and siblings how to retell a story. One parent said she didn't realize her child was learning so many big words in kindergarten until she heard her child retelling the stories.

The teachers, students, and I have had so much fun "playing" together with stories. I hope you'll have fun with these ideas as well. Feel free to tweak the ideas to fit your curriculum, standards, and objectives.

Assessment

Students' phonemic awareness can easily be assessed during the Pop or Plop game; their ability to use the vocabulary words appropriately can be observed during retelling activities.

READ, SPELL, AND TELL
Lynn Rubright
Speaking, Listening, Reading, Writing, and Visual Literacy

National Standards

NCTE: 6, 12; NCSS I: Culture; NCSS III: People, places and environment; CNAEA—Visual Arts 3: Choosing and evaluating a range of subject matter, symbols and ideas; CNAEA—Visual Arts 6: Making connections between visual arts and other disciplines.

NOTE: The activities presented in "Read, Tell, and Spell" easily can be adapted to use with any story or piece of literature studied in classroom grades three through seven.

Objectives

Demonstrate how "spelling words" can be chosen by students from a text being read in order to explore a story's deeper meaning through language arts, drama games, movement, music, reader's theater, and art. As students mine spelling words for meaning and usage, they will expand vocabulary while developing their spoken and written communication skills. This process leads to a natural understanding of story structure: setting, character, incident, conflict, crisis, and resolution.

For the past four years I have been using my chapter book, *Mama's Window* (Lee & Low Books, 2005), extensively across the curriculum in my Storytelling and Literacy Project for the Urban Arts Programs of the Center of Creative Arts (COCA) in the St. Louis (MO) Public Schools. In the spring of 2008, I completed a COCA author-storyteller residency at Jefferson Elementary School with fourth and fifth graders. The residency included exploring "tasty" words gleaned from the text of *Mama's Window* to uncover meanings from context clues. Dictionary and thesaurus searches, as well as spelling "drama" games, help students utilize the words in their daily vocabulary. Creative writing and a reader's theater activity culminated our study of Chapter 1.

Eleven-year-old Sugar (James Earle Martin Jr.) lives with his grumpy Uncle Free in a swamp in northwest Mississippi following the death of Sugar's mother. Both Sugar and Uncle Free are grieving the loss of Ida Mae Martin and are struggling to come to terms with their new, but unwanted, living arrangement. As he strived to be helpful to Uncle Free in his fishing business and to accept his new life, Sugar worked to keep alive his mama's dream of having a stained glass window placed in the New Sweet Kingdom Church. This necessitates Sugar fighting Stewie, a bully, and confronting the church building committee, which has diverted funds for the window fund to buy bricks for the new church. Ultimately, an anonymous donor makes it possible for the stained glass window to be put in place for the church dedication.

Mining Spelling Words from Text

Fourth and fifth graders from Jefferson Elementary School chose "spelling words" from their favorite sentences in Chapter 1 of *Mama's Window* and listed them on the board: aroma, aroused, irritated, cripple, ashamed, wobbly, splayed, tentacles, slimy, nudged, murky, mosquitoes, snippets, snuggled, grizzled, curdle, conjure, disability, insurance, sullenly, and tentatively.

1. Students read sentences from the book and explained the meaning of their selected word(s) from the context clues. "The familiar aroma of hot water cornbread frying in bacon fat aroused Sugar from a deep sleep." Jeremy said, "Aroma means 'smell' and aroused means 'woke up.'"
2. Students listed the words and their dictionary definitions in their journals:

aroma: noun: "distinctive, pleasant smell"
aroused: verb: "to awaken from sleep"

Ms. Thomas, the teacher, asked her fifth graders to write original sentences in their journals, applying some of these words to their own life experiences.

Aarionna wrote:

That lady looks **familiar**.
I was **ashamed** of my brother because he acts dumb.
The gym teacher has arms like **tentacles**.
The **mosquitoes** were so little I couldn't see them.
My uncle got money because of his **disability** of walking.

Shannise wrote: My grandparents get disability insurance because they were in a car accident.

Spelling Word Charades I (Variant of the Spelling Bee)

This Spelling Word Charade game is adapted from a spelling word pantomime game Ms. Thomas's students composed. After students carefully read the chapter and choose and study the spelling words, the class is divided into two teams. Spelling words are placed in a hat.

A student from Team One pulls a word from a hat and pantomimes the meaning of the word so that Team Two must guess the word. Example: Tony acts out his word, mosquitoes, by slapping imaginary buzzing mosquitoes. A student from Team Two guesses the word and must spell it correctly to win a point for his team. The team with most points wins Spelling Word Charades.

Spelling Words Charade II (Variation to Reinforce Understanding of Story Structure Through Storytelling)

A child from Team Two guesses the pantomime word presented by Team One and correctly spells it. He or she must then *tell* the section of the chapter from which the word came, including something about the setting, characters, and incident from which the spelling word was embedded. Note: In another variation, students improvise monologues and dialogues from scenes in *Mama's Window* using the same core spelling words.

Spelling Word Spell and Tell—Pass It On

Prepare large cards for each spelling word, numbering them one through twenty-one. The words are listed in order of how they appear in Chapter 1 of *Mama's Window*. Children line up in numerical order so they are positioned in a semicircle in front of the room. (The words are in order of how they appear in the story: aroma, aroused, irritated, cripple, ashamed, wobbly, splayed, tentacles, slimy, nudged, murky, mosquitoes, snippets, snuggled, grizzled, curdle, conjure, disability, insurance, sullenly, and tentatively.)

Each child holds up his or her spelling word card, spells it, and tells a small part of the section where the word appears in the story. To pass it on, the next person holds up his card, spells the word, and tells the next bit of story action embedding the spelling word in the tale. Round robin, the story of Chapter 1 unfolds, with children using natural language to tell the tale, practicing their skills of oral interpretation. *Note:* Have a spelling word card prepared for each child so the entire class is involved in the Pass It On spelling circle.

Daily Edit

Students write and punctuate a paragraph adapted from Chapter 1 in *Mama's Window,* correcting each misspelled spelling word and adding correct punctuation. Students can work alone or in small groups.

the arroma of his uncle free's cooking aroussed sugar as he snugled under the quilt mosqutoes buzzed around sugar he was ashamed of his grizled cripled uncle as he sat at the woobbly table cypress tress had tentakles that reached into the slimie murrky swamp water he ain't nothing but an old conjuur man who curddles milk with his evil eye sugar thought sugar sulenly

(correct spelling: aroma, aroused, snuggled, mosquitoes, grizzled, crippled, wobbly tentacles, slimy, murky conjure, curdles, sullenly)

This unedited paragraph with misspelled words can be duplicated for each child to work on individually or in small groups. It can be written on the board for students to copy in their journal, with the teacher leading a collective exercise in spelling and punctuation. This activity is an opportunity for children to practice handwriting skills.

Ms. Turner expected her fourth-grade students to find "juicy words" of their own to use in their *Mama's Window* creative writing activities—not just the words they found in the story text. In one exercise, Ms. Turner asked students to write "What Happened Next in Chapter Thirteen?" (*Mama's Window* only has twelve chapters). In groups of four, students worked collaboratively to create 18″ × 24″ "What Happened Next" books with illustrated covers. These books were the result of cooperative learning as students practiced the writing cycle: brainstorming, draft writing, dictionary work, rough draft, revision, and final editing. "What Happened Next in Chapter Thirteen?" books were displayed in the hall.

Here is "What Happened Next in Chapter Thirteen?" by Antonyo H., Aunjanee I., Davion H., and Erin C.

*"Sugar arrived at the church picnic. The trip exhausted him … rowing a boat and holding onto a three-layer **caramel** cake. The cake is for the potluck supper in honor of Reverend's twenty years of **ministry**. Then all of a sudden Stewie came up and said, "Why would someone want to eat that swamp cake. It probably got all bugs in it." "No, my Uncle free and I bought this from the store yesterday!" **retorted** Sugar. Sugar walked away and Stewie followed. Both **ambled** to the table where Uncle Free sat. "Hey boy! Put that cake on the table, and you stop playing behind Sugar's back. Are you afraid to make that **commotion** in his face? You two boys sit!"*

*They said grace together and ate. Sugar reached over the table to get the last piece of fried chicken. When Stewie **grabbed** Sugar's plate and started eating the chicken. Sugar, angry and <u>disheartened, bellowed</u>, "Say, why you take my food you ugly boy?" "I wanted to, Swamp Rat," answered Stewie, as he **examined** the crispy fried chicken leg. "That's not the right way to talk to folks," said Uncle Free, as he picked his teeth with the toothpick. So you both just stop and get along with each other." "Yes sir." After that day, Sugar and Stewie never spoke again."*

Ms. Turner's fourth graders became so involved in creating books inspired by *Mama's Window* that they researched and wrote "Swamp Books." (*Mama* is set in northwest Mississippi.)

Oral Interpretation: Reader's Theater

After studying spelling words from the text, playing drama games, and doing creative writing projects, it was time to read and tell Chapter 1 of *Mama* through Reader's Theater.

Reader's Theater

Mama's Window by Lynn Rubright

Chapter One

ALL: Sugar lay curled like a cat on the old iron cot.

Storyteller: Uncle Free's cabin in the swamp smelled like fish. The aroma of cornbread patties frying in bacon fat on the cookstove aroused Sugar from a deep sleep.

Sugar: Hummm. Somethin' smells good. Cornbread patties. Just like Mama used to make.

Uncle Free: James Earle! You awake?

Storyteller: But Sugar remembered he was now in Uncle Free's shack in the swamp. He covered his head under Mama's old crazy quilt.

Uncle Free: Get yourself up, James Earle! There's work to be done. Nets need mendin'. There's frogs to gig and fish to catch. And you gotta practice usin' one of the boats on your own.

Sugar: Aw, Uncle Free. It's Sunday. Mama never washed and ironed on Sunday. And I didn't tote laundry to the people she worked for in Wilson City on Sunday. So why we gotta fish on Sunday?

Uncle Free: Cause you gotta eat on Sunday, James Earle. Unless you want to go hungry all day. Besides you see me workin' over this here hot stove? You think I doin' that for my health? Answer me, boy!

Sugar: No sir, Uncle Free.

Uncle Free: Then get yourself over here and eat your breakfast while it's hot.

Sugar: Yes sir.

Storyteller: Sugar got dressed and quickly smoothed the crazy quilt over his cot. He sat down at the wobbly table and ate what Uncle Free had put before him. He tried not to think about the roots of the cypress trees next to the shack that reached into the water like tentacles.

Uncle Free: What is it now, James Earle?

Sugar: It's groundbreakin' day at the church, Uncle Free. Mama would have been there.

Uncle Free: You wanna go to the church groundbreakin', James Earle? I ain't stoppin' you. Take the little boat. Time you go out on the water by yourself, anyways.

Sugar: You be wantin' to come with me, Uncle Free?

Uncle Free: Naw. Gave up church goin' years ago. Church folks ain't my kind a folks.

(Reader's Theater script adapted by Lynn Rubright. Used with permission by Lee & Low Books.)

Figure 3.42. Mama's tissue-paper windows.

Figure 3.43. A portion of *Mama's Window* mural.

Similar short scripts can be written by teachers or students based on any story being read as part of the existing curriculum. Make copies for each student to use as an exercise in reading fluently with both expression and comprehension.

Art Extensions

Art extensions included fourth and fifth graders researching stained glass windows and making tissue paper stained glass windows to hang in their classrooms. Ms. Thomas and Ms. Hicks's fifth graders concluded the residency by making a magnificent *Mama's Window* mural twelve feet by three feet that is being mounted and preserved for use in future *Mama's Window* residencies.

Assessment

Entries by the students in their *Mama's Window* journals reflecting various Read, Spell, and Tell activities were regularly reviewed by teachers and students in peer-assessment groups. Students' ability to spell the chosen words and play the charade games effectively were observed and noted by the teachers.

Bibliography

- Norfolk, Sherry, Jane Stenson, and Diane Williams. *The Storytelling Classroom: Applications Across the Curriculum.* Westport, CT: Libraries Unlimited, 2006.
- Rubright, Lynn. *Beyond the Beanstalk: Interdisciplinary Learning through Storytelling.* Portmouth, NH: Heinemann, 1996. See appendix B "Storytelling, Movement, and Drama Exercises" for activities that can be adapted for language arts enrichment, including "Reading, Spelling, and Telling."
- Rubright, Lynn. *Mama's Window.* New York: Lee & Low Books, 2005. See http://www.lynnrubright for reviews and expanded interdisciplinary curriculum.

READING NATURE: A TREASURE HUNT
Heather Forest
Listening, Speaking, Writing, and Visual Literacy

National Standards

NCTE: 1, 4, 5, 6; NAS 1: Students should develop abilities necessary to scientific inquiry; NAS 2: Students should develop an understanding of properties of objects and materials; NAS 4: Students should develop an understanding of the properties of earth materials.

Literacy Development in the Storytelling Classroom

Objectives

Utilizing observation and inquiry to heighten awareness of the natural world, students will be encouraged to use both spoken and written words to describe details and qualities, compare and contrast, and honor diverse points of view.

Materials Needed for a Nature Treasure Hunt

(One for each team of gatherers)

- Treasure hunt list
- Paper bag
- Large sheet of paper

For the past thirty years, I have been visiting schools as a guest story-teller and author. Much has changed in the lives of children. Games have changed. As a child, my favorite pastime was playing outside, *investigating*. Walking outside as a child, I looked intently at the smallest natural things and always looked up at clouds. Mostly I loved the shapes and forms I could imagine. As fast as the wind would allow, I would see a face or a mountain or a moving, drifting swath of billowing white and grey pictures. As an adult, I have learned that one can "read" the sky for rain or shine or an impending storm. Now I "read" nature when I notice that the leaves on the trees are drooping and need some water. Reading the natural world is a kind of eco-literacy based on recognizing patterns and forms. In our contemporary world, children in technologically oriented lifestyles surrounded by televisions and computers spend much of their time inside of buildings. Richard Louv (2008) has dubbed this condition "nature deficit disorder." Exploring the natural world beyond the school's walls can offer inspiration across the curriculum. Here is a language arts activity that encourages a walk outdoors to enhance literacy.

Preparation

What is a natural object?

Observation and Comparison

- Have students look at and handle some objects that are handcrafted out of natural materials such as wood, glass, stone, fur, wool, etc.
- Have students look at and handle some natural objects such as small tree branches or assorted stones that have interesting shapes and have *not* been crafted by humans into their current shape or form.
- Have students look at and handle some objects made of plastic or other synthetic, man-made materials.

Activity

Bring students to a public park, backyard, or any outdoor wooded area. In small groups of three or four, have them take a bag and a treasure hunt list and gather a collection of some assorted natural objects. These objects must be things that have not been made or constructed by humans.

Treasure Hunt List

Give each group a treasure hunt list and ask them to work together to find natural objects to put in the bag that are a group-acceptable example of each of the things that is:

• Green

• Soft

• Hard

• Round

• Jagged

• Smooth

• Rough

• Scented

• Long

• Multicolored

• Hollow

• Sound producing

Or construct your own list.

After an agreed amount of time for collecting (fifteen to twenty minutes), groups gather to share and compare their findings.

Sharing

Visual Display

Each team of students arranges a pleasing display of the collected natural objects on a sheet of paper on a flat surface.

Contrast and Compare

Have students travel from display to display to view and admire the diversity of solutions found, comparing and contrasting the natural items selected for each quality. For example, ask students to notice differences in each group's version of the "round" things or "jagged" things collected. A representative for each group can remain at the display to curate and explain selections. Ask students to notice if any human-made items may have been inadvertently gathered, too.

Speaking and Listening Extension

Point of View: Gather as a group and have each group take turns orally telling:

1. How they came to decide and agree upon items for the bag?
2. Were there several acceptable solutions the group found for each item on the list? If so, why?

Writing and Reading Extension

Descriptive Poem

- Ask each group to select one found object from the display on the sheet.
- Select one student to be the *word-gathering scribe* who writes down the descriptive words contributed by students on a large piece of paper so everyone can read them.
- Sitting in a small circle, have students pass the chosen object around the group. When a student holds the object, he or she observes it closely and says one word to describe the object without repeating adjectives said before.
- When at least twenty words have been collected that refer in some way to the natural object's qualities, ask each student in each group to use the descriptive words to write a non-rhyming poem that celebrates and describes the object. More words can be added.

When the poems are completed, ask each student to read their writing out loud so that the group can compare solutions. Ask students to notice how each poem celebrates the same natural object and may use similar words but is different and unique.

Retelling Nature Tales

Making a connection from lived experience in nature to literature, ask students to read a collection of nature tales such as *Earth Care* by Margaret Read MacDonald, *Keepers of the Earth* by Michael Caduto and Joseph Bruchac, or *Celebrating the Earth: Stories, Experiences, and Activities* by Norma Livo.

- Ask students to select a favorite story about a natural object such as a plant, a rock, or a tree. Have students retell the tale in their own words using generous description of natural environments.
- Explore retelling the tale from the point of view of the natural object.

Assessment

Consider if students were able to follow both oral and written directions; showed a spark of interest in exploring an out-of-doors natural environment; accepted diverse solutions to a task; and were able to notice and describe details through both oral and written expression.

Selected Teacher Resources

- Caduto, Michael J., and Joseph Bruchac. *Keepers of the Earth: Native American Stories and Environmental Activities for Children.* Golden, CO: Fulcrum Publishing, 1997.
- Cornell, Joseph Bharat. *Sharing Nature with Children: A Parents' and Teachers' Nature-Awareness Guidebook.* Nevada City, CA: Dawn Publications, 1998.
- Cornell, Joseph Bharat. *Sharing the Joy of Nature: Nature Activities for All Ages.* Nevada City, CA: Dawn Publications, 1989.
- Livo, Norma J. *Celebrating the Earth: Stories, Experiences, and Activities.* Englewood, CO: Teacher Ideas Press, 2000.
- Louv, Richard. *Last Child in the Woods: Saving Our Children from Nature-Deficit Disorder.* Updated and Expanded. Chapel Hill, NC: Algonquin Books of Chapel Hill, 2008.
- MacDonald, Margaret Read. *Earth Care: World Folktales to Talk About.* North Haven, CN: Linnet Books, 1999.
- Stone, Michael K., and Zenobia Barlow. *Ecological Literacy: Educating Our Children for a Sustainable World.* Bioneers series. Berkeley, CA: Sierra Club Books; produced and distributed by University of California Press, 2005.

LIAR!

Ben Rosenfield, PhD

Speaking, Listening, Reading, and Writing

National Standards

NCTE: 1, 2, 3, 4, 5, 6, 7, 8, 9, 10, 11, 12.

Objectives

Students will use imagination, reasoning, and the ability to analyze and judge various pieces of information to form a cohesive story that stretches the truth and persuades listeners.

Materials

Collections of tall tales and urban legends (see Bibliography)

Introduction

There's an old adage that advises, "If you don't know what to say, tell the truth." This article is for those who *do* know what to say. That is . . . LIE! This article is for those who seek to put the tall tale, urban legend, and liar's contest into elementary school curriculum. All are a uniquely American contribution to folk literature.

The young ought to be temperate in the use of this great art [lying] until practice and experience shall give them confidence, elegance, and precision which alone can make the accomplishment graceful and profitable. Patience, diligence, painstaking attention to detail—these are the requirements; these, in time, will make the student perfect; upon these, and upon these only, may he rely as the sure foundation for future eminence. Think what tedious years of study, thought, practice, and experience went to the equipment of that peerless old master who was able to impose upon the whole world the lofty and sounding maxim that "Truth is mighty and shall prevail"—the most majestic compound fracture of fact which any woman born has yet achieved. For the history of our race, and each individual's experience, are sewn thick with evidences that a truth is not hard to kill, and that a lie well told is immortal.

—Mark Twain, "Advice to Youth," April 15, 1882

Why Teach Tall Tales in School

The lie has been practiced and taught as the tall tale in our multicultural world, but is especially prevalent in American literature and storytelling. Tall tales are usually told in the first person and are outrageously funny and highly exaggerated; they never attempt to be anything related to plausibility. Sporting feats of superhuman strength, they often take the place of myths that explain phenomena of nature that have resulted from the intelligence, skill, or uncanny abilities of the hero. Tall tales are presented as true accounts without any semblance or expectation of convincing the listener to actually believe the presentation.

Encompassing myth and current culture, American heroes include Paul Bunyan (who may be French Canadian!), Pecos Bill, Johnny Appleseed, Wild Bill Hickok, Davy Crockett, Daniel Boone, Annie Christmas, Calamity Jane, John Henry, Mike Fink, Febold Feboldson, Molly Pitcher, Joe Magarac, Aylett C. "Strap" Buckner, and Alfred Bulltop Stormalong; the list is endless. These characters, somewhat based in reality, epitomize the labor and life of the common man, all the while possessed of superhuman strength or speed, wisdom, skill, and common sense—the nature of exaggeration.

We teach these tales because they give us a sense of self, of history, and of connection to our past. Our world is changing faster than we can keep up, and tall tales ground us in something permanent, always recognizable and strong, but simultaneously something familiar. We learn who we were and how America became great. Because these myths reveal our identity, we need to use our imaginations, higher-level thinking skills, and good writing skills to bring them into focus for ourselves and for those who experience our work. First assignment: research your folk hero and report to the class.

From Tall Tale to Urban Legend

The current tall tale is our beloved urban legend, a phenomenon that amazes and fools us all. An urban legend is a kind of myth that is told as if it's real. It usually claims to have happened to an acquaintance, friend, or relative and may even contain a grain of truth; but has been exaggerated, embroidered, and stretched into a barely plausible concoction of humor and horror, usually meant to outrage or shock the reader or listener. It's the big lie, so outlandish and often far-fetched that susceptible listeners will grasp onto the tiny shred of evidence contained within and believe the whole thing. It is modern folklore in the purest sense and deliciously wicked although sometimes misleading and hurtful.

These can be as simple as the Mrs. Field's Cookie recipe story, or as frightening as the tales of the Chupacabra now making their way through the Midwest and the nation, having started in Puerto Rico in the mid-1990s. Urban legends fulfill that storytelling need for the vast, ever-changing society that thrives in cyberspace. Urban legends have often been related to the current technology. Currently, that means e-mails decrying trespasses and injustices, for example, legends of palatial prisons in Illinois, hidden backgrounds of political candidates, Microsoft and AOL giveaways, tax changes, etc., all untrue but revisited and momentarily believed until their falseness is articulated.

Urban legends are usually terrible things about which we should be fearful or outraged. They are cautionary tales that not only entertain fears and prejudices, but remind us of our morays and tell us how to live in society. Don't stray from the path or the big, bad wolf will get you! Obey your parents, save your money, prepare for a rainy day or the long cold winter, don't build your house of sticks and straw, and be vigilant!

Both the tall tale and urban legend are delivered with "tongue-in-cheek" audacity. Teller and audience alike understand that the story is a lie, and a great amount of humor and goodwill is exchanged. Mark Twain told us to enjoy our life and our stories. "Humor is the great thing, the saving thing. The minute it crops up, all our irritations and resentments slip away and a sunny spirit takes their place." Second assignment: find and articulate two urban legends.

How Children Relate

Emerging writers naturally gravitate to the tall tale and urban legend. Listen in on the conversations our students have with one another. Remember your own as a child and you will hear and recall tales of hushed excitement and expectancy of dastardly deeds and often inappropriate behaviors that more often turn out to be false imaginings. Forming small groups to create, write, and rewrite stories, the conversations naturally and quickly are turned to "what if" and then, "Oh, they could . . ." and "THEN they would go. . . ." The possibilities are endless. Get the students started, give a little guidance to keep them on track, and enjoy the results. When they are ready to share the stories, they easily and naturally share the telling in meaningful ways, such as reading, narrating, orally relating, illustration, mime, or a myriad of other possibilities of expression.

The Liar's Contest

This creative, fun event begins in school with a unit on tall tales. Often combined with U.S. history, the folk heroes that sprang up explain a lot about U.S. climate, topography, economy, and attitudes. A big country has to have big heroes. Next, seeking knowledge of the urban legends that wind around the continent will provide students with hilarity, disbelief ("How can people believe this stuff?"), and a greater understanding of U.S. mores. Ask, "What do these tales say about us as people?" Ask your students to tell their story, tall tale, or urban legend.

Crafting the story begins with plausible (in the sense of real or actual) events and people, so that the story is grounded in the truth. The story's conflict can be stated in exaggeration and must be persuasive, and it is an easy leap from stretched truth to the lie. The solutions to the conflict can be wild and silly, growing larger and more grandiose with each passing attempt. The solution brings the story back to reality so that the teller and audience recognize the fun they had together.

Telling the tale takes planning and attention to detail. The teller needs to be in the moment and conscious of the audience, aware of the audience's acceptance of the story. Delivery includes tone, facial and physical expressions, and listening in order to persuade.

Here's an example from the Illinois Storytelling Festival, where an annual liar's contest is held: contestants signed in and told their stories in that order. The judges (including myself) took notes on the stories. Contestants ranged in age from four or five years old to octogenarians. One year, I was about to dismiss the audience and begin deliberations when a young woman ran to the front of the tent and began admonishing the audience for not only attending, but taking part in a contest of lies, especially on the "Lord's day," the Sabbath. When she finished, a stunned silence filled the tent. Then, reality hit—the audience burst into applause and gave her a standing ovation. She planned, judged the audience, and combined timing, exaggeration, and audacity with an idea that struck a chord in the community. She took home the trophy—a coveted 1965 Studebaker convertible donated by a local car dealer! Hmm.

My Day Job—School Principal

As a (now) retired elementary school principal, I dealt often with children and lying, so I have great respect for the truth and for ethics. I gave each child a chance to tell me his story and remember often overhearing those waiting outside my office, advising the next victim, "Whatever you do, tell him the truth!" I checked out those stories and if I discovered conflicting information, I returned to the child to clarify or give an opportunity to tell the truth. In school, mutual respect and trust are based on truthful relationships. The truth will set you free, but for critical thinking, one needs to recognize exaggeration, hyperbole, as well as a downright LIE.

Assessment

In recapping this article, there are several built-in assessments, some assignments, and some collaborations. In total, they are the reflections on this unit of study. 1) Working in small groups, each student will research a folk hero from a particular time in American history. They will collaborate on the backstory America's history and climate provides and they will report individually on their chosen hero. What tall tales can you tell about the folk hero? What do these tales say about American culture? 2) Find and share two urban legends. How does technology influence the urban legend? What is the context for the legend? What do these tales say about American culture? 3) Crafting a tale for a liar's contest: Working individually, craft a story for the liar's contest. The beginning must be plausible and there must be enough reality so that the character(s) and setting(s) are understood by the audience. There must be exaggeration, still grounded in truth, but that can lead to the lie. The conclusion is a return to a reality, transformed by the fun the teller and audience shared during the story.

GARRETT MORGAN: THE TRAFFIC LIGHT GENIUS
Mama Edie Armstrong, MHS, CCC/SLP
Speaking and Listening

National Standards

NCTE: 3, 4, 9, 11.

Objectives

Students will be able to recall the sequence of events within the story; retell the presented rhythmical story-poem about a great inventor; ask and answer questions within acceptable grammatical structures regarding the events in the story and their importance; explain the meanings of vocabulary selected from the story and song; present the "Song for Garrett Morgan" in sign language and voice; discuss two main reasons why people cannot hear or lose their hearing; discuss two potential dangers of not being able to hear (that is, traffic safety, etc.); and discuss feelings about the accomplishments of the key character in the story, and how they feel about their ability to do great things.

Several years ago, I wrote a story called "Garrett Morgan: The Traffic Light Genius." Although it was originally developed for three to five year olds, over the years, it has been expanded for use with older groups as well. The inclusion of communicative movement through the use of sign language for the accompanying original song "Garrett Morgan: The Traffic Light Genius" makes it more engaging. It contributes visual, auditory, kinesthetic, and fine motor dimensions to the literacy experience. It also allows us to explore the science of sound, the way we hear, and deaf culture; appreciate the accomplishments and challenges of people who are deaf; and explore another dimension of diversity that goes beyond ethnicity.

There is so much beyond academics that can be learned through our efforts to teach children history, literacy, and language development. Through the careful preparation of historical stories, children can be given a sense of cultural, family, and/or national pride. This can thereby lift their self-esteem, which is so necessary for success in life, however one defines success. In the interest of developing the whole child, they can be taught from an early age the importance of seeing history as honestly as possible. This will help them to realize that we can learn from events or activities that make us proud and also those that brought us shame. They can, therefore, be taught to celebrate their own personal accomplishments and also be open to learning from their mistakes. These stories can allow children to celebrate the glory of civilizations that demonstrated their ability to live together in peace. From these stories, children can learn to consider intelligent, creative ways of approaching problems. They also provide examples of strength in the face of adversity. Children can learn how there are people who, despite their circumstances, know how to find a bit of joy in life, engaging the healing powers of music, story, and laughter. They can also learn that one of the greatest gifts is to be able to tell one's own story.

There is an African proverb that states, "Until lions have their own historians, the story of the hunt will always glorify the hunter." By presenting history through the power of story, children can be taught to know and honor who they are and be inspired to move toward their full potential.

Activity

Ask the students what they might see outside that lets them know when it is all right to cross the street and when they must wait. Once they are prompted to respond with "a traffic light," ask them if they know who made the first traffic light. Once you tell them his name, ask the students if they think he was a Chinese American, a European or white American, or an African American (any combination of choices may be used *and varied*). Then explain to the students that Garret Morgan was a great black man, an African American.

Prompt the students to recall the colors used in traffic lights and what each color represents. Continue the conversation by asking where one might see a traffic light, why they think it is important that we have traffic lights, and what could possibly happen if we did not have them. Tell them that people now use this genius's traffic lights all over the world.

The presenter (teacher/parent/storyteller) should now tell or read the story of "Garret Morgan: The Traffic Light Genius," an original poem.

"Garrett Morgan: The Traffic Light Genius"

There was a man who was thinking one day,
"There are so many cars all down the way and,
Hey! That guy almost *hit* someone!
The children can't even safely have fun."
That man said, "I've got to *do* something here!"
So, he made something wonderful that got him a cheer!

He made a traffic light of red, yellow, and green.
It was the greatest thing anyone had seen!
The yellow says, "Get ready to *please* slow down."
The red says, "**Stop!**" But don't wear a frown because
Green says, "You can go again and cross the street.
But *do* be careful and use walking feet!"

That man was Garrett Morgan, a great Black man.
I wish I could have met him; I'd like to shake his hand!

So, now we cross safely to the other side
and we sing to Garrett Morgan our song with pride
and it goes like this . . .

© by Mama Edie Armstrong

(This tribute to Garrett Morgan can be recited using American Sign Language and voice.)

When the story is completed, prompt the students to recall the sequential elements of the story and allow them to ask questions. Encourage them to answer one another's questions. Students often like to "show" what they know. In this way, they will come to appreciate that at times they too can be a teacher. The students should then be directed to learn the accompanying song, "Song in Tribute to Garrett Morgan," done in a call-and-response style.

Assessment

Research basic information about the science of sound, the way we hear, and causes that contribute to one losing the ability to hear, especially the frequent bombardment of loud music, and share this information with the

Song in Tribute to Garrett Morgan

Go, stop! Look both ways.
Go, stop! Look both ways.
Go, stop! Look both ways.
Garrett Morgan made the traffic light.

Be careful when you cross the street.
Be careful and use walking feet.
Go, stop! Look both ways.
Garrett Morgan made the traffic light.

Garrett Morgan made the traffic *light!!!*

© by Mama Edie Armstrong

students. After a brief discussion as to why signals are important, talk about people who can see but cannot hear.

An optional activity would be to learn the song in a blend of American Sign Language and voice. This can lead to conversations about safety regarding people who have physical challenges (blindness, deafness, mobility limitations, etc.), and the need for us to take care of each other, despite the nature of our differences.

CHAPTER FOUR

Elementary Grades

IMAGINATION AND COMMUNITY
Jim May

Some thirty years ago, I taught a fifth-grade, self-contained classroom in a small, neighborhood elementary school in Woodstock, Illinois.

I sat at my desk on an early Tuesday morning after a three-day weekend in the silence of the empty school building taking slow breaths punctuated by the clanking of the boiler, the sudden tick of the minute hand on the wall clock, and the distant sound of the custodian slamming a door. In due time, the bell would ring, the school's outside doors would open like floodgates, and I would hear a rumbling on the stairs, signaling the ascent of my small hoard of learners, intent on living their days with gusto and earnest anticipation. What would I have for them today?

Though I had taught elementary school for some ten years, I had never gotten over the little chunk of terror that crept up in the early morning before the school day began; that little voice that whined, "What am I going to do today?" It is a truism and part of the essential mythology ("sacred beliefs") of any civilized country that education is the "key to success"; a good school and a gifted teacher are the great equalizers—able to help children better themselves and their families. Good schools and teachers are the key to any society's social mobility. It was up to me, then, and was my professional duty each school day to fulfill the truth of this mythic purpose amid the chaos, clutter, interpersonal conflicts, and serendipity that is the normal terrain when any group of twenty-five ten-year-olds, or any group of humans for that matter, is confined together in a small physical space in a competitive atmosphere and routinized, scheduled structure, five days a week, thirty-nine weeks a year.

It was for these altruistic reasons, and as a practical matter of survival and sanity, that I was on the constant lookout for interesting activities and ideas to keep my students engaged. I had noticed that they needed something to hold their interest in books and language beyond worksheets and reading "seat work" extolling the virtues of finding the "main idea" and using prefixes and suffixes.

In fact, I was distressed that, as far as my students were concerned, reading class was often the least popular of all the subjects that I taught, more than likely owing to our basal reader approach to reading. Using the basal reading text, it emphasized breaking down the reading process into a myriad of individual skills and provided volumes of worksheets for each of those skills. As a result, my reading teachers' edition resembled a law school text in terms of its sheer mass and fine print.

The cherubic, eager-for-knowledge faces of my fifth graders would sometimes haunt me in my sleep. Would I live up to what they expected and deserved from me?

The one literary aspect of our day that everyone did enjoy, teacher included, was our curriculum-mandated read-aloud time. I would read from a favorite book: *My Side of the Mountain, Where the Red Fern Grows, Bridge to Terabithia*, and others. My students would listen in serene repose, taking in the images and narrative. I'd feel satisfied: the room was quiet, the story the main focus of the moment—language as king. If nothing else worked that day, I would still feel that something was accomplished.

Mondays or Tuesdays after a three-day weekend were the hardest. But this day was different. On this particular October morning, I at least knew what I was going to do. I just didn't know if it would work. I was going to tell them a story that I had learned over the weekend. I was not going to read it out of a book.

As my students arrived that morning, I was still in the glow of a weekend spent at the National Storytelling Festival, surrounded by the tall, green mountains of eastern Tennessee. The little town of Jonesborough was filled with tents; the tents were filled with stories. That weekend I had listened to stories that fit my ear like easy melodies rising out of the hollows and streambeds.

The enduring and ancient beauty of that landscape seemed to be caught in those narratives, many of which were told by mountain people whose entire experience was shaped by a way of life rich in lore and tradition however hardscrabble the economy and few the material rewards. The stories, many from old folkloric traditions that had come across the Atlantic Ocean with the Scots, Irish, English, and German settlers of the Appalachians, contained the same depictions of the rural struggle for survival that I had seen played out among the tenant farmers and small-town characters of my own youth. I sat listening and thinking how much my late father would have enjoyed the tales.

In one particular tent, I had heard Jackie Torrence, an African American woman from Salisbury, North Carolina, tell a story called "Soldier Jack."

Jack, the trickster hero of the European and American folk cycle of Jack Tales, had quit the king's army because he was tired of "fightin' people he didn't even know just because the king was mad at them." Jack, the proverbial underdog and champion of the "little guy," was loose, on the road, and off to "seek his fortune" in those smoky mountains, just as he had been in the highlands of Scotland or the shadowy Black Forest of Germany.

I learned the story from a tape I made while sitting in the audience (the National Storytelling Festival allowed audiences to record in those days) and listened to it over and over as I drove back to Woodstock.

I told the story to my students first thing that Tuesday morning, once we had milk, lunch count, and the pledge behind us. As I was telling the story, I thought I sensed a look in many of my students' eyes that seemed to say, "This guy is a lot more interesting than he was Friday afternoon. I wonder what happened to him over the weekend?"

For my part, in ten years of teaching, I had never experienced the kind of intense listening and focus that my students were able to achieve during that twenty-minute story. Our roles as teacher and students seemed to fade into the background. We attained a kind of peerage, a unity of purpose; we became a community of listeners watching this character, Jack, who represented all of us, as he worked out the exciting, sometimes dangerous, but ultimately rewarding details of his life's adventure. Like pilgrims on the way to Canterbury, we shared a journey together: Jack's struggles, his heroism, and his success through his own guile and cleverness drew us into our own lives and concerns, and somehow, into the pleasure of each other's company. Consequently, I began learning and telling stories to my students at every opportunity.

In addition to the joy and focus my students found in the stories, storytelling became a kind of "classroom survival kit." Often, when things would be "going bad," the classroom in a tumult, teacher and students impatient and cranky, I would say, "Put your books away and clear your desk; I'm going to tell you a story." And, without fail, after a story, we would all tend to be civil with each other again, at least for awhile.

Six years after that October morning, I left teaching and have been a full-time professional storyteller for some twenty-three years. I have visited hundreds of schools and have experienced this same intensity, interest, and sense of community virtually every time I tell stories.

I have also found that there is professional literature that supports and expands upon my own observations, particularly regarding the intensity with which my students were able to focus on a narrative without visual aids or a screen of any kind.

In a 1992 article in *Parabola* magazine, Joseph Chilton Pearce cited studies compiled by Dr. Keith Buzzell, Jerry Mander, Mary Jane Healy, and others that claim "the damage of television has little to do with content but rather with the pairing of imagery in synch with sound. This provides a synthetic counterfeit of what the brain itself is supposed to produce in response to language as in *storytelling*. The child's mind becomes habituated to such sound-images, and the higher cortical structures simply shut down.

"The brain uses the same neural structures every time the TV comes on, and very few of the higher structures are developed. They simply lie dormant, and no capacity for creating internal imagery develops."

Conversely, according to Chilton Pearce, when the brain receives language without images, the brain, specifically the cerebral cortex (the area of the brain controlling most higher neural functions), creates new neural cells and pathways in order to comprehend the story. The brain actually grows! This is an *active* process—note the facial expressions of someone listening to an interesting story versus the glazed stare of a TV viewer. The TV (and DVD and computer screen) seems to present a counterfeit image of what the brain naturally creates, given the stimulation of language without images.

The images created in the students' brains, are, by their very nature, more satisfying and engaging than images created from outside because the images are unique, one-of-a-kind, and based on the experiences and creativity of the listener: "The movie was OK, but not as good as the book." A second grader once approached me after a storytelling session and said, "Thanks for the movies." His gratitude was dead serious; he had, of course, imagined his own movies.

So allowing students to hear stories without pictures is critically important, but I wondered over the years, what, if any, distinction there might be between storytelling and the read-aloud sessions my students and I so enjoyed in my fifth-grade classroom. If reading aloud accomplished everything that storytelling did, then why was I taking the time to learn stories "by heart," and what is the purpose and meaning of my full-time profession?

The similarities between read-aloud sessions and storytelling are obvious and yet, after having read aloud for hundreds of hours, I knew something was different about my storytelling; something in the students' response was unique; something "in the air" shifted when I told a story. But what was "in the air?"

I believe I found my answer, appropriately enough, while working with elders. Some years ago, I participated in an intergenerational literacy project sponsored by the Illinois Department on Aging. In this project, community elders were brought into the school to listen to children read. I was brought into the classroom to tell them stories.

One of the assumptions of the project was that children learn best when that learning involves a positive human relationship, a human connection! This immediately made sense to me. Two of the passions that have brought joy and satisfaction to my life are storytelling and birding (bird watching). Both of these were learned at the side of a very affectionate and patient father. He was a farmer and a collector of wild asparagus, hickory nuts, and jokes and stories. He was an avid observer of animals, nature, and the characters that populated our small farming community. In his loving presence, my mind opened to stories and nature. The neural framework, then, was set and ready to go years later, when becoming a storyteller and learning to find and identify hundreds of birds seemed joyful and fluid, rather than an academic task. At the foundation of these two activities, I believe, lies the relationship with my father.

Indeed, a relationship is built when a storyteller looks the listener in the eye. With each telling, the story is born anew for the particular listener at a particular time and place. A storytelling friend of mine began telling to her grandchildren, and of course, they responded with great enthusiasm. When my friend's kindergartner began school, and her teacher picked up a picture book for "story hour," the young one questioned, "Aren't you going to tell stories out of your head like Grandma Jo?" The little girl wanted to commune; she did not want the third party (book) interfering in the experience she had shared with her grandmother; she wanted the direct intimacy, the real thing, the relationship.

It seems imperative that this twenty-first century is one that will require a unified effort among humans the world over to forge a sustainable relationship with the planet and with one another. If we are to nurture the Earth and all human beings, we will have to imagine new solutions and strategies for agriculture, peace, and the creation of a global community. Albert Einstein claimed that imagination was more important than knowledge. Graham Greene, the English novelist, asserted that hatred is a failure of the imagination. With individuals, groups, and whole societies turning attention toward going "green," what better "garden" for the imagination than storytelling?

Bibliography

- Chase, Richard. *Jack Tales*. Boston, MA: Houghton Mifflin, 1943, 1971.
- McCarthy, William B., and Joseph Sobol, eds. *Jack in Two Worlds: Contemporary North American Tales and Their Tellers*. Chapel Hill, NC: University of North Carolina Press, 1994.
- Pearce, Joseph Chilton. "The Risk of Evolution," an interview with *Parabola*, Summer 1992, 54–60.

The following two articles are featured together because they demonstrate how a teller and teachers can collaborate for children's understanding. Both teller and teacher have important things to say and skills that encourage children's understanding of the possibilities of the oral tradition and the literate tradition. The resulting children's work samples are found in the teacher's article. The authors genuinely thank these teachers and tellers for this fine collaborative work.

THE PIPELINE BLUES: CRAFTING AN HISTORICAL STORY OF INDIRECT PERSUASIVENESS AND CITENZENSHIP

Beth Horner

Speaking, Listening, Reading, Writing, and Information Literacy

National Standards

NCTE: 3, 4, 5, 6, 11; AASL 1: Learners use skills, resources, and tools to inquire, think critically, and gain knowledge; AASL 2: Learners use skills, resources, and tools to draw conclusions, make informed decisions, apply knowledge to new situations, and create new knowledge; AASL 3: Learners use skills, resources, and tools to share knowledge and participate ethically and productively as members of our democratic society; AASL 4: Learners use skills, resources, and tools to pursue personal and aesthetic growth.

Objectives

The school hired Beth to bring the story as well as her back work in crafting the story to the fifth grade; when children understand the process of the art, they can more easily access the art form. Beth as the artist was compelled to create the story!

Materials and Resources

- Horner, Beth. *The Pipeline Blues*. CD. http://www.BethHorner.com, 2001.
- Horner, Beth. "The Pipeline Blues: A Tale of Environmental Triumph" in *The Scenic Route: Stories from the Heartland*. Indianapolis, IN: Indiana Historic Society Press, 2007.
- Wheeler, Jerome. "The Pipeline Blues" on *River Cowboys* by Jerome Wheeler Friends (CD). Columbia, MO: Blue Coaster Records, 2006.

The Artist's Plan

The backstory, metacognition!

There's just something about a song or story
that brings things into focus a whole lot sharper
than any stack of statistics.

—Jerome Wheeler

"The Pipeline Blues" is a story of indirect persuasiveness, citizenship, humor, sewage, an historical event in my own hometown, and of a song that galvanized a community and brought about change in environmental policy.

Inspiration

I was immediately struck by Jerome Wheeler's song "The Pipeline Blues" when I first heard it in 1999. Like any piece of effective art, it empowered me and affected me emotionally. I could relate to the memorably described characters and their journey. Instead of a pedantic, heavy-handed style, information was presented in a humorous way that allowed for my own thoughts on the problem. And the images were vivid. For example:

The next time you flush your stool,
Be thinking of us Boone County fools
Who have to drink downstream from our latrine.
Now, Columbia's got a sewer to the ocean,
Full of do-do-do-do-do-do-do.

I was smitten with the idea of creating a story about the song, written in 1988, the events that inspired it and its effect on a community.

Research

Not living in Columbia in 1988, I was only vaguely aware of the events surrounding the song. So I thoroughly researched the local newspaper archives and interviewed the journalists, politicians, community members, and people prominently mentioned in the articles. My interviews with Jerome Wheeler were invaluable for final fact checking and particularly in adding "color" to the story.

Crafting a Story: Guiding Principals

As I began to craft "The Pipeline Blues," I kept in mind my own six guiding principals:

- I tell stories in order to entertain, educate, and empower.
- I bring true stories of our past to life in order to better understand our present and to better inform and shape our future.

- Identification with a main character significantly increases interest in a story.
- Every story needs an element of suspense to keep the listener engaged and desirous of continuing to journey with the main character to the story's conclusion.
- Vivid characters and images are the colors that bring stories to life.
- Any story of an actual event must be written so that it becomes an experience universal to all listeners and one that impacts their current life experiences.

Crafting "The Pipeline Blues": Essential Questions

Crafting a story is seldom a straightforward process. At times, I became overwhelmed with the mounds of information and interviews that I had gathered, the numbers of characters involved, and the legal, political, and scientific aspects of the story. Over eight months, I created six versions of the story with different emphases and from different perspectives. Because I work orally rather than on paper, I recorded my thoughts and versions on audio recordings. I then ran each version by objective colleagues for creative input and by those I had interviewed for checks on my facts and interpretation of events.

During this process, I slowly crafted the final story by continually keeping my guiding principals in mind and by repeatedly asking myself the following questions:

1. Why do I want to tell this particular story?

   I decided that I wanted to document this event because I have passion for environmental issues and was proud of my hometown's actions. Even more, I wanted to illustrate the powerful effect of one person speaking out, of creative problem solving, and of artistic expression. I wanted to tell the story to inspire those working against overwhelming odds and to encourage proactivity. I also wanted to share my delight in Jerome's ingenious, humorous song.

2. Of the many stories and sub-stories within this one event and of their relation to several larger issues, on which specific story thread do I want to focus?

   This is always the most important, most difficult question. By returning to the question of *why* I wanted to tell the story, I was finally able to narrow my focus and settle on the specific story: the story of my hometown that developed a dangerous problem because it had grown too quickly without proper planning, of a citizen who took note of an illegal and unethical environmental policy and came up with an innovative solution (wetlands sewage treatment), and of a song that inspired a citizenry to open its eyes, fight city and state financial and legal powers, and create a precedent-setting change in public environmental policy.

   I could now answer other essential questions.

3. Who are the primary and secondary characters?

   Immediately, I decided that the town itself was a character—with strong points, flaws, needs, and desires. I then selected three very colorful, very different protagonists: Doug Elley (who first noticed the problem, persisted in bringing it before the city council, and suggested the wetlands sewage system), Tracy Barnett (the author of unceasing and pointed newspaper articles), and

Jerome Wheeler (a songwriter whose song galvanized the community). For antagonists, I selected the city council members and engineers who put financial concerns above the environment and public health.

4. How can I make this story of a specific event in a specific place into a story of characters and actions with which anyone could relate—a story of universal experience?

The overall theme of environmental safety is already uppermost in the national political scene. To bring it to a personal level, I brought out smaller themes existing in all people's lives: a problem sneaking up on you while you are just trying to keep up with day-to-day life, suddenly realizing that those in power have made decisions that might negatively impact you, continually having to consider all decisions in relation to financial costs, admitting wrong decisions, and deciding whether or not to stand up for your beliefs no matter the personal time or money involved.

5. What are the important episodes that move the plot along?

Which specific events should I put in or leave out? What are the small moments behind the big moments? There were so many episodes within this one event that it was difficult to decide which episodes to select to move the story forward. First, I outlined how the town's problem developed, the characters who discovered the problem, the obstacles they had to overcome to solve it, and the eventual victorious resolution. Second, after determining my main purpose for telling the story (question 1), the specific thread I would follow (question 2), and the main characters (question 3), I removed all episodes and characters that did not directly relate to or support them. Therefore, I had to edit Jerome's song to reflect my editing of the larger story. Third, I highlighted the smaller moments in each episode that I selected for inclusion, focusing intently on the actions and thoughts of my main characters—as if I was momentarily looking at them through a magnifying glass in slow motion.

6. Through whose voice should the story be told?

To tie the listener directly to the characters in Columbia, I decided to introduce the story through my own eyes, a person who had grown up in Columbia in the 1950s, 1960s, and 1970s. I selected specific and colorful examples from my own experience of how gradually, and without most people realizing it, my town grew beyond the capacity of its sewage treatment system. Beginning the story in the first person made the action immediate and real rather than something that happened in some unknown place to some unknown people.

7. To whom would I be telling the story?

One must consider the background and experience that the listener brings to the story. I initially created "The Pipeline Blues" for adult audiences in the United States with an exposition and plot that assumed an understanding of sewage treatment and a specific political process. When I told the story to fifth graders at Baker Demonstration School, I introduced sewage treatment through a young person's eye. I took students through my own early childhood experience with sewage management, which changed as my family progressed from an outhouse to indoor plumbing that emptied into a field to our eventual move into Columbia, where our sewage was added to thousands of other people's sewage. I also added brief details about the political process.

8. How do I structure the story?

Because the story is partially about a song, I decided to employ music as a structural device. I highlighted an edited version of Jerome Wheeler's song in the middle of the story. I then framed the story by beginning and ending with music.

The story begins:

This is a story about a town like so many towns all around
That grew til it was bursting at the seams.
This is a story about my hometown that went one way, then turned
around and said,
"Show me a better way to be."
AND, this is a story about a song, written, sung,
came along and totally changed the scene.
Do-Do-Do-Do-Do-Do-Do-Do-Do

The story ends:

Now Columbia's got a newer sort of notion
Of what to do 'bout their do-do-do-do.

To keep the listener engaged from start to finish, I maintained a thread of tension throughout. Rather than introducing all facets of the primary problem at the beginning of the story, I designed it so that just as the main characters meet one challenge, an additional obstacle is revealed. This constant slight suspense keeps the listener wondering if the protagonists will ever fully overcome the problem and makes the final resolution even sweeter.

9. What style and tone should I employ?

I decided to echo the style and tone of Jerome's song. I felt that listeners would stay more engaged and hear this particular material more fully if it was presented in an inviting, inclusive, humorous, and indirectly persuasive style. Rather than feeling lectured, scolded, or defensive, the listener would enjoy the story and listen with an open heart and mind. Thus, the story would provide a more empowering experience.

10. Color: How do I make each character and moment come alive?

After making all of the above decisions and determining that I had all the components of the story the way I wanted them, I went back over the story with a fine-toothed comb and "colorized" it with more vivid imagery, character description, humor, and detail.

For example, I changed my introduction of protagonist Doug Elley as "an old hippie" to the following: *A quiet, unassuming man with longish, graying hair and wire-rimmed glasses stood up. Eyeing him across the room, several of the city council members had the sneaking suspicion that this was a guy who lived some sort of progressive-alternative lifestyle. And, more than one of them feared that underneath his suit jacket and white shirt, there lurked a tie-dyed T-shirt—but not one that had been purchased recently. In other words, he looked like an old hippie. Well . . . he WAS an old hippie.* "Colorizing" the story is like putting icing on a cake. It adds deliciousness to substance, bringing out the flavor.

Permissions and Legalities

When telling a story of an actual event, one must double-check all facts and take extra steps. For legal and ethical reasons, I contacted each character in the story and obtained verbal permission for my characterization of them (even the antagonists). In addition, I gained permission from Jerome Wheeler to use his song and edit it as needed. Finally, I contacted an attorney to ensure that I was in no way slandering any individual, organization, or corporation mentioned in the story.

Epilogue

Since 2001, my story about Jerome's song and its impact on Columbia, Missouri, has gone on to inspire public policy and environmental action in other communities. Indeed, Jerome's indirectly persuasive song and the subsequent story have been much more effective than any stack of statistics could possibly be!

PERSUASIVE WRITING: MOVING BEYOND THE FIVE-PARAGRAPH ESSAY
Jackie Downey and Juli Ross
Speaking, Listening, Reading, Writing, Visual Literacy, and Information Literacy

National Standards

NCTE: 4, 5, 6, 7, 8, 9, 11, 12; AASL 1: Learners use skills, resources, and tools to inquire, think critically, and gain knowledge; AASL 2: Learners use skills, resources, and tools to draw conclusions, make informed decisions, apply knowledge to new situations, and create new knowledge; AASL 3: Learners use skills, resources, and tools to share knowledge and participate ethically and productively as members of our democratic society; AASL 4: Learners use skills, resources, and tools to pursue personal and aesthetic growth.

Objectives

After listening to *The Pipeline Blues* by storyteller Beth Horner, students will use spoken, written, and visual skills to persuade an audience.

Materials

• Horner, Beth. *The Pipeline Blues*. CD. http://www.BethHorner.com, 2001.
• CD player

- Materials for final representation (poster board, computer access, guitars, and more standard materials)

Instructional Plan

This collaborative project began with a meeting between storyteller Beth Horner and the classroom teachers. The three of us emphasized the importance of this first meeting because an open dialogue between the storyteller and the teacher is critical in setting the stage for the students. The purpose of this meeting was to develop a common language and understanding of 1) What it means to persuade, and 2) the audience (fifth-grade students Beth was addressing as well as the audience[s] the students would choose to persuade).

As a result of this meeting, we agreed to prepare the students in the classroom for Beth's story *The Pipeline Blues* by researching and sharing current environmental issues happening around the globe. We also agreed that we would integrate the geography of the area in our classrooms by locating and discussing the Missouri River in Boone County, Missouri. Finally, using Jerome Wheeler's song as an authentic form of persuasion, we felt strongly that the students should have the flexibility of choosing their method/style of persuasion.

We were able to give Beth the information she needed about our students in order to adapt her story for fifth graders. One of her goals was to have the students be able to relate and identify with the main character. The image of a "hippie" for a main character was established. This image, along with the topic of sewage, and the inclusion of a catchy song with the word "do-do" was sure to captivate our fifth graders' attention!

What We Did

We began this project with a visit from storyteller Beth Horner. She shared *The Pipeline Blues*, an entertaining yet inspirational story of how one man galvanized a community, and how his commitment to the environment led to an innovative way to deal with a common problem, sewage. The story ended with Jerome Wheeler's song, culminating with the line "The Talkin' Columbia Wetlands Project: Do-Do-Do-Do-Do-Do." At first, the students were singing the song for the mere silliness of it, but after some discussion, both with Beth Horner and after her visit, the students began to understand the persuasive nature of the song, how it made them feel, and the concept that the songwriter had used his voice to be an agent of change. Expanding on the idea, we asked our students to choose an environmental issue they felt passionate about changing and then explored the idea that they could use their own voices to be agents of change for their selected issues.

The next day we spent a good deal of our language arts block discussing what it means to persuade. Our students shared some wonderful real-life examples, such as commercials that during their favorite shows try to get them to buy a product, or the tactics they use on their parents and babysitters to get to stay up late. Connecting their real-life experiences to Beth's story, we discussed the idea that there are more ways to persuade an audience than writing a traditional five-paragraph essay. Most of our students had experience with persuasive writing in previous grades and for the most part had all written a persuasive essay at one time or another. While we gave the students the option to write an essay, we challenged and encouraged them to try a new method to persuade their audience with an alternative end product. Together we brainstormed a list of possible ways the students could persuade their audience: a poster, a PowerPoint presentation, a podcast, a fiction or nonfiction story, a song, a rap, a letter, an essay, etc. (bumper sticker, movie, flyer, or public service announcement).

Excited by the challenge of trying something different, our students dove into their projects. From the beginning we felt that it was essential that students select their own topic and although we offered the option of alternatives, most of our students chose a topic related to improving the environment or promoting environmental awareness. We took time during this initial phase to introduce the idea of writing to your audience, returning to this theme throughout the process. We actively encouraged our students to keep their topic, audience, and method of presentation fluid and flexible until they had done their research. This brought a reflectiveness to our students' projects. For example, before doing any research, Graham decided that he was going to write a rap for his peers about the effect plastic bags have on the environment. During his pre-writing conference, we asked him to focus on the tone of his piece and the language he would use when writing to his peers. To illustrate, we connected it back to Beth Horner's experience of changing her original story to appeal to a fifth-grade audience. Graham decided on funny and casual. Later, after he did some research, he decided that he could be more persuasive and create more change if he wrote a letter to the CEO of Dominick's Foods trying to persuade the company to stop supplying plastic bags to their customers. Other students modified their topics when, during the research phase, they found them to be too broad or too narrow. Giving students the opportunity to modify their paths, even late in the writing process, we were able to capture their passion and creativity.

Next we turned to the ReadWriteThink program for use in organizing the students' thinking and work. The persuasive strategy definitions worksheet served as a teaching tool and graphic organizer. We introduced the terms: claim, logos, pathos, ethos, and kairos, and modeled how to gather and organize the information. Then we let the students go to work. Many were interested in the topic of global warming. As they researched and gathered facts, it became evident that global warming was too broad to use to

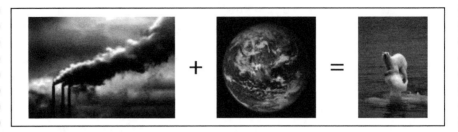

Figure 4.1. Cole's persuasive bumper sticker.

persuade an audience. Thus, the students utilized that topic and narrowed their focus to issues such as car emissions, energy and lightbulb use, and waste.

Students had the most difficulty working with pathos and ethos. Searching images on the Internet provided powerful emotional responses and served as a breakthrough for two students. Cole is a student with special learning needs. He has difficulty expressing himself in written language but has a global way of thinking and synthesizing. He decided he would like to make a bumper sticker as his project. He determined his message would reach a great number of people with this medium. We conferenced about what types of bumper stickers exist and the different messages we have seen. Cole's idea was to make a mathematical equation using images. Image one plus image two equals image three. This real-life application of persuasion was a result of the openness and flexibility of the project.

As students were completing their persuasive strategy definitions sheet, we had a discussion about assessment. Using the models of *authentic assessment*, popularized by Grant Wiggins (1989), and *performance assessment*, written about by Robert J. Marzano, Debra Pickering, and Jay McTighe, we decided to write a rubric together based on the ReadWrite-Think program. We asked the students to identify the most important components of the project, urging them to use the persuasive strategy definitions worksheet. We had a blank graphic organizer on the overhead, and as the students made suggestions, we filled in the categories to be assessed. We all agreed that the main point was critical and should be clear and concise. Next, students suggested that each category on the worksheet be transferred to the rubric. Caleb noticed overlap and made a case for a research category that encompassed research, logos, and big names. At this stage in the discussion, we pointed out to the students that the categories for the rubric be assessable. We asked how we would be able to identify if someone were persuasive or not and the components of a powerful and effective persuasive project. The remaining categories were urgency, appearance, and an overall section that we suggested as a way to evaluate if the project and the message were a good fit. Teachers and students used this rubric to assess the projects.

KELSEY'S PLASTIC BAG SONG

To the tune of: "Hey There Delilah"
By: Plain White Ts

Hey there Evanston, did you know that we use too many
Plastic bags, and it's really bad for the earth
Yes it is
You know that it's very true
Oh yes it's true

Will you help me?
To save the earth
Will you help me?
To stop global warming
Please help me!
By using plastic bags you kill
Harmless little animals, that don't know
What it is till it's too late then they die!
If you knew this you would cry
Oh yes you cry ☹ ☹ ☹

Will you help me?
To save the earth
Will you help me?
To stop global warming
Please help me!

Hey there Evanston, too many plastic bags
Get dumped into landfills everyday and it's not good, not good
About 4,800,000 a day and that's a lot!

Will you help me?
To save the earth
Will you help me?
To stop global warming
Please help me!

The End ☺
By: Kelsey Siegel

By Rachel Kornbluh

Global Warming: Cars

"The warnings about global warming have been extremely clear for a long time. We are facing a global climate crisis. It is deepening. We are entering a period of consequences.

-Al Gore

What are the consequences of global warming?

- Sea levels will rise and flood coastal areas
- Heat waves will happen more often, and will be more intense
- Droughts and wild fires will occur more
- There will be more mosquitoes carrying disease
- Species will go extinct

Why *should* we stop global warming with cars?

- If we drive less, we can save money on gas
- If all of the ice melts, all of Manhattan will go under water
- If we can stop global warming, we can save future lives.

What Is Global Warming?

Global warming is a time when the earth gets really hot. It's caused when a lot of carbon dioxide, from things like cars, get stuck in the world. The carbon dioxide absorbs lot's of the sunlight and starts heating up the world.

It's also caused when all of the carbon dioxide starts making a hole in the ozone layer.

We have too much of the carbon dioxide and if we keep up all of the driving and other things, we could have serious consequences . We could end up dying.

These Polar bears are suffering from global warming. On May 15, 2008 Polar bears went on the endangered list.

All of the artic ice is melting and by 2040, the polar bears may be ice-less.

How can we stop global warming with cars?

We can stop global warming massively with cars. Or more without them. If we stop using cars as much and every- one takes a bus, we would make a *huge* difference. Other good ways to stop are to walk or ride your bike to all of the close places. If we all work together, we can save the earth!

Figure 4.2. Rachel's persuasive flyer.

STORY SCAVENGER HUNTS
Mary Hamilton
Speaking and Listening

National Standards

NCTE: 11, 12.

Objectives

Students will tell and listen to stories relevant to curricular material, adjusting their vocabulary, body language, and other means of oral expression to effectively communicate with their listener and develop a community of inquiry.

Materials

Story prompts, see below

Instructional Plan

Take your students or workshop participants on a story scavenger hunt. How? You provide a list of story prompts, then invite participants to gather stories from each other.

Story scavenger hunts are a strategy my colleague Cynthia Changaris and I have been using for years. We especially like it as an opening activity for workshops and other instructional settings. People have a reason to talk with each other by playing the story scavenger hunt game. By telling and listening to each other, they begin building a community together.

Just as ordinary scavenger hunts contain a list of things to be found, our story scavenger hunts contain a list of stories to gather from others. Our lists are always headed by the instruction: find someone who will tell you, followed by a list of story possibilities. We also include the following advice: when you are asked by someone else to tell a story, tell only what you are willing to share. We include this advice because Cynthia and I know stories can be very personal. While we do want to build community, we do not want to make folks uncomfortable by invading their privacy.

Just like ordinary scavenger hunts, the list of stories to scavenge can be tweaked depending on the reason participants are gathered. When we've led workshops for teachers, we've included, "about a shining moment in their life as a teacher" and "about something he/she wishes someone had told them before they began teaching." With storytellers, we've included, "about their earliest memory of hearing a story" and "what happened to the first two pigs in 'The Three Little Pigs.'"

Story Scavenger Hunts Go to School

Teachers could use the story scavenger hunt strategy to begin the school year, especially in grades where students could be expected to be able to read the prompts either independently or with the help of a partner. I've been thinking lately about the types of prompts that would have students talking about their ordinary experiences that put into practice the everyday relevance of particular subjects. Here are some story prompts I've developed. I've arranged the ideas by subject application. You'll notice I have not listed language arts as a subject. All this talking and listing is language arts. Some prompts will elicit a narrative. Some will elicit descriptions. Some may elicit both. So, language arts all the way through! Math teachers, I have also not listed math separately because every math prompt I thought of also fit with other subjects, so look for "and math" repeatedly in the lists below.

Although this list provides lots of possibilities, I think five to seven prompts are enough for a typical story scavenger hunt. After all, you want everyone to talk and listen, not race around barely attending to one another.

Find Someone Who Will Tell You

Learn the details. Why was this happening? Who else was involved, if anyone? Why do they remember it? How do they feel about it now?

Science

- About a storm they will never forget
- About the strangest place they've ever seen grass growing
- About a time they sat in a tree for a long time
- About a time they were involved in growing something
- About an unforgettable outdoor walk
- About a time they smelled an unusual odor and how they finally figured out what it was
- About a time when they heard an unusual sound and how they finally figured out what it was

Science and Math

- About a collection they have and how they organize it

Social Studies

- About a time they got to vote
- About something that happened before they were born and how they learned about it
- Tell about a relative or friend who lives in another country
- Their three "rules" for using a cell phone and why they follow these rules
- How to say hello in three languages and how they learned to do this

- About a time they got into trouble for something they did not do
- About a time they should have gotten into trouble but didn't

Social Studies and Math

- About a time when they used a map
- About a time they had to figure out how to share something fairly
- About a time when arriving too late or too early caused a problem
- How to handle the situation when dividing teams and one person is left over (Math? They are handling a remainder. Social studies? Issues of fairness.)

Arts and Humanities

- What their favorite CD art looks like and why it is their favorite CD art
- About the ugliest object they've ever seen
- About their favorite photograph—it can be of them or someone else, but they need to describe it and tell you why they like it
- About their earliest memory of dancing
- About an object they love to look at and why they love to look at it
- About their favorite game of pretend when they were younger

Arts and Science

- About the best sunrise or sunset they've ever seen

Arts and Math

- About the most beautiful building they've ever seen.
- About a time when they folded paper to make something. (Math? Both of the above prompts can be related to geometry.)

Arts and Social Studies

- About a time they wore a costume—Why did they wear it? Did they want to wear it? What did it look like? (Why social studies? This could be a cultural or religious event that called for a costume—not special occasion clothing or an outfit worn for ritual purposes and not referred to as a costume.)

Practical Living and Math

- About a time they saved up to buy something

Practical Living and Social Studies

- About a time they dressed up for a special occasion—What was the occasion? Did they want to dress up? What did they wear? (Why social studies? Sometimes people dress up, but not in what the individual would call a "costume" for some cultural or religious events. Why practical living? It's worth being aware of different ways of dressing for different situations.)

- About a time when a misunderstanding caused a problem.

Practical Living, Physical Education, and Social Studies

- About the first time they were ever on a team (Did they have fun? What sort of team was it? What did the team do together?)

Physical Education and Social Studies

- About a time someone taught them how to play a game (Why social studies? Folklore—handing down of a game.)

Any and Every Subject Area!

- About a time when following directions would have made everything easier

Assessment

Look for students' ability to mingle appropriately with each other, their ability to express themselves orally (so respond with appropriate stories), and their ability to listen to others appropriately.

STUDENT STORYTELLING IN THE CLASSROOM AND BEYOND

Sue Black and Beverly Frett

Speaking, Listening, Reading, and Information Literacy

National Standards

NCTE: 1, 3, 4, 7, 11, 12; ACS 5: Students will demonstrate the ability to use interpersonal communication skills to enhance health, distinguish between verbal and non-verbal communication, and demonstrate attentive listening skills to build and maintain healthy relationships; AASL 1: Learners use skills, resources, and tools to inquire, think critically, and gain knowledge; AASL 2: Learners use skills, resources, and tools to draw conclusions, make informed decisions, apply knowledge to new situations, and create new knowledge; AASL 3: Learners use skills, resources, and tools to share knowledge and participate ethically and productively as members of our democratic society; AASL 4: Learners use skills, resources, and tools to pursue personal and aesthetic growth.

Objectives

Students will select a story and learn how to tell it. Students will learn the components of effective communication: visualization, summarization, identification of emotions and mood, addition of voice and gestures, question development, and connection to real life.

Materials

- A well-stocked 398.2 section of the library
- Bibliography for this article and this book

A fifth-grade student stands in front of 100 first graders and tells a story. He takes a deep breath. He feigns pushing his sleeves up to his elbows, pulling open the mouth of the dog, and reaching down, down, down to pull out . . . a cat! *That's* why the dog had been meowing. The first graders roar with laughter.

As storytellers, students have the opportunity to do it all—read, write, listen, and speak. They have fun experimenting with voice, facial expressions, emotion, and gestures that make the story "just right" for telling. As they present their story, the art of listening becomes a two-way street. By using good eye contact and reading body language, tellers communicate with their audience. That's not all! The activities and skills that they learn will be used across the curriculum and throughout life.

Start with a Story

The storytelling lesson begins with the students listening to their teacher tell a fable. Then they form small groups to process what they heard. As the teacher asks questions about the fable, the students answer orally in their small groups: Who are the main characters in the story? What do they look like? Where did the story take place? When did the story happen? What is the problem? Why is there a problem? How does each of the main characters feel about that problem? How is the problem resolved? What happens at the beginning of the story? What happens in the middle? What happens at the end?

Each small group then retells the fable round-robin style—one sentence at a time, passing the story around the circle until it is complete. Not only do students demonstrate their understanding of the story and story structure, they also practice listening and respect for what others contribute to the story. After each small group has retold the story, they find another small group and tell it again. Students delight in the discovery that stories change with each telling. Their homework? Tell the story again to someone at home.

Read! Read! Read!

Now that your students are excited, it's time for them to discover the 398.2 section in the library—folktales, fairy tales, legends, tall tales, and fables. Their goal is to read at least five different stories before making a final selection. Once they choose the story they will tell, they reread the story two more times. First time: read the story out loud to determine if you like the sound of it. Second time: read the story out loud and time it. A good rule of thumb for first-time student storytellers is to choose stories that are between five and seven minutes long.

Storyboard and Tell It Ugly

Once students have read the story three to four times, it is time to close the book and draw a storyboard. Students are asked to visualize the story and draw it, complete with color. Students fold a piece of paper into six or eight squares. They draw the main scenes of the story. No word bubbles are allowed—they must use visual language only. No fancy artwork is required. They cannot copy illustrations from the book. When they are done, they find a partner and use their storyboard for their first telling. The student points to each scene on the storyboard and tells the story in his or her own words. This is the "tell it ugly" stage. This first telling won't sound pretty or polished, but it is important to just to do it. As the students move away from the text and illustrations in the book to their own images, the words they use to describe those images become their own. As they continue to work with the story, each time they tell it again, it will sound just a little less "ugly."

Bringing the Story to Life

This is where student tellers dig in and add their own personalities to the story. They are challenged to experiment with voice: high/low, fast/low, and loud/soft. Ask: What emotions are in your story—anger, heartbreak, defiance, bravado, joy, sorrow? Does your voice match the emotion you are describing? Do your facial expressions and body language communicate those emotions? Students are also challenged to accurately depict actions, for example, churning butter; they may have to find accurate information in order to convey the story more effectively.

Dialogue provides aural action in a story. Model how easy it is to convert narrative to dialogue. Ask: Where can you add dialogue to replace some of your narrative? A great exercise to give students practice with this concept is to give them a line of narrative from a familiar story and ask them to brainstorm dialogue to replace the narrative. For example: the narrative Mama Bear uses to call her family to the table for breakfast becomes "Papa! Baby Bear! Breakfast is ready." It doesn't take students long to discover how much more alive a story sounds with dialogue to move it forward. Try some of these:

- Baby Bear complained his porridge was too hot.
- Papa Bear suggested they all go for a walk.
- Goldilocks saw three bowls of porridge sitting on the table.
- Goldilocks thought the chairs looked comfy.
- The boy thought watching sheep was really boring.
- The villagers told the shepherd boy they were very angry he had tricked them.
- The boy told the villagers he really had seen a wolf.
- The soldiers came to the house and told everyone there would be a ball at the castle.
- Cinderella really wanted to go to the ball, too.
- The fairy godmother told Cinderella to dry her tears.
- The fairy godmother told Cinderella to be home by midnight.
- The prince asked Cinderella to dance.

How about gestures? Give students the opportunity to brainstorm with one another ideas for adding simple, waist-up gestures that enhance, define, or replace a word. Is there a mirror or window they can stand in front of as they practice? Encourage students to have a reason for adding a gesture and making that gesture clean—solid, simple, and definitely not sloppy.

Walk, Talk, Listen, Respond

Get moving! (This is shared with the permission of storyteller Bob Kann.) Take your storytellers for a walk. Have each student find a partner. Decide who will be the first teller and who will be the listener. As students walk the halls of your school, or around the library or gym, they practice telling their story to their partner.

Try adding a little "popcorn" to your practice sessions. Divide your storytellers into two groups, tellers and listeners. Paired and seated in chairs, each teller faces a listener. On your command, each storyteller begins telling their story. After a minute or two, call out "Popcorn!" The storytellers stop telling immediately. They pop up from where they are sitting, trade places with someone else who is standing up, and resume telling to a new partner. Repeat until all stories are complete.

Listeners have a responsibility during this part of the storytelling unit— their job is to listen for the good stuff. What's working? What was communicated well? Which facial expressions and gestures worked well? What use of voice added to the story? Only after the listening partners have offered positive feedback can they then offer one suggestion to make the story even better. They should phrase that suggestion by asking, "Have you thought about . . . ?"

Assessment

Tell . . . and tell again: At this point, students are ready to tell their stories to small groups of peers or to a younger class. How do you measure success? When students stand in front of their audience ... smiling, proud, mistakes and all ... they'll be ready for more, and so will their listeners. That's success!

Use the **S.M.I.L.E.** checklist to track student progress:

Stand tall and sound proud.

_____ Student spoke clearly.

_____ Student told with confidence.

_____ Student stood with a relaxed posture and didn't fidget too much.

_____ Student handled mistakes without getting upset.

Make the story your own.

_____ Student sounded natural (not memorized).

_____ Student chose words that painted a picture.

_____ Student changed voice to suit the character(s) or mood.

_____ Student included some dialogue.

_____ Student added simple gestures that enhanced the story.

Interact with your audience.

_____ Student greeted audience with a smile.

_____ Student captured the attention of audience with a good beginning.

_____ Student made eye contact with audience.

_____ Student used facial expressions when appropriate to tell the story.

_____ Student varied the pace of telling.

Love your story.

_____ Student practiced story.

_____ Student told story with appropriate energy and enthusiasm.

End with a smile.

_____ Student finished story with a clear ending line.

_____ Student accepted the applause with a nod or smile.

_____ Student thanked audience.

[*Note: See Ann Bates's article Assessment in Chapter 1.*]

Related Resources

Books

- Collins, Rives. *The Power of Story: Teaching through Storytelling.* 2nd ed. Boston: Allyn & Bacon, 1996.
- Hamilton, Martha, and Mitch Weiss. *Noodlehead Stories: World Tales that Kids Can Read and Tell.* Little Rock, AR: August House, 2000.

- Hamilton, Martha, and Mitch Weiss. *Children Tell Stories: A Teaching Guide.* 2nd ed. Katonah, NY: Richard C. Owens, 2005.
- MacDonald, Margaret Read. *Three-Minute Tales: More Stories to Read & Tell When Time Is Short.* Little Rock, AR: August House, 2004.
- MacDonald, Margaret Read. *Five-Minute Tales: More Stories to Read & Tell When Time Is Short.* Little Rock, AR: August House, 2007.
- MacDonald, Margaret Read. *Shake-It-Up Tales: Stories to Sing, Dance, Drum, and Act Out.* Little Rock, AR: August House, 2000.
- Sima, Judy, and Kevin Cordi. *Raising Voices: Creating Youth Storytelling Groups and Troupes.* Westport, CT: Libraries Unlimited, 2003.

Web Sites

- Clow School TattleTales. http://clow.ipsd.org/lmc_storytellers.html (accessed March 2008).
- Kokie, Stan. November 1998. "Storytelling: The Heart and Soul of Education." PREL Briefing Paper; Pacific Resources for Education and Learning. http://www.prel.org/products/Products/Storytelling.pdf (accessed March 2008).
- McWilliams, Barry. 1998. "Effective Storytelling: A Manual for Beginners." http://www.eldrbarry.net/roos/eest.htm (accessed March 2008).
- National Council of Teachers of English Teaching. "NCTE Positions and Guidelines: Teaching Storytelling, a Position Statement from the Committee on Storytelling. http://www.ncte.org/positions/statements/teachingstorytelling.

EVERY PICTURE TELLS A STORY: VISUAL NARRATIVE AND CALDECOTT MEDAL AND HONOR WINNERS
Janice M. Del Negro, PhD
Visual Literacy

National Standards

NCTE: 4, 5, 6, 12; CNAEA—Visual Arts 1: Understanding and applying media, techniques, and processes; CNAEA—Visual Arts 2: Using knowledge of structures and functions; CNAEA—Visual Arts 3: Choosing and evaluating a range of subject matter, symbols, and ideas.

Objectives

The objectives are to introduce children to elements of visual literacy; to stimulate imagination and thought regarding symbols and visuals; and to communicate the connection between the visual and textual in picture books.

*"If a picture is worth a thousand words, imagine the value of many pictures
plus a thousand words."*
— Bette DeBruyne Ammon and Gale W. Sherman

"Visual literacy" is a term that ignites much debate and inspires many definitions. The first recorded use of the term was in 1969 by John Debes, an important figure in the history of the International Visual Literacy Association (IVLA). According to Maria Avgerinou on the IVLA Web site:

Visual literacy refers to a group of vision-competencies a human being can develop by seeing and at the same time having and integrating other sensory experiences. The development of these competencies is fundamental to normal human learning. When developed, they enable a visually literate person to discriminate and interpret the visible actions, objects, symbols, natural or manmade that he encounters in his environment. Through the creative use of these competencies, he is able to communicate with others. Through the appreciative use of these competencies, he is able to comprehend and enjoy the masterworks of visual communication.

Subsequent educators and researchers have broadened the meaning of visual literacy to include the understanding, interpretation, and implementation of illustrations, visual media, and technology. According to Philip Yenawine, visual literacy includes "the ability to find meaning in imagery [ranging] from simple identification—naming what one sees—to complex interpretation on contextual, metaphoric and philosophical levels ... Many aspects of cognition are called upon, such as personal association, questioning, speculating, analyzing, fact-finding, and categorizing." All of these skills are recognized as necessary for literacy.

Instructional Plan

For the purposes of this lesson, the definition of visual literacy borrows from several disciplines and includes the ability to make meaning from symbols, recognition and understanding of visual narrative, and the ability to retell the visual narrative either orally or in writing; the ability to decipher, interpret, and verbalize images and symbols; the ability to create verbal and written narrative from visual narrative; the ability to create various meanings from visual narrative; and the ability to use symbols and other visual images to create meaning.

Storytellers and those who read aloud dance through the field of juvenile picture books like Ferdinand through a field of daisies. A strong text lends itself with ease to reading aloud and storytelling, but the use of picture books to stimulate visual literacy expands possible picture book uses. Using picture books in the promotion of visual literacy in the classroom or library setting is an aesthetically enriching way to introduce elements of visual literacy to children.

Definitions of a picture book vary, however, as does the understanding of a picture book's audience. In *Children and Books*, Zena Sutherland defines "the true picture book" as one in which the illustrations are the dominant feature, with little or no text. Lukens further explains the picture book as being a book in which "the pictures exist to extend the textual meaning, going beyond what may be the simplicity of the words." A picture book blends textual and visual art; the images and language work interdependently to tell a story. The images in a picture book further the text, Bette DeBruyne Ammon explains, saying that the art not only reflects the text, but adds to it, going beyond words and adding depth of meaning.

The picture book is a format, not a genre; the picture book is not, as is often conventionally perceived, a book suitable only for preschoolers or pre-readers. Picture books range in appeal from birth through adult, and the rich variety available means that picture books can be used in any classroom, with any age level. Using picture books to promote visual literacy in the classroom or library setting means separating the poppy seeds from the ashes. Mediocrity is not motivational, so selection from the hundreds of trade picture books published annually is a critical process. Contemporary Caldecott Medal and Honor–winning picture books form a preselected visual and literary pool of titles for those seeking to reinforce narrative through visuals as well as language. Some of the finest art produced by some of today's best illustrators, using the latest technology, is showcased in the contemporary picture book.

The criteria for the Caldecott Medal almost ensure a marriage of text and image that results in an ideal aesthetic and pedagogic tool for visual literacy. The wide variety of picture book themes and subjects available lends themselves to use with a wide variety of ages and interest levels.

The Caldecott Medal, first awarded in 1939, is the oldest medal for children's picture book illustration in the United States. Caldecott criteria, refined over nearly seventy years of discussion and process, states:

> A picture book for children as distinguished from other books with illustrations, is one that essentially provides the child with a visual experience. A picture book has a collective unity of story-line, theme, or concept, developed through the series of pictures of which the book is comprised.

In identifying a distinguished picture in a book for children, the committee considers excellence of execution in the artistic technique employed; excellence of pictorial interpretation of story, theme, or concept; of appropriateness of style of illustration to the story, theme, or concept; of delineation of plot, theme, characters, setting mood, or information through the pictures; and excellence of presentation in recognition of a child audience.

The committee makes decisions based primarily on the illustration, but other components of a book are to be considered. In other words, the picture book is to be considered as an organic whole, with elements such as text, design, etc., considered. (For complete Caldecott criteria, go to http://

acrl.org/ala/mgrps/divs/alsc/awardsgrants/bookmedia/caldecottmedal/calde
cottterms/caldecottterms.cfm.)

Ideally, the best picture books, with text or wordless, provide a visual narrative or thematic experience. The strong narrative and thematic threads present in Caldecott winners makes them ideal for exercises in visual literacy; these award-winners offer nearly unlimited opportunities to promote visual literacy through practice deciphering visual images or symbols.

The 1997 Caldecott Honor–winning *The Graphic Alphabet* by David Pelletier (Orchard, 1996) is a playful, sophisticated look at the alphabet, with each letter constructed to indicate the word for which the initial letter stands. Bits of a gold capital A tumble down the side of the letter that starts the word "avalanche"; the triangular tip of an I, for "iceberg," bobs above a graphical sea.

The 2007 Caldecott Honor–winning title, *Gone Wild: An Endangered Animal Alphabet* by David McLimans (Walker Books for Young Readers, 2006), is another title that offers symbol-decoding opportunities: each letter morphs into an elegant depiction of an endangered animal, while decorative motifs provide additional deciphering opportunities. *Alphabet City* by Stephen T. Johnson (Viking, 1995) includes photo-realistic paintings of an urban setting in which the letters of the alphabet are formed by "found" objects or designs, and Suse MacDonald's *Alphabatics* (MacMillan, 1982) offers letters that grow into alphabet acrobats with the addition of heads, arms, and legs. None of these alphabet books is designed for letter identification by the pre-reading child, but they do lend themselves to the symbol-decoding of the older child who can already recognize the letters of the alphabet.

For those students willing to tackle the non-linear, David Macaulay's Caldecott medal-winning *Black and White* (Houghton Mifflin, 1990) offers multiple narratives that interweave such disparate elements as cows, trains, and burglars.

Titles that prove their strength through the manipulation of paper and die cuts include *First the Egg*, written and illustrated by Laura Vaccaro Seeger (Roaring Brook Press, 2007) and *Color Zoo* by Lois Ehlert (Lippincott, 1989). Books such as Donald Crews' *Freight Train* (HarperCollins, 1978) offer a visual presentation of action and motion.

Eric Rohmann's *My Friend Rabbit* (Roaring Brook Press, 2002) is a classic piece of linear narrative in which the story tells itself without text or unnecessary explanation. Other examples of strong linear narrative include Mo Willem's *Knuffle Bunny: A Cautionary Tale* (Hyperion, 2004); *When Sophie Gets Angry—Really, Really Angry* by Molly Bang (Scholastic, 1999); *The Gardener* (Farrar, Straus and Giroux, 1997) by Sarah Stewart; and *A Snowy Day* (Viking, 1962) by Ezra Jack Keats.

All three of Maurice Sendak's honor and award-winning trilogy of titles—*Where the Wild Things Are* (HarperCollins, 1964), *In the Night Kitchen* (HarperCollins, 1970), and *Outside Over There* (HarperCollins, 1981)—offer opportunities for interpretation of visual narrative. *Where the Wild Things Are* in particular is a title that can be used with or without the text, with or without the illustrations. That is, the text stands alone in its rhythmic insistence, and the pictures stand as a powerful example of visual storytelling; used together, image and text unite in a narrative marriage.

Mo Willems's *Don't Let the Pigeon Drive the Bus!* (Hyperion, 2003) and its subsequent iterations *The Pigeon Finds a Hot Dog!* (Hyperion, 2004), *Don't Let the Pigeon Stay Up Late!* (Hyperion, 2006), and *The Pigeon Wants a Puppy!* (Hyperion, 2008) combines forceful dialogue with graphic elements that add to the emotionality of the text.

Children interact with stories, listening, telling, and interpreting them through text and image. Visual literacy addresses several different learning styles, making visual literacy exercises effective multipurpose tools for the classroom or library.

David Wiesner's nearly wordless picture books *Tuesday* (Clarion, 1991), *Flotsam* (Clarion, 2006), *The Three Pigs* (Clarion, 2001), *Sector 7* (Clarion, 1999), and *Free Fall* (HarperCollins, 1988) have earned him three Caldecott Medals and two Caldecott Honors, a historic number of medals given to one illustrator. The strength of these titles lies in their strong visual narratives, the story told through pictures and few words, with the linear narrative thread running through each book despite the differences in illustration style and medium. Sample activities for Wiesner's (and other) titles include:

- Telling the story from the pictures
- Tracking individual images through an entire book
- Identifying written words (if any) and their purpose

Sample questions for Wiesner's *Tuesday*, the story of a strange night of flying frogs, include:

- How can you tell that time has passed?
- How are the frogs flying?
- What is happening on the last page?

Sample questions for *Sector 7*, the story of a cloud-making factory, include:

- How can you tell that the clouds have personalities?
- How do you know this is a place that makes clouds?
- What tells you that the boy has a friend?

Sample questions for *The Three Pigs* include:

- What happens when the pigs try to get away from the wolf?
- Is "The Three Pigs" the only story in this book?
- How do the pigs get from page to page, story to story?

Telling the story from the pictures and identifying eye-catching details in the illustrations offers children the opportunity for close interaction with visual narrative, as well as the chance to become comfortable with the interrelationship of image and text.

Assessment

Children tell or write their own stories or interpretations of visual narrative; students construct their own symbols for meaning-making.

Bibliography

- Ammon, Bette DeBruyne, and Gale W. Sherman. *Worth a Thousand Words: An Annotated Guide to Picture Books for Older Readers.* Englewood, CO: Libraries Unlimited, 1996.
- Avgerinou, Maria. "What is 'Visual Literacy?'" International Visual Literacy Association, http://www.ivla.org/org_what_vis_lit.htm.
- Avgerinou, Maria, with J. Ericson. "A Review of the Concept of Visual Literacy." *British Journal of Educational Technology* 28.4 (1997): 280–291.
- Bamford, Anne. "Visual Literacy White Paper." Art and Design University of Technology, Sydney, Australia. Commissioned by Adobe Systems Pty Ltd, Australia. Adobe Systems Inc., 2003.
- Begoray, Deborah L. "Through a Class Darkly: Visual Literacy in the Classroom." *Canadian Journal of Education* 26 (2001): 201–217.
- Brill, J. M., D. Kim, and R. M. Branch. "Visual Literacy Defined: The Results of a Delphi Study—Can IVLA (Operationally) Define Visual Literacy?" In R. E. Griffen, V. S. Williams, and J. Lee (eds.), *Exploring the Visual Future: Art Design, Science, and Technology.* Blacksburg, VA: The International Visual Literacy Association, 2001, 9–15.
- "Information Literacy Standards for Student Learning: Standards and Indicators." Prepared by the American Association of School Librarians. *Information Literacy Standards for Student Learning.* American Library Association and the Association for Educational Communications and Technology, 1998.
- Kovalik, Cindy, and Peggy King. "Visual Literacy." Kent State University College and Graduate School of Health, Education, and Services. http://www.educ.kent.edu/community/VLO/.
- Kress, Gunther. *Literacy in the New Media Age.* London: Routledge, 2003.
- Metros, Susan E., and Kristina Eoolsey. "Visual Literacy: An Institutional Imperative." *EDUCAUSE Review*, vol. 41, no. 3 (May/June 2006): 80–81.
- New London Group. "Pedagogy of Multiliteracies: Designing Social Futures." *Harvard Educational Review* 66.1 (1996): 66–92.
- Riesland, Erin. "Visual Literacy and the Classroom." New Horizons for Learning. March 2005. http://www.newhorizons.org/strategies/literacy/riesland.htm.
- Sims, Ellen. "Visual Literacy: What It Is and Do We Need It To Use Learning Technologies Effectively?" With Ros O'Leary, Julian Cook, and Gill Butland. Learning Technology Support Service, University of Bristol, UK. ASCILITE, 2002. http://www.ascilite.org.au/conferences/auckland02/proceedings/papers/ellen_sims_et_al.pdf.

- Stokes, Suzanne. "Visual Literacy in Teaching and Learning: A Literature Perspective." *Electronic Journal for the Integration of Technology in Education*, vol. 1, no. 1, http://ejite.isu.edu/Volume1No1/pdfs/stokes.pdf.
- Sutherland, Zena. *Children and Books.* 9th ed. New York: Longmans, 1997.
- Yenawine, Philip. "Thoughts on Visual Literacy." *Handbook of Research on Teaching Literacy through the Communicative and Visual Arts.* Mahwah, NJ: Lawrence Erlbaum Associates, 2005.

THE SHAPE OF MUSIC: REVEALING VISUAL NARRATIVES WITHIN ARTWORKS
Mike Gnutek
Visual Literacy

National Standards

NCTE: 3, 4, 7, 8, 9, 11, 12; CNAEA—Visual Arts 1: Understanding and applying media, techniques, and processes; CNAEA—Visual Arts 3: Choosing and evaluating a range of subject matter, symbols, and ideas; CNAEA—Visual Arts 4: Understanding visual arts in relation to history and cultures; CNAEA—Visual Arts 5: Reflecting on and assessing the characteristics and merits of their work and of the work of others; CNAEA—Visual Arts 6: Making connections between visual arts and other disciplines.

Objectives

Students will create on paper an original artwork reflecting what their minds paint when listening to different musical compositions. Students will learn that the liberal arts are interconnected and musical inspiration enhances artistic experiences.

Materials

- Nancarrow, Conlon. *Conlon Nancarrow: Studies for Player Piano, Nos. 1–20.* CD. Other Minds, 2008.
- Various artists. *Hideous Kinky: Soundtrack from the Motion Picture.* CD. Seattle, WA: Will Records, 1999.
- CD player.
- Oil pastels.
- 9″ × 12″ sketch paper.
- Pencils.
- Watercolors.

- Brushes.
- 12″ × 18″ watercolor paper.
- Photocopies of artworks by Wassily Kandinsky.

Instructional Plan

This integrated lesson is intended to teach students to develop what their minds see when listening to music as a means of artistic creation. It is similar to the way the mind develops mental pictures of characters and settings when reading a book. It is also intended to allow students to see the way finished abstract paintings can reveal oral narratives and autobiographies.

During the lesson, in order for the students to put this new way of seeing into practice, they needed to have a relevant and working vocabulary to assist them. Therefore, we began the lesson by discussing a few key terms of art. I explained the basic definitions of geometric shapes, organic shapes, realism, abstraction, formal balance, and informal balance by providing simple, visual examples.

Students then investigated the work of Wassily Kandinsky. While looking at color copies of his paintings, students answered the following questions on paper:

- How many geometric shapes do you see in this picture?
- How many organic shapes can you count?
- What kind of balance is in this artwork?

These questions were geared toward the knowledge and understanding spectrum of Bloom's Taxonomy, a six-level classification of intellectual behavior. They were intended simply to get students to describe what they were seeing. T. Lee Williams notes "... so much of what primary students think of as literacy comprehension is really just describing" (2007). He explains that teachers need to "help move students beyond basic description to developing their critical thinking skills" (2007). This quote demonstrates the need for probing questions. Too often, because of time constraints or other obstacles, this important line of questioning does not occur.

In order to get the students to see the possible stories in the paintings, I needed to continue the questioning with deeper analysis:

- Does this artwork have rhythm?
- How does it flow?
- What is one question you would ask Kandinsky about this artwork?
- What do you think inspired Kandinsky to create this painting?
- Why did he use the color blue?
- Why did he choose geometric shapes?

These questions were intended to connect students in a familiar way with Kandinsky's visual thought process and to get students thinking about the possible stories within the artworks. In other applications of this same lesson, I have introduced students to the artwork of Sonia Delaney. Much of her art is geometric-based and connects directly to the music that inspired her artwork. In fact, some of her paintings include the word "rhythm" in the title.

In the next session, we began the musical portion of the lesson. Students received no background information about the musical compositions or the composers they were about to hear. To usher in an unbiased and authentic experience, I provided no demonstration or finished examples. Each student received a piece of paper and oil pastels. Before playing the first musical composition entitled *Study #1* by Conlon Nancarrow, I explained the relative length of the piece and the requirement for the lesson. Students had to close their eyes and listen to the music for fifteen seconds before drawing the colors, shapes, and lines their minds envisioned, but they were able to employ any type of line creation or techniques gained from previous pastel projects. As the piece began, students anxiously closed their eyes. Once instructed to begin drawing, oil pastels feverishly took to paper. Most students used the entire two and one-half minutes to draw during this staccato and disjointed melody on player piano.

I gave the students the same instructions as they prepared for the second, drum-laden musical composition, *Baba Baba Mektoubi* by Jill Jilala, a North African chant that contrasts the Nancarrow piece. The same supplies were used to ensure that the only variable would be the musical composition. A second time, oil pastels feverishly took to paper and students utilized the entire length of the musical composition to draw. In other applications of this lesson, I have included *Diablo Rojo* by Rodrigo y Gabriela. Choosing unfamiliar music void of recognizable lyrics with contrasting rhythm and tempo allowed the students to work from a more authentic sense of self.

Students then began the process of composition and coloring. They selected one sketch and recreated it on a larger format watercolor paper using the same oil pastels. Some students noticed connections between the two sketches and merged the two into a single composition. Relying on their previous knowledge of watercolor usage, students added washes of color to enhance the artistic composition. Working in a large format allowed them to intensely explore each line or shape. In other applications of this lesson, students created artworks using acrylics on Bristol boards and cut up the two compositions using scissors. Then they rearranged and adhered the pieces on a new, smaller sheet of paper. This process forced the students to consider which brushstrokes were essential and which could be discarded. It helped get to the essence of each work and pushed the understanding of composition. Some students said that the process reminded them of fitting together a puzzle.

The lesson culminated with a critique of the work created as a result of this musical process. This became the foundation for the oral narratives in the paintings and the assessment of the artworks. Students followed a prescribed format when critiquing so they could begin to read the paintings. While displaying their completed works at the front of the classroom, the artists could not use preambles or explanations. Instead, they selected students to comment on the work as though they were reading a book. Students used the following response prompts to get the dialogue started:

- The beginning of this artwork for me is _____.
- What really caught my eye was _____.
- I think the artist used these colors and shapes because _____.
- This artist is really skilled at _____.
- I would enhance this artwork by _____.

As the teacher, I was allowed to comment after the students. Finally, the artists answered any questions posed during the critique and explained the intent.

To the students, many artworks demonstrated a linear narrative of sound, making clear an introduction and conclusion. In many artworks, amassing lines, shapes, and squiggles in the center of the paper revealed a steady crescendo of sound. In one example, a narrow channel bulged as it cut diagonally across the page. Students commented on its resemblance to a squid heading toward its home. In another artwork, students saw a twisted, neon-green forest with a black owl's head poking out of a tidal wave.

In other artworks, students employed a more nonlinear approach when they drew. They commented about how the artworks seemed to be more mid-story without an introduction or a conclusion. In one, a mass of scribbles exploded from the center and wound over and over around the perimeter of the page, making it challenging for students to identify the beginning and ending of the story. In another, yellow and orange scribbles covered a purple watercolor wash.

Some students expressed difficulty seeing abstract shapes and lines as the music played. Their stories about the music were more reality-based and, therefore, easier to interpret. Recording their mental pictures on the center of the page, they drew a beach, a horse galloping on a green field, and a pink castle. This seems to reveal the autobiography within each student, suggesting who they might be, their interests, their hobbies, and their passions. It explains what their minds were thinking at the time of creation.

The goal of this lesson was to help students find possible narratives within paintings and a new way to interpret the visual world around them. Students are increasingly bombarded by imagery in magazines, in museums, on television, on billboards, and on the Internet. We need to equip our students with the skills necessary to decipher what they are observing. We need to break free from the narrow and archaic understanding that literacy simply refers to vocabulary words, sentences, and printed text. By using a deeper form of questioning and suspending historical and contextual clues, students can begin to observe the potential stories within images and that a visual form of literacy, void of text, exists in our world today.

TAILYPO: CREATING VIVID CHARACTERS
Bobby Norfolk, Pam Beagle-Daresta, and Sherry Norfolk
Listening, Writing, and Visual Literacy

National Standards

NCTE: 4, 5, 6, 12; CNAEA—Visual Arts 1: Students intentionally take advantage of the qualities and characteristics of art media, techniques, and processes to enhance communication of their experiences and ideas; CNAEA—Visual Arts 2: Students generalize about the effects of visual structures and functions and reflect upon these effects in their own work; students employ organizational structures and analyze what makes them effective or ineffective in the communication of ideas; students select and use the qualities of structures and functions of art to improve communication of their ideas.

Objectives

Students will retell "Tailypo" in the form of a manga comic, with appropriate sequence, plot, setting, and characters; students will develop vivid written descriptions of the characters in their manga version of Tailypo.

Materials for Visual Art Project

Each student will need:

- Unlined paper
- Pencil
- Eraser

For an in-depth collaborative project or to deepen the basic experience, students will need:

- Fine-tip black pens (a Sharpie or Pilot pen)
- Water-based colored markers or watercolor paint sets
- Small, round watercolor paintbrush
- Large section of Kraft paper

What's the best way to teach kids to develop clear, vivid characters in their writing? There are many points of entry—the spoken word, the drawn image, and the living person. The more points of entry we provide, the more likely it is that each student will find the magical door to understanding.

In storytelling, the storyteller "sees" the image in his/her imagination, then uses words, facial expressions, body language, and gestures to conjure the same images in the listeners' imagination. The listeners infer a lot of the information from the paralinguistic clues. When asked to translate those images into drawings, then into descriptive verbal passages, interesting things happen!

In this lesson plan, we will move from the storyteller's images to concrete images on paper to words on a page to help students learn to write effective, evocative character descriptions.

The Storyteller's Performance (Bobby Speaks)

When I created my version of the African American classic "Tailypo," I had to envision the characters, setting, and action. The words and actions I use to create that imagery must be vivid enough for each listener to recreate those images in his or her imagination. Since I'm a storyteller, I'm not limited to words, and can use nonverbal or kinesthetic "language" to help my audience experience the story.

There are two main characters in the story: the old man and Tailypo. My characterization of the old man is aural-kinesthetic rather than linguistic; that is, he speaks in a creaky, cranky voice with a bit of a southern accent, and he moves slowly and arthritically—but he is never described.

Tailypo is somewhat described (although I deliberately leave some room for the listeners to create their own images). Along with the descriptive passages, I provide visual and auditory cues:

Tailypo has huge red eyes (this is the first hint of the presence of Tailypo, and it needs to be vivid). To accentuate the eeriness of the eyes, I cup my hands around my eyes and pulse them forward, at the same time making a throbbing sound effect: boom-boom-boom!

Tailypo has claws, and a long, bushy tail which appears between the cracks in the floorboards and wags. I pantomime the tail wagging and make the scratchy sound of the claws moving against the wood. When the old man cuts off the tail, I pantomime the writhing and flopping of the severed tail along with sound effects: thump-thump-thump.

Tailypo has a voice that "whistles in the wind." The descriptive words are evocative, but to me, creating that voice is essential! The repeated phrase, "Tailypo, Tailypo, who's got my Tailypo?" isn't very hair-raising if you just *describe* that voice—I use a guttural, raspy moan.

Tailypo has terrible claws. I make three-fingered claws, folding my thumbs and little fingers together and raking the air with my remaining "claws." A gruesome face accompanies those claws—Tailypo is really scary!

At the conclusion of the story, I talk to the audience: "I didn't give you any description of the creature except the huge red eyes, its claws, and its tail. What do you think it actually was?"

No answer is wrong—whatever they saw in their mind's eye is correct. I simply want to encourage them to begin visualizing the creature before I turn them over to the visual artist.

The Visual Artist's Workshop (Pam Speaks)

Now that students have heard Bobby's version of "Tailypo," they will be asked to retell and/or recreate the story in the form of a manga comic (also called sequential art). I chose manga because students are fascinated with this art form—and because manga has the same structure as a well-written story. In fact, it's essential to develop the story before you can draw. It's important to create characters that are engaging and significant to the story and are emotionally charged. Animating a comic character is descriptive—but it utilizes the *visual* alphabet rather than the *written* alphabet. Google "manga start" for drawing and story-creating exercises that can be downloaded and printed.

Okay—if your left-directed brain is already saying, "I can't teach this!" tell your brain to take a break and go to Starbucks. You already do this in your classroom—the structural components of a written story are the same as those of a drawn story. Writing starts with a first draft; a drawn image starts with a preliminary drawing. Either is a means of getting your ideas down before editing and fully developing the composition in words or images. The real difference is the alphabet: letters are symbols for sounds that create words; varied lines create drawings or *images* of what the words represent.

We will eventually create a full storyboard, developing setting, action, and plot, but the focus of this article is about developing *characters*. Bobby created his characters in his imagination; now the students will visualize their own characters, retelling the essence of the story from their own perspective. Characters are developed through *emotion, action*, and *appearance*.

I try to direct students to their drawing through questions that help them clarify words into images, and then make suggestions on how to draw the form. First we discuss "Tailypo"—a challenging character to draw, especially since it is typically not seen in its entirety! The lesson goes something like this:

What image of Tailypo do you have from Bobby's story and how did this character make you feel? See that image in your mind; give it shape and color—these derive from how the character makes you feel!

There are many ways to approach drawing; let's begin with abstracting the overall or biggest shape of our subject. I think of Tailypo's eye shape as a parallelogram, with sharp exaggerated angles that create scary eye corners and eyebrow lines that have that same sharp and jagged line. I am aware of the tension in my body and draw with that scary, mean feeling I have and want to convey.

Being a good artist, like being a scientist, you are trained to be a good observer. Look at your neighbor's eyes and ask him to make scary, angry eyes. See how the shape changes. We know the eyes are red—kick them up a notch

Figure 4.3.   Give me back my Tailypo!

by adding some yellow, green, or blue. We do not see Tailypo's body, which keeps him scary and more mysterious. What color surrounds his eyes: candy-pretty pink or dark elusive blues and blacks?

How can you convey the eyes popping out of the darkness, getting smaller and larger, moving away and right up in your face? Can you feel and hear Tailypo's claws? What shape does that noise make? Is it soft and flowing or deep, cutting, and jagged? Draw it the way you feel it.

Now for the tail. I might think about a cat with arched tail and bristling back, so I would make a baseline for the tail, maybe with a sharp angle near its end. I'd give it shape with sharp lines for hair sticking out or standing up, remembering the hairs are longer at the base where it would come out of the body and getting progressively shorter as they move to the tail's tip.

While I am talking and asking questions, I am drawing—and yes, I make mistakes and bad drawings! Even the best artists have to really concentrate to do a good drawing, but I am modeling the activity and giving the students a starting point.

I take aspects of each student's drawing, cut them out, and place them on a large piece of Kraft paper to create a collaborative storyboard in the form of a manga. Use the students' drawings to sequence the story and add the appropriate environments, dogs, old man, and word bubbles.

The questions for creating a visual story are the same as for creating a good written story. Whom or what are the eyes looking at, where are they, and can you show me? Draw the dogs running off, and show the old man in his bed, eyes all around him in the dark. Have fun! Writing takes practice, as does

Figure 4.4.   Manga storyboard.

drawing. I believe thinking in more than one realm and stepping out of the familiar makes us look a little harder, recognize more, and build observation and communication skills. Let everyone draw and change things and explore the story—it is the act of creating, not always the final result, that teaches.

The final products will be complete storyboards with clear visions of the story and all of its components. One of the strengths of manga is the empathy the characters project, engaging the reader deeply with the emotions of the story.

With the characters fully developed in visual imagery, the students will now begin to describe those same characters with words alone!

The Creative Writing Workshop (Sherry Speaks)

Bobby has engaged the kids in creating mental images of the story and its characters; Pam has helped them develop these into their own visual images; my job is to help them translate those images into words on a page.

There has a been a lot of research about the way human beings communicate, and it is surprising to many people to learn that only approximately 8 percent of communication employs words—the other 92 percent is all of the paralinguistic language described above! That fact clearly explains the difficulty children face when asked to *describe* a character—they immediately begin showing the height and shape with their hands, the attitude with faces and bodies, etc. But creative writing is all about using *words* to create images, and that's what we'll be doing in this workshop.

Every student has now given a lot of thought to what the characters look like, and they have visual representations of those characters—but in a written story, the words create the pictures, so now we need to select the best descriptive words to capture the images in print. Looking carefully at the characters they have created, we brainstorm a list of adjectives for Tailypo. This process turns on the left side of the brain, accessing all of those little-used vocabulary words. After each student jots down the best choices for their creation, they continue with the other characters. For this article, we'll limit the focus to Tailypo.

Next, I ask the students to stand and "become" Tailypo in their story. It takes a little time to get past their self-consciousness, but once they're all in character, I ask them to begin moving as *their* Tailypo moves. When their actions begin to individuate, I ask them to stop and think of the best verbs to describe the way Tailypo moves: does he lope, run, skulk, slither? We jot those words down, too.

Then we play emotion lotto: I have a set of cards, each with a different "emotion" word printed on it (disgusted, ecstatic, lethargic, insecure, etc.). Each student draws a card and tries to portray the emotion through facial and postural clues, and the class guesses the word. Harder (and more fun) than you'd think—but effective! Now we're ready to tackle the personality of the character.

Looking at their illustration, the students choose words that describe Tailypo's attitude and personality: how is he feeling at the beginning of the story? How does he feel when he loses his tail? How does he feel when he gets it back? Students can look at the cards to get some ideas. We jot down the words and continue.

Next question: what is the most important thing about Tailypo? Is it the length of his tail, the smell of his breath, the sharpness of his claws? Since this feature is the most important, it's essential that the reader gets a very clear picture of it. Rather than give the length of the tail in inches, we will compare it to something that is familiar and conjure up a clear image. Is it as long as a school bus? Long enough to use as a jump rope? Would it stretch from the top of the Empire State Building down to the ground? These similes create vivid pictures in the minds of the reader—so now the students are asked to develop similes that will allow their readers to visualize this important feature. This assignment is spectacularly interactive—kids tend to think out loud, and the responses bounce back and forth across the room, resulting in some really colorful phrases!

One more step: developing a metaphor for the creature, a body part, or his actions. There's a lot of confusion about "metaphor" and "simile." Most kids—and many adults—think that they're synonymous. A simile is used to compare one thing to another; a metaphor is used to symbolize or represent something. For instance, "The Tailypo was as quick as a wink" (simile); "He was a cyclone, tearing through the house in a whipping, flailing frenzy" (metaphor). I usually encourage kids to work in pairs or small groups to develop suitable metaphors for each others' stories.

Now each student has created a collection of adjectives, verbs, and emotions, along with at least one simile and a metaphor that can be used to describe the Tailypo. They have the tools to write a character description that will evoke vivid images in the minds of their readers.

It takes a little time to help students move from images in their heads to visual images to words on a page, but this step-by-step approach is effective and will translate into characters that practically leap—or crawl or flip—off the page!

Assessment

Mangas can be assessed with your art teacher's rubric; written character descriptions can be assessed with a rubric that includes vivid and appropriate use of adjectives, verbs, similes, and metaphors.

Resources

- Galdone, Joanne. *Tailypo: A Ghost Story*. Clarion Books, 1984.
- Holt, David. *Tailybone and Other Strange Stories*. High Windy Audio, 2000.
- Public Library of Charlotte and Mecklenburg County's "Bookhive." Jackie Torrence tells "Tailypo" at http://www.plcmc.org/Bookhive/zingertales/default.asp?storyID=6.
- Wahl, Jan. *Tailypo!* New York: Holt, 1991.

HIDDEN MEMORY: A FAMILY HISTORY PROJECT
Anne Shimojima
Information Literacy

National Standards

NCTE: 7, 8, 9, 12; AASL 1: Learners use skills, resources, and tools to inquire, think critically, and gain knowledge; AASL 2: Draw conclusions, make informed decisions, apply knowledge to new situations, and create new knowledge; AASL 3: Share knowledge and participate ethically and productively as members of our democratic society; AASL 4: Pursue personal and aesthetic growth.

Objectives

To read the backstory of how a storyteller crafted a family story about migrating and assimilating in the United States.

Materials

- Computer with iPhoto program and iMovie program or similar programs
- Old family photographs
- Tape recorder

The Artist's Plan

In my family, stories about World War II were never told. Since we are Japanese American and some were imprisoned in internment camps, there were plenty of stories. But many Japanese American families are reluctant to talk about their wartime experiences. Several years ago, I decided that with the older generation aging, the time had come to uncover our story.

The first step was to collect old family photographs. I also decided to interview my ninety-one-year-old aunt for information about my grandparents' emigration from Japan and her memories about life in Portland, Oregon, and then the forced removal to the Tule Lake internment camp in California. Collecting family historical documents followed, and I finally found myself creating digital slideshows of the photographs, a DVD of the slideshows, and a booklet with copies of the interview and the historical documents for each member of the family.

As an elementary school library media specialist, one of my priorities is to teach my students information literacy skills—to locate, organize, analyze, and evaluate information. In my school district, we use the Big6 information literacy model created by educators Bob Berkowitz and Mike Eisenberg. Our goal is for students to internalize this research framework so that they will have the skills to become information seekers and lifelong learners. It was only after my family project was completed that I realized that the entire process fell into this six-step framework.

1) Task Definition

Initially, my only goal was to create a hardbound book of old family photos. But I soon realized that we needed to know more. I needed to interview my aunt, the only remaining family member of my father's generation. I was also on the hunt for any other family documents or information I could find.

2) Information-Seeking Strategies

I asked my family members for any old family photos they could send me and started thinking about what government and private institutions I could write to for family historical documents.

3) Location and Access

I interviewed my aunt over three visits, tape recording her each time. During the last two visits, I asked her to tell me about old photographs. One that I showed her was a photo of herself at the age of about two, dressed in a little kimono. I thought she would talk about the kimono, but instead she saw the house behind her and told me about the bath in it that her father had brought from Japan and how her mother had heated water each night for the bath. As I discovered, photographs can prompt many story gems.

Believing that my grandparents were married in Portland, Oregon, where they settled, I wrote to Multnomah county and the Oregon State Archives, trying to find a copy of their marriage license. No copy was found, but the mystery was solved when a cousin from Colorado sent my grandmother's photo album and personal papers, a treasure trove I never even knew existed. Included were photos of my grandparents in Japan and their early Portland days. I had never seen photographs of my grandparents as young people; I was seeing them in their early years for the very first time.

I also wrote to the Japanese American National Museum for information on picture brides, for we believe my grandmother was one. My grandfather, unable to afford the long journey back home, sent his photograph, and she traveled across the world to marry a stranger, something that thousands of young Japanese women did.

4) Use of Information

The Japanese American National Museum sent a copy of the ship manifest in which we found my grandmother's name listed as her married name, proof that she married first in Japan by proxy and then, according to the marriage license, again on the day after she landed in Seattle. Now I knew why there was no marriage license in Oregon.

It took about twelve hours to transcribe my aunt's interviews. Finding Japanese written on the back of many of the old photographs, I took them to another aunt who, being from Japan, could translate for me. It was this step that uncovered a photograph of my grandfather, taken on the very day he left Japan in 1906, and identified photographs of my two great-grandmothers.

Meanwhile, I was busy scanning and retouching more than 400 photographs sent to me by my relatives. The retouching was made easy with the iPhoto program on my Macintosh computer.

5) Synthesis

Now that I had all of the photographs scanned, I could use the iPhoto program to create and order a hardbound book of photographs. I chose to take the best from our first three generations: *Issei*—my grandparents, the first generation to live in the United States; *Nisei*—my parents, the second generation; and *Sansei*—my generation, the third. I included photographs through my generation's high school days. But with a fourth generation and hundreds more photographs, I needed another way to document our family's journey. I used the iMovie program to create digital slide shows for each generation, which I then turned into a DVD for viewing. In addition, I converted the tape recording of my aunt's interview to CD to give to her children.

By now I was planning to give copies of everything to my family members for Christmas. Along with the DVD and the book of photos, I created booklets containing the transcribed interview; the photo commentary; our family tree, including the Japanese branch, which I had collected on a trip to Japan many years earlier; and copies of my grandparents' passports, marriage license, and War Relocation Authority records.

6) Evaluation

My family members did not know what I was doing, just that I was "working on a family project." When we gathered for our family Christmas dinner, I invited them all to the family room and announced that I had something to show them. From the first photograph of my young, handsome grandfather that flashed on the screen, they were captivated. Seeing everyone smile, laugh, and exclaim over the pictures made all of the hard work of the previous six months worthwhile. Photographs of each succeeding generation took us through the years and showed a family becoming more American, but still in touch with its roots.

Thank-you letters from my out-of-town cousins later confirmed that I had given an important gift, one that highlighted our common family roots and gave us a sense of heritage and tradition.

This family project could be recreated with students. They can collect family photographs and scan them into a book or document, interview family members, gather family stories, have family members comment on family photos, and create a family tree. Older students may want to search for family documents like marriage licenses, school degrees, and passports. They can weave the photos and stories into a digital storytelling project in which they creatively present their family's history. Such a project is intrinsically fascinating and gives each student a sense of personal history and his or her place in the world. This project meets standards in information literacy, language arts, and social studies, and requires each student to carry out an information search using, organizing, and analyzing multiple resources, and synthesizing the information into a creative whole.

A year after the project was complete, I was asked to perform in the JustStories storytelling festival in Techny, Illinois, an event dedicated to stories of diversity, social justice, immigration, and peace. Realizing that my usual folktale and fairy-tale repertoire wasn't quite appropriate, I decided to create a story that told of my family's journey from Japan and through the internment camps of World War II. It was based primarily on my interview with my aunt, but I realized that I needed to find out more information about the camps themselves, the climate of the country and the political realities that made the camps possible, and details about camp life in Tulelake, California. I was off on another research adventure. This time my search took me through books and Web sites, where I found old photographs and viewed footage of videos about the camps and the war, read memoirs of internees, and marveled at the courage and endurance of the Japanese American people and the Japanese American soldiers who fought for the United States.

The actual performance of my story took place in front of a large audience that included four of my family members. My aunt, subject of the interview, heard her story performed, and afterward proudly came to the front of the room to be introduced.

Several months later, I was able to tell a shorter version of this story to my fourth graders during their immigration unit. While they have heard me tell stories since their kindergarten days, I was unsure how they would react to something so personal and so historical. I needn't have feared. Their quiet attention and respectful listening told me that they were, indeed, hearing what I was trying to convey. I know that telling folktales and fairy tales to my students over the years has created a strong bond between us. Now they were hearing something about my own family and history that gave them a different insight into me as a person and as a representative of my culture.

The journey that took me from my grandfather's departure from Japan in 1906 to our family today was a fascinating one, where every photo was a glimpse into the past and each discovery taught me about my family and myself. An important step in understanding who we are is knowing where we come from. This is a journey that anyone can take. All that is needed is curiosity, patience, the willingness to ask questions, the patience to listen, and a few good research skills.

The Shimojima family story is available at http://www.racebridges forschools.com in both text and audio files with a free lesson plan and discussion questions.

STORYTIME FAMILY STYLE—BUILDING GENERATIONAL BRIDGES
Teresa B. Clark
Listening, Speaking, Reading, Writing, and Information Literacy

National Standards

NCTE: 7, 12; CNAEA—Theater 1: Script writing by planning and recording improvisations based on personal experience and heritage, imagination, literature, and history; CNAEA—Theater 2: Acting by assuming roles and interacting in improvisations; CNAEA—Theater 5: Researching by finding information to support classrooms; AASL 1: Learners use skills, resources, and tools to inquire, think critically, and gain knowledge; AASL 2: Learners use skills, resources, and tools to draw conclusions, make informed decisions, apply knowledge to new situations, and create new knowledge; AASL 3: Learners use skills, resources, and tools to share knowledge and participate ethically and productively as members of our democratic society; AASL 4: Learners use skills, resources, and tools to pursue personal and aesthetic growth.

Objectives

Students will learn the proper ways to collect and document oral histories; students will enhance their listening skills as they communicate effectively with their interview subjects; students will identify main ideas and supporting details as well as other story elements as they partner, listen, and share their stories; students will enhance their writing skills as they collect raw data and form it into a story; students will interpret meaning through group conversation by sharing the mental images they experienced and the messages they gained from the stories they listened to and collected; students will develop and enhance their analytical skills as they coach one another in the storytelling and story writing process; students will increase their communication skills as they craft their selected oral histories into oral storytelling performances.

Storytime—Family Style!

Brody was a lost boy. His teacher warned that he never came to school clean and rarely spoke, and she therefore was worried he would fail at collecting and telling a family story.

Six weeks later, to conclude the storytelling-family style unit of study, Brody stood directly in front of his mother's wheelchair, microphone in hand, ignoring the packed auditorium. Looking her square in the eye, he declared his promise to fulfill her hopes and dreams for him, since she would not live to see him reach adulthood. Few eyes in the audience were dry. The school administration finally understood. Brody was no longer a lost boy.

Brody's mother had multiple sclerosis, and somehow, no one had known it. When Brody was finished, he threw himself into his mother's arms as the crowd exploded in applause. It has been said it's hard to hate (or taunt, or complain about) someone once you know their story. That was certainly the case with Brody.

The moment transformed Brody, the student body, and the school staff. The school staff, because they finally understood the story behind Brody's situation. The student body, because they witnessed firsthand not only the trial Brody and his mother faced but the strength of the love between them. And finally, Brody himself was transformed. His confidence dramatically increased. He was no longer a little boy with a secret. He had found his voice. He was a boy with a story that had touched everyone. Once he learned people would listen to what he had to say, he found the words to share far more frequently.

Figure 4.5. Storytelling builds generational bridges.

Instructional Plan

The family, or "Storytime—Family Style!" is especially effective at enhancing multigenerational storytelling; it is recognized in every culture as the first level of literacy. Students gain a stronger identity and connection to individuals in their families. Family storytelling bridges the generations. The benefit is twofold as the students are listened to and listen to their elders.

This process involves learning effective oral history collection skills. Students are trained to successfully interview and know when to interview and why. Thought-prompting questions and techniques are discussed. Options are discussed for keeping the interview subject comfortable and relaxed. Listening skills are reviewed. Successful interviewing is not in the setting or the questions but is in the listening skills of the one asking the questions. Collected histories are transcribed. Tips are given in regard to selecting and polishing a single tale from the interview to tell and write. The process requires conversation and interaction with others. Trust and respect in the story groups is established. Acceptable parameters are set, and the students self-govern as they practice their tales. The culminating event is an evening program featuring the student storytellers telling their tales to the stars of their stories—the interviewees.

Purpose: Through a creative blend of computer technology and storytelling skills, students discover the joy of learning about the past from those who have lived it. Students practice interviewing skills, document the information they gather, create an entertaining story from the data, and then share their story in a performance setting. If computer technology is unavailable or too challenging, the process can be completed without the technology.

Session I: Students are trained in oral history collection methods.

Assignment: Students record and document an oral history interview from a relative or neighborhood elder.

Session II: Students transcribe from their recordings and notes a word-for-word record of the interview in a computer file, print out a copy, and save it to a disk.

Assignment: Students complete their transcriptions and choose a specific incident to turn into a story.

Session III: Students learn how to storyboard the sequence of an incident and begin developing it into a story by handwriting it. A discussion is held about the creative process of handwriting a story versus entering the data to a computer.

Assignment: Students complete handwriting their stories.

Session IV: Students enter the final draft of their story into the computer and print it out. They read their stories to their group.

Assignment: Students storyboard the final story sequence.

Session V: Students learn storytelling performance skills and begin using them in group practice.

Assignment: Students are to continue telling their tale frequently to various listeners.

Session VI: Students perform their stories for their group. A discussion is held about the differences of their original written tale and their current oral tale. Students come to understand that no oral story is ever "complete."

Assignment: Students draw a picture to illustrate their story for the class book. They compile a class book with a final copy of their oral history transcript, their story, and their illustration to display at the storytelling performance.

Performance

Students perform their stories for the class, students, and invited guests. Students present a transcript of the interview and their story to the interviewee.

If the subject is not at the final performance, arrangements are made to deliver it. Students encourage the performance guests to look at the class book.

Assessment

Storytelling is more than a performance art: it is a life skill. Performance is the end product, but it is only one way to identify that learning is taking place. In essence, if students are talking to each other, learning is taking place. Students learn when they are sharing their stories with each other, when they are sequencing their stories in storyboard form, when they are discussing strengths of the story, and when they stand and deliver anything orally. Students are learning when they encourage one another or listen attentively to their peers and when they practice good audience manners. Learning is taking place when camaraderie develops within the story groups and between the interviewer and the interviewee. Learning also is taking place when the students successfully transition their oral stories into well-crafted written stories.

The following characteristics mark a successful collaboration: students use oral skills to share personal experiences; they identify mental imagery as a tool for story interpretation; they act as positive, respect-filled story coaches; and they analyze their visual imagery and understandings experienced with written and oral versions of the same story.

Fun and chatter are the first signs of a successful collaboration! Encourage interaction. If you can sit at the back of the room and hear excited conversation wash over you in waves from story group to story group, you are having a successful collaboration. Laughter, sound effects, and experimenting with facial expressions are the first characteristics of a successful collaboration. Next come the storyboard and writing phase.

Consider asking the students to answer these questions as a form of assessment:

- What oral skills did you use to share personal experiences?
- How did personal experiences become a part of your storytelling?

- Describe how you used mental imagery as a tool for story interpretation.
- Cite one example of how you acted as a positive, respect-filled story coach or received positive coaching.
- What did you see in your peers (and yourself) which contributed to the successful performance of stories for others?

WHAT'S IN A NAME?

Sadarri Saskill

Speaking, Listening, Writing, and Information Literacy

National Standards

NCTE: 7, 8, 9, 10; CNAEA—Visual Arts 3: Choosing and evaluating a range of subject matter, symbols, and ideas; NCTE—Foreign Language 4: Comparisons—develop insight into the nature of language and culture; AASL 1: Learners use skills, resources, and tools to inquire, think critically, and gain knowledge; AASL 4: Learners use skills, resources, and tools to pursue personal and aesthetic growth.

Objectives

Explore how stories, in a variety of formats, can be used as a vehicle for understanding the importance and significance of names in English and other languages. Improve listening, speaking, and writing skills in the target language. Use research and other techniques to craft and present a personal name story. Create a culturally safe classroom environment while enhancing student self-esteem and appreciation for cultural diversity.

Instructional Plan

This lesson plan can be used with a variety of grade levels, settings, and student populations. It is particularly helpful with English-language learners (ELLs) for whom there are many acronyms. ELL is used in this article for non-native students of English.

One of the easiest ways to get students warmed up to storytelling and story writing is to begin with something as simple as a name.

General Stories About Names

First, we delve into stories where a name has particular significance to the plot. Stories can be read or told. One example is Rumpelstiltskin, a story of a dwarf character who threatens to take away a young woman's child if she can't guess his name. Before the story, we discuss the German origins of the name Rumpelstiltskin and how names can lead us to so many clever discoveries. There is the classic Brothers Grimm version, as well as variants to explore. One of these stories is *Ananse and the Lizard: A West African Tale* by Pat Cummings. In this humorous Ghanaian-influenced folktale, Ananse the spider gets caught up in his own tricks when trying to win the hand of the chief's daughter by guessing her name. Also available are films such as *Muppet Classic Theater* and animated shorts from the old Rocky and Bullwinkle "Fractured Fairy Tales" segment. A rock 'n' roll audio version by Dave Rudolf completes the list.

With ELLs, as well as other student populations, there is often parity between oral language and its relationship to the written page. Because of this, when focusing on this particular connection, I provide students with written copies of song lyrics, poems, and the like. I find this to be especially helpful regarding regional accents and geographically specific vocabulary. When we speak naturally, we do not always use distinct word boundaries as they are laid out on the page. If we did, we would sound robotic, mechanical. This can be challenging to an ELL, but can be overcome with repeated exposure and practice. Add other phonemic processes to the mix, such as epenthesis, assimilation, and elision, and we begin to see how oral language can be quite complex. Consequently, a word-rich environment from day one is essential. Access to as many learning tools as possible can be provided (dictionary, thesaurus, word walls, word banks, books, computers, whiteboards, audio player/recorder, etc.). Using storytelling in all its forms is a fun way to enhance literacy skills for all ages.

Personal Stories About Names

As a segue into the next portion of the lesson plan, I read the story *The Day of Ahmed's Secret* by F. P. Heide and J. H. Gilliland. Culturally rich, the story moves through a typical day of young Ahmed, a boy living in Cairo. The theme of names pops up along the way and concludes with Ahmed being able to read and write his own name in Arabic for the first time. After reading, we discuss the meaning of Ahmed's name. Another book choice might be the bilingual Hmong/English picture book *New Life in America,* which describes what motivates a seven-year-old girl named Yer to learn to read and write. Next, I share a funny story about my name, Sadarri. Finally, I share the following name story from Somsamy Xiong, an ELL teacher and friend:

"It was the year 1976. The United States had pulled out of Vietnam. The Hmong became targets and had to flee from the country of Laos. My parents were one of the first to be able to come to the United States. At the time, my mother was nine months pregnant with me. On the way to the States my mother went into labor. When the plane landed in Seattle, Washington, my mother was rushed to the hospital. My dad named me Somsamy, which means "modern" because we were starting a new life, a new generation, in a new, modern country."

This simple yet powerful name activity was used in a storytelling/creative writing residency with junior high students. Baily, from Princeton, Illinois, wrote us: "... It was more fun than any other stuff I have ever done ... I'm not scared to talk in front of people anymore!" At the elementary level, I told students to go home and ask questions like: How did I get my name? Where did it come from? What does it mean? Was I named for someone? Students were not limited to the English language when making their inquiries. It is important for them to learn how to synthesize information into English, as this mimics real-life scenarios.

One student, Jensen, found out he was named after a soap opera star, and a Wisconsin fourth grader, Aurora, shared scientific information about the aurora borealis, the northern polar lights named for the Roman goddess of the dawn and the Greek god of the north wind. This name story dialogue establishes a basis for continued family communication and serves as a springboard to other family stories. As Illinois student Ryan said, "I really enjoyed the name stories ... I got to share how I was named and then learned about something that happened to my parents when they were kids."

Perhaps not all answers about the origin of the child's name are known. Other options must be available: Students can share the story of their nickname and where it came from; interview an adult in their home about the adult's name story; choose a different name that the student admires and tell a story about it; or tell a name story, real or imagined, about a pet or doll. Baby-name books and Web sites add information to the developing narratives. Web sites may or may not be valuable. The resulting tales can be just the bare bones or can be expanded for a "meatier," more extensive writing project.

Students' name stories may be read or told. Students should be informed beforehand that they will be sharing publicly. They need to be conscious of revealing anything they wish to keep private. Insults and other negative language usage should also be avoided. Stories will vary in tone; some humorous, some thought provoking, some eye-opening. Since language acquisition levels vary from student to student and class to class, here are a few additional related activity choices.

Related Activities

- Acrostic poem: students write the first letter of their name vertically down the side of the page. Next to each letter, they write a word or sentence of self-description.

- Teach the name-game song. Example: Rico, Rico bo Bico / Bonana fanna fo Fico / Fee fy mo Mico / Rico. Follow the pattern for student names as the class sings along. (This reinforces phonemic awareness.)

- In American Sign Language (ASL), instead of spelling out a name, a person is given a sign name. This usually is the first letter of a person's name joined to a sign that represents a particular characteristic or personality descriptor. Students can be taught the first letter of their name in sign language and look up descriptive ASL signs either in a book or online.

- Another version of this concept is to form a circle and have the children choose an action that represents their name and show it to the group. It does not have to be a true ASL sign; it can be an interpretive sign symbol. Play begins with one student saying his or her name while performing the selected action. Then he calls out another name and performs that action. The student who has been called then repeats his own name with the action and calls out yet another name and corresponding action. Play continues as such. Variant: If someone forgets or stalls too long, they have to sit out.

- A computer Egyptian hieroglyphics program can be used to print out the letters of a student's name. Using online hieroglyph translators and charts, students can match English alphabet letters to their hieroglyph counterparts and draw out their name to be used on a poster, bookmark, or other craft project. Conversely, students can translate letters or messages from the hieroglyphs. Students may even create their own symbols to represent the letters of the English alphabet. These activities especially validate languages that use alternative alphabets or writing systems.

- More advanced students can research the name of a favorite fictional character (superhero, literary character, pop-culture persona, etc). After finding out the meaning of the name, students write about how the character is similar to or different from the actual meaning of the name.

- Continue the lesson using surnames. You can find free genealogy sites on the Internet and access information through, for example, the Ellis Island, New York, databases. Students can make a family crest with a few selected words describing what their surnames represent. They can also study other cultures that have family crests (that is, Scottish, German, and African).

- Make a colorful collage poster of self-descriptive words and expressions.

- Make a class book, an audio recording, a video recording, or a PowerPoint presentation of all student name stories.

- Discuss in detail customs for choosing names across a variety of cultures and compare them to any cultures represented within the classroom (Native American, Nigerian, etc.).

Assessments

Assessments vary. Students can be evaluated on their name story presentations by a rubric of requirements predesigned by (or with) the classroom teacher. Additional avenues include flashcard matching (hieroglyphs/English), artwork, classroom discussion, or other related writing assignments.

Resources

Books, CDs, and DVDs

- Cummings, Pat. *Ananse and the Lizard: A West African Tale.* New York: Henry Holt and Company, 2002.
- Heide, Florence Parry, and Gilliland, Judith Heide. *The Day of Ahmed's Secret.* New York: Mulberry Books, 1995. Heiner, Heidi A. SurLaLune Fairytales. http//www.SurLaLuneFairytales.com. Cross-cultural fairytale and folktale variants, bibliographies, links, and essays.

- Rudolf, Dave. *Not So Grimm Fairy Tales.* CD. Park Forest, IL: Gambler Publishing, 2003.
- "Rumpelstiltskin" and "Rumpelstiltskin Returns." *Rocky & Bullwinkle: The Best of Fractured Fairy Tales: Volume 1.* DVD. Directed by Steve Moore, 1961. San Diego, CA: Genius Products, Inc., 2005.
- "Rumpelstiltskin." *Muppet Classic Theater.* VHS. Directed by David Grossman. Burbank, CA: Walt Disney Studios, 1994.
- Yang, Sheng. *New Life in America.* Brillion, WI: Zander Press, 2006.

Web Sites

- American Sign Language Browser. http://commtechlab.msu.edu/sites/aslweb/browser.htm. Communication Technology Lab, Michigan State University.
- Ashliman, D. L. *The Name of the Helper.* University of Pittsburgh, 2000–2001. http//www.pitt.edu/~dash/type0500.html. Versions of Rumplestiltskin-like tales.
- Baby Name Addicts. http://www.babynameaddicts.com. This site has a search feature and categories by theme (birds, music, soap operas, Disney characters, etc.).
- Campbell, Mike. "Behind the Name: The Etymology and History of First Names." http://www.behindthename.com. This site has a search feature that locates names that sound like the name entered. Other options include searching a geographic location or popular names from mythology, astronomy, literature, the Bible, etc.
- Character Naming Resources. http://www.writing-world.com/links/names.shtml. This is actually a literary character-naming resource to links that deal with naming and name origins.
- Make Your Own Cartouche. http://www.hbschool.com/activity/cartouche/cartouche.html. Students can make their own Egyptian cartouche using hieroglyphics that represent the letters of their name. Harcourt School Publishers.
- Millmore, Mark. Ancient Egyptian Hieroglyphic Writing. http://www.eyelid.co.uk/hiero1.htm. This site has a hieroglyphic alphabet translator feature and instructions for making a hieroglyphic eCard. 1997–2008. Hieroglyphs. Discovering Egypt.

BEGINNING READING—A FAMILY AFFAIR: MAINSTREAMING KOREAN STUDENTS THROUGH ESL STORYTELLING

Luiz DaSilva, PhD

Speaking, Listening, Reading, and Writing

National Standards

NCTE: 1, 2, 3, 4, 6, 9, 10, 11.

Objectives

The goal is to assist in various ways Korean students in English schools in São Paulo, Brazil, in learning and using English in order to accomplish school work and in order to establish peer friendships.

Reading via a large emphasis on storytelling has been the tool used for mainstreaming Korean students, grades K-8, in English-speaking schools in Brazil. Fortunately, the children come to us literate in their own language and this makes the job a lot easier. As their English is limited, teachers, aides, parents, and private tutors rely on storytelling to bring the new students into the daily lessons. Folktales across cultures are key.

From kindergarten on, the newcomers are exposed to practical language—it is an immersion program. The approach is individual most of the time, with the tutor providing a rich interaction of language and folktales. A student's work is integrated during the main teaching, beginning with reading aloud one-, two-, three-, and four-syllable words. When necessary, a bilingual Korean native speaker assists the new student. However, most of the assistance given to the student, at school and privately, helps him or he feel accepted in class.

As a private tutor, I focus my teaching first on the classroom goal and then I supply the student with reading material on his or her own level. As we begin our sessions, I often start with a story. The student retells the story in English. By telling and reading the same story over and over, the student begins to absorb the sounds and illustrations. Quite often, the student may already know the story from a Korean book and will read it again as homework. Then he or she reads the new English version to every member of the family. Grades one and two usually copy the story in their notebook. Next, they retell the story in their own words. Finally, they reproduce the story in writing, with the aid of the illustrations. As the student produces more and more writing techniques, such as spelling, vocabulary, and grammar, those in grades four and up are helped through a classroom content base.

The bright side of this process is the total support given by the family. The mothers in particular are dedicated to their child's English learning and academic progress. Many students have daily private lessons with different teachers in order to improve their mechanics, listening, and speaking abilities. They often surprise the teachers by performing beyond our expectations.

Since the students do not speak Portuguese and the teachers do not speak Korean, the only source of communication for both parties is through the English language. They are immersed in the language even during recess and lunch to reinforce the learning. Consequently, after one year in our schools, many youngsters are as fluent in English as they are in Korean. In their second year in Brazil, some feel more comfortable speaking English because all their communication away from home is in English. English becomes their main access to the world beyond the family.

One of the most intriguing ways they practice communication in public is the "show and tell" presentations. This weekly exercise is mandatory for all students. Therefore, they rehearse it at home so many times that the performance, funny at first, ends with the students rejoicing. The teachers never get tired of assisting them. Perhaps it is because the children want to be successful; they have a tradition of obedience and respect.

Teachers and administrators are very pleased with the attitude, progress, and performance of each student in class. A few years ago, when increasing numbers of Korean children started to make a difference in schools, administrators were unsure how they would handle the needs. The "bridge" or intervention program defined above helps us integrate these students into our classrooms, and Koreans are welcome in all the five English-speaking schools in São Paulo without reserve. The students have made a healthy contribution through their determination, performance, and behavior. From victory to victory, the Korean students are climbing to the mountaintop of knowledge.

Rich—A Story of Success

There is an old idiom that says, "Necessity is the mother of invention." The pristine need of Korean students to continue their education abroad puts them in the category of being the quickest foreign learners in the American schools in Brazil. Korean students are at the top rank among new transfer students in grades K-12.

Storytelling is the number one method used in the schools of São Paulo to assist the mainstreaming of this population. In addition to the regular grade-level classes, most students are requested to take private lessons to guide them into the new rhythm imposed by the educational system. Therefore, as they join the new schools and attend classes, they are either matched with a fellow student who translates for them, or they go through the motions of "sink or swim." Often parents help by providing extra assistance along with the private tutoring.

In February 2007, a boy named Richard was transferred to Brazil with his father, who was embarking on a new post in a multinational company. There was no time to prepare the child for the new school challenges. Rich was a fourth grader, but because of his lack of English, he attended first-grade English class. A classmate helped him and, at home, a tutor gave him educational and moral support to cope with the transition. In April, I was hired to assist him. We worked on all levels of communications. He enjoyed classical fairy tales the most because he had read them in Korean. Storytelling became the method and strategy to help Rich learn English. Regarding his other subjects, Rich brought his books home and we went over his lessons, one by one.

In late May, after three months in our school, during a teacher-parent-tutor conference, it was suggested by the school that Rich leave it because they felt they could not provide him with the help he really needed. I proposed an immersion course during the school break (June and July) and suggested that a new evaluation be conducted in August. During this time, Rich blossomed. He attended the fifth-grade class during the new school year and did not need any more in-class translations. In addition to homework and reading comprehension, he did all that was demanded in class and brought home extra work for practice. Little by little he was becoming independent and his first-quarter report card boasted a reading comprehension on a third-grade level. Over

Christmas break, he read *Charlotte's Web* by E. B. White and gave an oral presentation in class.

During the parent-teacher conference in February, his mother was informed that Rich's progress was amazing and he was becoming an asset to the class. Even though he still needed to increase his English vocabulary, other skills such as his reasoning, comprehension, and class participation brought him to the same level as the rest of his peers. Rich not only enjoys attending school, but was anxious to participate in all of the activities. His jolly attitude made assisting him effortless. If he frowned when he did not understand a word problem, the teacher's aide was always ready to help. His third-quarter report card was really something to boast about. Rich concluded the fifth grade and the teacher believes that he will have no difficulty in sixth grade, provided that his improvement remains steady.

Even though his parents still remain mediocre in their English communication, Rich has served as interpreter at informal meetings. He is an active group member in oral presentations and community involvement. Rich now serves as a *cicerone* (cultural guide) to a Korean newcomer in his class. He remembers so well how this helped him last year that he does it cheerfully. Based on his progress in English, the family has decided that the next vacations will be devoted to the reinforcement of English writing, reading comprehension, and learning Portuguese. This story is a tribute to a dedicated student and teachers of bilingual education who can make a difference using storytelling as a tool.

USING PICTURE BOOKS AS A "JUMPING-OFF" PLACE FOR STORYTELLING

Darlene Neumann

Speaking, Listening, Reading, Writing, and Visual Literacy

National Standards

NCTE: 1, 4.

Objectives

Students will listen carefully to a picture book that is read aloud and reread it; students will tell about an event from their own life that is related to a picture book; they will write the story of this life experience after telling it to an audience; they will retell a story changing some of the literary elements.

Every time a picture book is read, a new window is opened into the world for readers and listeners alike. The fun of reading a picture book doesn't have to stop when the book ends. Sharing common experiences through reading aloud is a comfortable yet exciting way to step into the world of storytelling.

The shared experience of reading picture books can trigger memories that are begging to be told. These lesson plans use picture books that are likely to trigger memories of deeds fair and foul.

Elements of a Good Story

Duke, Kate. *Aunt Isabel Tells a Good One.*

Aunt Isabel, a mouse, and a little mouseling make up a story before bedtime, giving the reader elements of a story well-told according to Aunt Isabel: when, where, who, what happens, a problem (to keep the story from being dull), villains, danger, and a happy ending.

Make a chart using Aunt Isabel's elements. Have students tell the "when" or the "where," etc., that the mouse uses while telling the story. When all elements of the mouse's story are recorded on the chart, have the class retell her story using the chart. Tell the class that you would like to change some of the events when you reread the story. Ask students for suggestions of changes. Reread Aunt Isabel's story using a few of the students' suggestions.

One student took the book home to read to his mouse. He reported that his mouse thought the book was too long, so he left out some of the elements. The story didn't work as well, but his mouse didn't know the difference and went to sleep anyway.

Adding or Changing Animals in an Existing Story

Pearson, Tracey Campbell. *Bob.*

Bob, a rooster who doesn't know how to crow, searches for someone who can teach him. Because this is a pattern book, it is very easy to add or change animals and sounds. Kids can join in the barnyard confusion as Bob uses his new skills.

Read the book but stop just as Bob gets home. An animal is coming down the lane! It's a fox, and the kids will need to help scare it away. They need to choose whether to be the cow, the frog, the cat, or the dog, but everyone can be the rooster. On the page where the animal sounds happen, each child can repeat his or her chosen sound at least five times all together. Be sure to tell them what signal you've chosen for stopping so they can do the "cock-a-doodle-do" together.

While I do not use props when I perform stories, I do use them occasionally in teaching storytelling. This pattern story lends itself well to using plastic barnyard animals when working with younger children or those with special needs. Since plastic farm animals can be found easily and cheaply, each child can have a set of them to use while retelling the story. Retelling worked well in a group. Special-needs children benefited from working in a group but still needed help with dialogue. Having the plastic animals arranged in sequence helped all of the children remember the sequence of events.

Changing the setting and animals completely changed the story. Children replaced the barnyard with a jungle. They lined up the farm animals, replacing each with a jungle animal. Children determined which animal had a problem and what the problem was. One group of first graders changed the problem from a rooster not knowing how to crow to a monkey not knowing how to climb trees. He asked many animals in the jungle for help. Finally, a little caterpillar told him to use his arms to grab branches, but, since she was a caterpillar and not a monkey, she could only tell him what to do, not show him how to do it.

This book lends itself well to drawing story maps not only for the picture book, but also for their adapted stories.

Trouble Stories

Shannon, David. *No, David!*

There is trouble on almost every page of this book, and almost every child can tell a story about something that he or she did which was very close to what David did.

Krosoczka, Jarrett J. *Baghead.*

This is an easy book to use with storytelling because almost everyone has a haircut story involving either a person or a pet. After reading *Baghead*, ask if anyone in the group has ever cut their own or anyone else's hair. Stories will abound.

One deaf child shared this story. She decided to cut her doll's hair. It got shorter and shorter because she tried to make it even, but she wasn't worried at all. She got up the next morning and was shocked to find out the doll's hair hadn't grown back even a little bit. She hid the doll, hoping its hair would grow back before her mom found the doll. She finally realized the doll's hair was never going to grow back. Her mom didn't get mad because Mom had done the very same thing when she was a little girl!

Students wrote their stories in comic-book style. Children told their stories to other class members.

Researching a Person and Telling His or Her Story

This exercise works well for fourth and fifth graders. Third graders will need extra help in reading research material.

Chandra, Deborah. *George Washington's Teeth.*

This book can be a model for researching a famous person with a problem that he or she encountered and had to overcome. Just as the title implies, this book is about problems George Washington had with his own teeth and his first set of false teeth. They were not, as rumor has it, wooden. They were made out of hippopotamus ivory and cow's tooth, carved by hand, and held in his mouth with metal springs. Actual photos of George Washington's teeth can be found online.

Have students read about famous people and choose a person whose story moves them. Consider these questions: Does the person have a weakness or shortcoming in his or her personality? Is there a physical problem or characteristic that concerned or hindered this person? How was the problem overcome? Or was it ever overcome? Tell that person's story, inspiring the audience, making them feel this was or is one of the most important people in the world.

A Tribute to a Hero

Polacco, Patricia. *Thank you, Mr. Falker.*

When Patricia Polacco began attending school, she had great difficulty learning how to read. Her classmates called her dumb. Her fifth-grade teacher, Mr. Falker, tried to stop the teasing.

When Mr. Falker found Patricia hiding on the playground after an episode of name-calling, Patricia admitted that she couldn't read. Every day after school, Mr. Falker and the reading teacher met with Patricia, and she learned to read. She remained so grateful to her fifth-grade teacher that she dedicated this book to him. Patricia saw Mr. Falker at a wedding thirty years later and was finally able to tell him how he had changed her life.

Invite students to think of a hero who helped them, and tell about the situation. This story can be intensely personal. To help remove the teller from the situation, this story can be told in third person. *A bully should never be named, however. Bullies sometimes outgrow their bad behaviors.*

Assessments

Each student will tell a story from his or her own experience that relates to one of the categories of picture books that have been read. Each student will use a story map to summarize a story for telling. Each student will tell and write a story about getting in trouble.

Bibliography

- Chandra, Deborah. *George Washington's Teeth.* New York: Farrar, Straus and Giroux, 2003.
- Duke, Kate. *Aunt Isabel Tells a Good One.* New York: Dutton Children's Books, 1992.
- Krosoczka, Jarrett J. *Baghead.* New York: Alfred A. Knopf, 2002.
- Pearson, Tracey Campbell. *Bob.* New York: Farrar, Straus and Giroux, 2002.
- Polacco, Patricia. *Thank you, Mr. Falker.* New York: Philomel Books, 1998.
- Shannon, David. *No, David!* New York: Blue Sky Press, 1998.

FROM MYTH TO SUPERHERO: CONNECTING ANCIENT STORIES TO OUR MODERN WORLD

Tracy Walker

Speaking, Listening, Reading, Writing, Visual Literacy, and Information Literacy

National Standards

NCTE: 2, 3, 8, 12; CNAEA—Theater/Drama 2: Students use variations of locomotor and nonlocomotor movement and vocal pitch, tempo, and tone for different characters. They assume roles that exhibit concentration and contribute to the action of classroom dramatizations based on personal experience and heritage, imagination, literature, and history; CNAEA—Theater/Drama 5: Students communicate information to peers about people, events, time, and place related to classroom dramatizations; CNAEA—Visual Arts 1: Students use different media, techniques, and processes to communicate ideas, experiences, and stories; CNAEA—Visual Arts 6: Students identify connections between the visual arts and other disciplines in the curriculum; AASL 1: Learners use skills, resources, and tools to inquire, think critically, and gain knowledge; AASL 2: Learners use skills, resources, and tools to draw conclusions, make informed decisions, apply knowledge to new situations, and create new knowledge; AASL 3: Learners use skills, resources, and tools to share knowledge and participate ethically and productively as members of our democratic society; AASL 4: Learners use skills, resources, and tools to pursue personal and aesthetic growth.

Objectives

Through writing, listening, the visual arts, and speech, students will work cooperatively to explore major characters of Greek mythology. They will gain an understanding of the link between ancient stories and modern mythology found in comic books and graphic novels. Using this information, students will then individually create their own superhero and origin story.

Materials

- Classroom space where students can work effectively in groups
- Computers with Internet access
- Access to school media center
- Poster board
- Marker, crayons, other art materials as desired
- Rulers

- Scissors
- Paper and pencil for writing
- Paper for individual drawings
- Myths for student skits

Good gods! The characters of Greek mythology and the stories that surround them are a wonderful way to demonstrate universal themes and origin stories by connecting them with modern myths found in comic books and graphic novels. I have used these activities for both mythology units and as exercises when exploring graphic novels.

I begin this unit by discussing the origin of the Greek gods and goddesses and telling the creation myth of Nyx, Uranus, and Gaia. We also discuss origin stories so students have knowledge of their purpose and the role they play.

Once we have explored these initial steps, it's time for students to be divided into groups for their first mission. Each group is assigned a different deity. I do this by asking each student to consult the Oracle, which is usually a unique box or bag I have created. Inside I place the names of the principal gods/goddesses of the Greek pantheon (Zeus, Athena, Apollo, Aphrodite, Mars, Hades, Artemis, and Poseidon—give or take depending on the size of the class). Every student will draw one god or goddess slip from the Oracle. Once each has drawn a name, there should be three to four students in each group.

Using library and Internet resources, it will be the mission of each group to research their god or goddess by answering the following questions:

- How did this god/goddess come to exist?
- What is he or she the god/goddess of? (Mars is the god of war, for example.)
- What powers does this god/goddess possess?
- Does this god/goddess have any helpers?
- What is the symbol of this god/goddess?

After the groups have completed their research, they will work together to create a poster depicting their god or goddess, incorporating the answers to the above questions. Each group will then present their posters to the class to give a better idea of each of the major deities.

Next, each group will be given a myth that is primarily about their god/goddess. They will then work together to tell the story to the class. At this point, I go over good telling tips and work with each group as they develop their story. Once the groups are ready, they will share these stories with the class.

The second stage of this project involves students working individually and applying the knowledge they have gained from their group work (and class discussion) to create their own mythological character and origin story. As a group, we reflect on the Greek origin story and discuss our modern genres of comic books and graphic novels. Examples can be found in characters such as Spider-Man, Superman, and Wonder Woman, who each have their own origin stories that explain how they came to be and how they attained their powers.

I begin this part of the unit by sharing with the students that Marvel—the publisher of Spider-Man and the X-Men comics—is searching for the next great superhero to add to their famous lineup. Each student is given the mission of creating a superhero of their very own, complete with origin story. They begin by answering the following questions, which I usually put in the form of a memo from Marvel asking students to provide the following information:

- What is your superhero's name?
- How did your superhero come to be? (For example: Was he/she/it born with the powers? Did he/she/it develop them on their own, like Batman? Did he/she/it obtain the powers through an accident, like Peter Parker (Spider-Man)? And exactly what power does the superhero possess?)
- Many superheroes have secret identities (for example, Clark Kent is secretly Superman). Does yours? If so, what is it?
- What superpowers or skills does your character possess?
- What equipment, gadgets, or inventions aid your character?
- What mission does your superhero pursue? (For example, does he or she work to rid the world of threats to the environment, etc?)

Every superhero needs a supervillain, as well. Once students have completed information on their superheroes, it's time for them to do the same for their supervillains.

We need to know the following about your supervillain:

- What is his/her/its name?
- What are the methods used to battle your superhero?
- Why does your supervillain oppose the work of your superhero?

Once students have answered these questions, they are ready to write the origin story of their superhero. The origin story should include information from the above questions, including those on the supervillain. Next, students will create a visual depiction of their superhero. Finally, they will tell their origin stories to the class. If students choose, they may integrate their visual in the telling of their story.

There are a number of ways to expand on this unit. For example, origin stories of other cultures can be explored, and there are a myriad of ways to integrate social studies into this project, as well.

In my experience, students have responded well to this project—particularly boys. Several small miracles have occurred: students who are not traditional verbal and logical learners, but those who are more inclined toward kinesthetic and visual learning, enjoyed getting to express themselves in the varied formats used. I also found that comic books and graphic novels helped to create interest in reading for some students who were not stimulated by more traditional books. An example, while working with a group of students, one boy went above and beyond in creating his own superhero and origin story. After the project was complete and he had shared his origin story with the class, he expanded to create his own comic book using the superhero he had created. This was particularly rewarding because his teacher explained that he was difficult to motivate. While very bright, he rarely completed homework assignments and seemed disinterested in many classroom activities. With this project, however, he used visual, written, and spoken storytelling skills that connected with his life and interests.

Assessment

Using information gleaned from reading and listening to research on Greek gods and goddesses, students will be asked to apply this knowledge to create and tell the origin story of a NEW superhero! Understanding is documented throughout the activities by actively monitoring students during group and individual work and during class discussion. Students will be asked how the Greek origin myth is similar to the origin stories used for comic book and graphic novel characters. They will be asked to make connections between the characteristics of the Greek gods and goddesses and those of superheroes. Rubrics may be used for the writing, visual, and oral portions of this project, as well.

Related Resources

The following books and Web sites are helpful when teaching this unit.

- Amery, Heather. *Greek Myths for Young Children.* London: Usborne Books, 1999.
- D'Aulaire, Ingri. *D'Aulaire's Book of Greek Myths.* New York: Doubleday Books for Young Readers, 1962.
- The Myth Man presents Myth Mania: Greek Mythology Today and Myth of the Month. http://mythman.com/ (accessed March 21, 2008).

EXPLORING THE WESTWARD EXPANSION THROUGH STORYTELLING
(Using Learning Centers)
Evornia Kincaid, EdD
Speaking, Listening, Reading, and Writing

National Standards

NCTE: 3, 5, 11.

Objectives

Through the use of learning centers using related literature, children will be better able to identify and use story literary terms; predict (who, when, where, and what happened); create writing topics based on the reading of a book; employ basic elements of storytelling; work in collaborative groups to practice storytelling skills; keep a literature response journal; and compare and contrast and create a story and tell it.

Introduction

Research shows that the traditional way of teaching our twenty-first-century children should be modified to meet their needs. According to an article written in *Essay Forum* (2006), "Having a wide range of effective approaches and knowing how and when to use them is the way to go." Teaching using learning centers will allow students to connect what they are learning with each other, with other subjects, and with the outside world. Exploring the Westward Expansion will allow children to develop in two areas: compare and contrast historical events and develop storytelling skills through reading, writing, speaking, listening, viewing, and visualizing.

Before introducing the centers, the children and their teacher will discuss selected aspects of the movement of people to the West. One introductory method is KWL, which helps students make a connection to the topic of Westward Expansion before getting into the centers. KWL is an instructional technique created by Donna Ogle (1986). It was introduced for classroom use to encourage students to use their prior knowledge, to generate questions, and to affirm what new information was acquired. Students brainstorm what they know before teaching occurs:

- What I **K**now
- What I **W**ant to know
- What I **L**earned (accomplished after unit is studied)

Another introductory method is webbing, which is used to help students brainstorm and write down all their ideas about a topic in order to make connections to what is being introduced. Next, those brainstorms are organized into topics for study.

Concurrent to learning center assignments, students will be reading short novels, picture books, and nonfiction literature to broaden their understanding and/or to pursue a special interest about Westward Expansion.

Opening Celebration

The classroom is decorated with western artifacts. Upon the arrival of the students, western music is playing to set the mood. The teacher is wearing clothing from that era (cowboy hat, boots, kerchief. long flannel shirt and/or pants with chaps, or a long dress with a bonnet). The teacher asks students what they know about the Westward Expansion and uses KWL to chart responses or make a story web.

Literacy Development in the Storytelling Classroom

- Develop a word wall for new words, that is, west, expansion. Students will find words from the stories to add to the word wall.
- Use the U.S. map as a visual to locate specific places.
- Focus on moving from east, west, north, and south.
- Select a related book that will be introduced such as *Wagon Wheels* by Barbara Brenner
- Discuss the brief narrative historic account on the back cover of the book.
- Discuss the genre of writing (historic fiction).
- Discuss elements of our own stories that should be remembered.
- Model the story elements—whole classroom.
- Share the selected story with the class.
- Re-discuss the story elements after reading the story.
- Have students journal the story elements.
- Have students report to their assigned centers.

Developing Learning Centers

The teacher establishes the centers and assigns no more than five or six students per center (traveling groups). As students use the centers, the teacher moves throughout to make sure that the students understand the assignments. The teacher must decide what the students are to learn (and accomplish) at each center, all with the idea that at the end of the center experience, students are expected to understand the story elements well enough to write and create their own narratives about the Westward Expansion and share them with the class. Students will journal each day before going to the centers (listed below).

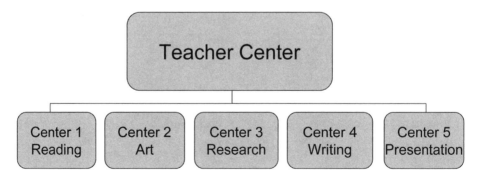

Learning Centers Format

Figure 4.6.

The Reading Center

Students will use the selected class book or they may choose their own from the variety of books and articles offered. Sample categories: tall tales, picture books, and young adult novels; bringing law to the West: bad buys of the Western Expansion; eyewitness books; books on foods, medicines, and herbs; hazards; daily life; transportation: covered wagon, stagecoach, and railroad; immigrant populations, etc. Students will submit the titles and authors of all books they have read, some from each category offered. They will make index cards of words they have learned and place the new words on a word wall.

The Art Center

In this center, students will 1) design a booklet for their stories, and 2) accomplish one piece of handwork, such as wood burning or crafting a leather good such as a wallet. These activities are easily attainable at craft stores; their importance to the unit of study cannot be overlooked. The senses involved such as smell and texture are important to the language that will appear in the student stories.

The Research Center

Students will research Westward Expansion. This will help them reinforce Internet skills in order to be more creative with their stories. Students can work independently or with a buddy. This center includes books and Internet accessibility. Materials: a computer for Internet research, social studies texts, and related nonfiction books.

The Writing Center

The teacher will give clear instructions and examples. The teacher models the five-sentence paragraph. In this center, students will work on basic skills for writing a flowing paragraph. They will learn what a topic sentence (or main idea) is and how to add supporting details. In this center, students will hone their writing skills by constructing paragraphs for their stories. They will have the option to change the ending of the original story told, or create their own stories.

The Presentation Center

Students will share their written stories with a buddy or with their traveling group before sharing it with the full class. Also, a traveling group may decide to write a play and this is their practice space.

Activity Time: Day One

- Develop a storyboard based on *Wagon Wheels* by Barbara Brenner.
- Use story elements (character, setting, plot, theme/mood, conflict, and solutions).
- Students will base their storyboards on *Wagon Wheels*.

- Students will use drawings to represent each story element.
- Developing a storyboard will help students to better understand story elements before developing their own stories.

Day Two

Students will be assigned to four different centers. A team leader will be assigned in each group to help anyone needing assistance and to aid special-needs children. In some cases, I will have my assistant work with special-needs children. Centers: reading, writing, art, and research.

Day Three

Students will rotate centers, adjusting student assignments if necessary and including the research center.

Day Four

Students will rotate centers. They are reminded daily before beginning the center work that all of this work has a language arts emphasis. Their work should move from knowledge of Westward Expansion to the ability to organize this information into a written and spoken narrative.

Day Five

Students will continue to develop and edit their stories.

Day Six

Presentation center: Students will share their written stories with each other, checking for story conventions, authenticity, historical accuracy, and interest. Students should also be encouraged to speak clearly and with emotion. A teacher can also work with students on stance, intonation, confidence, and enthusiasm.

Day Seven

Wrap up: Students will share their created stories with the whole class as an oral presentation. Students' artwork should be displayed with the stories.

Modifications

Special-needs children will experience the same journey as the rest of the students. They will be assigned support people to help them. Gifted and talented students will go to the independent center to do further research on Westward Expansion. They write a brief report of this research to place in their book.

Supplies

- Copies of the book *Wagon Wheels*
- Dictionaries
- Poster board
- Maps
- Markers, color pencils, pencils, crayons, and glue
- Construction paper
- Notebook for journaling

Assessments

Students will be assessed on their written stories, art booklets, journals, and storytelling.

Resources

- Brenner, Barbara. *Wagon Wheels*. New York: Harper and Row, 1978.
- Coerr, Eleanor. *Buffalo Bill and the Pony Express*. New York: HarperCollins, 1996.
- Kramer, Sydelle. *Wagon Train*. Grosset Dunlap, 1997.
- MacLachlan, Patricia. *Sarah, Plain and Tall*. New York: Harper Row, 1985.
- Sandin, Joan. *The Long Way Westward*. New York: Harper Row, 1989.
- Thompson, Gare. *A Homesteading Community of the 1880s*. Washington, DC: National Geographic Society, 2002.

TEACHING HISTORY, LANGUAGE, LITERACY, AND CULTURAL PRIDE THROUGH STORYTELLING, MUSIC, AND MOVEMENT
Mama Edie Armstrong, MHS, CCC/SLP

National Standards

NCTE: 4, 9, 10.

Objectives

All students need to recognize themselves in the classroom and in the curriculum studied; those who are challenged need classroom accommodations and wherever possible they and their special curricula need to be included (mainstreamed) into the classroom community.

When I was in elementary school, I did not like history. All the dates and wars and presidents on some level had me wondering, "What does any of this have to do with me?" I did not like geography either. I found interest in studying the cultures of the various peoples, but didn't really care about population counts, the names of mountain ranges, or their distance above sea level.

My keen interest in social studies really began when my mother started telling me stories of her life and of our people in the early 1900s. She told me stories of the great migration of black people fleeing north from various southern states to escape the brutal and unjust Jim Crow laws. With my parents having both been born in 1911, and with emancipation occurring between 1863 and 1865, slavery was not at all far behind them. It had only been about fifty years, not even a lifetime for many; and both of my parents' people were from the South. This history was very relevant for me. I became visible in this history. It is this sense of relativity, of personal connection, that we need to provide for children in order for them to find meaning in the stories of our past. These stories also provide fantastic material for literacy and language development.

My personal experiences growing up, even in the North during the 1950s and 1960s, reflected double standards and unjust Jim Crow laws that were imposed upon people of color, even though they were illegal. In fact, the eradication of such attitudes and double standards continues to this day.

My experience was connected to real and personal history that my parents and grandparents spoke of, a history they lived. They told stories related to my African American, Italian, and First Nations ancestry. I couldn't enjoy cowboy and Indian movies as I thought others did. These films had a different meaning for me, for us, especially when I would see my elderly grandmother fussing and throwing her soft house slippers at the television as the cavalry pillaged Indian villages; she shouted, "Leave 'em alone! Leave 'em alone!" These stories seemed to make authentic and realistic references to people and events I either knew, was related to, or had played a significant role in the lives of my people. Our history, as my family elders presented it, allowed me to somehow see myself in this continuum; that's what gave it meaning to me. In my work, introducing children to a sense of connection has been essential in helping them see the importance of our history and of their own significance in this continuum. They become visible.

The life stories I was told were not all about unhappy times. Many stories told by my grandparents, uncles, and aunts had my cousins and me falling out laughing during our visits to each others' homes or during our large family reunions. Whether happy, sad, or completely fabricated from uniquely intelligent and creative imaginations, they knew how to make these stories come to life!

I'm certain I didn't like social studies in school because the presentation was irrelevant and therefore very boring. Little about my culture was included. I was unable to comprehend that there was anything that could serve to make me proud or give me a reason to want to connect. As we teach, and *whatever* we teach, it is key to employ a sense of personal connection to the learner in a way that is engaging and alive.

In the late 1970s, I started providing classroom language stimulation sessions while working within the Chicago public schools. This practice began one day after I went to pick up a child for individual speech therapy. I was told he was absent. So, rather than returning to my office, I asked his teacher if she would like me to engage the entire classroom with a language development activity. She eagerly said, "Yes!" and that's how it began.

I facilitated the class the activity I planned for the absent child. The children were very receptive and easy to engage, and they demonstrated their comprehension of the concepts introduced. I offered to come into Mrs. Christian's classroom whenever I could to provide more of the same. Again, she excitedly accepted.

Word traveled about Mrs. Armstrong, the speech clinician, providing language sessions in Mrs. Christian's room. Other teachers wanted me in their classrooms. While it was impossible to accommodate everyone, once a week I began going into the classrooms of my speech-enrolled children with severe learning disabilities. The main focus of the lessons was guided by the speech/language goals and objectives on my enrolled students' individualized education plans (IEP), and everyone in the classroom benefited.

And then we found the power of story! Entering a teacher's class one day, I found her "fit to be tied." She was exasperated that her ten- to twelve-year-old children with learning disabilities had twice miserably failed her test on the American Revolution. I suggested, "OK, have a seat. Let me see what I can do." I dove full force into black dialect with the class of all African American students, becoming "Ol' George, III," saying things like, "You better SEND me my money or I'll send my boys over there after you!" The new Americans replied, "We not sendin' you *nothin'!* We ain't getting nothin' for it! We don't even have nobody over there to speak up for us! So, if you bad, SEND your boys on over here! We'll show 'em a thing or two!"

Next, I became the First Nations people, hiding in the hills, crouching down low, peering quickly from left to right, poised with bow and arrow, ready to take aim. I became the new Americans, brandishing shotguns and just waiting for the first sight of a British red coat. I was Paul Revere AND his horse, rearing up on its hind legs, looking very impressive, as the famous warning was shouted, "The British are coming! The British are coming!" and then "galloping" across the front of the classroom. The children and the teacher laughed and laughed. But of more significance is that she retested on the American Revolution in standard English—and the students all passed.

In this one exercise about history and geography, the children gained new vocabulary; had practice in producing target speech sounds; began to distinguish between a monarchy and a democracy; learned what it means to have "the third" behind your name; understood "taxation without representation"; and learned why it is each person's responsibility to fight for freedom. I knew then that I had discovered something special by connecting with storytelling. I asked students to connect how they thought and spoke with what is required in

Chicago public school classrooms ... and it made sense to them in their language. I've been using the power of story in performances, multimedia productions, and workshops, teaching many things to all ages and cultures ever since.

One day, the developer and program coordinator of our speech assistants program, which was a pilot for the country, paid me an unexpected visit. And there I was, in a location not on my schedule (an administrator's nightmare). She sat quietly in the back of the room as I continued my lesson, asking afterward, "What was that?" When I explained what I was doing and why, she simply nodded her head, saying, "Hmm." At our next speech assistants meeting, she distributed a form that was to be used in required weekly classroom language sessions. She mentioned to us what she had observed during her visit to one of my sites. In this way, we contributed to the beginning of the increasingly popular practice of providing speech therapy in the classroom, or mainstreaming, or "least restrictive environment," or "every child needs to be included." As more speech and language pathologists address issues of literacy, the classroom provides the perfect environment for reaching the greatest number of children.

Providing services in the classroom has allowed me not only to teach language concepts and to provide fun exercises for articulation, but also to address issues of self-esteem and cultural pride. The children were guided in their use of descriptive language as they were asked to explain their answers to my questions, which also reflected their level of language comprehension and critical-thinking skills. They were also given, through the presentation of original songs, poetry, and stories from history, a knowledge and appreciation of other cultures and a sense of themselves belonging to a cultural group that has and continues to contribute much to the world.

CHAPTER FIVE

Middle School and Beyond

USE YOUR WORDS: REIMAGINING LITERACY
Greg Weiss

"Oralcy precedes literacy."
—Elizabeth Ellis

"The art of writing is inseparable from the act of having something to say."
—Wallace Douglas

For many, it begins at about the age of two. The child is agitated, gets flushed, starts making sounds of distress—all signs of the coming torrent of tears. Not a problem, Mom knows the "I'm hungry" cry, from the "Pick me up" cry, from the "I need a change" cry ... but it does not work this time. Instead, in her encouraging maternal voice, she says, "Use your words, tell me what you want." The odyssey of spoken language begins. Actually, it began even earlier, when baby would mimic the facial expressions and sounds of adoring onlookers. This laid the foundation for language acquisition. Now, the child will discover the purpose behind those fun sounds, sculpting nonverbal noise into verbal speech. The young brain will associate an image with each different sound/word.

So, what is the big deal? It is all normal and natural. That is precisely the point. As educators, we get caught up in all the jargon, "best practices," and mandates, forgetting and even short-changing certain fundamentals of how the ever-developing mind prefers to function. The essential link between brain function and literacy cannot be understated. Literacy is not just thinking, reading, and writing. Nor is it simply speaking. Literacy is a process. To neglect *any* aspect of that process will impair the result, or outcome. Breaking it down, the process of literacy is about our mental images seeking expression. The two-year-old mentioned above has just begun to make the connection that certain needs can and should be expressed with specific sounds—*words*. Later the child will learn that these *sounds* have a written code—things called *letters* arranged into set patterns become *written words*. Words are put down on paper and grow into sentences, paragraphs, pages, and books! So, that is why Mom and Dad always say the same thing every time they get to the picture of Jack being chased down the beanstalk by the Giant!

Fast-forward from age two to school days. Somewhere in the elementary years, we downplay or downright drop the necessary intermediate step(s) in the literacy process. As it becomes more complex, with the addition of reading, we lose sight of the vital importance of imagining (creating mental pictures) and verbalizing—not merely answers to the teacher's questions in a class discussion, but the chance to take time to develop our thought pictures into articulate spoken responses, like speeches, oral reports, and stories.

Like so many of life's and school's worthy lessons, addressing all parts of the literacy process takes time, and time is precious to teachers. We have so much to accomplish and our education systems are forever placing new demands, in the interest of addressing declining test scores and the education initiative du jour. While this will not be a popular viewpoint, it is nonetheless worth stating that none of the ideas/programs currently being presented on teacher institute days have anything *new* to offer. In fact, the best of them (and some of them are actually pretty good) take a common-sense notion that has been around forever and dress it up in fresh, catchy sound-bites and acronyms. Regarding testing, the trend seems to be that even more testing, and teaching how to take tests, is the answer. This means actual instructional time has been compromised in most schools. No wonder teachers become defensive and covetous of what little time they do get for authentic teaching. That said, why should educators forego the efficiency of the commonly used approaches to teaching literacy for one that requires a greater imposition of their time?

The answer—the current models don't get the job done, and since literacy is at the core of just about all educational processes, it is worth taking all the time needed to do the job right. We need to address all the components of literacy if we want students to become fully, functionally literate.

Reading and writing are very important and are the easiest to test/measure (no matter that most standardized test employ examples of reading out of context). In this regard, the literacy model we are using looks like Figure 5.1.

READ→THINK→WRITE

Figure 5.1.

In this model, writing becomes the ultimate measure, the *written word* the be-all and end-all. However, our brains do not prefer to function this way.

Try this simple test with your students. Ask them to close their eyes and provide them a verbal prompt/image—I use *apple pie*. Then ask them to share whatever came to their minds. With the suggestion, apple pie, the responses inevitably include images of "steaming homemade lattice crusted pies sitting on window ledges to cool," "Grandmother in her apron in the kitchen," "family holiday gatherings," "those red rectangular boxes from McDonald's," etc. In all my years of teaching, none of my students have ever responded, "I saw the letters a-p-p-l-e p-i-e." What does this prove? Simply that our minds are wired for images—imagining—imagination. The act of putting these images into words is an abstract process, which is best served when we support it with the component of speech. By including oral response, we place speaking back into its proper place in the literacy continuum. Working out our thoughts by speaking/hearing them aloud engages our minds in a way that can make the act of writing less intimidating and more accessible. Infusing our curriculum with projects that require as many verbal as written products will serve to strengthen both. The new literacy model *might* look like Figure 5.2:

However, this is too easy and too scientific. How often have we found that simple models are generalizations, which tend to leave out important details? In my thinking, literacy is much more *art* than *science*, so my preferred model actually looks more like Figure 5.3:

Admittedly it isn't as precise and clean, but it mirrors the reality of the art of literacy. Each component is an equal partner in this model, and it becomes abundantly clear that the elimination of any one would be to the obvious detriment of literacy. If we want our students to display solid, balanced literacy, then our teaching not only needs to address equally all its aspects, but to allow for their necessary interplay. While this approach is not easily quantified on a Scantron answer sheet, nor does it translate well to multiple-guess standardized tests, students who have been educated with this as their foundation will likely score better on those onerous exams, if they are indeed the barometer by which student achievement will continue to be measured.

There is a real *danger* in this approach—students who are exposed to this type of literacy education will learn to trust *themselves* as the source of creative ideas/impulses. They will not feel that all the answers to life's questions are to be found in a textbook. They will find joy in complex verbal exchanges; their vocabularies will grow and become rich with words

READ→THINK→SPEAK→WRITE

Figure 5.2.

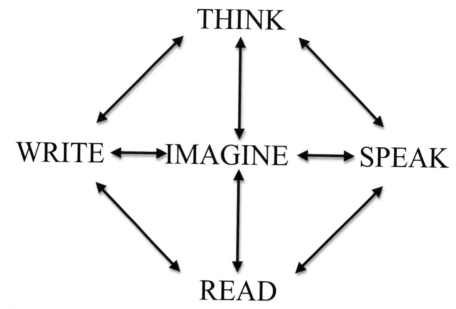

Figure 5.3.

containing more than one or two syllables. They will believe it is as important to speak their minds as it is to write their thoughts—and their writing will improve. These students will *tell* and even *write* great stories.

So, instead of letting time be our enemy and letting the strictures of the education system get in the way of what we should be doing, it's time we did something truly revolutionary—revisit some of life's earliest lessons—encourage students to "use (speak) their words".

When teachers collaborate and share their talents, children understand that they too should collaborate. In these articles, two teachers who understand how to give children their voices asked them to remember winter moments and create beautiful winter adornments. These activities emphasize that words have a sensory base, that in the beginning, all the world is sensory for the child and that art and language and literacy are simply layers of expression. The collaboration culminates with a spoken-word event where students share their fine work with their families and their school community. Enjoy!

CREATIVE BOOK MAKING: STORIES OF THE SEASONS
Susan Gundlach and Lea Basile Lazarus
*Speaking, Listening, Reading, Writing, Visual Literacy,
and Information Literacy*

National Standards

NCTE: 1, 2, 3, 4, 5, 6, 7, 8, 9, 10, 11, 12; CNAEA—Visual Arts 1: Understanding and applying media techniques and processes; CNAEA—Visual Arts 2: Using knowledge of structures and functions; CNAEA—Visual Arts 3: Choosing and evaluating a range of subject matter, symbols, and ideas; CNAEA—Visual Arts 5: Reflecting upon and assessing the characteristics and merits of their work and the work of others; CNAEA—Visual Arts 6: Making

Figure 5.4. Student announcers at Presentation Day program.

connections between visual arts and other disciplines; AASL 4: Learners use skills, resources, and tools to pursue personal and aesthetic growth.

Authors' Objectives

The book's authors include this specific example of integrated learning that drives toward a spoken-word performance. This project demonstrates what the authors know about keeping curriculum whole, about not using a standardized test to measure performance, and about finding joy in integrating our experiences as we move/expand into new places in our lives. These are sixth-grade students who are encouraged by their teachers to 1) reexperience their sensory understanding of the natural world; 2) develop artistic and language responses to those experiences; 3) create and enjoy developing a book about the experiences; and 4) tell the story of their creations in a public event.

Teachers' Objectives

Through this seven-week project, our sixth-grade art students combine art and writing to create different forms of books. The four-term art cycle lends itself to seasonal themes, one season for each term. Each book is a collection of words, images, and art techniques that together convey the meanings and feelings of a given season. Our books for this particular term have eight pages.

The book project has two strands, which we will describe separately, although, in reality, both proceed simultaneously throughout the art class term. For purposes of this article, we will focus only on our winter books.

"Well, if you make your visual very detailed, it might 'tell a story' to the person looking at it. If you make your writing detailed, it can make a visual picture in your mind."

—Lizzy D., student

Each art student will create a book that includes several pieces of artwork and journaling and at least one original poem that tells the story of a seasonal memory. The unifying theme for the book will be fall, winter, spring, or summer, depending on the student's art schedule. Throughout the project, students will explore connections between visual imagery and text. They will also learn ways to use as models the works of poets and artists studied in this unit. At the end of the term, students will present their books and read their poems at a program for classmates, parents, and school administrators.

Instructional Plan for Writing the Winter Poem

Susan Gundlach, Visiting Artist

Figure 5.5. Thumbnail photos of the eight pages.

Day One

"You need to brainstorm or think about it before you start to write."
—Charlie D.

To put ourselves in a winter mood, we begin by discussing different examples of art and writing that were inspired by the season. Samples include photographs of much-magnified snowflakes (Wilson A. Bentley); writing and sketching in nature journals (Claire Leslie); and sculptures made of ice, snow, and other natural materials (Andy Goldsworthy). We have a lot of fun analyzing the different shades of white that show up in the various media. Photographs by Ansel Adams are also thought-provoking. After we talk about the visual artworks, I read aloud from Ted Kooser's collection of short poems, *The Blizzard Voices.*

Next, individually and as a group, the students make many lists of sensory images on notebook paper—winter sights, sounds, smells, textures, tastes, and activities. We pay extra attention to winter colors, listing and naming them (piney green, snow shadow, dry stalks, December clouds). These lists will be used often when the students are creating their poems and designing their journal pages. List-making gets the writers thinking in terms of specific images and insures that everyone will start on the poem planning/writing with lots of ideas in mind—no "blank-sheet-of-paper" angst.

Another important list that begins now is the catalogue of winter memories, memories that will form the basis for the poems the students will compose—their winter "stories." At this point, the students can share brief versions of their memories, thus building a sense of group interest and

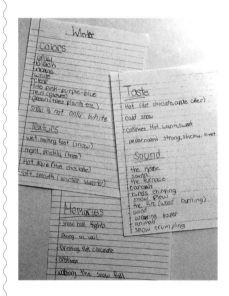

Figure 5.6–5.7. Samples of students' lists.

enthusiasm. Of course, they love to reminisce about experiences from their short lives (building a snowman at age five, walking through the woods with Grandpa, sitting indoors and watching the snow falling outside), and the telling reminds others of moments they may not have remembered on their own. It is important for the students to realize that these memories do not have to be "spectacular" experiences, but rather may be simple, quiet times that have stuck in their minds.

Day Two

First we take a few minutes to add to the lists of winter memories.

Then we read some winter poems and analyze them for such elements as structure, imagery, and use of repetition. A particularly successful model has been Ted Kooser's "That Was I," a poem that is interesting and accessible to middle schoolers. I show the class a poem I wrote that was inspired by Kooser, and I also show them winter poems written by the previous year's sixth graders. They especially enjoy one that tells about the perils of skitching, which is the practice of grabbing onto the rear bumper of a moving car on a snowy day, thereby "hitching" a ride and "skiing" on the icy street. (For younger students, Valerie Worth's little gems in *All the Small Poems and Fourteen More* work well as models.)

Day Three

"We use writing to draw a picture in the reader's or listener's mind."
—David E.

With all of their notes handy, the students are ready to choose which of their memories they will use for their poems. Because Kooser's poem is actually three stanzas, each of a different memory, some students may also decide to use three memories—so, one longer story or three short ones. In either case, I encourage them to write three stanzas, and to try a version of Kooser's repetition of the words "That was I" at the beginning and ending of their stanzas.

To get started, I ask the children a few questions that lead to yet another list: How old are you in this memory? Where does it take place? What time of day is it? What is the weather like? What are you wearing? Who is with you? What colors, sounds, smells, etc. catch your attention as you think about this memory? Once finished with those notes, the students write for the remainder of the period.

I collect the drafts, and, over the next few days, read them and comment on each one.

Figure 5.8. Students writing their poems.

Examples of Poems

The Skater

By Susan Gundlach, teacher *(Editor's note—All people in the classroom are artists, together.)*

You might have wondered about me, that silhouette
so carefully stepping sideways,
right foot, left foot, right foot, left foot,
slowly descending the steep wooden stairs,
from the top of the bluff down to the frozen lake.
You may have thought I looked nervous,
taking my time like that, but really I was
just trying to balance on my skates.

And there I was, that tiny speck you could hardly see,
swirling and spinning all alone across the
now solid water of Lake Mohawk, racing from one side
to the other, humming a secret tune to myself—
a ten-year-old gliding through the world, under a
blue crystal sky, on a perfect winter day.

And did you notice me, a tired and hungry skater, heading
back across the thick, crackling ice, as the lake sent
audible lightning echoes ahead of me, sounding
under my weight. A younger child would have been afraid
of those fearsome groans, but I loved the noisy ice,
and I knew it would bring me home.

(inspired by Ted Kooser's "That Was I")

*****

Student Poems

You Saw the Snow
By Kathryn Achuck

You saw the snow,
I know you did.
The soft chalky snow
That drifted to the ground
And lay still until the wind blew it.
I know you saw the snow.

You saw the snow,
I bet you did.
The pure white snow,
That you thought looked
Like powdered sugar.
And did you see
Those huge mounds,
Those barriers, those walls,
You thought would protect you
From the harsh winds?
I bet you saw the snow.

Well, I saw the snow,
While looking out my window,
Sipping cocoa that burned my tongue,
while clutching my blanket tight.
I saw the snow.

*****

Sledding
By Rachel Lichtenberg

I was the tiny girl in blue you saw.
The shivering girl on the peak of the hill

Sitting behind her cousin.
On the scarlet and white wooden sled.
Gripping the sides with excitement crawling up her spine
And biting cold turning her cheeks and nose red.
I was the tiny girl in the blue you saw.

I was the squealing girl you saw,
As the sled flew down the icy hill.
As the spidery trees rushed past her and her cousin in a blur
And the powder sprayed at them.
As they hit a huge bump and flew into the air,
I was the squealing girl you saw.

I was the girl you saw who looked like a living snowman.
The one rolling down the hill,
Having a great time with her cousin.
I was the girl who looked like a living snowman.

*****

The Ice Hero
By Nick Anaclerio

I stood tall
On top of my cheap plastic pitifully amateur snowboard
at the peak of the only vaguely good sledding hill
around the flat Chicago area I called home.

Strangely, the long stretches of time
I had spent sitting at the computer,
watching my ice hero character
with his bent knees,
extended arms,
and will to snowboard down that slope
without falling on his sorry behind,
were about to pay off.

For a few moments I was that ice hero
Watching intently on the snow ahead.
I felt the euphoria that came with sliding forward
Without tightening a single leg muscle,
Without lifting a foot.
That was I who made it down that hill
for the first time.

*****

There I Was
By Liz Gibbons

There I was
In the crunchy white snow
Enjoying my cousin's amazed delight
At his first icy snowfall.
You may have thought we were strange,
Two children, screaming and fighting,
But we were just playing.

There I was
Stuffing cold snow
Down my cousin's warm jacket.
You may have thought we were strange
In the freezing cold, with no gloves on our red hands,
But we were just playing.

There I was
Coughing and sneezing next to my cousin
When we both got sick
And he couldn't go back to Florida.

You may have thought we were strange,
Two children, both shivering and wet
Because we'd been playing.

Trees
By John Brady

That was I, standing among the rows of silent trees set upon iced racks.
I stood waiting and waiting for a car to break the silence of the snow.
I stood waiting, facing away from the frigid winds. That was I.

There I stood, head down, hood up, arms crossed against the cold.
I stood feeling the snow and wind against my coated back.
I stood, my hands warm and dry, but my feet wet and cold. There I stood.

There I huddled, into the rows of snow-covered trees still green in the frozen
land. As I huddled, waiting and waiting for a customer to break the silence,
there came a pair of headlights shining through the snow. At last, a customer.

*****

The Winter Chase
By Sally Myers

Did you see me? Racing down the hill, skis gliding down the slope. Using my
poles to push me harder, go faster. I pushed with all my might so I could be the
first! Turning, twisting, and curling down the mountain like a snake I went!

Heart beating fast, sweaty hands tightening, gripping the poles in my wool gloves. Pumping as if the race would never end! Yes, that was I.

Did you see me? My skates pounding on the ice. Crackle, crackle, came from the ground. My eyes wandered around the rink for a place to stop, to catch breath, face beet red, I kept running. Skates right, left, right, left, I went. The race continued. Yes, that was I.

Did you see me? Snow melting on the tip of my tongue. My sled sinking into the snowy slope. Rotating in circles, the world spinning right there before my eyes. I gripped the edges, heart fast, boom boom, chest puffing, I wouldn't stop. It was a race, as I chased that hill away. Yes, that was I.

Day Four (At Least a Few Days Later)

"I really like my poem because it's fabulous!"
—Charlie M.

We are off to the computer lab! I return the poems and we have a brief discussion of positioning line breaks and experimenting with the look of the poem on the page.

The students revise, edit, and type their poems, saving them in Group Share so that I will have access to their work.

Subsequent Days

• I meet with individuals during art class for further revising and editing.
• I format the poems to fit the size of the winter book pages.

Winter Life
by Matt Rauner

There I worked, amidst the swirling snow, Packing, Rolling, Crunching, Three solid balls of snow...

Figure 5.9. Student poem.

- I organize a booklet of the poems from all three winter term art classes.
- We also create a huge bulletin board display that holds samples of student art, photographs of students working, and copies of all the poems that were written that term.

Last Week of the Term

"Nothing means more to me than being able to share a very important memory with my classmates and parents."

—*Josie S.*

We prepare for the class presentation programs. Each student practices his or her poem with me, reading slowly and clearly. Announcers for the programs also have their own practice sessions.

For the big day, we cover the art room tables and display the books. Each student sits by his or her book. Announcers (preferably one boy and one girl—although we have had as many as six) begin the program by explaining how the students wrote their poems and how they made the books. They show samples of student work to illustrate each step of the process. Then they announce the readers, and the students step forward and wow their audience, not only with the brilliance of their poems but also with the seriousness with which they present their writing and art. It is so interesting and moving (and often surprising!) to parents and other guests to see the children in such a dignified light. After the readings we have refreshments, and our guests have an opportunity to view the books and talk with the students—the perfect end to a wonderful project.

Figure 5.10–5.11. Students reading their poems aloud at presentations.

Figure 5.12–5.14. Sketches/diagrams showing how a book is constructed.

Instructional Plan for Making the Book/Creating Winter Art

Lea Basile Lazarus, middle school art teacher

Setting up the Collaboration

Even before Sue begins her writing process, I start talking with the students about the collaboration. I discuss such matters as how we will combine writing and art in various ways; how they will use their journal notes to create artistic pages for their books; how they will fashion winter color collections by combining inventive words and winter images. I also assure them that Sue will make the poem-writing process very easy.

Book Form

"The value of putting my art and writing into book form is so that they blend together, then creating a whole new piece of work."

—*Isabella B.*

What should our books look like? How will they open? What size will the pages be? Each season has unique qualities, so I try to design a book form that complements the season and the artwork that will eventually be placed in it. With snowflakes and starry forms in mind, I came up with a winter book that appears to be fairly typical but can actually be opened into a star shape (inspired by "star books" in *Cover to Cover: Creative Techniques for Making Beautiful Books, Journals, & Albums* by Shereen LaPlantz [Sterling, 1998]).

As you can see, there are eight pages to be filled. The following section describes the set of art pieces/writings our students produced for this project. Many of the assignments encourage them to explore relationships between written text and visual imagery.

Preparing the Book Pages

Each student is given four 18″ × 7″ strips of watercolor paper, which will eventually be folded to make eight pages. After reviewing their lists of winter colors, the students apply "winter color" washes to their book pages. I demonstrate how they might create recognizable images or simply make abstract designs with the washes, which will then become backgrounds for the art they will be producing. The book is not assembled until all of the artwork is completed. Some pieces will be glued onto pages, and some will be done right on the wash-covered watercolor paper.

Materials

- 18″ × 7″ watercolor paper
- Watercolor paints
- Watercolor brushes

Page 1. Decorated Journal Page

"Our drawing was inspired by the lists we made."

—*Devon W.*

According to artist Gwen Diehn, a decorated journal page uses "visual elements that enhance the written words and communicate facts, emotions, moods, and stories." For this piece, again the students refer to the winter journal lists they have made: colors, textures, sights, sounds, smells, activities, and memories. I show them samples of professionally made decorated journal pages and pages created by other students. Then they decide how they will represent winter through this art form. What kinds of lettering will they use? What images will be effective? The writing and drawing are done right on the pages, so the wash will determine the colors for this piece.

Figure 5.15–5.16. Journal page.

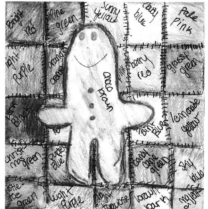

Figure 5.17–5.18. Color collection.

Materials

• Book page
• Fine black Sharpies

Page 2. Winter Color Collection

"When we wrote our poems, I based mine on my color. I wrote what I saw, a visual in my head, written down."

—Meg S., student collection

For this page, the students refer to their list of winter colors and creative names, and each chooses at least six to present in his or her collection. They can draw realistic images or abstract designs that they fill in with their winter colors. These drawings are made on separate squares of white drawing paper and then glued onto the book pages.

Materials

• Watercolor paper
• Pencils
• Watercolor pencils
• Fine black Sharpies

Figure 5.19–5.20. Ink trees.

Pages 3–4. Black Ink Trees

To create silhouettes of bare trees, students use black ink and straws. Sixth graders generally have difficulty drawing branches, so this activity helps them visualize how a tree is formed. A blob of ink is dropped on an unfolded (double) page, and then the student blows through a straw onto the ink. As the ink lines "move," they branch into V shapes, thus creating abstract tree forms.

Materials

- Black India ink
- Short lengths of straws (4″)
- One unfolded, open book page (18″ x 7″)
- Paintbrushes

Page 5. Block Prints

The theme for this assignment is "winter animals." We study woodcuts by Wisconsin printmaker Audrey Christie, noting especially how she uses contrast and texture to make her dynamic prints. For our blocks, we use Soft-Kut 4″ × 6″ printmaking blocks, a soft material that is much easier to carve than wood or linoleum.

Materials

- Soft-Kut print blocks
- Carving tools
- Brayers
- Water-based printmaking ink
- Construction paper cut in rectangles larger than the print blocks

Figure 5.21–5.22. Students making paper, and close-ups of handmade paper squares.

Page 6. Original Poem

Note: Obviously the pages can be assembled in whatever order you prefer.

Page 7. Front Cover

Earlier in the term, we made clay tiles using the snowflake form as the base for the design. These tiles now serve as papermaking molds. By pressing paper pulp into the tile, each student creates a beautiful piece of embossed white paper to be glued onto his or her book cover. (The tiles are then glazed, becoming additional pieces of artwork!)

Materials

- Paper pulp (white, recycled)
- Molds

Page 8. Back Cover

"Crystal was born on January 4, 1996. She has one brother and a lot of fish. She enjoys playing soccer and doing art . . . "

The back cover is our About the Artist page, which displays a self-portrait and a brief statement written by the student. The pencil portrait is created from a graphed-out black-and-white photo taken in class. The students

Figure 5.23–5.25. "About the Artist" pages.

learn how to graph, how to use different graphite pencils, and how to shade their drawings.

Materials

• Photograph of each student
• Rulers
• Graphite pencils
• Paper

Assessment

So, was the project a success? Regardless of skill level, each student did complete his or her poem, artwork, and book, and everyone participated enthusiastically in the final presentations. It must be said that the effect of all the books displayed together was quite gorgeous! But especially impressive (and maybe a bit surprising) to us was the level on which the children were able to see relationships between writing and art. They talked about making their colors and naming them (one boy said he made his color collection to go with his poem); about creating a self-portrait and writing a statement to go with it; about working back and forth between words and visuals; and about how memories trigger words, stories, and images.

And even more unexpected was the students' ability to reflect on the book as an object, like an artist's portfolio, that is greater than the sum of its parts: "The book better showcases your works. They may be OK apart, but together they are great!"—Matt F. Another boy put it this way: "The book lets you see what you have done; the book is a piece of artwork."—Matt S. Seeing the individual pieces formally put together, the children seemed more aware of what they had accomplished during the term, and, as one student said, "Everyone could see how hard we worked."

This project turned out to be challenging and exciting for our students and for us as teachers. Each term we have moved through the process a little differently, trying new ideas, leaving out others, and learning from past classes. We hope you will try a version of this project with your students. We are sure everyone will enjoy making seasonal stories with words and images, and then sharing their art and writing with each other.

Bullet Speed
By Michael Molitor

Did you really notice me
On my first ski trip,
Scorching down the mountain,
At bullet speed?
So you *did* notice me?

A fantastic sight it was,
Swerving and swiveling,
Through nature's beauty,
At bullet speed.
You really caught a glimpse of me?

A sentimental memory it was,
Knocking into my dad,
Bringing joy and laughs,
At bullet speed.
I guess you truly remembered me.

Figure 5.26. Student and parent at Presentation Day.

Bibliography

Art

Benke, Britta. *Georgia O'Keeffe: The Artist in the Desert.* New York: Barnes and Noble, 2000.

Bentley, Wilson A. *Snowflakes in Photographs.* New York: Dover, 1962.

Goldsworthy, Andy. *A Collaboration with Nature.* New York: Abrams, 1990.

Koch, Maryjo. *Seed Leaf Flower Fruit.* San Francisco: Collins, 1995.

Leslie, Claire Walker, and Charles E. Roth. *Keeping a Nature Journal.* Pownal, VT: Storey Books, 2000.

Montgomery, Elizabeth. *Georgia O'Keeffe.* New York: Barnes and Noble, 1993.

Book Making

Diehn, Gwen. *The Decorated Journal Page.* New York: Lark Books, 2003.

LaPlantz, Shereen. *Cover to Cover.* New York: Lark Books, 2000.

Poetry

Fletcher, Ralph. *Ordinary Things.* New York: Atheneum Books for Young Readers, 1997.

Harrison, Michael, and Christopher Stuart-Clark. *A Year Full of Poems.* New York: Oxford, 1996.

Kooser, Ted. *The Blizzard Voices.* Lincoln, NE: University of Nebraska Press, 1986.

_____. *Delights and Shadows.* Port Townsend, WA: Copper Canyon Press, 2004.

Larrick, Nancy, ed. *Piping Down the Valleys Wild.* New York: Dell, 1968.

Oliver, Mary. *New and Selected Poems: Volume One.* Boston: Beacon Press, 1992.

Oliver, Mary. *New and Selected Poems: Volume Two.* Boston: Beacon Press, 2005.

Worth, Valerie. *All the Small Poems and Fourteen More.* New York: Farrar, Straus and Giroux, 1994.

HISTORIC ACCOUNTS AS NARRATIVE PROSE
Diane Williams
Speaking, Listening, Reading, Writing, and Information Literacy

National Standards

NCTE: 1, 2, 3, 4, 5, 6, 7, 8, 9, 11, 12; AASL 1: Learners use skills, resources, and tools to inquire, think critically, and gain knowledge.

Objectives

Students will use prior knowledge to become performance ethnographers; students will create narrative verse or prose to tell a story; students will write an essay suitable for an oral presentation; and students will use elements of orality to translate written language.

Session Goals

To create a thematic unit of social studies or history using narrative verse as the vehicle for interpretation, writing, and presenting a course of study as an oral storytelling presentation.

Lately, I have been enamored with narrative prose. Of course, it has been a staple of my life, but I had no idea of the depth and breath of narrative verse. It was during a writers' workshop with the Alabama poet laureate, Sue Walker, that I fell in love. One of the examples she shared with the workshop participants was a book titled *Out of the Dust* by Karen Hesse (Scholastic, 2005). I immediately purchased a copy, and to my surprise, I found that it was a 1998 Newbery Medal award winner. What impressed me was the fact that the story was written almost as if it were a journal of a young girl's life, and yet it was very poetic. I imagined that the story and its historic context would entice other young people to read, as well as to write their own narrations.

What really fascinated me more than anything else was the fact that narrative prose, narrative poetry, narrative verse—whichever form you decide to use as a format for writing and capturing story, IS storytelling! Narrative prose is written in the ordinary language people use in speaking or writing. It is expository and narrative. Examples from the literary world would be fairy tales, fables, legends, fantasy, mystery, biographies, autobiographies, science fiction, and short stories. Narrative poetry is the oldest form of poetry. It is generally written as a novel in verse. It can be short or long and is usually collected in interrelated groups of recollections. The narratives tell about action, intentions, outcomes, and personal experiences of people, although it doesn't always include all of the story elements.

Classic examples of narrative poetry and narrative prose are "Lady Janet and Tam Lin," as well as "Robin Hood," and I have seen both titles written as prose and poetic verse. Edgar Allen Poe's "Annabelle Lee" and "The Raven" are other examples. "The Song of Hiawatha" by Henry Wadsworth Longfellow is still another example. I'm sure that storytellers and teachers can name a few of their own favorites.

Lesson Plan

In working with students in the classroom, generally I establish a course of study. As an artist going into a school, I work with the teacher to determine what their students will be learning that semester. For the purpose of this article, the course of study is the historic establishment of the rail system across the United States. But teachers can use any social studies or history study. If you want to make the learning even more interesting, you can create an interdisciplinary thematic unit and you could even turn the classroom into the time period being studied complete with setting, pictures, and props.

Here is the story that I usually share with students to give them an idea of the direction that I would like to see them take with their writing. This piece is written for eighth graders. For younger students, I would change a few of the harsh realities of the lifestyle of the men who worked to build the railroad.

As a project-based arts education activity, I usually like to end by singing one of the songs from the gandy dancers, the hardworking men who built the railroad. I made up my own tune, but I found the words in one of anthropologist/author Zora Neale Hurston's collections. Based on the last part of the narrative, I also use information about the dance to teach students how to do the gandy dancers' dance. It mimics the way the men sang and worked on the rail system. This is a great way to engage students from beginning to end. The dance is easy enough that no one will have two left feet.

"The Railroad"
Diane Williams
(Note: the story opens with the playing of a few bars on a harmonica.)

All that's left is this harmonica,
but when Chalmus would play, folks would come out of the canvas city
—the temporary tent shelters—
and folks would sit down around the old oak tree.
Kids and grown folks alike loved to hear what he had to say.
And they loved to hear him play.
They could see it as clear as day.
They would sit there and he would point to the grove of fig trees.
That's the way he always started the story.
He'd point and say, "Right over there."
That's where it all started—here in Corinth.
Chalmus was head man in the railroad camp in Corinth.
The railroad was going to connect Corinth with Hamburg,
a point on the Tennessee River.
You see, Mississippi ranked among the first five rail systems
to be built in the United States.

The second was built in Woodville, Mississippi, in 1838 on Judge
McGehee's plantation.
Chalmus was proud to be a part of the action.
This was the beginnings of the iron highways across America.
It offered the hope of freedom,
But Chalmus didn't think so at first.

He remembered one Friday that he was going to quit.
He told the other workers that he would hide if he had to,
but he wasn't going back.
The work was too hard.
He stayed out in the woods all weekend carousing and
acting like a hound dog.
Until his friends came to him with a warning—
"Don't you spit in the well from which you may want to drink one day,"
they said.
"If you get caught out here we're going to have to use
our shovels and dig your grave."
Next work day, Chalmus was back on the job.

Chalmus told a story about Heddy to get everyone's attention.
He told about the time Heddy wanted to die.
She wanted slavery time to end so bad that she was going to
end it for herself.
She laid down on that track.
And he'd point and say, "Right over there."
He saw it with his own eyes.
Heddy was a woman child and those times were too hard.
(And slavery wasn't going to end for at least a few more years.)

The plantation workers worked even harder picking cotton
once the railroad was built.
Working on the railroad was a tough job, but it was a race to connect the
East and West Coast, and the North and South for trade.
You see, in Mississippi the trains toted that cotton up the
Mississippi River to Memphis.
Every evening when Heddy came home from picking cotton, she said,
"I smells like dirt, I don't want to live no more.
From dust I came and to dust I will return. Lord don't care!"
Everyone told her that the Lord do care.
And that's why those that were alive were alive.

Chalmus said that when he found her laying on the railroad tracks,
he snatched her up.
He must have stared at her for a whole five minutes before
he said anything.

*And when he did, he said, "Chile you ain't doing nothing but
mixing up homemade sin."
Heddy got scared that lightning was going to strike her dead.
She had done some things wrong in her time,
but mixing up homemade sin was Devil's work.
She didn't want no part of that . . .
Heddy didn't go back to the railroad track for a long time.*

*Finally, she forgot about that time.
She forgot because Chalmus would sit her down with the rest of the folks.
And he'd tell her stories right along with the rest of them.*

*He told her about the time her mama snuck down near those fig trees
and watched the gandy dancers work their rhythm, keeping time.
So that the men could get the job done.
First the surveyor checked out the land.
Had to make sure no Indians impeded their progress.
And after that, the grader made sure everything was smooth.
And after that, some of the men laid down the crossties.
And after that, the rails were laid.
They were laying bridge rails back then.
And after that, the iron spike was placed.
And after that, the spike was hammered in.
A dozen men laid at least two miles of track a day.*

*This was going on all across America from the late 1700s to the mid-1800s.
A man died for every mile of track that was laid and that's no
exaggeration.
He was either killed by the fierce nature of the wilds or God knows what.
It took a tough and rugged man to help build the railroad tracks.
Work gangs suffered from floods, bubonic plague, extreme cold, cholera,
landslides, anthrax, and bandits.*

*Most of the time these were drinking men.
At night they would drink.
They would keep up enough of a stink to harelip hell.
They would still be skunked the next day.
It seemed that there was much that they wanted to forget.*

*It is said that a golden spike was driven into the last crosstie in
Utah by a nameless laborer.
Actually, it wasn't hammered, it was simply dropped into a
pre-drilled hole.
Actually, it wasn't a golden spike either, but an iron spike.
But storytellers have told the golden spike version for years.*

Thomas Durant, president of the Union Pacific Railroad,
was supposed to place that last spike,
but he was too unsteady after a night of drinking to even make an attempt.

Well, anyway, Heddy's mama watched them as they worked.
She heard the railroad songs and she saw their peculiar shuffle.
There was a methodical harmony and rhythm to what they
did—a lining rhythm of sorts.
She walked back home dancing a jig.
She danced that dance every day, and then she got an idea that would
liven up that rail camp.
No one had even seen her dance that jig. So she held a contest.
Chalmus remembered it with the juice joy of laughter.
She said if anyone could guess how to do her gandy dance,
they would win a prize.
The prize would be two peach cobblers.
Everyone in that rail camp tried out.
One of the women almost guessed the dance.
She rocked left, right, left, right, eight times, but then she messed up on the
rest of the dance.
One of the fellows tried out and he almost guessed the dance.
He rocked back and forth eight times.
And then pushed both arms double time—left, right, left, right.
But he didn't know how to end the dance.
It seemed that no one could guess, and finally it was time to go.
Everyone went back to their makeshift homes.

Heddy's mama went to her tent and danced one more time so that she
wouldn't forget.
But Chalmus saw her.
By the light of the candle in her tent, he saw her shadow dancing.
Chalmus learned how to do that dance, but he didn't want Heddy's
mama to know.
The next day he went to his best friend and asked him to do that dance
at the next contest.
But his friend said that he didn't know now to dance.
Chalmus's friend was a very large man and he was a very good friend.
Chalmus taught him the dance and he danced at the next contest and won.
Folks looked and Heddy's mama looked.
Chalmus's friend was so large it was hard to tell if he was doing the
dance right.
But he won nonetheless and won those two peach cobblers.
Chalmus and his friend celebrated out in the woods.
While they danced around in a circle, those pies disappeared.
Chalmus never did explain that one.

> *But from that day until this one, folks would gather under that tree to*
> *hear Chalmus's stories.*
> *The time would always end with the gandy dance.*
> *The dance mimicked the hard work of the men who built the*
> *rail system in Corinth.*
> *Unless a person was ailing, when Chalmus finished storytelling,*
> *everyone jumped up and the fun began.*
> *Chalmus would sing the gandy dancer's song and everyone danced.*
> *And the folks couldn't wait until the next time they heard*
> *Chalmus playing his harmonica over by the trees.*

Older students can do research to learn how the rail system was established as a resource for trade in the United States, followed by a class discussion of what everyone has learned about the topic.

Next, I give students as many tools as possible to consider as they begin to write their stories. Each tool is explained and in some cases we use the tools as an exercise so that the students will become familiar with how I want them to incorporate their selection of tools.

Writing Tools

- Story elements (character, setting, theme, problem or conflict, event sequence, and resolution).
- Point of view.
- Descriptive words, use of imagery.
- Repetitive phrases.
- Idioms (example: cut to the chase, as easy as pie, six of one/half a dozen of the other).
- Metaphor (describes a first subject as being equal or equal to a second object in some way. It compares seemingly unrelated subjects as a way to enhance the description of the first subject.)
- Hyperbole (a figure of speech in which statements are exaggerated. It may be used to evoke strong feelings or to create a strong impression, but is rarely meant to be taken literally.)
- Similes (a technique that uses words such as "like" or "as" to compare two ideas. Example: Carol was switching like a flag blowing in the breeze as she walked.)
- Word rhyme (if writing narrative poetry.)
- Alliteration (applies to the phonetic repetition that occurs in the first position/first letter of words. Example: Come ... dragging the lazy languid line along.)

Storytelling Tools

- Cadence
- Pausing/pacing
- Intonation
- Attitude
- Emotional intelligence
- Expressive intonation
- Accent(s)
- Character voice

This kind of activity in the classroom is relative to project-based arts education because it is an activity that is dependent on the classroom group work, but it is also an independent activity that appeals to middle school students because it takes curriculum learning off the pages of the book. It becomes more authentic than traditional standardized learning because the students are engaged in creating stories and demonstrating other skills that they have learned (such as writing).

The activity is easily adapted to the typical classroom setting and should be monitored and evaluated based on the built-in assessments. Project-based arts education's task format is product, performance, and extended constructed response. Students will take information they have learned about a subject and create the product of a written story. They will present their stories in an oral presentation, and an extended response could be the creation of a song, dance, theater play, visual arts component, or interdisciplinary thematic course of study (as mentioned previously).

What's important for the success of this activity is that the expectations have to be clear. In short, students will write a story using the information gleaned from a social studies or historic unit of study. The stories can take a variety of individual directions because of point of view.

As mentioned earlier, the students as a class should have already reviewed information on the study of the building of the rail system across America, or they can research the information as homework and prepare for a class discussion on what they have learned. With this information in mind, they will think about the possibilities of their written stories. If necessary, you can prompt your students by asking questions such as:

- What do you think it was like for the men who worked to build the rails?
- What about their families and/or their communities?
- If you were to make a movie about this subject, what would be the story elements?
- Who are the characters? How does the story begin?
- Write about the action that takes place in a day, a week, a month, or a year.

Ironically enough, with narrative prose, students do not have to deal with the crisis or problem in the story, not in the sense that there is a situation that has to have a resolution, but the narrative prose must have action. The narrative prose is written almost as if one were saying: this is what happened at this time, or around this time period, or around this situation, or on this particular day. It is so close to the written story as we know it that it is almost hard to explain, but it is more in line with recounted, thought-out memories.

Assessments

When students learn historic facts and can translate that information into a story by making inferences, by creating a bird's-eye view into the lives of characters and events, and by contextualizing the economy, social, and cultural riches, and when they can clearly juxtapose the prominent difference in time periods/eras and even incorporate the antiquated language by shrouding the story around facts, then the assessments will be evident.

Resources

- Hurston, Zora Neale, *Mules and Men* from the collection of *Jonah's Gourd Vine* (1934), *Mules and Men* (1935), and *Their Eyes Were Watching God* (1937). New York: Quality Paperback Books, 1990.
- Teachers can use any area of history and social studies as a resource for this activity.
- Williams, Diane. *Mississippi Storytelling: A Heap of Comfort.* CD. Canton, MS: Don Forbush Productions, 2008.

WAKING THE MYTHIC MIND
Megan Wells
Speaking, Listening, Reading, Writing, and Visual Literacy

National Standards

NCTE: 1, 2, 3, 4, 8, 9, 10, 11.

Objectives

By developing mythical imaginations through a step-by-step process, students learn how to reanimate myths from the page to embodiment. Once animated, the students engage with the myth on a multisensory level. This dimensional experience imprints their imaginations with deep and applicable human truths.

Materials

- Simple: a variety of the world's myths to read and a safe room where they can be read aloud.

- Intermediate: a variety of the world's myths plus visiting adults to interact with; art supplies to color or paint; and a variety of costume pieces from the world's cultures and props.
- Advanced: a handout of Joseph Campbell's *Hero's Journey*, plus art supplies to build masks; and a small theater and an audience to witness the final performances.

Instructional Plan

Introduction

I am standing in a middle school gymnasium getting ready to tell Greco-Roman myths. In the front row, six thirteen-year-old girls slide their fold-up, chairs making loud clangs as the metal legs bang into each other. They don't even notice the noise they make in their determined urgency to be close to their "group." They form a chimera with their fusion of parts.

The teenage boys defy the chairs, too. With arms up, hands folded behind their heads, they lean the four-legged chairs up into two-legged saddles. Are the front chair legs/horse hoofs ready for battle?

These students ARE myth, but they don't yet see themselves, so they look at the storyteller from behind "I'm cool" masks and dare me to take them somewhere.

I think, "Myths in middle school . . . perfect."

The Bigness of Myths

The middle years are hard on the identity as the young teenager is being torn, by their bodies and time, from the free-spirited world of childhood. They feel like they are on an escalator they can't stop, up up, up, to the manic adult world that petrifies them. On the other hand, they are powered by a potent drive toward the independence and sexual callings of adulthood. Children? Bah! Who wants to remain a silly child?

Is it any coincidence that myths contain heroes and heroines struggling with the same issues of identity? Who am I? What is my fate? Who is the fairest? How will I master the Minotaur at the center of the labyrinth? Who will betray me? Why can't I turn into a tree and stay SAFE from all these GRABBING boys? Why do I wish I WAS Medusa?

World myths are psychologically large enough for this age group. The characters and story lines are ripe with images big enough to grip this self-conscious age and travel the adolescent imagination out of the anxious present into bigger ideas of who they are and who they can become.

The exciting invitation for the teacher is to help students animate myths from written words into their three-dimensional imaginations.

Better Heard Than Read

Myths were created through oral and ritual experiences and refined over the ages by telling and retelling to multiple generations. They are dense gatherings of human wisdom, and as such do not reflect everyday reality. Myths were created to be public and experiential.

Myths Are Like Puzzles

Myths are full of symbols and metaphors. The characters and monsters are representations of the emotional and psychological world. Like poems, they require interaction. What's a chimera? Why a lion's head and a goat's body? Where does a chimera sleep? What does it eat? Hmm? Myth symbols inspire engagement.

Myths Are Not Factual, Yet They Are True

At first reading, it is sometimes tempting to conclude that myths are old thoughts by ancient humans, like curious museum pieces, useful only as a clue to an age gone by. However, with a more penetrating look, hidden within the stories are ageless clues to human experience; deep truths that help even modern humans learn how best to behave with each other and our planet.

Activities to Animate Myths

There are many ways to excite the middle school student into the multidimensions of myths. Since every school has different resources, and each classroom has its cast of personalities, here's a list of proven activities for you to mix and match to customize your own myth experiences.

If it becomes difficult to carve out an entire unit of myths, integrating myth into more standard subjects such as ancient Egypt can be accomplished. Isis and Osiris can be a read aloud when studying the Nile Valley. At each change in the season, or during a time of extreme weather, read a myth together in class. Or, the Campbell's hero's journey can be a prompt for journal writing.

More Ideas

- Have students read the myths aloud. (Always.)
- Find a talented parent or the drama teacher to come in and read the myths aloud. Select a reader who fits the characteristics of the myth, a fellow teacher, or someone in the school or community to read a specific god/goddess or hero/heroine story to the class. Can the gym instructor or a local fireman read the Hercules myth? Can the principal come in and read Zeus?
- Hire a professional storyteller skilled at myth-telling.
- Have students "cast" the myths from celebrities. What would Zeus be like if he were played by Robert De Niro, Bill Clinton, or Abraham Lincoln? What about Aphrodite? Could she be played by Angelina Jolie, Lindsay Lohan, or Princess Diana?

- Join with the art teacher. Have students make masks of the characters. Then they can write a "monologue" from the point of view of the character through the mask. For example, create a mask of Persephone. Student then write a monologue from Persephone's point of view (a trip to the underworld.) They can read their monologues aloud.

- Join with the drama teacher. Have students write the myths into playscript. Have them act the plays out in front of each other. (You can combine this with the previous activity and let them use their masks when they are acting.) Have students rewrite the myths into modern or future times. (What would the Perseus/Medusa myth be like if it happened in space on some alien planet?)

- Have students select myths from different cultures and do a comparison/contrast report about the two myths.

- Have students create new myths by selecting characters from different cultures and bringing them together. What if Amaterasu (the Japanese sun goddess) fell in love with Loki (the Nordic trickster god), but they were thwarted by the Skeleton Woman (the Inuit vampire).

- Have students compose music to convey mythical characters. Stretch the musical ear by having students study the instruments associated with the culture of the myth. Music/songs can be composed for each character using these instruments or language.

- Provide materials for students to construct/create a game board following a mythical hero's journey. (Snakes pour from Medusa's head, every player but Medusa returns to START.) Play the games!

Assessments

In the students' active recreation of myths, does their work demonstrate the relationship between the ancient story and themselves? There are many engaging ways to help the middle student mine the rich material of myths. Once the stories are animated off the written page, the students' imaginations begin to fly. Humor, of course, comes first. It is important to let students use their humor as the first level out of their self-consciousness. If you are patient with their giggles and sarcasm, after a while the depth of the stories cannot be helped. You will be amazed to experience the emotions released by your students as they encounter the riveting wisdom in these marvelous tales.

A POETIC APPROACH TO STORYTELLING
Oni Lasana
Speaking, Listening, Reading, Writing, and Visual Literacy

National Standards

NCTE: 1, 2, 3, 4, 5, 6, 8, 9, 11, 12.

Objectives

Students learn about the life and work of Paul Laurence Dunbar, an important writer and poet in American and African American literature; students gain an understanding and appreciation of Dunbar's mastery of writing poetry through analysis of metaphor and idioms; students recite and review formally and casually, giving them an opportunity to get to know and understand the poetry as it relates to Dunbar's life, the African American experience after the Civil War, as well as students' life today by expressing themselves creatively, poetically, and socially in writing; students present dramatic and entertaining oratory interpretations as performance for classmates, teachers, parents, and/or a community assembly.

Poetry recitation is on the rise; it offers a diverse and multifaceted way of looking at stories. Probably going back 100 years or more, there have been recitations in schools, churches, and at community events. Our foreparents talk about childhood recitations where literature is interpreted by the stories they represent. The one who best interprets and understands the story is remembered for imparting a window from which we can view some semblance of a beginning, a middle, and an end. The words of a poet are often metaphoric and set to a pattern, rhythm, or flow. We think of musicians and filmmakers as storytellers, but poets—the likes of Dunbar—are also storytellers. His writing of both standard and dialect poetry offers a full resource for classroom learning on most grade levels.

This interactive lesson plan offers a unique and creative opportunity in many areas of study, such as English, history, theater, music appreciation, and art. Students will learn, be engaged, and will perform the lyrical poetry of Dunbar for its historic focus, educational, entertainment, and timely literary value.

By engaging students in classic poetry recitation, you can also help them make story connections. Looking at classic poetry created by a poet whose work threads through a time period based on a particular theme can be rewarding. It's all about the ingredients, in this case, poetic verse, a theme, and possibly a cultural and historic time element.

If you want to see kids get fully engaged in the lesson, consider adding an element that appeals to them: music! Adding music to performance poetry—ah! Now there's a concept. Music doesn't quite turn poetry into hip-hop, but it certainly adds a flavor all its own.

For the purpose of this lesson, the focus will be Dunbar's "Sympathy" (also known as "I Know What the Caged Bird Feels"). At the end of this article, you will find other suggestions that can be used for future class projects. Students can take this activity and become experts in applying the information to other areas of social studies and history by interpreting what they have learned by writing narrative verse. Narrative verse and narrative prose is a thoughtful way to capture stories as we see and live them every day.

The works of Dunbar provide the foundation upon which students can create their own narrative verse and prose. Just remember that it is about the journey rather than the resolution. You can find a collection of Dunbar's poetry on the Internet at the University of Dayton's Paul Laurence Dunbar Web site at http://www.dunbarsite.org/gallery.asp.

A Brief History of Dunbar

Paul Laurence Dunbar (1872–1906) was born and raised in Dayton, Ohio. He was the son of former slaves and a member of the first generation of African Americans to be born into freedom in the United States. Dunbar published his first book of verse at the age of nineteen. He borrowed the money to publish his book and paid it back from independent book sales. From 1896 to 1905, Dunbar published twelve books, more than any African American before 1950. At the age of thirty-three, he died of tuberculosis at his home in Dayton. He was featured on the U.S. postage stamp in 1975, and his home is now a historical state landmark and museum.

Activity

Using Dunbar's standard poem "Sympathy" (also known as "I Know What the Caged Bird Feels"), I begin this lesson with a class review:

• Review/read the poem at http://www.angelfire.com/pa/doindunbar/DunbarPoetry. html.

• Listen to a reading of the poem at http://www.dunbarsite.org/gallery/Sympathy.asp.

• Discuss the time period represented by the poem and lead a discussion relating to the connections that students can make to this time period.

• Discuss words and phrases that are new or unfamiliar to students.

• Read the poem to students and lead them in a discussion on the meaning of the poem by gleaning as many inferences as possible from the metaphors and imagery. A sample analysis can be found on 123helpme.com at http://www.123helpme.com/preview. asp?id=18764.

In presenting the poem "Sympathy" to students, they must first understand what Dunbar was trying to say with this poem. He wrote it some thirty years after slavery had ended, but the thought of not being free was still a consideration. African Americans did not have equal opportunities. As a poet, Dunbar made a comparison of a person held in captivity to that of a caged bird.

After students have had time to become familiar with the poem, I lead a discussion centered about adding soft background music behind a dramatic recitation of the poem. What type of music best fits the rhythm and pacing of the poem? What type of music complements what the poem is trying to say? We consider calypso, blues, jazz, and other types of contemporary music. The music engages the students—and they will use it later to write their own stories based on the poem.

As the conversation about the poem continues, the students recite the poem to the music. Kinesthetic movement is added to the creation of a memorable performance (start out reciting the first stanza of the poem without movement—depicting the caged bird, then adding a gentle swaying from side to side). In selecting instrumental music to fit the poem, I have always found a way to incorporate freestyle movement to a brief musical interlude. Student volunteers will enjoy this moment of self-expression.

This activity can take place over the course of a three-day period. On the second day, students should be ready to write stories based on what they've learned from Dunbar's poem. I offer a variety of choices, such as:

- Write about your reactions to circumstances you have experienced (such as having to stay inside during inclement weather, or parents implementing punishment for breaking a rule).
- What do you think freedom means to the bird in the story?
- What does freedom mean to you?
- Dunbar observed a situation from his era—write about an observation you have made based on social circumstances today.

Dunbar wrote "Sympathy" based on his observation of a caged bird and how that bird must have felt. In all of his poems, point of view is an important element. Whether to tell the story from the perspective of the bird, or as an observer to the plight of the bird, is relevant to the success of the story and therefore important to literacy development in the storytelling classroom. In teaching history and social studies, changing point of view can give students a "bird's-eye view" and perspective that piques their interest.

There are many possibilities for creating stories. I've always allowed students to make a decision on whether they want to write a traditional story, an animal story, or a folktale. The stories should be crafted using story elements and should be appropriate for verbal retelling. If time permits, this lesson can be taken a step further with editing and rewriting of the stories and, once complete, placed in a class booklet. But for the purpose of this activity, students should be prepared on the third day to become individual storytellers standing in front of the class and telling their stories. The classroom telling can serve as practice for a future assembly performance in front of other students or even as a presentation to parents.

I assist students who may not be familiar with storytelling by encouraging them to take the time to review the elements of their story. Once students are comfortable with theme, character(s), setting, plot, problem, resolution, and a possible moral (and in the simplest of terms—a beginning, a middle, and an ending), they are free to tell their stories. I assure them that the words they've written do not have to be exactly the same as the ones they use to tell the story, and encourage the use of sensory images (the five senses), as well as descriptive words and phrases. We also explore the use of sounds to depict action wherever possible when they tell their story.

Isn't it amazing how poetry can inspire storytelling? Your students have been engaged in poetic recitation. They have written original stories and made decisions on the type of music to enhance the poetic recitation of "Sympathy." If things have gone well, on the last day, there should be a festival-like atmosphere as each student prepares to tell his or her story. They should also be prepared to be good listeners, rallying support for one another.

Conclusion

Students can focus on the southern and northern styles of speech from the time period referenced by Dunbar's work as it relates to the Civil War, the Underground Railroad, or southern living in future class projects. Each session can feature one dialect and one standard poem by Dunbar.

Another resource that you can use to take a poetic approach to storytelling can be found at the Poetry Out Loud Web site at http://www.poetryoutloud.org. It includes a diverse listing of poems and a teacher's guide.

Assessment

Poetic recitation and storytelling enhances students' abilities to speak in public. The more they do it, the more confident they become. Connecting to the riches offered by classic and contemporary poetry can benefit students' learning as they express themselves when engaged in a discussion about what literature means to them and what it means to writers. Research has shown that the vehicle of multiple intelligences learning can reach students who are becoming bored with traditional ways of learning. Multiple intelligences and emotional intelligences are both part of the learning in this activity.

Getting students involved in writing their own stories can be assessed by referencing the story elements and the use of sensory imagery and descriptive words.

Some Additional Ideas

Dunbar wrote hundreds of poems appropriate for review, study, performance, and storytelling. To find poems by other authors and tips on recitation, as well as lesson plans, visit http://www.poetryout.org. Here are some additional activities to consider:

Activities

Suggested poem: "Sympathy," aka "I Know What the Caged Bird Feels"
Lesson: the value of freedom
Art aid: chalk or water paint drawings of caged and free birds
Presentation: recited as a group to modern soul music: "What About Us" by Timbaland

Suggested Poem: "We Wear the Mask"
    Lesson: reasons for hiding true feelings
    Art aid: African mask making
    Presentation: recited as a group to Caribbean music: "Mr. Brinks" by
    Dean Fraser
Suggested poem: "A Preference"
    Lesson: appreciation of natural southern foods for survival
    Art aid: decorate a drinking cup.
    Presentation: lines shared, all perform

Resources

- http://www.poetryoutloud.org.
- http://www.dunbarsite.org/gallery.asp.
- An Analysis of Paul Laurence Dunbar's "We Wear the Mask," http://www.123helpme.com/view.asp?id=19393.
- Braxton, Joanne M., ed. *The Complete Works of Paul Laurence Dunbar.* Charlottesville, VA: University of Virginia Press, 1993.
- Wiggins, Lida Keck. *The Life and Works of Paul Laurence Dunbar.* Whitefish, MT: Kessinger Publishing, 2007.

TAKING THE RIGHT MYTH-STEPS
Larry Neumann
Listening, Speaking, Reading, Writing, and Information Literacy

National Standards

NCTE: 3, 4, 6, 7; AASL 2: Learners use skills, resources, and tools to draw conclusions, make informal decisions, apply knowledge to new situations, and create new knowledge; AASL 4: Learners use skills, resources, and tools to pursue personal and aesthetic growth.

Objectives

Develop a love of mythology, refine research skills, and share personal stories; and develop a personal version of a classical myth.

Materials Required

- Variety of books on Greek myths
- LoopWriter Software
- Books in the Percy Jackson and the Olympians series by Rick Riordan
- *Tell It Together: Foolproof Scripts for Story Theatre* and *Greek Myths, Western Style: Toga Tales with an Attitude* by Barbara McBride-Smith

The series of books by Rick Riordan is based on the premise that Olympian gods never died, but continue to live and interact with certain mortals. Olympus has moved, and is now hidden high above Manhattan, accessible by a special elevator in the Empire State Building. The young hero, Percy Jackson, is a likeable boy who has a record of getting into trouble of the most mysterious kind in numerous experiences in a variety of schools. The main character's problems and personality are magnets that draw young readers into this world and the wider world of classical mythology.

To set the stage for this unit, a quick storytelling activity was used in which students recalled a time when they got into trouble but it really wasn't their fault. After a few moments of reflection, they brainstormed what happened, how it started, who got them into trouble, and why it wasn't their fault. Each student found a partner to tell about what happened. Partners switched and repeated the process. Students were invited to share their stories with the class.

The teacher introduced Riordan's *The Lightning Thief* as a book with a main character who gets into lots of trouble through no fault of his own. After reading the introduction to the book, students portrayed Percy Jackson. We discussed his examples of unusual occurrences mentioned in the introduction. Next, everyone had a chance to speak a line or two as Percy, and each student added something to the story. We began with a starter phrase, "Hi, I'm Percy Jackson, and you are going to have a hard time believing my story." The incorporation of storytelling activities into many aspects of the unit helped prepare students for the final project. Part of what really hooked fifth graders was the idea that the adventures of myth could be real today. Whether or not their individual story had a modern setting, they loved to consider the possibilities.

Students read and discussed *The Lightning Thief* sequentially with paced readings set as assignments, but the magic of the series soon took hold and students quickly moved through all three books available in the series: *The Lightning Thief*, *The Sea of Monsters*, and *The Titan's Curse*.

Research about the gods of Olympus paralleled the reading of the novels. Students researched mythological heroes such as Perseus, Heracles, and Theseus. Monsters of myths were also hot topics of research. Basic information, including task or quest, special powers or abilities, and outcome of adventure, was noted on graphic organizers. After a few days of independent work, students shared stories of the gods, heroes, and monsters. Listeners recorded information as classmates shared kernels of stories. Research continued to inform their reading of the novel as they began to appreciate Riordan's use of classical myths. Students also were listening to decide which hero they would like to portray in the storytelling portion of the unit.

Another aspect of the unit relied upon Barbara McBride-Smith's updated myths in her book, *Tell It Together: Foolproof Scripts for Story Theatre*. This invaluable resource heightened the excitement about different versions of mythological stories. In small groups, students practiced reading a story theater version of a myth before presenting it to the entire class. The humor and liveliness of these tellings gave another burst of energy to the unit. These stories were compared to research on classical myths. The story theater scripts also helped make the students more comfortable with performing before their peers.

Greek Myths, Western Style: Toga Tales with an Attitude, a collection of McBride-Smith's stories about characters from Greek myths, helped students appreciate changes the author made in modernizing and setting stories in her chosen world of central Texas. A sample of these stories was read to the class.

Celebrating the knowledge acquired through researching Greek myths, students used an activity generated by LoopWriter software. Each student held a set of cards. The designated starting card began with a name of a character from Greek mythology. The first student began by reading her card: "I have Perseus. Who has the goddess of wisdom and weaving?" The student who had the proper card continued, "I have Athena. Who's got the three-headed dog?" The first space is filled in with a character's name, and the second space has a clue to another character. The game continues until the first name is repeated and the loop is complete. Students enjoyed the challenge of improving their time for the whole loop. Everyone got a chance to review information about characters as the game progressed. Because they did not know when they would have to share another of their cards, each student listened carefully. Students could create their own game by writing clues to go with heroes, monsters, and events from Greek mythology.

Finally, students began working on their final project, which was to tell their own version of a hero story from mythology. As the students worked on hero stories, some decided to update their hero much in the same way that Riordan had done in *The Lightning Thief*. Students practiced telling their stories in partners. While one told, the other listened to make sure that elements of the original myth could still be recognized in the retelling. After a few practices with partners, some students volunteered to tell to the entire class.

One student's myth was entitled, "Herk, the Body Builder, and His Twelve Days of Community Service." In this story, Herk was sentenced to twelve days of community service, handling problems such as defeating the Hydra and retrieving the Cerynitian Bullet. Herk defeated the Hydra by shooting off its heads and employing a gang who loved to play with flamethrowers that singed the heads so they would not grow back. The Cerynitian Bullet was to be reclaimed from a gang of hunters called R Tee Mus. "Bellhop Eraphon, the Partier," and "Perseus and His Lamborghini" were offered in addition to the classical versions of a number of hero stories.

A class of seventeen students read forty-four Riordan novels during the three-week unit of study. One mother e-mailed to thank me for helping her son get excited about reading. Another mother told of dinner-table discussions about the Greek gods and an excitement about reading that exceeded assignments at school. Students were so involved in the Riordan books that they began talking to friends, who ran to the school library, the public library, and every teacher's bookshelf to get copies of the books.

Some students who had previously been reluctant writers could hardly contain their excitement once they became involved in their own versions of myths. After telling their story, each one wanted to write it so they would always have a copy. They decided that the written version was really what they needed to preserve their ideas.

Individual class members could share their stories with other classes to interest others in a unique and exciting series of myths made modern.

Assessments

Students were assessed on research skills based upon their reports to the class. They were assessed on their storytelling skills in their final project by use of a checklist of oral language skills and story structure. Finally, an objective test on the Greek myths was administered.

Bibliography

- LoopWriter software. Austin, TX: The Curriculum Project, Inc.
- McBride-Smith, Barbara. *Greek Myths, Western Style: Toga Tales with an Attitude*. Little Rock, AR: August House, 1998.
- McBride-Smith, Barbara. *Tell It Together: Foolproof Scripts for Story Theatre*. Little Rock, AR: August House, 2001.
- Riordan, Rick. *The Lightning Thief: Percy Jackson and the Olympians, Book 1*. New York: Hyperion Books for Children, 2005.
- Riordan, Rick. *The Sea of Monsters: Percy Jackson and the Olympians, Book 2*. New York: Hyperion Books for Children, 2006.
- Riordan, Rick. *The Titan's Curse: Percy Jackson and the Olympians, Book 3*. New York: Hyperion Books for Children, 2007.

STEALTH TEACHING: ENGAGING RELUCTANT WRITERS

Sherry Norfolk
Speaking, Listening, Writing, and Visual Literacy

National Standards

NCTE: 4, 11, 12.

Objectives

Students will create, tell, and write original stories based on collaborative drawings.

Materials

- Blank paper
- Pencils
- Imagination

Several years ago, my husband Bobby and I were invited to perform at the Beyond the Border International Storytelling Festival in St. Donats Castle, South Wales. As part of their outreach program, he and I were driven to five middle schools in the nearby valleys to work with the "disenfranchised" youth (kids on the verge of dropping out of school for good). Our assignment: to encourage interest in writing and telling stories. Our time frame was two and a half hours per school.

Bobby performed a forty-five-minute assembly in each school. He always started by asking the students if they liked to read. The answer was always a resounding "No!" He asked them why they didn't read, and the answers were always variations on a theme: "It's boring." And indeed it probably *was* boring, because if you can't visualize the characters, scenery, and actions, the words on the page are meaningless. It's just decoding—and that's *very* boring!

Bobby never failed to capture his audience and help them create those elusive images in their minds that didn't appear when they read those boring books. But *my* job was to get them writing—a task that the schools had apparently failed to accomplish in ten or eleven years, yet I was supposed to achieve in less than ninety minutes!

How to get them started? I needed to capture their attention quickly, break through years of apathy toward school and antipathy to writing and reading, and move them toward narrative. I needed to jump-start their imaginations and engage their dormant visualization skills. Not a simple task, since the students who had been laughing and listening intently in the assembly program turned sullen as soon as they returned to the classroom. Stealth teaching was in order. I passed out pencils and blank paper and gave them these instructions:

- Write your name in one of the corners, then put down the pencil.
- In a few minutes, you're going to get one minute to draw anything you want on the page—as long as it's appropriate for school! No words; no anatomically correct people!
- When the minute is up, you'll exchange papers with someone, and you'll have one minute to add anything you want to the picture you receive (the same rules apply!).
- At the end of that minute, you'll switch again, making sure you don't get your own picture back. Again, you'll have one minute to add to the picture.
- When the minute is up, you'll get your own page back—and it will not look the way you had intended! Look at it carefully and create a story about what is happening on the page. Make sure to include everything in the picture.
- Now find a partner and tell your stories to each other.

Well, this clearly wasn't what they had expected. Some of the hostility evaporated as they listened to the instructions; it was replaced by curiosity. What was this all about?

As soon as I gave the word, they began to draw, and silence descended. Switches were made; they returned to silence and drew in earnest, although a few chuckles could be heard from time to time. A bit of chaos always ensued with the second switch as everyone tried to find a different person with whom to swap, but silence fell once more as the drawing continued.

When the drawings returned to their starting point, laughter broke out all over the room. Gasps of surprise, shouts of hilarity—then I reminded them to make up a story to tell to a partner. Giggles continued to bubble up as students ruminated, then eagerly grabbed partners and began to tell. Then, without being instructed to do so, students reached for each others' drawings and made up their *own* stories about them as well.

After everyone finished exchanging stories in small groups, I asked if anyone would like to share their story and picture with the whole group. There was never any hesitation—and it was usually the surliest of the group who jumped up first. One after another, students shared their stories and then asked if they could tell stories about their classmates' pictures.

Next came my favorite part: in every group, someone would ask if they could write down their stories! I graciously allowed them to do so, and watched as they joyfully fell into writing. Mission accomplished!

When we left, the kids were still writing. A team of volunteers from the arts council provided follow-up on the writing project, which reportedly developed into some successful local publications.

For many students, writing is a dreaded and hateful task. When faced with writing a story, imaginations fail to conjure up anything remotely interesting. The mind—and the page—remains blank. This simple exercise is as effective with second graders as it is with adults in providing a new point of entry into narrative.

Assessment

Listen to and assess the ability of the student to create and tell a story that includes all of the details of the drawing in a cohesive and coherent manner. Written stories should also include descriptions and details that describe the images on the page.

APPENDIX OF NATIONAL STANDARDS AND ABBREVIATIONS

STANDARDS FOR THE ENGLISH-LANGUAGE ARTS

1. Students read a wide range of print and non-print texts to build an understanding of texts, of themselves, and of the cultures of the United States and the world; to acquire new information; to respond to the needs and demands of society and the workplace and for personal fulfillment. Among those texts are fiction and non-fiction, contemporary and classic.

2. Students read a wide range of literature from many periods in many genres to build an understanding of the many dimensions (for example, philosophical, ethical, and aesthetic) of human experience.

3. Students apply a wide range of strategies to comprehend, interpret, evaluate, and appreciate texts. They draw on their prior experience, their interactions with other readers and writers, their knowledge of word meaning and of other texts, their word-identification strategies, and their understanding of textual features (for example, sound-letter correspondence, sentence structure, context, and graphics).

4. Students will adjust their use of spoken, written, and visual language (for example, conventions, style, and vocabulary) to communicate effectively with a variety of audiences for different purposes.

5. Students employ a wide range of strategies as they write and use different writing-process elements appropriately to communicate with different audiences for a variety of purposes.

6. Students apply knowledge of language structure, language conventions, (for example, spelling and punctuation), media techniques, figurative language, and genre to create, critique, and discuss print and non-print texts.

7. Students conduct research on issues and interests by generating ideas and questions and by posing problems. They gather, evaluate, and synthesize data from a variety of sources (for example, print and non-print text, artifacts, and people) to communicate their discoveries in ways that suit their purposes and audiences.

8. Students use a variety of technological and informational resources (for example, libraries, databases, computer networks, and video) to gather and synthesize information and to create and communicate knowledge.

9. Students develop an understanding of and respect for diversity in language use, patterns, and dialects across cultures, ethnic groups, geographic regions, and social roles.

10. Students whose first language is not English make use of their first language to develop competency in the English-language arts and to develop an understanding of content across the curriculum.

11. Students participate as knowledgeable, reflective, creative, and critical members of a variety of literary communities.

12. Students use spoken, written, and visual language to accomplish their own purposes (for example, for learning, enjoyment, persuasion, and the exchange of information).

Standards for the English Language Arts, by the International Reading Association and the National Council of Teachers of English, copyright 1996 by the International Reading Association and the National Council of Teachers of English. Reprinted with permission.

The National Standards

Throughout the book, the same highly respected sources have been cited for the national standards in each subject area. The following abbreviations are used when referencing the sources for these standards:

AASL—American Association of School Librarians
ACS—American Cancer Society
CNAEA—Consortium of National Arts Education Associations
HCOF—Head Start Child Outcomes Framework
ISTE—International Society for Technology in Education
NAS—National Academies of Science
NASPE—National Association for Sport and Physical Education
NCSS—National Council for the Social Studies
NCTE—National Council of Teachers of English
NCTM—National Council of Teachers of Mathematics
NETS—National Education Technology Standards

SUGGESTED RESOURCES

Judy Sima

STUDENT RESOURCES—SINGLE TITLES

Ada, Alma Flor. *Medio Pollito/Half Chick*. New York: Dragonfly Books, 1997.

Amoss, Berthe. *The Cajun Gingerbread Boy*. New Orleans: MTC Press, 1994.

Andersen, Hans Christian, and Jerry Pinkney. *The Ugly Duckling*. New York: HarperCollins, 1999.

Baker, Keith. *Big Fat Hen*. New York: Harcourt Brace, 1994.

Bang, Molly. *When Sophie Gets Angry—Really, Really Angry*. New York: Scholastic, 1999.

Baumgartner, Barbara. *The Gingerbread Man*. New York: DK Ink, 1998.

Benke, Britta. *Georgia O'Keeffe*. New York: Barnes and Noble, 2000.

Bentley, Wilson A. *Snowflakes in Photographs*. New York: Dover, 1962.

Bernhard, Emery, and Durga Bernhard. *How Snowshoe Hare Rescued the Sun: A Tale from the Arctic*. New York: Holiday House, 1993.

Blair, Eric. *The Gingerbread Man*. Minneapolis: Picture Window Books, 2005.

Brenner, Barbara. *Wagon Wheels*. New York: Harper & Row, 1978.

Brown, Margaret Wise. *Goodnight Moon*. New York: Harper & Row, 1947.

Browne, Marcia. *The Bun: A Tale from Russia*. New York: Harcourt Brace, 1972.

Cabrera, Jane. *Old MacDonald Had a Farm*. New York: Holiday House, 2008.

Campbell, Joseph. Phil Cousineau, ed. *A Hero's Journey: Joseph Campbell on His Life and Work*. Novato, CA: New World Library, 2003.

Cauley, Lorinda Bryan. *The Pancake Boy: An Old Norwegian Folktale*. New York: G. P. Putnam's Sons, 1988.

Chandra, Deborah. *George Washington's Teeth*. New York: Farrar, Straus and Giroux, 2003.

Suggested Resources

Coerr, Eleanor. *Buffalo Bill and the Pony Express*. New York: HarperCollins, 1996.

Compestine, Ying Chang. *The Runaway Rice Cake*. New York: Simon & Schuster Books for Young Readers, 2000.

Crews, Donald. *Freight Train*. New York: HarperCollins, 1978.

Cummings, Pat. *Ananse and the Lizard: A West African Tale*. New York: Henry Holt and Company, 2002.

De la Mare, Walter. *The Turnip*. Boston: D. R. Godine, 1992.

Del Negro, Janice. *Lucy Dove*. New York: DK Publishers, 1998.

———. *Willa and the Wind*. New York: Marshall Cavendish, 2005.

Diehn, Gwen. *The Decorated Journal Page*. New York: Lark Books, 2003.

Duke, Kate. *Aunt Isabel Tells a Good One*. New York: Dutton Children's Books, 1992.

Egielski, Richard. *The Gingerbread Boy*. New York: HarperCollins, 1997.

Ehlert, Lois. *Color Zoo*. New York: Lippincott, 1989.

Ernst, Lisa Campbell. *Goldilocks Returns*. New York: Simon & Schuster Books for Young Readers, 2000.

Faulkner, Keith. *The Wide Mouth Frog*. New York: Dial, 1996.

Fleming, Denise. *Mama Cat Has Three Kittens*. New York: Henry Holt, 1998.

Forest, Heather. *The Animals Could Talk*. Little Rock, AR: August House Audio, 1994.

Fox, Mem. *Hattie and the Fox*. Seattle, WA: Bradbury Press, 1987.

Galdone, Joanne. *Tailypo: A Ghost Story*. New York: Clarion Books, 1984.

Galdone, Paul. *The Three Bears*. New York: Clarion, 1972.

Gallina, Michael. *Bebop with Aesop*. Indianapolis, IN: Shawnee Press, 2005.

Ginsburg, Mirra. 1997. *Clay Boy*. New York: Greenwillow Books, 1997.

Golding, William. *Lord of the Flies*. New York: Berkley, 2003.

Goldsworthy, Andy. *A Collaboration with Nature*. New York: Harry N. Abrams, 1990.

Gonzalez, Lucia. *The Bossy Gallito/El Gallo De Bodas: A Traditional Cuban Folktale*. New York: Scholastic, 1994.

Heide, Florence Parry, and Judith Heide Gilliland. *The Day of Ahmed's Secret*. New York: Mulberry Books, 1995.

Hennessy, B. G. *The Boy Who Cried Wolf*. New York: Simon & Schuster, 2006.

Hester, Denia. *Grandma Lena's Big Ol' Turnip*. Morton Grove, IL: Albert Whitman & Co., 2005.

Hurston, Zora Neale. *Jonah's Gourd Vine*. Philadelphia, PA: Lippincott, (1971) c. 1934.

———. *Mules and Men*. Bloomington, IN: Indiana University Press, (1978) c. 1935.

———. *Their Eyes Were Watching God: A Novel*. New York: Perennial Library, (1990) c. 1937.

Johnson, Stephen T. *Alphabet City*. New York: Viking, 1995.

Keats, Ezra Jack. *The Snowy Day*. New York: Viking, 1962.

Kimmel, Eric A. *Anansi and the Moss-Covered Rock*. New York: Holiday House, 1990.

———. *The Gingerbread Man*. New York: Holiday House, 1993.

Koch, Maryjo. *Seed Leaf Flower Fruit*. San Francisco: Collins, 1995.

Kramer, Sydelle. *Wagon Train*. Grosset & Dunlap, 1997.

Krosoczka, Jarrett J. *Baghead*. New York: Alfred A. Knopf, 2002.

LaPlantz, Shereen. *Cover to Cover*. New York: Lark Books, 2000.

Leslie, Claire Walker, and Charles E. Roth. *Keeping a Nature Journal*. Pownal, VT: Storey Books, 2000.

Lester, Helen. *A Sheep in Wolf's Clothing*. Boston: Houghton Mifflin, 2007.

———. *Tackylocks and the Three Bears*. New York: Houghton Mifflin Books for Children, 2002.

Macaulay, David. *Black and White*. New York: Houghton Mifflin, 1990.

MacDonald, Margaret Read. *El Conejito: A Folktale from Panama*. Little Rock, AR: August House, 2006.

MacDonald, Suse. *Alphabatics*. New York: MacMillan, 1982.

Mackinnon, Mairi. *The Gingerbread Man*. London: Usborne Books, 2007.

MacLachlan, Patricia. *Sarah, Plain and Tall*. New York: Harper & Row, 1985.

Marshall, James. *Goldilocks and the Three Bears*. New York: Dial Books for Young Readers, 1988.

May, Jim. *The Boo Baby Girl Meets the Ghost of Mable's Gable*. Elgin, IL: Brotherstone, 1992.

McLimans, David. *Gone Wild: An Endangered Animal Alphabet*. New York: Walker Books for Young Readers, 2006.

Meyers, Cindy. *Rolling Along with Goldilocks and the Three Bears*. Bethesda, MD: Woodbine House, 1999.

Montgomery, Elizabeth. *Georgia O'Keeffe*. New York: Barnes and Noble, 1993.

Morgan, Pierr. *The Turnip: An Old Russian Folktale*. New York: Philomel, 1990.

Olfers, Sibylle von. *The Story of the Root-Children*. Edinburgh, Scotland: Floris Books, 1980.

Oxenbury, Helen, and Aleksei Tolstoy. *The Great Big Enormous Turnip*. New York: Macmillan, 1972.

Parish, Peggy. *Amelia Bedelia*. New York: Harper Trophy, 1992.

Parkinson, Kathy. *The Enormous Turnip*. Niles, IL: Albert Whitman & Company, 1986.

Pearson, Tracey Campbell. *Bob*. New York: Farrar, Straus and Giroux, 2002.

Peck, Jan. *The Giant Carrot*. New York: Dial Books for Young Readers, 1996.

Pelletier, David. *The Graphic Alphabet*. New York: Orchard, 1996.

Penner, Fred, and Renee Reichert. *The Cat Came Back*. New York: Roaring Brook Press, 2005.

Polacco, Patricia. *Thank You, Mr. Falker*. New York: Philomel Books, 1998.

Riordan, Rick. *The Lightning Thief: Percy Jackson and the Olympians, Book 1*. New York: Hyperion Books for Children, 2005.

———. *The Sea of Monsters: Percy Jackson and the Olympians, Book 2*. New York: Hyperion Books for Children, 2006.

——— *The Titan's Curse: Percy Jackson and the Olympians, Book 3*. New York: Hyperion Books for Children, 2007.

Robinson, Gail. *Raven the Trickster: Legends of the North American Indians*. New York: Atheneum, 1982.

Rohmann, Eric. *My Friend Rabbit*. Roaring Brook Press, 2002.

Rosales, Melodye. *Leola and the Honeybears: An African-American Retelling of Goldilocks and the Three Bears*. New York: Scholastic, 1999.

Rowe, John A. *The Gingerbread Man: An Old English Folktale.* New York: North-South Books, 1996.

Rubright, Lynn, and Duane Smith. *Mama's Window.* New York: Lee & Low Books, 2005.

Sacre, Antonio. *The Barking Mouse.* Morton Grove, IL: Albert Whitman & Company, 2003.

Sandin, Joan. *The Long Way Westward.* New York: Harper & Row, 1989.

Seeger, Laura Vaccaro. *First the Egg.* New Milford, CT: Roaring Brook Press, 2007.

Sendak, Maurice. *In the Night Kitchen.* New York: HarperCollins, 1970.

————. *Outside Over There.* New York: HarperCollins, 1981.

————. *Where the Wild Things Are.* New York: HarperCollins, 1964.

Seuss, Dr. *Horton Hatches the Egg.* New York: Random House Children's Books, 1966.

Shannon, David. *No, David!* New York: Blue Sky Press, 1998.

Squires, Janet. *The Gingerbread Cowboy.* New York: HarperCollins, 2006.

Stevens, Janet. *Goldilocks and the Three Bears.* New York: Holiday, 1986.

————. *The Three Billy Goats Gruff.* San Diego: Harcourt, Brace, Jovanovich, 1987.

Stewart, Sarah. *The Gardener.* New York: Farrar, Straus and Giroux, 1997.

Thomason, Dovie. *The Animals' Wishes.* Barrington, IL: Rigby Reed, 2000.

Thompson, Gare. *A Homesteading Community of the 1880s.* Washington, DC: National Geographic Society, 2002.

Tingle, Tim. *Crossing Bok Chitto: A Choctaw Tale of Friendship and Freedom.* El Paso, TX: Cinco Puntos Press, 2006.

————. *When Turtle Grew Feathers: A Folktale from the Choctaw Nation.* Atlanta, GA: August House LittleFolk, 2007.

Tolstoy, Aleksei. *The Great Big Enormous Turnip.* New York: Scholastic, 1969.

Tolstoy, Aleksei, and Niamh Sharkey. *The Gigantic Turnip.* Brooklyn, NY: Barefoot Books, 1998.

Wahl, Jan. *Tailypo!* New York: Holt, 1991.

Wiesner, David. *Flotsam.* New York: Clarion, 2006.

Washington, Donna. *A Big, Spooky House.* New York: Hyperion Books for Children, 2000.

————. *Free Fall.* New York: HarperCollins, 1988.

————. *Sector 7.* New York: Clarion, 1999.

————. *Three Pigs.* New York: Clarion, 2001.

————. *Tuesday.* New York: Clarion, 1991.

Willems, Mo. *Don't Let the Pigeon Drive the Bus!* New York: Hyperion, 2003.

————. *Don't Let the Pigeon Stay Up Late!* New York: Hyperion, 2006.

————. *Knuffle Bunny: A Cautionary Tale.* New York: Hyperion, 2004.

————. *The Pigeon Finds a Hot Dog!* New York: Hyperion, 2004.

————. *The Pigeon Wants a Puppy!* New York: Hyperion, 2008.

Williams, Sue. *I Went Walking.* Pine Plains, NY: Voyager Books, 1992.

Wood, Audrey. *Silly Sally.* New York: Harcourt Brace & Company, 1992.

Yang, Sheng. *New Life in America.* Brillion, WI: Zander Press, 2006.

Zemach, Margot. *It Could Always Be Worse: A Yiddish Folktale.* New York: Farrar, Straus and Giroux, 1992.

Ziefert, Harriet. *The Turnip*. New York: Viking, 1996.

Zunshine, Tatiana. *A Little Story About a Big Turnip*. Columbus, OH: Pumpkin House, 2003.

STUDENT RESOURCES—COLLECTIONS

Amery, Heather. *Greek Myths for Young Children*. London: Usborne Books, 1999.

Andersen, Hans Christian. *The Complete Hans Christian Andersen Fairy Tales, Deluxe Edition (Literary Classics)*. New York: Gramercy Books, 2006.

Basile, Katrina. *The Scenic Route: Stories From the Heartland*. Indianapolis, IN: Indiana Historic Society Press, 2007.

Chase, Richard. *Jack Tales*. Boston: Houghton Mifflin, 1943, 1971.

D'Aulaire, Ingri. *D'Aulaire's Book of Greek Myths*. New York: Doubleday Books for Young Readers, 1962.

Del Negro, Janice. *Passion and Poison: Tales of Shape-Shifters, Ghosts, and Spirited Women*. New York: Marshall Cavendish Children's Books, 2007.

DeSpain, Pleasant. *Twenty-Two Splendid Tales to Tell from Around the World*. Little Rock, AR: August House, 1994.

Dunbar, Paul Laurence. *The Complete Poems of Paul Laurence Dunbar*. New York: Dodd, Mead, 1967.

———, and Joanne M. Braxton, ed. *The Complete Works of Paul Laurence Dunbar*. Charlottesville, VA: University of Virginia Press, 1993.

Fletcher, Ralph. *Ordinary Things*. New York: Atheneum Books for Young Readers, 1997.

Hamilton, Martha, and Mitch Weiss. *Noodlehead Stories: World Tales that Kids Can Read & Tell*. Little Rock, AR: August House, 2000.

Harrison, Annette. *Easy-to-Tell Stories for Young Children*. Jonesborough, TN: National Storytelling Press, 1992.

Harrison, Michael, and Christopher Stuart-Clark. *A Year Full of Poems*. New York: Oxford University Press, 1996.

Hayes, Joe. *Tell Me a Cuento/Cuentame un Story*. El Paso, TX: Cinco Puntos Press, 1988.

Holt, David, and Bill Mooney. *More Tellable Tales*. Little Rock, AR: August House, 2001.

Kooser, Ted. *The Blizzard Voices*. Lincoln, NE: University of Nebraska Press, 1986.

———. *Delights and Shadows*. Port Townsend, WA: Copper Canyon Press, 2004.

Larrick, Nancy, ed. *Piping Down the Valleys Wild*. New York: Dell, 1968.

MacDonald, Margaret Read. *Earth Care: World Folktales to Talk About*. North Haven, CT: Linnet Books, 1999.

———. *Five-Minute Tales: More Stories to Read & Tell When Time is Short*. Little Rock: AR: August House, 2007

———. *Three-Minute Tales: More Stories to Read & Tell When Time is Short*. Little Rock, AR: August House, 2004.

———. *Three-Minute Tales: Stories From Around the World to Tell or Read When Time is Short*. Little Rock, AR: August House, 2004.

———. *Twenty Tellable Tales: Audience Participation Folktales for the Beginning Storyteller*. Bronx, NY: H. W. Wilson, 1986.

———. *Shake-It-Up Tales: Stories to Sing, Dance, Drum, and Act Out*. Little Rock, AR: August House, 2000.

May, Jim. *The Farm on Nippersink Creek*. Little Rock, AR: August House, 1994.

McBride-Smith, Barbara. *Greek Myths, Western Style: Toga Tales with an Attitude*. Little Rock, AR: August House, 1998.

Munds, Ellen, and Beth Millet, eds. *The Scenic Route: Stories from the Heartland*. Indianapolis, IN: Indiana Historical Society Press, 2007.

Oldfield, Margaret. *Lots More Tell and Draw Stories*. Minneapolis, MN: Creative Storytime Press, 1973.

———. *More Tell and Draw Stories*. Minneapolis, MN: Creative Storytime Press, 1969.

———. *Tell and Draw Stories*. Minneapolis, MN: Creative Storytime Press, 1963.

Oliver, Mary. *New and Selected Poems: Volume One*. Boston: Beacon Press, 1992.

———. *New and Selected Poems: Volume Two*. Boston: Beacon Press, 2005.

Osborne, Mary Pope. *American Tall Tales*. New York: Knopf, 1991.

Parkhurst, Liz, ed. *The August House Book of Scary Stories: Spooky Tales for Telling Out Loud*. Atlanta, GA: August House, 2009.

Pellowski, Anne. *The Story Vine: A Sourcebook of Unusual and Easy-to-Tell Stories from Around the World*. New York: Aladdin, 1984.

Perrault, Charles. *The Complete Fairy Tales of Charles Perrault*. New York: Clarion, 1993.

Tingle, Tim. *Spirits Dark and Light: Five Supernatural Tales from the Five Civilized Tribes*. Little Rock, AR: August House. 2006.

———. *Walking the Choctaw Road*. El Paso, TX: Cinco Puntos Press. 2003.

———, and Doc Moore. *Spooky Texas Tales*. Little Rock, AR: August House, 2006.

———, and Doc Moore. *Texas Ghost Stories: Fifty Favorites for the Telling*. Lubbock, TX: Texas Tech University Press, 2004.

Washington, Donna. *A Pride of African Tales*. New York: Amistad Press, 2003.

Wiggins, Lida Keck. *The Life and Works of Paul Laurence Dunbar*. Whitefish, MT: Kessinger Publishing, 2007.

Worth, Valerie. *All the Small Poems and Fourteen More*. New York: Farrar, Straus and Giroux, 1994.

STUDENT RESOURCES—MULTIMEDIA

Hideous Kinky: Soundtrack from the Motion Picture. CD. Seattle, WA: Will Records, 1999.

Holt, David. *Tailybone and Other Strange Stories*. CD. High Windy Audio, 2000.

Horner, Beth. *The Pipeline Blues*. CD. http://www.BethHorner.com, 2001.

LoopWriter Software. Austin, TX: The Curriculum Project, Inc., 1999.

Moore, Steve, director. *Rocky & Bullwinkle: The Best of Fractured Fairy Tales, Volume 1*. San Diego, CA: Genius Products, Inc., 2005.

Nancarrow, Conlon. *Conlon Nancarrow: Studies for Player Piano Nos. 1–20*. CD. San Francisco: Other Minds, 2008.

Rosen, Gary. "The Three Bears," in *Animal Playground*. CD. New York: Putumayo World Music, 2007.

Rudolf, Dave. *Not So Grimm Fairy Tales*. CD. Park Forest, IL: Gambler Publishing, 2003.

"Rumplestiltskin." *Muppet Classic Theater.* Videocassette. Burbank, CA: Walt Disney Studios, 1994.

"Rumpelstiltskin" and "Rumpelstiltskin Returns." *Rocky & Bullwinkle: The Best of Fractured Fairy Tales, Volume 1.* DVD. San Diego, CA: Genius Products, Inc., 2005.

Saskill, Sadarri. *Shake Your "Tale" Feathers.* CD. Kenosha, WI: Global Communication, 2001.

Sima, Judy. "The Turnip." *Good Character.* StoryWatchers Club. Adventures in Storytelling. DVD. Indianapolis, IN: Sax Media, 2006.

StoryWatchers Club. *Adventures in Storytelling.* DVD series. Indianapolis, IN: Sax Media, 2006.

Thomason, Dovie. *Fireside Tales.* CD. Somerville, MA: Yellow Moon Press, 2001.

———. *Lessons from the Animal People.* CD. Somerville, MA: Yellow Moon Press, 1997.

Wheeler, Jerome. *River Cowboys.* CD. Columbia, MO: Blue Coaster Records, 2006.

Williams, Diane. *Mississippi Storytelling: A Heap of Comfort.* CD. Canton, MS: Don Forbush Productions, 2008.

TEACHER RESOURCES—CLASSROOM THEORY AND PRACTICES

American Association of School Librarians. *Information Literacy Standards for Student Learning.* Chicago, IL: American Library Association and the Association for Educational Communications and Technology, 1998.

Ammon, Bette DeBruyne, and Gale W. Sherman. *Worth a Thousand Words: An Annotated Guide to Picture Books for Older Readers.* Englewood, CO: Libraries Unlimited, 1996.

Avgerinou, Maria, with J. Ericson. "A Review of the Concept of Visual Literacy." *British Journal of Educational Technology* 28.4 (1997): 280–291.

Bamford, Anne. "Visual Literacy White Paper." Art and Design University of Technology, Sydney, Australia: Adobe Systems Pty Ltd, 2003.

Barrett, Terry. *Interpreting Art: Reflecting, Wondering, and Responding.* New York: McGraw-Hill, 2002.

Begoray, Deborah L. "Through a Class Darkly: Visual Literacy in the Classroom." *Canadian Journal of Education* 26 (2001): 201–217.

Biemiller, Andrew, PhD. *Reading Research to Practice: A Series for Teachers.* Cambridge, MA: Brookline Books, 1999.

Blachowicz, Camille, and Donna Ogle. *Reading Comprehension: Strategies for Independent Learners.* 2nd ed. New York: Guilford Press, 2008.

Brand, Susan Trostle, and Jeanne M. Donato. *Storytelling in Emergent Literacy: Fostering Multiple Intelligences.* Albany, NY: Delmar, 2001.

Burnham, Rita, and Elliot Kai-Kee. "The Art of Teaching in the Museum." *The Journal of Aesthetic Education,* vol. 39, no. 1 (Spring 2005): 65–76.

Caduto, Michael J., Joseph Bruchac, Ka-Hon-Hes, and Carol Wood. *Keepers of the Earth: Native American Stories and Environmental Activities for Children.* Golden, CO: Fulcrum Publishing, 1997.

Suggested Resources

Changar, Jerilynn, and Annette Harrison. *Storytelling Activities Kit: Ready-to-Use Techniques, Lessons, and Listening Cassettes for Early Childhood.* West Nyack, NY: Prentice Hall, 1992.

Collins, Rives. *The Power of Story: Teaching through Storytelling.* 2nd ed. Boston: Allyn & Bacon, 1996.

Cornell, Joseph Bharat. *Sharing Nature with Children: A Parents' and Teachers' Nature-Awareness Guidebook.* Nevada City, CA: Ananda Publications, 1979.

———. *Sharing the Joy of Nature: Nature Activities for All Ages.* Nevada City, CA: Dawn Publications, 1989.

Danoff, Susan. *The Golden Thread: Storytelling in Teaching and Learning.* Kingston, NJ: Storytelling Arts Press, 2006.

Davis, Donald. *Writing as a Second Language.* Little Rock, AR: August House, 2000.

Duffy, Gerald G., PhD. *Explaining Reading: A Resource for Teaching Concepts, Skills, and Strategies.* New York: The Guilford Press, 2003.

Griffen, R. E., V. S. Williams, and J. Lee, eds. *Exploring the Visual Future: Art Design, Science, and Technology.* Blacksburg, VA: The International Visual Literacy Association, 2001.

Hamilton, Martha, and Mitch Weiss. *Children Tell Stories: Teaching and Using Storytelling in the Classroom.* 2nd ed. Katonah, NY: Richard C. Owens, 2005.

Hannaford, Carla. *Smart Moves: Why Learning is Not All in Your Head.* Alexander, NC: Great Ocean Publishers, 1995.

Harrison, Annette. *Easy-to-Tell Stories for Young Children.* Jonesborough, TN: National Storytelling Press, 1992.

Hart, Betty, PhD, and Todd R. Risley, PhD. *Meaningful Differences in the Everyday Experiences of Young Children.* Baltimore, MD: Paul H. Brookes Publishing Co. Inc., 2000.

Harvey, Stephanie, and Anne Goudvis. *Strategies That Work: Teaching Comprehension to Enhance Understanding.* Portland, ME: Stenhouse Publishers, 2000.

Hirsch, E. D., Jr., PhD. *The Schools We Need: Why We Don't Have Them.* Garden City, NY: Doubleday, 1996.

Joy, Flora. *Treasures from Europe: Stories and Classroom Activities.* Westport, CT: Teacher Idea Press, 2003.

Kemper, David, Ruth Nathan, and Carol Elsholz. *Writers' Express: A Handbook for Young Writers, Thinkers, and Learners.* Wilmington, MA: Write Source, Great Source Education Group, 2000.

Kress, Gunther. *Literacy in the New Media Age.* London: Routledge, 2003.

LaRue, Thurston. *The Complete Book of Campfire Programs.* New York: Association Press, 1958.

Livo, Norma J. *Celebrating the Earth: Stories, Experiences, and Activities.* Englewood, CO: Teacher Ideas Press, 2000.

Louv, Richard. *Last Child in the Woods: Saving Our Children from Nature-Deficit Disorder.* Updated and expanded. Chapel Hill, NC: Algonquin Books of Chapel Hill, 2008.

McBride-Smith, Barbara. *Tell It Together: Foolproof Scripts for Story Theatre.* Little Rock, AR: August House, 2002.

McCarthy, William B., and Joseph Sobol, eds. *Jack in Two Worlds: Contemporary North American Tales and Their Tellers.* Chapel Hill, NC: University of North Carolina Press, 1994.

Metros, Susan E., and Kristina Eoolsey. "Visual Literacy: An Institutional Imperative." *EDUCAUSE Review*, vol. 41, no. 3 (May/June 2006): 80–81.

Norfolk, Bobby, and Sherry Norfolk. *The Moral of the Story: Folktales for Character Development*. 2nd ed. Little Rock, AR: August House, 2006.

Norfolk, Sherry, Jane Stenson, and Diane Williams. *The Storytelling Classroom: Applications Across the Curriculum*. Westport, CT: Libraries Unlimited, 2006.

Pearce, Joseph Chilton. "The Risk of Evolution," an interview with *Parabola* (Summer 1992): 54–62.

Rubright, Lynn. *Beyond the Beanstalk: Interdisciplinary Learning through Storytelling*. Portsmouth, NH: Heinemann, 1996.

Ryokai, K., C. Vaucelle, and J. Cassell. *Journal of Computer Assisted Learning*, vol. 19, issue 2 (2003): 195–208.

Sebranek, Patrick. *Write on Track: A Handbook for Young Writers, Thinkers, and Learners*. Wilmington, MA: Write Source, Great Source Education Group, 1996.

Sebranek, Patrick, Dave Kemper, and Carol Elsholz. *The Writing Spot*. Wilmington, MA: Write Source, Great Source Education Group, 2005.

Sebranek, Patrick, Dave Kemper, and Verne Meyer. *All Write: A Student Handbook for Writing and Learning*. Wilmington, MA: Write Source, Great Source Education Group, 2002.

Sebranek, Patrick, et al. *Write Away: A Handbook for Young Writers and Learners*. Wilmington, MA: Write Source, Great Source Education Group, 1996.

———. *Write One: A Handbook for Young Writers*. Wilmington, MA: Write Source, Great Source Education Group, 2005.

———. *Writers Inc: A Student Handbook for Writing and Learning*. Wilmington, MA: Write Source, Great Source Education Group, 2001.

Sima, Judy, and Kevin Cordi. *Raising Voices: Creating Youth Storytelling Groups and Troupes*. Westport, CT: Libraries Unlimited, 2003.

Stone, Michael K., and Zenobia Barlow. *Ecological Literacy: Educating Our Children for a Sustainable World*. Bioneers series. Berkeley, CA: Sierra Club Books; produced and distributed by University of California Press, 2005.

Sutherland, Zena. *Children and Books*. 9th ed. New York: Longmans, 1997.

Swinger, Marlys. *Sing Through the Day: Eighty Songs for Children*. Farmington, PA: Plough Publishing House, 1999.

Terban, Marvin. *Scholastic Dictionary of Idioms*. New York: Scholastic, 1996.

Yenawine, Philip. *Handbook of Research on Teaching Literacy through the Communicative and Visual Arts*. Mahwah, NJ: Lawrence Erlbaum Associates, 2005.

Zimmerman, Susan, and Ellin Oliver Keene. *Mosaic of Thought: Teaching Comprehension in a Reader's Workshop*. Portsmouth, NH: Heinemann, 1997.

WEB SITES

American Sign Language Browser. Communication Technology Lab, Michigan State University. http://commtechlab.msu.edu/sites/aslweb/browser.htm.

Ashliman, D. L. "The Name of the Helper." University of Pittsburgh, 2000–2001. http://www.pitt.edu/~dash/type0500.html.

Avgerinou, Maria. "What is 'Visual Literacy?' "International Visual Literacy Association. http://www.ivla.org/org_what_vis_lit.htm.

Ayvar, Carrie Sue. "Como se dice Storyteller? How do you say Cuentista?" http://www.carriesueayvar.com.

Baby Name Addicts. http://www.babynameaddicts.com.

Baldwin, Jackie. http://www.story-lovers.com.

Black, Judith. "Telling Stories to Children." http://http://www.tellingstoriestochildren.com.

Black, Sue. http://www.sue-black.com.

Brisas Elementary School. "Original Fables Inspired by Aesop." http://www.kyrene.k12.az.us/schools/brisas/sunda/fable/fable.htm#amy.

Burns, Jeri, and Barry Marshall. http://www.storycrafters.com.

Caldecott Medal. http://acrl.org/ala/mgrps/divs/alsc/awardsgrants/bookmedia/caldecottmedal/caldecottterms/caldecottterms.cfm.

Campbell, Mike. "Behind the Name: The Etymology and History of First Names." http://www.behindthename.com.

Clark, Teresa. http://www.writeonspeakers.com/teresa_clark.htm; e-mail: teresa-clark@blogspot.com.

Clow School TattleTales. http://clow.ipsd.org/lmc_storytellers.html.

Craddock Center's Children's Enrichment Program. http://www.craddockcenter.org.

Danoff, Susan. http://www.susandanoff.com.

Dudding, Kate. http://www.katedudding.com.

Dunbar, Paul Laurence. http://www.dunbarsite.org/gallery.asp; "An Analysis of Paul Laurence Dunbar's We Wear the Mask." http://www.123helpme.com/view.asp?id=19393.

East Tennessee State University. Storytelling Master's Program. http://www.etsu.edu/stories/.

Forest, Heather. Story Arts. http://www.storyarts.org.

Gnutek, Mike. http://www.bakerdemorg/teaching/biographies.htm.

Hamilton, Mary. http://www.maryhamilton.info.

Heiner, Heidi A.SurLaLune Fairytales. http://www.SurLaLuneFairytales.com.

Horner, Beth. http://www.BethHorner.com.

Howard, Sarah. http://www.playprettyproductions.com.

Ifft, Mary Anne. "Vocabulary & Idioms." De Anza College. http://faculty.deanza.edu/ifftmaryanne/stories/storyReader$255.

International Storytelling Center. http://www.storytellingfoundation.net.

Internet TESL Journal. "ESL: Idioms and Slang." http://iteslj.org/links/ESL/Idioms_and_Slang.

Irwin, Andy Offutt. http://www.andyirwin.com.

Johnson, Charles "Wsir." http://www.wsirarts.com.

Joy, Flora. http://www.storytellingworld.com.

Kokie, Stan. "Storytelling: The Heart and Soul of Education." PREL Briefing Paper; Pacific Resources for Education and Learning. http://www.prel.org/products/Products/Storytelling.pdf, November 1998.

Kovalik, Cindy, and Peggy King. "Visual Literacy." Kent State University College and Graduate School of Health, Education, and Services. http://www.educ.kent.edu/community/VLO.

Kuniko Theater. http://www.educ.kent.edu/community/VLO.

Kuniko Theater. http://www.kunikotheater.com.

Lakeshore Learning Materials. http://www.lakeshorelearing.com.

Lark in the Morning. http://www.larkinthemorning.com.

Lasana, Oni. http://www.onilasana.com.

Long, John R. "Aesop's Fables Online." www.aesopfables.com, 2008.

"Make Your Own Cartouche." Harcourt School Publishers. http://www.hbschool. com/activity/cartouche/cartouche.html, 2008.

May, Jim. http://www.storytelling.org/JimMay.

McWilliams, Barry. "Effective Storytelling: A Manual for Beginners." http://www. eldrbarry.net/roos/eest.htm, 1998.

Millmore, Mark. "Ancient Egyptian Hieroglyphic Writing." http://www.eyelid. co.uk/hiero1.htm, 1997-2008.

Myth Mania: "Greek Mythology Today and Myth of the Month." http://mythman. com/.

National Council of Teachers of English Teaching. "NCTE Positions and Guide-lines: Teaching Storytelling, a Position Statement from the Committee on Story-telling. http://www.ncte.org/positions/statements/teachingstorytelling.

National Storytelling Network. http://www.Storynet.org.

Norfolk, Sherry. http://www.sherrynorfolk.com.

Pearson Education, Inc. "Paint by Idioms." FunBrain.com. http://www.funbrain. com/idioms, 2000–2008.

Poetry Out. http://www.poetryout.org.

Price, Marilyn. http://www.marilynprice.com.

Race Bridges for Schools. http://www.racebridgesforschools.com.

Riesland, Erin. "Visual Literacy and the Classroom." New Horizons for Learning. http://www.newhorizons.org/strategies/literacy/riesland.htm, March 2005.

Rosenfield. Ben. http://www.storytelling.org/Rosenfield.

Rubright, Lynn. http://www.lynnrubright.com.

———. *Mama's Window.* http://www.leeandlow.com/booktalk/rubright/html.

Sacre, Antonio. http://www.antoniosacre.com.

Saskill, Sadarri. http://www.globaltales.com.

———. "The Jazzy Three Bears." http://www.prattlibrary.org/home/eStory.aspx.

Shimojima, Anne. http://www.storytelling.org/shimojima.

Sima, Judy. http://www.JudySima.com.

Sims, Ellen, et al. *Visual Literacy: What It Is and Do We Need It To Use Learning Technologies Effectively?* Learning Technology Support Service, University of Bristol, UK: ASCILITE, 2002. http://www.ascilite.org.au/conferences/ auckland02/proceedings/papers/ellen_sims_et_al.pdf.

Sperling, Dave. Dave's ESL Cafe: ESL Idiom Page by Dennis Oliver. http://eslcafe. com/idioms, 1995–2007.

Stagebridge. http://www.stagebridge.org.

Stenson, Jane. http://www.storytelling.org/Stenson.

Stokes, Suzanne. "Visual Literacy in Teaching and Learning: A Literature Perspec-tive." *Electronic Journal for the Integration of Technology in Education*, vol. 1, no. 1. http://ejite.isu.edu/Volume1No1/pdfs/stokes.pdf.

Storytelling in Schools. http://www.storytellinginschools.org.

Storytelling—It's News! http://www.storynet-advocacy.org/news.

Thomason, Dovie. http://www.doviethomason.com.

Tingle, Tim. http://www.choctawstoryteller.com.

Suggested Resources

———. *Crossing Bok Chitto: Teachers' Guide*. Cinco Puntos Press. http://www.cincopuntos.com/pdf/crossing_bok_chitto_guide.pdf.

Torrence, Jackie. *Tailypo*. Public Library of Charlotte and Mecklenburg County's "Bookhive." http://www.plcmc.org/Bookhive/zingertales/default.asp?storyID=6.

VSA Arts Research Symposium. "Framework and Tools for Evaluating Arts in Education." http://www.vsarts.org/evaluation.

Washington, Donna. http://www.DonnaWashington.com.

Wells, Megan. http://www.meganwells.com.

Williams, Diane. http://www.dwteller.com.

Write Source. http://www.thewritesource.com/.

Writing World. http://www.writing-world.com/links/names.shtml.

Index

Index

Index

Index

ABOUT THE EDITORS

About the coauthors of the award-winning *The Storytelling Classroom: Applications Across the Curriculum* (Libraries Unlimited, 2006) and *Literacy Development in the Storytelling Classroom*:

Sherry Norfolk

Sherry Norfolk is an internationally acclaimed storyteller, appearing at the International Storytelling Center, the Singapore Storytelling Festival, and many more festivals, schools, libraries, and universities nationwide. Her strong, clear, direct stage presence immediately connects to audiences of all ages. AND ... that VOICE! Perhaps there lives in her chords a pantheon of BOTH gods and goddesses! Her use of tones, timbres, and rhythms in her telling breathes life into her rich repertoire of folktales from around the world. Engaging and entertaining, compelling and educational, Sherry's programs are tailored to each audience and venue. In addition to an electric stage presence, she embodies the term "teaching artist"—that is, an artist who can not only talk the talk, but walk the walk. Sherry leads residencies and workshops internationally, introducing children and adults to story making and storytelling. She is on the roster of seven state arts councils, a testimony to her value as a teaching artist. Her dedication to and deep interest in children and literacy have been recognized with national awards from the American Library Association, the Association for Library Service for Children, the National Association of Counties, and the Florida Library Association. Sherry and her husband Bobby are coauthors of *The Moral of the Story: Folktales for Character Development* (August House, 1999) and six picture books. Sherry currently serves on the National Storytelling Network Board of Directors. Web site: http://www.sherrynorfolk.com; e-mail: shnorfolk@aol.com.

Jane Stenson

Jane Stenson is an award-winning kindergarten teacher at the Baker Demonstration School, affiliated with National-Louis University, in Wilmette, Illinois, where she is an adjunct professor. She tells stories in her classroom and has made storytelling (hers AND the children's) a major part of the school's curriculum. Every day she tries to find just the right story to match the children's interests and behavior! As permanent storyteller-in-residence, Jane presents programs throughout the PreK to eighth grade classrooms associated with curricular goals. Further, as producer of the Betty Weeks Storytelling Series, she brings storytellers into the school for mini-residencies and concerts. Jane's goal is to encourage teachers and storytellers to work together and share knowledge about how children learn best: through storytelling. As a community performer, Jane tells from the world's folktales and personal stories about growing up in the Connecticut woods and raising her own children. Beautifully crafted, these stories resonate with humor, sometimes to the point of silliness as well as her general playfulness with language. Jane loves words and words harnessed to a well-crafted tale is just what she's about! Web site: http://www.storytelling.org/Stenson; e-mail: jstenson@bakerdemschool.org.

Diane Williams

Diane Williams is a storyteller and teaching artist. She has worked with students on all grade levels, as well as conducted presentations for student teachers on the college level. Her work in the classroom includes involvement with a variety of education alliances and associations, as well as the Department of Defense's Dependent Schools throughout Germany. Diane's perspective on storytelling ranges from oral history collecting in communities, to storytelling with symphony orchestras, ballet companies, galleries, and museums. She has taught docents, forensic students, and teachers how to use the elements of storytelling to enhance their communications and social skills. She has worked on numerous occasions as a storyteller/trainer for Mississippi's Library Commission, Library Association, Volunteer Services, and Early Childhood Education Association, and she is on the Speakers Bureau for the Humanities Council. Diane is the former board chair for the National Storytelling Network, a past president of Guess Who's

Talking Now—Toastmasters, a life member of the National Association of Black Story-tellers, and the founder of at least four storytelling groups. She is the recipient of the Mississippi Humanities Council's Special Chair's Award; the ORACLE Award for Regional Leadership and Service from the National Storytelling Network; and the Zora Neale Hurston award from the National Association of Black Storytellers. Diane is currently the arts industry director for the Mississippi Arts Commission, where she has worked for more than six years. Diane is the author of *Annie Mae Jumps the Broom*, a children's book on DVD, and a CD titled *Mississippi Storytelling, a Heap of Comfort*. Web site: http://www.dwteller.com.

ABOUT THE CONTRIBUTORS

Mama Edie Armstrong is a bilingual (Spanish) storyteller, speech and language pathologist, and vocal percussionist. Her articles and original stories have been included in publications such as the first anthology of the National Association of Black Storytellers, the edition of Margaret Read MacDonald's *Tell the World: Storytelling Across Language Barriers*, *Chicago Percussion and Rhythm Magazine*, and a cultural magazine in Chandigarh, India. Known also for the inclusion of sign language and multicultural instruments and dolls, Mama Edie performed on two award-winning storytelling DVDs. She has served as workshop presenter for educational and storytelling conferences and as keynote speaker for the B'nai B'rith "Unity in Diversity Conference," the Illinois Speech, Language, and Hearing Association and for the Illinois Association of School Social Workers. E-mail: MamaEdie2@aol.com.

A third generation bilingual (Spanish/English) storyteller, **Carrie Sue Ayvar** has collected and told tales for most of her life. A respected Chautauqua Scholar and historical portrayal artist, she received the National Storytelling Network's 2007 ORACLE Award for Service and Leadership. Trained as an Artist in Education at the Kennedy Center for the Performing Arts, she was recognized with the Sun Award for Advancing Teaching and Learning Through the Arts. She has served on the board of the Florida Storytelling Association and as the Florida state liaison with the National Storytelling Network. She is a vivacious storyteller and popular consultant in arts integration. Web site: http://www.carriesueayvar.com; e-mail: cayvar@aol.com.

Jackie Baldwin is the publisher-writer-editor of ten books of adaptations from fairy tales, folktales, and myths; the creator of Story-Lovers (http://www.story-lovers.com), including SOS: Searching Out Stories, one of the largest Internet archives of story sources; a multimedia writer-producer-director for twenty-five years of PBS TV programs; the producer of Teller-to-Teller seminars for professional storytellers; a teacher of creative writing and film/video production; a consultant for SCBWI; and host of a weekly storytelling radio program. She received the 2006 National Storytelling Network's ORACLE award for outstanding national service as well as more than thirty other national and international awards. E-mail: jackie@storyloversworld.com.

Ann Bates is an assistant professor of reading and language at National-Louis University, where she teaches courses in reading diagnosis and assessment and corrective reading and directs a clinical practicum for graduate students. Ann's interests include the use of authentic and informal assessment measures to guide instructional planning in both classroom and clinical settings. E-mail: Abates@nl.edu.

Pam Beagle-Daresta is a paneled teaching artist with the Georgia Council for the Arts, the South Carolina Arts Commission, and Young Audiences of St. Louis and Atlanta. Her residency work includes murals, printmaking, papermaking, and book arts. She works in collaboration with museums/art organizations and educational institutions to create art-centered educational programs and professional development. E-mail: pdarest@hotmail.com.

Judith Black is one of the nation's foremost storytellers. Winner of the National Storytelling Network's ORACLE Award/Circle of Excellence Award, she performs and teaches at festivals, universities, schools, museums, and theaters throughout the nation. Her original tales of American history have been commissioned by the U.S. Department of the Interior, National Public Radio, and the Massachusetts Foundation for the Humanities. Her original stories and folktales bridge students to cultures and experiences that will transform their lives. She has been an adjunct faculty member at Lesley University for more than twenty-five years, teaching graduate students of education how storytelling can extend a school's cognitive, curricular, and social/emotional objectives. Based in Marblehead, Massachusetts, she teaches an annual storytelling class out of her home. Web sites: http://www.tellingstoriestochildren.com and http://www.storiesalive.com; e-mail: jb@storiesalive.com.

Storyteller, writer, and teaching artist—it's an awesome combination! **Sue Black** combines her passion for telling original and traditional stories from around the world with her delight in teaching students and their teachers to tell and write stories. Don't be surprised if you want to move, chant, sing, think, imagine, and dream right along with Sue. E-mail: sue@sue-black.com.

Jeri Burns, PhD, and **Barry Marshall** are **The Storycrafters.** Their natural, energetic style has been featured in major festivals, schools, and libraries in the United States and abroad, including the National Storytelling Festival. In addition to being internationally renowned musical storytellers, they are award-winning radio show hosts, recording artists, writers, and teaching artists. The Storycrafters are adjunct college faculty at Southern Connecticut State University in New Haven, Connecticut, in the graduate degree program in the oral tradition, through the University's School of Information and Library Science. Web site: http://www.storycrafters.com; e-mail: info@storycrafters.com.

Kim Cheves is an arts specialist and storyteller working primarily in underprivileged areas of the Appalachian region. She combines music, movement, and story to create fun and meaningful learning experiences for children. Her passion to help underprivileged children achieve strong literacy skills is evident in her work. E-mail: outbackms@tds.net.

Teresa B. Clark is a storytelling teaching artist. From schools, to conferences, to festival platforms, she presents and advocates for storytelling. Her quest is to help people reconnect with themselves, their hopes, and their dreams. She tells so her listeners will remember what it's like to feel and become motivated to share. Web site: http://www.writeonspeakers.com/teresa_clark.htm; e-mail: teresaclarktells@hotmail.com; blog: teresaclark.blogspot.com.

Catherine Crowley is a storyteller who apprenticed with master teller Elizabeth Ellis. She was a featured teller at the Tejas Storytelling Festival, and on stage at the Meyerson Symphony Hall in Dallas, Texas, and as well as the Frisco Storytelling Festival. After getting her master's degree in education with a specialization in storytelling from East Tennessee State University, she became an overseas ESL instructor. She has worked in Korea and Taiwan, and currently has spent two years teaching English at Sohar University in Oman. Her favorite way to teach English is through storytelling. E-mail: crowleycj@att.net.

Susan Danoff is a storyteller, teaching artist, and writer. She trains teachers in the art of storytelling and works with organizations seeking to build community. She is the author of *The Golden Thread: Storytelling in Teaching and Learning*, a book that was inspired by her many years as a storyteller in schools where she has worked extensively with low-income and special-needs school districts. Every summer Susan offers weeklong storytelling workshops at Princeton University. Her CD *Women of Vision* is a 2008 Parents' Choice Gold Award winner and a National Parenting Publications Awards (NAPPA) Gold winner. Web site: http://www.susandanoff.com; e-mail: susandanoff@ aol.com.

Luiz DaSilva, PhD, received his reading specialization degree from the University of Southern Mississippi. He has taught college-level and high school students in Florida. He currently teaches and tutors English to foreign students in São Paulo, Brazil, where he lives with his wife and sons. E-mail: luizdasilva@hotmail.com.

Janice M. Del Negro, PhD, is an assistant professor at the graduate school of library and information science at Dominican University in River Forest, Illinois. Professor Del Negro's first picture book, *Lucy Dove* (1998), won the Anne Izard Storytelling Award; her second picture book, *Willa and the Wind* (2005), was an American Library Association Notable Book. Del Negro's latest book, *Passion and Poison* (2007), a collection of supernatural tales for young adults, received starred reviews from *The Horn Book* and *School Library Journal*. E-mail: jdelnegro@dom.edu.

Jackie Downey has been an educator for eight years. She has spent the last four growing with and learning from her fourth and fifth graders at Baker Demonstration School in Wilmette, Illinois. Jackie brings her passion for literature, current events, and nature into her daily teaching practice. She received her bachelor of arts from the University of Colorado at Boulder and her master's in the art of teaching from National-Louis University. E-mail: Jdowney@bakerdemschool.org.

Mary Gay Ducey is a children's librarian at a branch of Oakland Public Library and staff trainer for volunteer story readers placed in Oakland Head Start programs. She is also a freelance storyteller, storytelling educator, and organizer. She has performed and taught throughout the United States, Canada, and Ireland. She has been a featured storyteller at the National Storytelling Festival and has appeared on *Mr. Rogers' Neighborhood*. Her one-woman show, *Union Maid*, was developed from a commission developed for and presented at the Smithsonian Institution's Museum of American History. Gay has taught storytelling at UC Berkeley's School of Library and Information Studies and Berkeley's Education Extension and Dominican University. She remains an adjunct instructor at Santa Rosa Junior College. Gay has presented workshops for librarians, storytellers, parents, and educators across the United States including King County Library System, Northern California Reading Conference, and the Oklahoma Institute of the Arts. E-mail: mducey@earthlink.net.

As a professional storyteller and author, **Kate Dudding** enjoys bringing history to life—giving a voice to people from the past. She has told stories at many venues in the northeastern United States. As a storytelling advocate, Kate has collected more than 350 articles about storytelling since June 2004, including more than 200 articles dealing with education, and put summaries of these articles on http://www.storynews.org, the advocacy Web site of the National Storytelling Network. She is a 2008 recipient of the National Storytelling Network's ORACLE Award for Regional Leadership and Service. Web site: http://www.katedudding.com; e-mail: kate@katedudding.com.

Limeul Eubanks is a visual artist and art educator. He holds a Master of Fine Arts (MFA), an MEd in special education, art education, and gifted and talented, and a BA in art and dramatic arts. He has served as administration representative and president-elect of the Louisiana Art Education Association, community representative of Louisiana Alliance for Arts Education, Talented Art Evaluator of the Louisiana Department of Special Education, and board member of the Mississippi Alliance for Arts Education. He has served on the Mississippi Art Education Association board as membership chairperson, elementary division representative, and is now president-elect. Eubanks is employed as the Visual and Performing Arts and Library Media Specialist for the Mississippi Department of Education. E-mail: limeuleubanks@aol.com.

Lynette Ford is a fourth-generation storyteller, a member of the Greater Columbus (Ohio) Arts Council's Artists-in-Schools Program, and an Ohio teaching artist with the Kennedy Center for the Performing Arts' Ohio State-Based Collaborative Initiative. Lyn facilitates interactive workshops for storytellers, educators, and other mentors, and nurtures the skills of young storytellers, in both the oral and literary traditions, through school residencies (especially at Herbert Mills Elementary in Reynoldsburg, Ohio!), classroom visits, and young-author sessions at Thurber House. E-mail: friedtales@aol. com.

Heather Forest is a storyteller, recording artist, author, and educator. Her unique minstrel style of storytelling interweaves poetry, prose, original music, and the sung and spoken word. For the past thirty years, Dr. Forest has toured her performance repertoire of world tales to theaters, festivals, schools, and reading conferences throughout the United States and abroad. She has authored seven children's picture books, two folktale anthologies, and eight recordings of storytelling. She is the creator of a popular educational Web site Story Arts Online, http://www.storyarts.org. Her recordings have won an American Library Association Notable Record Award and two Parent's Choice Gold Awards. Her folktale collections have won the Storytelling World Anthology Award. She holds a master's degree in storytelling and reading from East Tennessee State University and a PhD in leadership and change from Antioch University. She is a recipient of the National Storytelling Network's Circle of Excellence Award and an adjunct professor of oral tradition in the Library Science Department at Southern Connecticut State University. For the past twenty-five years, she has lived on a perennial flower farm in Huntington, New York, with her husband Lawrence Foglia, an environmental educator, and their two children, Lucas and Laurel. E-mail: heather@storyarts.org.

As a library media specialist with more than thirty years of experience in elementary education, **Beverly Frett** has seen firsthand the benefits of storytelling to and with children. Its curricular integration and advocacy have become a passion. She shares her experience and enthusiasm when she promotes storytelling in this high-tech world as a conference presenter, the webmaster of the Clow School Student Storytellers' Web site (http://clow.ipsd.org/lmc_storytellers.html), and academic advisor for the Clow School TattleTales. E-mail: beverly_frett@ipsd.org.

Mike Gnutek is a lifelong learner and passionate about the arts. He received his undergraduate degree in English and graphic design from Bradley University and his master's degree in interdisciplinary arts and educational studies from Columbia College in Chicago. With roughly five years of design experience, Mike worked as a Web designer for RollingStone.com and as art director designing children's books for Publications International, Ltd. He enjoys ceramics, photography, and printmaking. He currently teaches art at the Baker Demonstration School in Wilmette, Illinois, and relishes the daily opportunity to help children to develop into creative and self-directed artists who will successfully embark on the world beyond the classroom. Classroom blog: http://blog.bakerdemschool.org/mgnutek; e-mail: http://mail.bakerdemschool.org/mgnutek.

Susan Gundlach taught for sixteen years at the North Shore Country Day School in Winnetka, Illinois, serving as English department chair for grades K-12. She then moved to the Winnetka Public Schools, where she taught sixth-grade English and history for a decade. After retiring from full-time teaching, she was recruited back as a part-time artist-in-residence. At that time, she and the school's art teacher, Lea Lazarus, began their collaboration on a project that combines art and writing through bookmaking. This project, implemented in sixth-grade art classes, is now in its fourth year. Sue has written many articles on such subjects as collecting and writing family stories; including ancient literature in the study of ancient cultures; and integrating art into the English-social studies curriculum. She has also conducted workshops on these topics. E-mail: gundlacs@sbcglobal.net.

Mary Hamilton is a storyteller, recording artist, and workshop leader. Since 1983, she has worked with all ages in hundreds of venues. Her education includes a bachelor's in secondary education/English major and a master's in library science, both from University of Kentucky. The Kentucky School Media Association gave Mary the 1999–2000 Jesse Stuart Award for her storytelling in Kentucky schools. The Kentucky Arts Council selected her for both their arts education and touring-artist rosters. With her colleague Cynthia Changaris, she designs and conducts storytelling workshops and retreats through their partnership, Scheherazade's Legacy. Web site: http://www.maryhamilton.info.

Since 1979, **Annette Harrison** has been a dynamic storytelling performer, author, and educator. She wrote two successful storytelling books, *Easy-to-Tell Stories* (National Storytelling Press, 1992) that won the Benjamin Franklin Education Award, and *Storytelling Activities Kit* (Prentice Hall, 1992), with Jerilynn Changar, PhD. For five years, Annette co-hosted *Gator Tales*, a weekly children's television program on CBS. Annette draws the listeners in with her amazing dramatic abilities and her joyous energy. She is truly a "kid magnet" and a master storyteller. E-mail: netharbar@aol.com.

Storyteller **Beth Horner** is a former librarian, having worked at Yale University and Champaign, Illinois, public libraries. A festival favorite across the country since 1983, Beth has performed at the National Storytelling Festival, served on the National Storytelling Association's board of directors, and been awarded the National Storytelling Network's Circle of Excellence ORACLE Award. She delights in performing in schools and in conducting writing and story performance residencies for students. Her story, "The Pipeline Blues," was recorded for *Live From National Geographic* and used as a basis for her work on narrative with NASA engineers and educators. Web site: http://www.BethHorner.com; e-mail: BethHorner@earthlink.net.

Sarah Howard is the children and youth services coordinator for the Daniel Boone Regional Library system in Columbia, Missouri. She also teaches as an adjunct instructor in the School of Information Science and Learning Technologies for the University of Missouri. She and her husband Thom perform music and stories at other libraries, schools, and learning events. Web site: http://www.playprettyproductions.com; e-mail: sarahbirdie@gmail.com.

Andy Offutt Irwin is a touring storyteller/songwriter/show-off from Covington, Georgia. Among other gigs, he has been a featured teller at the National Storytelling Festival; a teller-in-residence at the International Storytelling Center; a guest artist at La Guardia Arts, the high school for art, music, and the performing arts in New York (the *Fame* school); and a keynote speaker/performer at the Library of Congress-Viburnum Foundation Conference on Family Literacy. His old real jobs include artist-in-residence in theater at Oxford College of Emory University (1991–2007), and writer, director, and performer for SAK Theatre at Walt Disney World. He thinks he's funny. E-mail: andy@andyirwin.com.

Charles "Wsir" Johnson is an ethno-folk artist, multi-instrumentalist, and storyteller. For nineteen years, much of his work has been influenced by ancient African and Old World cultures. He is a craftsman of musical instruments such as the diddley bow, cigar box guitars, West African akontings, gamelan ngonis, ceramic drums, saxophones, bamboo African flutes, and gourd banjos. He is a life-learner who explores the historical, social, and cultural connections that coexist within the traditions of world music, specifically blues, jazz, and roots. Education programming includes curriculum-connected concepts that integrate storytelling and traditional folk instruments with math, science, art, social studies, history, geography, language, and music lessons. Web site: www.wsirarts.com; e-mail: wsirarts@hotmail.com.

Flora Joy has been described as a "founder" in the world of storytelling. The following are a few examples of programs or events that she began: 1) *Storytelling World*, an international journal for which Flora has continued to serve as editor since its first issue in the 1980s. This journal is currently part of the

National Storytelling Network's *Storytelling Magazine*, 2) The Annual Storytelling Resource Awards Program, 3) the National Storytelling Youth Olympics, and 4) the master's degree program in storytelling at East Tennessee State University (where she taught for forty-one years and is currently a professor emeritus). She has won many prestigious awards, including the National Storytelling Network's Lifetime Achievement award. Web site: http://www.storytellingworld.com.

Evornia Kincaid, EdD, has worked in the educational field for more than thirty years. As a teacher, she regularly presents on using learning centers to incorporate storytelling in the classroom. Currently, she teaches communicative arts to pre-service elementary teachers at Jackson State University and psychology to undergraduate students at the University of Phoenix. Evornia is a member of the Good News Gospel Storytelling group. She is married and has four children.

Oni Lasana is a poet, storyteller, musician, and teaching artist. She offers performances, workshops, and an audio CD on the poetry of Paul Laurence Dunbar. She is also a reenactor of the life of Harriet Tubman. She lives in Pennsylvania. Web site: http://www.onilasana.com; e-mail: onilasana@aol. com.

Lea Basile Lazarus received her BA in art education from the College of New Jersey, and her MFA, with a concentration in printmaking, from the Art Institute of Chicago. She has been teaching for twelve years, the last eight at the Skokie School in Winnetka, Illinois. Do Your P'Art, a not-for-profit organization that enables city students and suburban students to establish relationships through the arts, has been an important part of her teaching experience in Winnetka. Recipient of a Teacher Fulbright to Japan in October 2003, Lea spent three weeks abroad learning about Japan's culture, art, and education system. For twenty years, Lea has owned and operated a business specializing in the decorative and functional arts. E-mail: leabasile@comcast.net.

Pam Lindsey, a children's music consultant, created a curriculum-enhancing fine arts program for young children that promotes literacy while exposing children to the arts. Pam Lindsey's HeARTSongs was the original model chosen and adopted by the Craddock Center's Children's Enrichment Program (http://www.craddockcenter.org) that annually serves more than 1,400 Head Start and preschool children in Georgia, Tennessee, and North Carolina. Pam has recently developed HeARTSongs Grandbuddies, an intergenerational program that combines her love of children and music with her love for senior adults. These classes meet weekly to bring children and seniors together to build ongoing, mutually beneficial relationships through songs, music, and stories. Web site: http://www.heartsongs.us.

Jim May is an Emmy-Award-winning storyteller and author and a former elementary school and college teacher who has performed live for more than one million school children in the Chicago area and across the country over the last twenty years. His children's picture book, *The Boo Baby Girl Meets the Ghost of Mable's Gable* (Brotherstone, 1992), is in its second printing and is a favorite of teachers, librarians, and parents, especially during the Halloween season. His collection of stories for adults and young adults, *The Farm on Nippersink Creek*, won a best book award from the Public Library Association and was praised by *Publishers Weekly*, *Booklist*, and the *Cleveland Plain Dealer*. Jim appears regularly in the major festivals and much of his work is educational keynotes, staff training, and school residencies. Web site: http://www.storytelling. org/May; e-mail: maystory@earthlink.net.

Darlene Neumann is a storyteller and library media specialist. With her clear, pleasing voice and engaging facial expressions, she paints compelling pictures, inviting children and adults to laugh, cry, and revel in the joy of stories. Darlene tells world folktales and shares bittersweet stories about growing up on a southern Illinois farm. She has told at festivals, international schools, and public libraries, and has conducted storytelling workshops at library and educational conferences and universities. She coordinates an annual storytelling festival at her school in which each fourth and fifth grader, and some younger students, tells a story. Darlene helps the students choose, learn, and tell their stories. She is an adjunct professor in storytelling at National-Louis University in Wheeling, Illinois. She and husband Larry sing and tell in tandem as "Two Voices." E-mail: ldneu@comcast.net.

Larry Neumann teaches gifted students at the Pleasantdale Middle School in Burr Ridge, Illinois. He has worked extensively on stories about the Wright brothers and works with storytelling in middle school classrooms. He has written several musicals and produces an annual musical at his school. He conducts storytelling workshops and performs at festivals, schools, and a variety of other venues. He and his wife Darlene are the tandem tellers, "Two Voices," sharing stories in word and song. E-mail: ldneu@comcast.net.

Bobby Norfolk is an internationally known performer and teaching artist. This three-time Emmy Award winner and Parents' Choice honoree is one of the most popular and dynamic story educators in the country. He is in the 2009 Circle of Excellence. E-mail: bobbynorfolk@charter.net.

Nancy Perla baked and read with her late grandmother Alice Yerak in Cleveland, Ohio, in the late 1950s. Currently she is the director of extended care and an early intervention teacher at the Baker Demonstration School in Wilmette, Illinois. She has a master's degree in elementary education from National-Louis University. E-mail: nperla@comcast.net.

Marilyn Price is a professional puppeteer, storyteller, and educator. With many specialties to her credit, including but not limited to professional development training, imagination stretching, story and program development, and much-sought-after performances, she travels from coast to coast and enjoys challenges of all kinds. Her wide assortment of performance venues ranges from Ellis Island, New York, to libraries, schools, and faith communities. A veteran of more than thirty-five years in the business of telling and listening, Price lives in Evanston, Illinois. Web site: http://www.marilynprice.com.

Delanna Reed is a full-time instructor of storytelling in East Tennessee State University's Storytelling Program. She has a strong background and many years of experience teaching and coaching oral interpretation, forensics, and storytelling.

Dr. Ben Rosenfield shares tales from his childhood growing up in the Ohio River Valley, as well as stories of his own creation. A retired elementary school teacher/principal, he helped write and clarify the language arts standards used in Illinois schools. Featured at storytelling festivals and on TV and radio, Rosenfield tells original stories, ghost stories, family and folktales, multicultural stories, country yarns, and more. He is the creator and artistic director of the highly popular Halloween extravaganza, "Scare on the Square," in Woodstock, Illinois, and has long hosted the liar's contest at the Illinois Storytelling Festival in Spring Grove. Web site: http://www.storytelling.org/Rosenfield.

Juli Ross is a national board certified teacher and currently teaches at the Baker Demonstration School (Wilmette, Illinois), where she has been teaching fourth and fifth grade for thirteen years. She holds a master's degree from National-Louis University and an undergraduate degree from Michigan State University. Ross has presented at national conferences in the areas of teacher leadership and integrated curriculum. She is a reluctant storyteller and has grown tremendously through this journey of collaboration. E-mail: jross@ bakerdemschool.org.

Lynn Rubright, professor emeritus, Webster University, St. Louis, Missouri, is an author-educator and co-producer of the Emmy-Award-winning video documentary, *Oh Freedom After While: The Missouri Sharecropper Protest of 1939*. Recipient of a National Storytelling Network's Circle of Excellence Award (1996) and the National Storytelling Network's 2007 Lifetime Achievement ORACLE Award, she teaches storytelling workshops at Webster University, the University of Missouri, and in St. Louis and around the world. She is a co-founder of the Metro Theater Company in St. Louis and the St. Louis Storytelling Festival. Lynn presently is author/storyteller-in-residence for the Center for Creative Arts (COCA) Urban Arts Storytelling and Literacy Project in St. Louis area schools, where she brings *Mama's Window* (and other stories) to life across the curriculum. Web site:

http://www.lynnrubright.com; e-mail: lynntells@aol.com; for *Mama's Window*: http://www.leeandlow.com/booktalk/rubright/html.

Antonio Sacre is an internationally touring storyteller, writer, and solo performance artist based in Los Angeles. He has been a featured storyteller at the Kennedy Center for the Performing Arts, the National Storytelling Festival, the National Book Festival at the Library of Congress, and museums, schools, libraries, and festivals worldwide. His recordings have won numerous national awards, and his retelling of the story "The Barking Mouse" was published as a picture book by Albert Whitman & Company in March 2003. His next two picture books will be published by Harry N. Abrams Books for Young Readers in 2010. Web site: http://www.antoniosacre.com.

Sadarri Saskill is a Chicago-born multilingual storyteller whose passion for writing and teaching has transported her performances, workshops, and creative writing residencies worldwide. She holds a BS in education with concentrations in world languages, ESL, theater, and psychology. Sadarri often performs with her husband and daughters, incorporating Spanish, French, Haitian Creole, sign language, and other languages. Her hilarious character voices have been recorded by several national textbook publishers while her own recordings have won Parents' Choice, NAPPA, Pegasus, and Storytelling World awards. Sadarri served as a magazine correspondent for *Storytelling Magazine* and her writings can be found in numerous publications. Web site: http://www.globaltales.com; e-mail: globaltales@yahoo.com.

Anne Shimojima has been a school library media specialist for more than thirty years and is currently at Braeside Elementary School in Highland Park, Illinois. A storyteller for more than twenty years, she performed at the Exchange Place at the National Storytelling Festival in 2001. Anne has taught graduate courses in storytelling and for seven years was on the board of directors of the Wild Onion Storytelling Celebration in Chicago. She has performed in schools, libraries, museums, and festivals, and gives workshops on the use of storytelling in classrooms and library media centers. Web site: http://www.storytelling.org/shimojima.

Judy Sima is an award-winning storyteller, author, and educator. Her performances and workshops have been featured at conferences, festivals, schools, and libraries throughout Michigan and across the country. As a school librarian for more than thirty-five years, she introduced many young people to the art of storytelling through her middle school storytelling troupe. Judy's book, *Raising Voices: Creating Youth Storytelling Groups and Troupes* (Libraries Unlimited, 2003, coauthored with Kevin Cordi), has received numerous awards and accolades, including the Storytelling World Honor Award, the VOYA Five-Foot Bookshelf, and the Anne Izard Storytellers Choice Award. Judy has been telling stories professionally since 1987. She is a frequent presenter at the National Storytelling Conference, the International Reading Conference, and the American Association of School Librarians. Her many articles have been featured in *Storytelling Magazine*, *Library Talk*, *Book Links*, *Oasis Magazine*, *Tales as Tools*, *Beginner's Guide to Storytelling*, *Telling Stories to Children*, and *The Storytelling Classroom*. Web site: http://www.JudySima.com; e-mail: Judy@JudySima.com.

Randy Taylor is a Wolf Trap Early Learning Teaching Artist with the Alliance Theatre in Atlanta and is on the rosters of Young Audiences, the Woodruff Arts Center, and the Georgia Council for the Arts. He currently teaches early childhood education at DeKalb Technical College.

Dovie Thomason is an award-winning storyteller, recording artist, and author, recognized internationally for her ability to take her listeners back to the "timeless place" that she first "visited" as a child, hearing old Indian stories from her Kiowa Apache and Lakota relatives, especially Grandma Dovie and her Dad. For more than two decades, Dovie's work has been exclusively in the preservation and continuation of Native cultural arts, utilizing the art form of traditional Native storytelling. She has developed a wide variety of programs for all ages, with the intent of sharing an indigenous perspective on Native cultures, stories, and concerns. Web site: http://www.doviethomason.com.

Tim Tingle is Oklahoma Choctaw and a frequent speaker at tribal events, literary conferences, and festivals. His recent work includes "Rolling Way the Rock," the story of Choctaw Clarence Carnes, the youngest inmate ever sentenced to Alcatraz Federal Prison. Tingle premiered the piece at the 2006 International Symposium of Artists of Conscience in Victoria, British Columbia, and performed a one-hour solo version at the 2008 National Storytelling Festival. His first children's book, *Crossing Bok Chitto*, was an Editor's Choice in the *New York Times Book Review* and won the 2008 American Indian Youth Literature Award, presented by the American Library Association. Web site: http://www.choctawstoryteller.com; E-mail: timtingle@hotmail.com.

Tracy Walker is the youth services specialist at the Dawson County Library in the north Georgia foothills of the Appalachian Mountains. As such, Tracy shares stories with the children at the library, as well as county elementary and middle schools, Head Start, and prekindergarten programs. She holds a BA in anthropology and an MEd in middle grades education. Tracy has also shared stories at festivals, including the St. Louis Storytelling Festival, the Roswell Magnolia Storytelling Festival, and TaleSpin in Chattanooga. E-mail: tswalker3@mindspring.com.

Cathy Ward has taught gallery programs at the Werner Center for the Arts in Columbus, Ohio, and the Art Institute of Chicago. She currently teaches first grade at the Children's School in suburban Chicago. Cathy has a BA in humanistic studies from Saint Mary's College in Notre Dame, Indiana. She holds an MA in art education from The Ohio State University and an MAT in elementary education from National-Louis University. E-mail: cward@ thechildrensschool.info.

Donna L. Washington is an author and award-winning storyteller and multicultural folklorist who has been sharing stories with audiences for more than twenty years. Her amazing vocal pyrotechnics and dynamic physicality make her stories come alive and enthrall and delight audiences from ages four to 104. She has been featured at numerous festivals, schools, and libraries across the country. Donna is an accomplished author of three children's books with more on the way and has seven multiple-award-winning CDs. She spends her days roaming the country doing workshops for librarians and educators as well as performing for schools, libraries, festivals, and anyone else who will listen to her. She lives in Durham, North Carolina, with her husband Dave, son Devin, daughter Darith, and two kittens. Web site: http://www.DonnaWashington. com.

Greg Weiss has been a teacher for almost three decades. He has spent most of that time teaching middle school speech and drama in Homewood, Illinois. As a storyteller, he has performed and presented workshops in the Midwest and beyond. Greg has served on the executive board of the Northlands Storytelling Network. He freely admits that his article resulted from several spoken dialogues with people who are probably glad it is finally in print so he will stop talking about it so much. E-mail: gjweiss@earthlink.net.

Megan Wells is a writer/storyteller living in La Grange Park, a suburb of Chicago, Illinois. With a BFA/MFA in theater, Megan worked in the professional theater until she discovered the folk and fine art of storytelling in 1989. Since then, Megan has been exploring the dynamic dance between story's conversational narrative and theater's emotional arc. She works in three arenas: story as a teaching tool in educational venues; story as an innovation tool for businesses and communities; and story as a wisdom tool in festival and theatrical venues. E-mail: megan@meganwells.com.

Mary Kay Will is a teacher-librarian in a pre-K-5 school in DeKalb County, Georgia. She has been involved in libraries since she was in fifth grade as a volunteer in her hometown library. Mary Kay worked in libraries throughout high school, college, and graduate school, served as a public children's librarian in New Jersey and as branch manager for DeKalb County Public Library. She returned to working with children in the elementary school in 2002, and loves being able to use stories in a school setting where children ask for stories over and over again.

About the Contributors

A native of Japan, **Kuniko Yamamoto** started performing professionally in her hometown of Osaka. She received national exposure performing on Kansai National TV in 1985. Kuniko traveled to the United States to study with Tony Montanaro the following year, then toured with Leland Faulkner's Light Theater bringing ancient Japanese tales to life with shadows and magic. Since creating her solo show, she has appeared at Epcot Disney, the Kennedy Center for the Performing Arts in Washington, DC, and the National Storytelling Festival, touring across the country. From native villages in Alaska to proscenium theaters in Florida, Kuniko performed at more than 2,000 theaters, schools, colleges, and festivals. E-mail: kuniko92@verizon.net.